PROPHECIES OF THE BIBLE

the Smart Guide to the Bible™ series

BE SMART · BE INSPIRED ™

Daymond Duck
Larry Richards, General Editor

NELSON BOOKS
A Division of Thomas Nelson Publishers
Since 1798

www.thomasnelson.com

Prophecies of the Bible
The Smart Guide to the Bible™ series
© 2007 by GRQ, Inc.

Published by Nelson Reference, a Division of Thomas Nelson, Inc., P.O. Box 141000, Nashville, Tennessee 37214.

Originally published by Starburst Publishers under the title *Prophecies of the Bible: God's Word for the Biblically-Inept*. Now revised and updated.

Scripture quotations are taken from The New King James Version® (NKJV), copyright 1979, 1980, 1982, 1992 Thomas Nelson, Inc., Publishers.

To the best of its ability, GRQ, Inc., has strived to find the source of all material. If there has been an oversight, please contact us, and we will make any correction deemed necessary in future printings. We also declare that to the best of our knowledge all material (quoted or not) contained herein is accurate, and we shall not be held liable for the same.

General Editor: Larry Richards
Managing Editor: Lila Empson
Associate Editor: W. Mark Whitlock
Scripture Editor: Deborah Wiseman
Assistant Editor: Amy Clark
Design: Diane Whisner

ISBN 1-4185-0995-7

Printed in the United States of America
 07 08 09   9 8 7 6 5 4 3 2 1

Introduction

Welcome to *Prophecies of the Bible—The Smart Guide to the Bible*™. This is the third book by Daymond R. Duck (Revelation was his first; Daniel was his second) in a new series that makes the Bible fun and educational. This is not the usual book on Bible prophecy. It is a new commentary that will change your outlook on Bible prophecy forever.

To Gain Your Confidence

Dr. Bob Jones Sr. said, "Simplicity is truth's most becoming garb." I wholeheartedly agree. Complicated speech is an unnecessary barrier that often stands in the way of my comprehension. Nothing is more worthless to me than a book filled with big theological terms and words I do not understand.

I wrote *Prophecies of the Bible—The Smart Guide to the Bible*™ for people who like things simple and straightforward. No complicated stuff. I set a goal to educate without boredom. Sure, I want to be accurate. But I do you a disservice if my words are not conversational, natural, and simple. I haven't done away with theological terms. I've just made them accessible to everyone.

A Word About Prophecy

Prophecy is what God says about the future. God can predict things to come before they happen. Prophecy is unique because it reveals God's plans. And God can and will do what he says. God says, "Remember the former things of old, for I am God, and there is no other; I am God, and there is none like Me, declaring the end from the beginning, and from ancient times things that are not yet done, saying, 'My counsel shall stand, and I will do all My pleasure'" (Isaiah 46:9–10 NKJV). Simply put, God knows the future. It is in his hands. What he says is prophecy. And what he says cannot be altered.

During Bible times God spoke to men of high character. Those special men wrote down God's words. God was the originator, and men were the recorders. And the parts they wrote that deal with future events are called prophecy.

About forty different writers wrote the Bible over a period of several hundred years. They recorded it in sixty-six volumes, called books, which are broken down into two sections: an "Old" Testament of thirty-nine books and a "New" Testament of twenty-seven books. Centuries later, scholars took what the writers had recorded and divided the text into chapters and verses.

All of the men who recorded God's words were Jews, except possibly Luke. (Luke was definitely a scholar in Jewish matters, but some authorities think he was Greek by ancestry.) As much as 40 percent of what those men wrote is prophecy. In this book I talk about the issues that people seem most interested in today.

A Word About Prophets

There is a plague of false prophets today, a plague of people who say they know the truth. But in fact, you can't trust these false prophets to give you the truth or to interpret it. Unfortunately, many prople who claim to speak for God hide the truth more than they reveal it. Some of these people may be theologians, seminary professors, and even preachers, but they're no better than the average newspaper horoscope or the local psychic in understanding prophecy.

The Bible says that we shouldn't add to or take anything away from what it says. Check it out for yourself—look up Deuteronomy 4:2; 12:32; Proverbs 30:6; or Revelation 22:18–19. People who aren't careful to do this go against a very basic teaching of the Bible. A person speaking from a deep understanding of God won't say anything that will contradict the Word of God. But a person speaking for the wrong reason will say a lot that simply isn't true. As the Bible says, God "overthrows the words of the faithless" (Proverbs 22:12 NKJV).

"What is truth?" Pontius Pilate asked Jesus (John 18:38 NKJV). That's a good question, but Pilate wasn't asking Jesus because he wanted to know the answer. Pilate was a cynic, and he was implying that truth is whatever those in authority want it to be. But truth is not what whoever's in a high position wants it to be. Truth is the Bible. When Jesus prayed, he said, "Your word is truth" (John 17:17 NKJV). The bottom line is this: the only modern-day prophet worth listening to is the one who sticks to the Bible. Such a speaker or teacher believes the Word and glorifies God.

A Word About Timing

When we think about prophecy, we usually think of the future. But first, here are four important questions worth exploring:

1. *Are prophecies fulfilled literally?* I interpret the Bible literally in its plain sense. Others who write or speak on prophecies may interpret the Bible in symbolic or allegorical ways. Such people believe that prophetic passages are just great ideas or timeless truths, and they wonder what the fuss is about.

2. *What prophecies have already been fulfilled?* Some prophecies, such as the first coming of Jesus, have been fulfilled. I believe other prophecies, such as the Church Age, are

being fulfilled now, and still other prophecies are for the future. Some Bible experts disagree; they believe all prophecy has already been fulfilled.

3. *What prophecies have not been fulfilled?* The second coming of Christ is one prophecy that has not yet happened. I believe the Tribulation Period has not yet occurred. Other Bible scholars think the famines, earthquakes, and floods we are experiencing today are those predicted in the Bible. Still other scholars believe nothing is currently being fulfilled. For them, it's all about the future.

4. *When and how will the unfulfilled prophecies be fulfilled?* I believe that on some occasions the Bible gives enough information to know the exact time a prophecy was, or will be, fulfilled. On other occasions it provides enough clues to place the prophecy in a certain time period—even if we don't know the exact day or hour that time period will arrive.

One other thing about timing: some prophecies are referred to as "double fulfillment" or "double reference" prophecies. Double fulfillment or double reference means that part of the prophecy refers to one event or time period, and part of it refers to a different event or time period. There is wide agreement among conservative prophecy experts that every prophecy will be totally fulfilled but that some prophecies will go through phases or stages before that happens. We also agree that one phase may be in one time period and another phase in a different time period, and the length of time between the two may range from the blink of an eye to thousands of years.

This book moves from one prophecy to the next from Genesis to Revelation. At the end of my discussion about each prophecy, I will tell you if the prophecy has been fulfilled, is still unfulfilled, has been partially fulfilled, or is continuously being fulfilled. We know that God inspired the Bible because of the fulfilled prophecies. And those fulfilled prophecies are evidence that God will literally fulfill the remaining prophecies at his chosen time.

Symbols, Symbols, and More Symbols

The Bible is filled with symbols, but we don't have to guess what they mean because they are often interpreted for us. Some symbols are explained within the context of the prophecy. Others are explained in a different passage of Scripture. I believe God did this to make us study the entire Bible. You do not need a Ph.D. to understand symbolism. You only need to search the Scriptures.

Why Study Bible Prophecy?

We are living in dangerous times. Quite often, the explanations of New Age astrologers, channelers, mystics, and psychics are being treated with respect. With regularity, the false doctrines and false prophecies of cults are valued more than the true doctrines and true prophecies of Christianity. Here are ten good reasons to study *Prophecies of the Bible—The Smart Guide to the Bible™*:

1. The Bible prophets received their messages from God, so what they said is the Word of God.

2. The accuracy of Bible prophecy proves the divine inspiration of the Scriptures.

3. Bible prophecy teaches us many things about God, politics, and faith.

4. Bible prophecy gives us assurance and hope in difficult or uncertain times.

5. Bible prophecy promotes evangelism, causes us to witness, and moves us to pray.

6. Bible prophecy aids perseverance during trials.

7. Bible prophecy causes us to watch for things to be fulfilled.

8. Knowing Bible prophecy increases our ability to help others.

9. Because so much Bible prophecy has already been literally fulfilled, we can logically expect the rest to be literally fulfilled.

10. If we do not study Bible prophecy, our understanding of the entire Bible will remain biblically inept.

How to Use *Prophecies of the Bible—The Smart Guide to the Bible™*

This book is divided into two main parts corresponding to the two main divisions of the Bible: Prophecies in the Old Testament and Prophecies in the New Testament. Part One is subdivided into five chapters: Prophecies in the Pentateuch, Prophecies in the Books of History, Prophecies in the Books of Poetry, Prophecies in the Major Prophets, and Prophecies in the Minor Prophets. Part Two is subdivided into four chapters: Prophecies in the Gospels and Acts, Prophecies in the Letters Written by the Apostle Paul, Prophecies in the Letters Written by Other Apostles, and Prophecies in the Book of Revelation.

A Word About Words

There are several interchangeable terms: Scripture, Scriptures, Word, Word of God, God's Word, Book, etc. All of these mean the same thing and come under the broad heading called the Bible. I will use each one at various times, but I will use "Bible" most of the time.

The word *Lord* in the Old Testament refers to Yahweh, God, whereas in the New Testament it refers to God's Son, Jesus Christ.

Tips to Help You

The Bible was written for all people, and God wants everyone to understand it. He even wants everyone to understand Bible prophecy. The Holy Spirit can do wonders to help you. Here are ten tips:

1. Begin with prayer.

2. Do not forget that God is infallible, and he does not make mistakes.

3. Do not forget that God is all-powerful, and he can do anything he wants to do.

4. Do not forget that God cannot lie, so what he says will be fulfilled exactly as he says.

5. Unless it is clear that symbols are being used, the prophecy should be interpreted literally.

6. When it is clear that a symbol is being used, find another passage of Scripture that interprets the symbol.

7. Look for normal, commonsense interpretations, not bizarre explanations.

8. Remember that some prophecies are about individuals (e.g., the Antichrist), some are about groups (e.g., the 144,000), some are about cities (e.g., Bethlehem), some are about nations (e.g., Russia), and some are about world empires (e.g., Babylon). But most prophecies are about one of three main groups: Israel (the Jews), the Gentiles (the non-Jews), and the church (Christians). The common thread in most prophecies is the Messiah (Jesus).

9. Remember that there are several different gatherings and destructions of Israel, several different rises and falls of Gentile nations, and two comings of Jesus.

10. Remember that some prophecy is sealed up and cannot be understood until God is ready to reveal it.

About the Author

Daymond is the best-selling author of *On the Brink, An Easy-to-Understand End-Time Bible Prophecy; The Book of Revelation—The Smart Guide to the Bible*™; and *The Book of Daniel—The Smart Guide to the Bible*™. He is the coauthor of *The End-Times Survival Handbook*. And he is a contributing author to *Forewarning—The Approaching Battle Between Good and Evil; Foreshadows of Wrath and Redemption; Piercing the Future—Prophecy and the New Millennium*; and *Prophecy at Ground Zero*.

Daymond worked his way through college and graduated from the University of Tennessee with a B.S. in agricultural engineering. In 1979, at the age of forty, he entered the ministry and became a bi-vocational pastor. He completed the five-year Course-of-Study Program at Emory University for United Methodist Pastors. He has twice served as honorary state chaplain for the Tennessee Rural Carriers, is a prophecy conference speaker, and is a member of the Pre-Trib Study Group in Arlington, Texas. Daymond and his wife, Rachel, make their home in Dyer, Tennessee. They have three children and five grandchildren.

About the General Editor

Dr. Larry Richards is a native of Michigan who now lives in Raleigh, North Carolina. He was converted while in the Navy in the 1950s. Larry has taught and written Sunday school curriculum for every age group, from nursery through adult. He has published more than two hundred books that have been translated into twenty-six languages. His wife, Sue, is also an author. They both enjoy teaching Bible studies as well as fishing and playing golf.

Acknowledgments

I wish to acknowledge the many long hours of hard work and invaluable help from my loving wife, Rachel. She worked behind the scenes, but her encouragement and commitment kept me going, and her research, definitions, suggestions, and editing made this difficult task much easier.

Thanks, honey.

Understanding the Bible Is Easy with These Tools

To understand God's Word you need easy-to-use study tools right where you need them—at your fingertips. The Smart Guide to the Bible™ series puts valuable resources adjacent to the text to save you both time and effort.

Every page features handy sidebars filled with icons and helpful information: cross references for additional insights, definitions of key words and concepts, brief commentaries from experts on the topic, points to ponder, evidence of God at work, the big picture of how passages fit into the context of the entire Bible, practical tips for applying biblical truths to every area of your life, and plenty of maps, charts, and illustrations. A wrap-up of each passage, combined with study questions, concludes each chapter.

These helpful tools show you what to watch for. Look them over to become familiar with them, and then turn to Chapter 1 with complete confidence: You are about to increase your knowledge of God's Word!

Study Helps

The thought-bubble icon alerts you to commentary you might find particularly thought-provoking, challenging, or encouraging. You'll want to take a moment to reflect on it and consider the implications for your life.

Don't miss this point! The exclamation-point icon draws your attention to a key point in the text and emphasizes important biblical truths and facts.

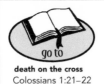

death on the cross
Colossians 1:21–22

Many see Boaz as a type of Jesus Christ. To win back what we human beings lost through sin and spiritual death, Jesus had to become human (i.e., he had to become a true kinsman), and he had to be willing to pay the penalty for our sins. With his <u>death on the cross</u>, Jesus paid the penalty and won freedom and eternal life for us.

The additional Bible verses add scriptural support for the passage you just read and help you better understand the <u>underlined text</u>. (Think of it as an instant reference resource!)

How does what you just read apply to your life? The heart icon indicates that you're about to find out! These practical tips speak to your mind, heart, body, and soul, and offer clear guidelines for living a righteous and joy-filled life, establishing priorities, maintaining healthy relationships, persevering through challenges, and more.

This icon reveals how God is truly all-knowing and all-powerful. The hourglass icon points to a specific example of the prediction of an event or the fulfillment of a prediction. See how some of what God has said would come to pass already has!

What are some of the great things God has done? The traffic-sign icon shows you how God has used miracles, special acts, promises, and covenants throughout history to draw people to him.

Does the story or event you just read about appear elsewhere in the Gospels? The cross icon points you to those instances where the same story appears in other Gospel locations—further proof of the accuracy and truth of Jesus' life, death, and resurrection.

Since God created marriage, there's no better person to turn to for advice. The double-ring icon points out biblical insights and tips for strengthening your marriage.

The Bible is filled with wisdom about raising a godly family and enjoying your spiritual family in Christ. The family icon gives you ideas for building up your home and helping your family grow close and strong.

Isle of Patmos
a small island in the
Mediterranean Sea

something significant had occurred, he wrote down the substance of what he saw. This is the practice John followed when he recorded Revelation on the **Isle of Patmos.**

What does that word really mean, especially as it relates to this passage? Important, misunderstood, or infrequently used words are set in **bold type** in your text so you can immediately glance at the margin for definitions. This valuable feature lets you better understand the meaning of the entire passage without having to stop to check other references.

the big picture

Joshua
Led by Joshua, the Israelites crossed the Jordan River and invaded Canaan (see Illustration #8). In a series of military campaigns the Israelites defeated several coalition armies raised by the inhabitants of Canaan. With organized resistance put down, Joshua divided the land among the twelve Israelite

How does what you read fit in with the greater biblical story? The highlighted big picture summarizes the passage under discussion.

what others say

David Breese
Nothing is clearer in the Word of God than the fact that God wants us to understand himself and his working in the lives of men.[5]

It can be helpful to know what others say on the topic, and the highlighted quotation introduces another voice in the discussion. This resource enables you to read other opinions and perspectives.

Maps, charts, and illustrations pictorially represent ancient artifacts and show where and how stories and events took place. They enable you to better understand important empires, learn your way around villages and temples, see where major battles occurred, and follow the journeys of God's people. You'll find these graphics let you do more than study God's Word—they let you *experience* it.

Chapters at a Glance

Part Two: Prophecies in the New Testament

Part One
Prophecies in the
Old Testament

Prophecy Basics

Two Kinds of Prophecy

This book is about prophecies—**fulfilled** and **unfulfilled**. The fulfilled prophecies are identified and we know when their fulfillment took place. The unfulfilled prophecies are identified too, but we have only a general idea about when they will be fulfilled. We don't know the day or the hour, but we do know when they will be fulfilled in relation to other events. These events have special names: **Tribulation Period**, **Rapture**, **Second Coming**, and **Millennium**.

Tribulation Period

Jesus was prophesying about the end of the age when he said, "For then there will be great tribulation, such as has not been since the beginning of the world until this time, no, nor ever shall be" (Matthew 24:21 NKJV). Contrary to what some say, the world is not moving toward a **New World Order** characterized by peace, cooperation, and prosperity. It is plunging toward distress characterized by calamities such as war, <u>famine</u>, **pestilence**, natural disasters, and death. This future period of distress is called the Tribulation Period. According to the Bible, the Tribulation Period will be seven years long, and the last three and a half years are called the <u>Great Tribulation</u> Period. More is said about this later under the discussion of Daniel's prophecies.

Rapture

There is wide agreement among those who study Bible prophecy that several passages of Scripture teach a future resurrection of deceased church members, a sudden gathering of those who are <u>still alive</u> at that time, and a "catching away" of these people into heaven. This expected "catching away" is usually called the Rapture. Some call it the Rapture of the Church. But while there is wide agreement

go to

famine
Revelation 6:1–7

Great Tribulation
Matthew 24:21

still alive
1 Thessalonians
4:13–18

fulfilled
has taken place

unfulfilled
will take place in the
future

Tribulation Period
seven years of God's
wrath against the
wicked on earth

Rapture
when the church is
removed from the
earth

Second Coming
the return of Jesus at
the end of the
Tribulation Period

Millennium
the thousand-year
reign of Christ on
earth

New World Order
another name for
world government

pestilence
a fatal contagious or
infectious disease

that the Rapture will happen, there are differing opinions about when it will happen in relation to the Tribulation Period. Most experts believe the Rapture will occur before the Tribulation Period. Their belief is called the Pre-Tribulation Rapture Theory. A small minority of experts believe the Rapture will occur at the middle of the Tribulation Period and their belief is called the Mid-Tribulation Rapture Theory. Another group believes the Rapture will occur at the end of the Tribulation Period and their belief is called the Post-Tribulation Rapture Theory. This book agrees with the majority by taking the Pre-Tribulation Rapture position. The diagrams of these theories should help you understand these concepts.

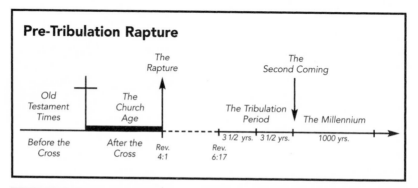

Pre-Tribulation Rapture

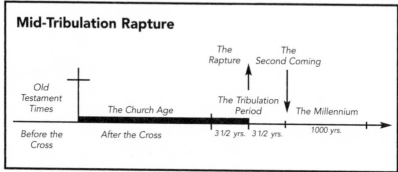

Mid-Tribulation Rapture

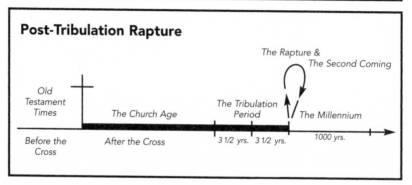

Post-Tribulation Rapture

The word *Rapture* is not in the English translations of the Bible, but the concept is. The first New Testament texts were written in Greek, and the Greek word *harpazo*, meaning "suddenly taken away by an irresistible force," was used. When the Greek texts were translated into Latin, *harpazo* was replaced by the Latin word *rapere*. When the Latin texts were translated into English, a problem arose: *harpazo* and *rapere* wouldn't translate into just one English word. So instead of using an awkward combination, they have taken the Latin word *rapere* and Anglicized it into the word *Rapture*.

Second Coming

Two of the most important events mentioned in the Bible are the two comings of Jesus: the first to die for the <u>sin of the world</u>, and the second to put an end to all sin. That's right, Jesus is coming <u>back</u> to put an end to Satan's influence here on earth. He will bind Satan, restore Israel, renew this creation, and reign here on earth for a while. Earth will be a wonderful place to live once again.

Millennium

It is important to know what the Millennium is because this book discusses prophecies being fulfilled in relation to that period of time. But understanding the Millennium gets confusing because there are three different beliefs about it: premillennialism, amillennialism, and postmillennialism. All three include the second coming of Christ and believe the saved will spend eternity with God.

Premillennialism was the first belief to appear, historically speaking. The word *millennium* is Latin, and it means "a thousand years." A <u>thousand</u>-year reign of Christ is mentioned six times in the book of Revelation. Putting "Pre" in front of "millennium" suggests Christ will return before the thousand-year reign. By interpreting the Scriptures literally, the early church came to the conclusion that Jesus will return to earth, destroy Israel's enemies, establish a kingdom, sit on the throne of David in Jerusalem, and rule over the world for a thousand years. Under his rule, all of the covenants with Israel will be literally fulfilled during that thousand-year reign; and peace, justice, and righteousness will prevail over the earth. Premillennialists believe that in the distant future, after the kingdom

go to

sin of the world
John 1:29

back
John 14:1–4;
Acts 1:11

thousand
Revelation 20:1–7

premillennialism
Christ will return
before his thousand-
year reign

amillennialism
the thousand-year reign has been replaced by the Church Age

postmillennialism
Christ will return after his thousand-year reign (Church Age)

Christianized
converted to Christianity

is purged of sin, Jesus will turn it over to the Father, and it will be merged with his kingdom. This is the view of many conservative Protestants and is the one set forth in this book.

The chart on Millennium Theories shows the three main views of the Millennium. All three views say society is in the Church Age, but postmillennialism says the church will convert the world before Jesus returns. Premillennialism and amillennialism believe in a Rapture, but at different times, and postmillennialism doesn't believe in a Rapture at all. Premillennialism is the only view to espouse a Tribulation Period. And amillennialism doesn't believe in an earthly kingdom.

Millennium Theories

Church	Age	Rapture	Tribulation	Millennium
Premillennialism	Now	Before Tribulation	After Rapture	Second Coming ushers in kingdom with Jesus on throne in Jerusalem
Amillennialism	Now	Occurs with Second Coming	Not applicable	No earthly kingdom
Postmillennialism	Now and getting better	None	Not applicable	Before the Second Coming

Amillennialism appeared about three hundred years after premillennialism. Putting an *a* in front of the word *millennium* means "no millennium" or "no thousand years." Those who embrace amillennialism believe all the prophecies about Israel refer to the church, that the kingdom is the church, that the Millennium is the Church Age, and that the New Earth is heaven. They believe Satan was bound at the first coming of Jesus. Instead of Jesus coming to sit on the throne of David in Jerusalem to rule over the world, they believe we are in the Millennium (Church Age) now and Jesus is ruling over the earth through the church. For them the Rapture is the Second Coming. This is the view of most Catholics and liberal Protestants.

Postmillennialism did not surface until the seventeenth century. This belief ignores or explains away most prophecies. Postmillennialism suggests that the world is constantly getting better, that the whole world will eventually be **Christianized**, and that Christ will not come back until it is. Postmillennialism means Christ will return after the Millennium, after the world is Christianized.

Instead of Christ coming to establish his kingdom, postmillennialists believe the church is building that kingdom. This belief almost died out in the mid-twentieth century, but is making a comeback under the names of Dominion Now, Dominion Theology, and Reconstructionism.

Prophecies in the Pentateuch

Chapter Highlights:
- **Corruption on Earth**
- **God's Covenants**
- **The Coming Ruler**
- **Choices for Israel**
- **The Coming Tribulation Period**

Let's Get Started

The first five books of the Old Testament are often called the **Pentateuch**. The word *Pentateuch* is a combination of two Greek words meaning "five books" or "five scrolls." Except for the book of Job, these five books are the oldest books in the Bible. Most authorities believe God gave the information contained therein to an Israelite leader named <u>**Moses**</u>. Moses recorded the information in the form of a continuous story beginning with Creation and ending with his death.[1]

Some other names for the Pentateuch are the Law, the <u>Law of Moses</u>, the Mosaic Law, and the **Torah**. The word *Torah* is Hebrew and it means "instruction, guidance, or Law." Devout Jews believe the Pentateuch contains laws given by God. Devout Christians believe it also contains prophecies given by him. Christians also believe Moses was a <u>prophet</u> and every little detail of what he prophesied will be fulfilled. Jesus says, "Do not think that I came to destroy the Law or the Prophets. I did not come to destroy but to fulfill. For assuredly, I say to you, till heaven and earth pass away, one jot or one tittle will by no means pass from the law till all is fulfilled" (Matthew 5:17–18 NKJV).

go to

Moses
Exodus 3:1–22

Law of Moses
Luke 24:44

prophet
Deuteronomy 34:10–12

Pentateuch
the first five books of the Old Testament

Moses
the first prophet

Torah
Pentateuch, Law of Moses, Mosaic Law

Birth			Death
Moses in Pharaoh's Palace	Moses in Exile in Midian	Moses in the Wilderness	
1525 BC	1485 BC	1445 BC	1405 BC

what others say

Larry Richards

The Old Testament is a collection of 39 books, which were written between 1450 BC and 400 BC. They tell the story of God's special relationship with one human family, the family of Abraham, Isaac, and Jacob, which became the Jewish people.

died
Deuteronomy
34:1–12

created
Genesis 2:4–7

Garden of Eden
Genesis 2:15

> Through this people God revealed himself to all mankind. And through this people God set in motion a plan to save all who would believe in him from the terrible consequences of sin.[2]

Some critics say Moses could not be the author of the first five books of the Bible because the fifth book provides information about things that happened after he <u>died</u>, for example the inclusions about Moses' death. But Jesus told us things about his own death before he died, that he would be killed and raised from the dead three days later. It is possible that Moses was able to foresee his own death experience. Jesus said, "With God all things are possible" (Mark 10:27 NKJV). This doesn't prove Moses wrote the first five books of the Bible, but it does mean the critics could be wrong.

GENESIS

Life in a Nutshell

GENESIS 3:14–19 *So the LORD God said to the serpent: "Because you have done this, you are cursed more than all cattle, and more than every beast of the field; on your belly you shall go, and you shall eat dust all the days of your life. And I will put enmity between you and the woman, and between your seed and her Seed; He shall bruise your head, and you shall bruise His heel." To the woman He said: "I will greatly multiply your sorrow and your conception; in pain you shall bring forth children; your desire shall be for your husband, and he shall rule over you." Then to Adam He said, "Because you have heeded the voice of your wife, and have eaten from the tree of which I commanded you, saying, 'You shall not eat of it': Cursed is the ground for your sake; in toil you shall eat of it all the days of your life. Both thorns and thistles it shall bring forth for you, and you shall eat the herb of the field. In the sweat of your face you shall eat bread till you return to the ground, for out of it you were taken; for dust you are, and to dust you shall return." (NKJV)*

Some call this the first prophecy in the Bible. When God <u>created</u> Adam and Eve, he placed them in a beautiful place called the <u>Garden of Eden</u>. He had created many different trees, and he told them they could eat from any tree in the garden except <u>the Tree</u> of the Knowledge of Good and Evil. They disobeyed and that is sin; sin always has a price. God decreed seven **judgments** because of <u>sin</u>:

1. Satan is cursed for as long as he lives.

2. Satan's head will ultimately be crushed.

3. Throughout history there will be conflict between the serpent's **offspring** and the woman's offspring, between good and evil.

4. Throughout history women will undergo pain during childbirth.

5. Throughout history women will have to <u>submit</u> to their husbands.

6. Throughout history men will have to work to feed themselves.

7. Throughout history human beings will die.

go to

the tree
Genesis 2:16–17

sin
Romans 5:12

submit
Ephesians 5:24

judgments
acts of God intended to punish

offspring
children, descendants, that which comes from something

Armageddon
a great battle between good and evil at the Second Coming

what others say

Wayne Barber, Eddie Rasnake, and Richard Shepherd

Sin had shattered the oneness with God that they had experienced. Instead of a oneness with God there was division and running away from God. Instead of honesty between themselves and their Creator, there was blame and excuses. The oneness between Adam and Eve was gone as well. In its place were separation, accusations, and disharmony. With Adam's disobedience, sin entered the human race. Instead of life and oneness with God, they experienced death and separation.[3]

Ed Hindson

Satan's doom is already assured, but the battle is far from being over. He still "prowls around like a roaring lion looking for someone to devour" (1 Peter 5:8 [NIV]). He has fallen from heaven (Isaiah 14:2). He was condemned in Eden (Genesis 3:14). He accuses the believers (Revelation 12:10). Eventually he will be cast out of heaven permanently and will expend his wrath on earth (Revelation 12:7–12). Ultimately he will be defeated at **Armageddon** and cast into the abyss (Revelation 19:11–20:3). Finally he will be thrown into the lake of fire (Revelation 20:10). . . . He may be a defeated foe, but he has every intention of keeping up the fight to the very end.[4]

second death
Revelation 20:14

Lake
Revelation 20:10

messianic
having to do with
the Messiah

Men have seed (sperm), but there is no such thing as a woman's seed. Therefore, many scholars say the phrase "her Seed" predicts a miracle birth. And the miracle birth they have in mind is the virgin birth of Jesus. This is why this prophecy is called "the first **messianic** prophecy in the Bible."

Because we have anesthetics, painkillers, well-equipped hospitals, etc., childbirth is less painful in this country than it once was. But these modern conveniences have been available only for the last few decades. Most are not available at all in many foreign countries. After thousands of years, this prophecy is still true.

This prophecy is continually being fulfilled, but it will not be completely fulfilled until some point after the Millennium. Satan suffered a major defeat when Jesus died on the cross to take away our sin. The curse will be suspended during the thousand years of the Millennium when Satan is bound (Revelation 20:2), but he will be set free again for an unspecified length of time (Revelation 20:3). Following that, Satan will die the <u>second death</u> when he is thrown into the <u>Lake</u> of Fire and this prophecy will be completely fulfilled.

He will die the second death. It is encouraging to know that Jesus will ultimately defeat Satan, and what God started in the Garden of Eden will be completed in eternity. Adam's fall and everything Satan has done in the past, or will do in the future, will not thwart God's original plan. But we should also know that the struggle between good and evil, the woman's offspring and Satan's offspring, will be a long, drawn-out affair. The judgment of God is sure, but he is very patient.

God Will Not Be Thwarted

Genesis	Revelation
Satan entered the Garden (3:1)	Nothing that defiles will enter New Jerusalem (21:27)
Satan's opposition to God and man began (3:15)	Satan will be cast into the Lake of Fire (20:10)
Sorrow and pain began (3:16)	No more sorrow and pain (21:4)
The ground was cursed (3:17)	No more curse (22:3)
Adam would return to dust (3:19)	No more death (21:4)
Adam barred from Tree of Life (3:21–24)	Access to Tree of Life regained (22:14)

In the Days of Noah

GENESIS 6:11–13 *The earth also was corrupt before God, and the earth was filled with violence. So God looked upon the earth, and indeed it was corrupt; for all flesh had corrupted their way on the earth. And God said to Noah, "The end of all flesh has come before Me, for the earth is filled with violence through them; and behold, I will destroy them with the earth." (NKJV)*

Adam and Eve's sin was the beginning of a moral crisis on earth. Their son Cain <u>killed</u> his brother Abel. Cain left the <u>presence</u> of God and moved away and society worsened. When Cain's great-great-great-grandson Lamech came on the scene, he was a **polygamist** married to <u>two women</u>. And by Noah's day, almost two thousand years after Adam, great **wickedness** covered the earth. So God decided to destroy his creation with a flood.

killed
Genesis 4:8

presence
Genesis 4:16

two women
Genesis 4:19

wickedness
Genesis 6:5

Ararat
Genesis 8:1–4

guilty
Numbers 14:18

hates
Proverbs 6:16–19

polygamist
one who has more than one mate

wickedness
all sin

depraved
wicked, corrupt

what others say

Bruce A. Tanner

Sin is not only a degenerative disease but also a contagious one. Like gravity, sin can be expected to exert a continuous downward pull on individuals and on society. It did not take fallen man long to learn the ways of sin.[5]

Robert T. Boyd

There are no fewer than thirty-three separate records from distinctly different people groups that tell of a worldwide flood. The similarities between these accounts and Moses' description of the flood in Noah's time are remarkable.[6]

Some say the Flood was a local flood limited just to the Middle East. If that is true, how is it that Noah's ark came to rest near the top of a 17,000-foot mountain called <u>Ararat</u>?

God is very loving, but he is also holy. He is very patient, but man is not free to do any evil thing he wants to do. God cannot and will not overlook the sin of a **depraved** society forever. He will punish the <u>guilty</u>. Here are seven things God <u>hates</u>:

1. A proud look

2. A lying tongue

3. Hands that shed innocent blood

4. A heart that devises wicked plans

5. Feet that are swift in running to evil

6. A false witness who speaks lies

7. One who sows discord among brethren

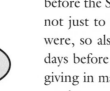

The flood portion of this prophecy has been fulfilled, but Jesus drew a comparison between the wickedness on earth during the days of Noah and that which will exist during the Tribulation Period just before the Second Coming. This promise applies to the entire world, not just to the nation of Israel. He said, "But as the days of Noah were, so also will the coming of the Son of Man be. For as in the days before the flood, they were eating and drinking, marrying and giving in marriage, until the day that Noah entered the ark, and did not know until the flood came and took them all away, so also will the coming of the Son of Man be" (Matthew 24:37–39 NKJV). The bad news is that humankind is going to become more and more evil. But the good news is that Jesus is going to return and put an end to it.

A Promise to Remember

GENESIS 8:22 *While the earth remains, seedtime and harvest, cold and heat, winter and summer, and day and night shall not cease. (NKJV)*

Following the Flood, Noah's first act was to build an altar and offer a **sacrifice** to God. He was specifically humbling himself, giving thanks to God for saving him and his family, and declaring his __faith__. God was pleased with this and promised that as long as the earth exists, there will always be seasons.

This prophecy is continuously being fulfilled, and it will continue to be fulfilled until the earth is destroyed sometime after the Millennium. Here God promises that seasons will always be distinct.

God's Covenant with Abram (Abraham)

GENESIS 12:1–3 *Now the LORD had said to Abram: "Get out of your country, from your family and from your father's house, to a land that I will show you. I will make you a great nation; I will bless you and make your name great; and you shall be a blessing. I will bless those who bless you, and I will curse him who curses you; and in you all the families of the earth shall be blessed." (NKJV)*

God's **covenant** with Abraham is also called the Abrahamic covenant. God said to Abraham:

- Get out of your country (Ur of the Chaldeans).
- Go away from your family.
- Go away from your father's house.
- Go to a land I will show you.

If Abraham would do these four things, God promised he would do seven things. Some scholars break these promises down into the following categories:

National Promise

- "I will make you a great nation."

Personal Promises

- "I will bless you."
- "I will make your name great" (i.e., make you famous).
- "You shall be a blessing" (i.e., a benefit to others).

World Promises

- "I will bless those who bless you."
- "I will curse those who curse you" (the people and nations in the world who do evil to Abraham and his nation).
- "I will bless the whole world through you" (the Messiah will be a descendant of Abraham).

go to

faith
Hebrews 11:6–7

earth
Revelation 21:1

Abraham
Galatians 3:6–16

Ur of the Chaldeans
Genesis 11:31

faith
trust in God

covenant
an agreement
between two parties

From the very beginning of the world, God has dealt with his people through covenants. These covenants are sometimes called the driving force of Bible prophecy because they spell out the actions or agreements that God intends to follow through on in the future. Some are conditional, meaning God will not fulfill his part unless the other party fulfills their part. And some are unconditional, meaning God will do what he said even if the other party doesn't do anything. Since Abraham left his country, friends, family, and father's house, and moved to the land God showed him, God has now obligated himself to fulfill all the promises he made in this covenant. They are literal and destined to be literally fulfilled. If they are not fulfilled, the Bible is wrong or God lied. Most conservative Christians cannot accept either one of these possibilities.

Fast Facts on the Driving Force of Bible Prophecy

Covenant	Scripture
Edenic Covenant	Genesis 1:28–30; 2:15–17
Adamic Covenant	Genesis 3:14–19
Noahic Covenant	Genesis 8:20–9:17
Abrahamic Covenant	Genesis 12:1–3; 13:14–15, 17
Mosaic Covenant	Exodus 20–23
Davidic Covenant	2 Samuel 7:4–17; Psalm 89:3–4
Palestinian Covenant	Deuteronomy 30:1–10
New Covenant	Jeremiah 31:31–40; Hebrews 8:6–13

what others say

Wayne Barber, Eddie Rasnake, and Richard Shepherd

One would look in vain for an explanation of why he [Abraham] was selected for God's purposes. The only answer we have is that by **grace**, God sought him out. God had a unique purpose for Abraham's life. He called him from a pagan culture to make a new nation—one that would follow God.[8]

Henry M. Morris with Henry M. Morris III

The nations that have befriended the Jews (notably the United States and, to a lesser degree, England, France, and others) have indeed been blessed. Those that have persecuted the Jews (Egypt, Babylon, Assyria, Rome, Spain, Nazi Germany, and others—Russia's time is coming!) have eventually gone down to defeat and humiliation.[9]

Abraham and Noah are both recognized in the New Testament for their great <u>faith</u> because they trusted in God when he asked them to do something unusual. Noah believed God when he said he was going to destroy the world with a flood, so Noah built an ark and was saved. Abraham believed God when he made all those promises, so he moved to Canaan and they started coming true. How should we respond to the prophecies of God?

The covenants reveal what God plans to do in the future. By keeping his covenants, God gives us evidence of his existence and how he moves in history.

First, he binds himself to do specific things. Then, he views his covenants as promises he is obligated to keep because his honor and reputation are at stake. Finally, he fulfills them in every detail because he wants his people to know he can be trusted. Prophecy is a record of promises made and promises kept.

This covenant was made with Abraham, not the church. The church is a recipient of the spiritual blessings because God by his grace included it. As a party of the covenant he can do that. But the church has not replaced Israel. The material blessings (land, its size, etc.) belong to that nation only. God's blessings will fall on those who are kind to the Jews, and his curses will fall on those who mistreat them.

Abraham left the place where he lived and went to the land of Canaan (see Illustration #1, Abraham's Travels). He was <u>seventy-five</u> years old when he departed. Ten years after he arrived, a servant of his wife bore him a son named <u>Ishmael</u>. Fourteen years later, when Abraham was one hundred years old, his wife, Sarah, bore him a son named <u>Isaac</u>. It is clear that God intended for his covenant with <u>Abraham</u> to pass through this son. Isaac's descendants would become the great nation of Israel, and they would be the instru-

go to

Canaan
Genesis 12:6–7

faith
Hebrews 11:7–19

seventy-five
Genesis 12:4

Ishmael
Genesis 16:1–16

Isaac
Genesis 17:1–27

Abraham
Matthew 1:1

key point

Canaan
Israel

atone
make reconciliation with God

ments of blessing and curses in the world. This prophecy is continuously being fulfilled through the existence of Israel. It was partially fulfilled at the first coming of Jesus, and it will be completely fulfilled after the Millennium when Satan is cast into the Lake of Fire.

Forever Is a Long Time

> GENESIS 13:14–17 *And the LORD said to Abram, after Lot had separated from him: "Lift your eyes now and look from the place where you are—northward, southward, eastward, and westward; for all the land which you see I give to you and your descendants forever. And I will make your descendants as the dust of the earth; so that if a man could number the dust of the earth, then your descendants also could be numbered. Arise, walk in the land through its length and its width, for I give it to you." (NKJV)*

The Lord appeared unto Abraham a second time, and on this occasion God told Abraham he would give the land of Canaan to him and his descendants **forever**. God was saying, "I will not give you and your descendants the land and expect to get it back at a later date." The land of Canaan is Israel's forever.

God also told Abraham he would have a great number of descendants. They would number more than anyone could count.

God gave the land to Israel, but there is a problem. Muslims do not believe Israel's God is God. They worship Allah and believe he gave the land to them. This makes the land conflict a theological conflict. The question is, Whose god is God or who worships the true God? The media and multitudes are lining up against Israel, and at the same time setting themselves against God. It will take the Tribulation Period and the second coming of Christ to settle the issue. But make no mistake, the Word of God says he will do just that.

Israel has occupied the land several times, but because of sin God has allowed them to be removed for temporary periods of time. So the land portion of this prophecy is continuously being fulfilled, but it will not be fully realized until the Millennium. The "great number of descendants" portion of the prophecy has already been fulfilled.

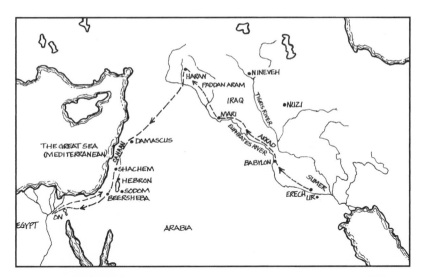

Illustration #1
Abraham's Travels—
Abram and his wife,
Sarai, traveled from
Ur of the Chaldeans,
through Haran and
Egypt, to Canaan.

Egypt
1 Kings 4:21; 8:65

Lots and Lots of Land and a Covenant to Boot

Promised Land
another name for
the land of Israel

GENESIS 15:18 *On the same day the LORD made a covenant with Abram, saying: "To your descendants I have given this land, from the river of Egypt to the great river, the River Euphrates." (NKJV)*

God appeared unto Abraham a third time, and on this occasion he spelled out the boundaries of the land he was giving to Abraham and his descendants. It covers an area that runs from the river of Egypt, which is a reference to the Nile River, to the river Euphrates.

Some say this is more land than Israel has ever occupied. It includes all of modern Israel, all of the West Bank territories, part of Egypt, and part of Iraq (see Illustration #2). But more important, God made a covenant with Abraham. He bound himself to give the land of Canaan to Abraham and his descendants.

> ### what others say
>
> #### Randall Price
>
> If we look at current maps of Israel, we will see that the nation comprises only a small portion of the area originally promised to the Patriarchs for their future descendants (the 12 tribes of Israel) as an everlasting possession. When Abraham received the title deed to God's **Promised Land** the geographical boundaries were significantly greater than those occupied by the modern state: "from the river of Egypt as far as the great river, the river Euphrates" (Genesis 15:18). Later these boundaries were made even more specific to Moses (Numbers 34:2–12).[11]

go to

covenant
Daniel 9:4

Among scholars there are differences of opinion about whether or not Israel has ever possessed all the land God promised. But they are not divided about the fact that Israel will possess all of the Promised Land during the Millennium. So this is designated unfulfilled with reservations. When God makes a covenant, he sets up a standard by which he can be measured. He exposes himself to being evaluated.

Israel's God

GENESIS 17:7–8 *And I will establish My covenant between Me and you and your descendants after you in their generations, for an everlasting covenant, to be God to you and your descendants after you. Also I give to you and your descendants after you the land in which you are a stranger, all the land of Canaan, as an everlasting possession; and I will be their God. (NKJV)*

The Lord repeated his promise to give all the land of Canaan to Abraham and his descendants and, once again, he added something else. He would be the God of Abraham and his descendants throughout all generations. No matter what, he would keep his <u>covenant</u> and never turn his back on Abraham's descendants.

Illustration #2
The Promised Land—The shaded area indicates present-day Israel. The area encompassed by the dashed line indicates the area Jews will occupy in the millennial reign of Christ.

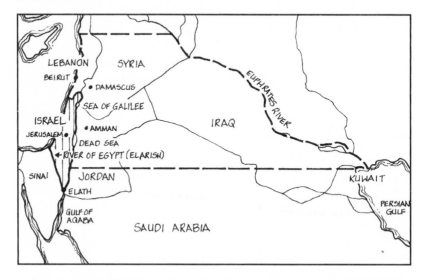

At times Israel has been an evil nation. Idolatry and unbelief have filled the land. On at least two occasions, God let foreigners destroy the nation (Babylon and Rome). But God is faithful and has never ceased to be Israel's God. Christians sin, but that doesn't mean God will break his promise to save them. Everlasting means forever, whether it is everlasting life as in John 3:16 or an everlasting covenant as in Genesis 17:7–8. If God can break an everlasting covenant, Christians may not have everlasting life. But Christians do have everlasting life and the land is Israel's forever.

God gave "all the land of Canaan" to Israel. The Arabs and their Palestinian allies are trying to take control of Israel and Jerusalem piece by piece, and many world leaders are helping them. But God said all the land belongs to Abrahamic offspring (Israel).

Hagar
Genesis 16:1–4

Ishmael
Genesis 16:15–16

Why Israel Will Receive the Promised Land

Why the Jews Will Receive the Promised Land	Scripture
God knows the future and will not cast Israel away	Romans 11:1–2
God is faithful and will not break his covenants	Leviticus 26:44–45; Psalm 89:30–37
God is forgiving and full of mercy	Jeremiah 31:31–37; Romans 11:30–32
The gifts of God can't be taken back	Romans 11:29

In spite of the fact that Israel has returned to the land in unbelief, this prophecy is constantly being fulfilled. The relationship between God and Israel is not what it should be, but things will change when the Jews accept Jesus as the Messiah at his second coming. That will start the Millennium, and they will occupy all the land God promised to them. God will always be Israel's God. God's unconditional covenants depend upon God, not Israel.

Announcing a New Arrival

> GENESIS 17:19 *Then God said: "No, Sarah your wife shall bear you a son, and you shall call his name Isaac; I will establish My covenant with him for an everlasting covenant, and with his descendants after him." (NKJV)*

God's promise to give the land of Canaan to Abraham and his descendants could be fulfilled only by Abraham having a child. When his wife, Sarah, decided she could not conceive, she suggested that Abraham father a child by her maidservant Hagar. Abraham did as she suggested, and Ishmael was born. That was a great thing for an eighty-six-year-old man, but it was not what God had intended. He appeared to Abraham and announced that his wife, Sarah, would

Isaac
Genesis 21:12;
25:1–7

sons
Genesis 16:10–12;
21:1–8

ninety
Genesis 17:17

concubines
secondary wives

indeed have a baby, it would be a male child, his name would be Isaac, and God's covenant would be renewed with this child and his descendants.

Abraham even asked God to accept Ishmael and let the everlasting covenant for possession of the land go through him. If God had agreed, the land would have gone to the Arabs. But God said no (Genesis 17:18–21). Later, Abraham fathered several sons by his wives, his **concubines**, and their servants. God blessed all of them, but the covenant he made with Abraham passed through Isaac.

God often provided signs so people can remember and know that he made covenants. Some of this is shown in the following chart.

Signs of God's Existing Covenants

Covenant	Sign	Scripture
Covenant with Noah	Rainbow	Genesis 9:12–17
Covenant with Abraham	Circumcision	Genesis 17:11
Covenant with Moses	Sabbath	Exodus 31:13
New covenant (Church/Israel)	Communion Cup	Luke 22:20

Those who oppose Israel need to pay attention to God's attitude toward that nation. When they set themselves against Israel they are setting themselves against God as is shown in the next chart.

How God Refers to Himself in the Bible

Phrase	Number of Times He Used It
The God of Abraham	16
The God of Isaac	8
The God of Jacob	22
The Lord God of Israel	108
The God of Israel	203

When Abraham was one hundred years old and Sarah was ninety, the portion of this prophecy that pertains to Isaac was fulfilled. The remainder is continuously being fulfilled from generation to generation.

A Blessing for All

GENESIS 18:17–18 *And the LORD said, "Shall I hide from Abraham what I am doing, since Abraham shall surely become* *a great and mighty nation, and all the nations of the earth shall be blessed in him?" (NKJV)*

The inhabitants of two cities that existed in Abraham's lifetime were particularly **evil**, so God decided to destroy them. But he had a special relationship with Abraham, and that prompted a question, "Should I hide my intentions from Abraham, since I have promised that he will become a great nation and a source of <u>blessing</u> to all people?"

go to

blessing
Acts 3:24–26

Sodom
Genesis 19:27–28

world
John 3:16–18

covenant
Psalm 25:14

test
Genesis 22:1

evil
sinful, wicked

soliloquy
talking to oneself

> **what others say**
>
> ### W. H. Griffith Thomas
>
> How beautiful is the suggestion made by the Divine **soliloquy**! "Shall I hide from Abraham that thing which I do?" God's friends are permitted to know His secrets because they are His friends. Abraham is regarded by God as having a right to know what was about to be done (Psalm 25:4; Amos 3:7).[12]

God revealed his plan to Abraham and then destroyed the cities of <u>Sodom</u> and Gomorrah. Abraham's descendants eventually became the nation of Israel. During the Millennium, Israel will be the great nation predicted in the Bible. All the earth was blessed when Abraham's descendant named Jesus died for the sins of the <u>world</u>. More blessings will be realized at Jesus' second coming. Those in <u>covenant</u> with God have a special relationship with God.

Abraham Passes with Flying Colors

GENESIS 22:15–18 *Then the Angel of the LORD called to Abraham a second time out of heaven, and said: "By Myself I have sworn, says the LORD, because you have done this thing, and have not withheld your son, your only son—blessing I will bless you, and multiplying I will multiply your descendants as the stars of the heaven and as the sand which is on the seashore; and your descendants shall possess the gate of their enemies. In your seed all the nations of the earth shall be blessed, because you have obeyed My voice." (NKJV)*

God had a special relationship with Abraham, but he still decided to <u>test</u> him by asking him to sacrifice his son Isaac as a burnt offering. With simple childlike faith, Abraham was about to obey when God stopped him. God could see that Abraham was willing to go all the way and that was enough. He hadn't intended for Isaac to be killed. The angel of the Lord appeared and told Abraham that his willingness to obey God would be rewarded: Israel would become a very powerful nation, one that would occupy the territory of its enemies.

Prophecy

The number of Abraham's descendants is constantly growing. All the nations were blessed at the first coming of Jesus. Israel will possess the promised cities and territories at the second coming of Jesus and continue through the Millennium.

God's Covenant with Isaac

GENESIS 26:3–4 *Dwell in this land, and I will be with you and bless you; for to you and your descendants I give all these lands, and I will perform the oath which I swore to Abraham your father. And I will make your descendants multiply as the stars of heaven; I will give to your descendants all these lands; and in your seed all the nations of the earth shall be blessed. (NKJV)*

Not long after Abraham moved to the land of Canaan there was a <u>famine</u> in the Promised Land. God did not tell Abraham to relocate, but Abraham had family, servants, and animals to feed so he temporarily moved to Egypt. The event in this passage of Scripture took place about seventy to eighty years after Abraham returned to the land of Canaan.

Abraham had died, and his son Isaac was a grown man. When a second famine came to the land, God did not want Isaac to do what his father had done. So God appeared to Isaac and asked him not to go to Egypt. God wanted Isaac to stay in the Promised Land, and God promised to

- be with him
- bless him
- give the land to him
- carry out the covenant he made with Abraham
- give him a great number of descendants
- give the land to his descendants
- make one of his descendants a blessing to the whole earth

famine
Genesis 12:10; 26:1

world
John 1:29; 11:27

what others say

W. H. Griffith Thomas

Trials are permitted to come into the life of the best and holiest of men, and it is by this means that God sometimes teaches His most precious lessons… Egypt was not the promised land, and there were dangers there to body and to soul from which it was necessary that Isaac should be safeguarded.[14]

God blessed Isaac by giving him the land and many descendants. All the earth was blessed many generations later when his descendant Jesus came into the <u>world</u> the first time. More blessings will be realized at Jesus' second coming. Abraham's descendants will possess all the land during the Millennium.

God's Covenant with Jacob (Israel)

GENESIS 28:13–15 *And behold, the LORD stood above it and said: "I am the LORD God of Abraham your father and the God of Isaac; the land on which you lie I will give to you and your*

go to

Jacob and Esau
Genesis 25:19–26

birthright
Genesis 25:29–34

blessing
Genesis 27:1–40

birthright
the oldest son's right to inherit

blessing
an oral last will and testament

patriarchs
early fathers, head of the family

descendants. Also your descendants shall be as the dust of the earth; you shall spread abroad to the west and the east, to the north and the south; and in you and in your seed all the families of the earth shall be blessed. Behold, I am with you and will keep you wherever you go, and will bring you back to this land; for I will not leave you until I have done what I have spoken to you." (NKJV)

Isaac had twin sons named <u>Jacob and Esau</u>. The one born first was Esau, and that gave him a **birthright** to inherit the covenant God made with Abraham and Isaac. But Esau was foolish. The birthright meant very little to him, and he sold it to Jacob for a bowl of stew. Several years later, Jacob deceived his father and tricked him into giving him his **blessing** as the head of the family. When Esau learned about it, he planned to kill Jacob, but Jacob fled the country. On his first night away from home, God appeared to Jacob and said he was giving him everything he promised to Abraham and Isaac. Thus the all-important covenant land went to Jacob.

what others say

Wayne Barber, Eddie Rasnake, and Richard Shepherd

Jacob experienced seven revelations from the Lord in his journeys, and in those revelations we discover Jacob learning to follow God—to hear His word and obey. Those revelations occurred around five significant turning points in Jacob's life, turning points designed by God to fulfill the destiny He had for Jacob. But not only for Jacob, they were also part of God's destiny for His people Israel, for His Son the Messiah, and for all His redeemed throughout the ages—all those who have been, are now, or ever will be on the journey of following God.[15]

Abraham, Isaac, and Jacob are sometimes called the **patriarchs**. As such, each was the male head of their family or clan. The Jews recognize them as the beginning of the nation of Israel.

God blessed Jacob (Israel) with twelve sons, and this is continuously being fulfilled because their descendants eventually became the nation of Israel. Jesus came from this nation. More blessings will be realized at his second coming. They will possess all the land during the Millennium.

Jacob Gets a New Name

> GENESIS 35:10–12 *And God said to him, "Your name is Jacob; your name shall not be called Jacob anymore, but Israel shall be your name." So He called his name Israel. Also God said to him: "I am God Almighty. Be fruitful and multiply; a nation and a company of nations shall proceed from you, and kings shall come from your body. The land which I gave Abraham and Isaac I give to you; and to your descendants after you I give this land." (NKJV)*

go to

handmaids
Genesis 32:1

Bethel
Genesis 35:1, 6

Israel
Genesis 32:22–30

Jacob was out of the land for about twenty years. He returned to the land of Canaan with two wives, two **handmaids**, and eleven children, and moved around until God told him to settle in <u>Bethel</u>. At that point God told him not to go by the name of Jacob anymore—his new name would be <u>Israel</u>. God said a nation and kings would descend from him, and God repeated his promise that the land given to Abraham and Isaac now belonged to Jacob and his descendants.

handmaids
servants

Who or What Is Israel?

Who/What	Scripture
The territory God promised to Abraham and his descendants	Genesis 15:18–21
The grandson of Abraham, Jacob, whose name was changed to Israel	Genesis 32:28
The children of Israel otherwise known as the descendants of Israel	Genesis 32:32
The twelve tribes of Israel that descended from Israel's twelve sons	Genesis 49:1–28
The Northern Kingdom of Israel or ten northern tribes of Israel	1 Kings 12:16–24
The Israel of God or the Jews who have accepted Jesus as the Messiah	Galatians 6:16

Jacob's name became Israel, and his descendants became the nation of Israel. Some even became kings. The nation of Israel occupied the land at various times during the Old Testament period. They occupy part of it today, will receive all of it at the Second Coming, and will occupy all of it during the Millennium.

prophecy

Judah
Genesis 49:1–2,
8–12

lion's cub
Genesis 49:9

enmity
Genesis 3:15

toil
Genesis 3:17–19

Jacob
Isaiah 49:26

Lion
Revelation 5:5

good shepherd
John 10:11

King of kings
Revelation 19:16

rod of iron
Revelation 2:27

scepter
the rod or staff car-
ried by a king or
sovereign ruler

enmity
hostility or animosity

The Coming Ruler

GENESIS 49:10 *The scepter shall not depart from Judah, nor a lawgiver from between his feet, until Shiloh comes; and to Him shall be the obedience of the people. (NKJV)*

When he was dying, Israel called his twelve sons together to reveal things about their future. One of his sons was named Judah. Israel called Judah a lion's cub. Israel said the **scepter** will belong to the tribe of Judah "until Shiloh comes; and to Him shall be the obedience of the people." This means God's Messiah and coming Ruler of the nations will be from the tribe of Judah. Among scholars there is wide agreement that *Shiloh* means "rest" or "peace." Adam's sin brought the curse of **enmity** and toil. Hence there will be no peace on earth, and people will be required to labor for a living until the second coming of Jesus. In Genesis 49:24 (NKJV), God's Messiah is called "the Mighty God of Jacob," "the Shepherd," and "the Stone of Israel."

The twelve tribes of Israel are named after the descendants of Jacob (Israel). Jacob had twelve sons. One son was named Levi, and his descendants are called the Tribe of Levi (or Levites). The Levites were selected to be the priests, so they were not counted among the twelve tribes. Omitting them left eleven tribes. One son was named Joseph. He was sold into slavery in Egypt. Joseph married an Egyptian, so his descendants were part Egyptian. He had two sons, Ephraim and Manasseh, who were made heads of tribes instead of their father. Omitting Joseph left ten tribes, but adding his two sons made twelve tribes. The tribe of Judah was selected to be the leader of all the tribes.

Some of the names of Jesus are Lion of the tribe of Judah, Mighty One of Jacob, and the good shepherd. Jesus is the King of kings and Lord of lords who will rule with a rod of iron during the Millennium.

LEVITICUS

The Big If . . . (The Mosaic Covenant)

go to

Egypt
Exodus 1:1–22

plagues
Exodus 7:14–12:30

Moses
Exodus 2:1–4:17

rain
Deuteronomy 28:12

enemies
Deuteronomy
28:23–25

land
Deuteronomy
28:33–37

the big picture

Leviticus 25:1–26:46

The twelve sons of Israel (Jacob) multiplied and moved to Egypt. During a span of several hundred years, Israel's descendants had become slaves. So God raised up Moses to lead them out of the land of Egypt to Mount Sinai. There God gave the land of Canaan to them, but they had to let the land rest every seventh year, help the poor, observe the Sabbaths, etc. If they obeyed, he would bless them. If they disobeyed, he would punish them. If the punishment did not work, he would eventually put them off the land and let it rest one year for each seventh year they wrongfully planted a crop. But he would not cancel his covenant or permit all of the people to be destroyed. After the land rested the proper number of years, he would restore the nation.

plagues
something that causes a great deal of suffering

Pharaoh
a title given to the main ruler in Egypt

Another famine came and the descendants of Israel wound up in Egypt. The Israelites stayed in Egypt for 430 years, and their numbers increased to several hundred thousand, some say perhaps as many as two million. This population explosion troubled the Egyptians. They were afraid the Israelites would soon outnumber and overpower them. So the Egyptians took the Israelites as slaves. God responded by sending **plagues** to force **Pharaoh** to let them leave, and by raising up an Israelite named Moses to lead them.

Moses led his people to Mount Sinai, and it was there that God made a special covenant with the nation. If Israel would obey him, God promised to bless the nation with rain, good crops, fruit, peace, victory over her enemies, and safe dwelling. If Israel would not obey, God would make the nation afraid, send diseases, and let the nation's enemies defeat her. If the nation continued to disobey, God would punish the people seven times more with poor crops. If that did not work, God would punish them seven times more with plagues of wild animals. If that failed, God would punish them seven times more with diseases and famine. If they still disobeyed, God would punish them seven times more, they would cannibalize their children, the land would become desolate, the people would be scattered among the nations, and the land would rest to make up for all those years they wrongfully planted crops.

go to

blessings
Deuteronomy
28:1–8

Jeremiah
Jeremiah 25:1–13

Nebuchadnezzar
2 Chronicles
36:11–21

It is very important to understand this prophecy. It is the key to understanding why the Jews would be off the land for seventy years during the Babylonian captivity (not letting the land rest) and why they would be punished seven times more (7 X 70 = 490 years) for their other sins (adultery, lying, idolatry killing the prophets, etc.). Beginning with Moses, the Jews were faithful to God for many years and they enjoyed the <u>blessings</u> he promised. But by the time the period of Judges arrived, the nation was going through cycles of rebellion, punishment, repentance, and restoration. Every time the Jews rebelled God punished them.

Every time they repented, God restored them. He was always very patient and reluctant to apply the curse. He loved the children of Israel and wanted to maintain a special relationship with them. By the time Jeremiah came along the nation was divided. The Northern Kingdom called Israel had been destroyed and the Southern Kingdom called Judah was in rebellion.

They had stolen seventy crops (one crop every seven years) and were breaking all of God's other Commandments. Speaking through Jeremiah God told them he would put them off the land seventy years to rest the land and recover the seventy stolen crops. Later, he spoke through Daniel and said they would suffer seven times more (490 more years) for breaking the other Commandments. This explains the Babylonian captivity. Then, Daniel chapter 9 will explain the 490 years and it will become clear why prophetic scholars expect a seven-year Tribulation Period.

God told the Jews to let the land rest every seventh year. Letting the land rest every seventh year was a great test for the nation. If the people trusted God enough to not plant crops, God would bless them. If they did not trust him enough to do that, God would afflict them. The message for us today is trust God and he will take care of us.

Israel broke the covenant again and again. Finally, <u>Jeremiah</u> warned the people to repent or God would put them off the land. When the people refused to heed the warning, God let King <u>Nebuchadnezzar</u> of Babylon defeat them. Multitudes of Jews were killed. Others were taken to foreign lands. Seventy years later, more than forty thousand returned. In AD 70 the Romans conquered the land. Multitudes were killed again, but not everyone. In AD 135

prophecy

those who were left were scattered and their property was sold. This prophecy has been fulfilled.

NUMBERS

Remember Balaam

go to

scepter
Genesis 49:10

Balaam
Micah 6:5

loved
2 Peter 2:13–16

error
Jude 11

NUMBERS 24:14–19 *"And now, indeed, I am going to my people. Come, I will advise you what this people will do to your people in the latter days." So he took up his oracle and said: "The utterance of Balaam the son of Beor, and the utterance of the man whose eyes are opened; the utterance of him who hears the words of God, and has the knowledge of the Most High, who sees the vision of the Almighty, who falls down, with eyes wide open: I see Him, but not now; I behold Him, but not near; a Star shall come out of Jacob; a Scepter shall rise out of Israel, and batter the brow of Moab, and destroy all the sons of tumult. And Edom shall be a possession; Seir also, his enemies, shall be a possession, while Israel does valiantly. Out of Jacob One shall have dominion, and destroy the remains of the city." (NKJV)*

Moab and Edom
two small kingdoms in southern Jordan

idolatry
worshiping false gods

The story of Balaam is one of the strangest in the Bible. He was a living contradiction who knew a lot of Scripture but set most of it aside. He was an unusual prophet who mixed divine revelation with pagan practices, a man of faith who sold out to Satan. He said something we often hear at Christmas: "A Star shall come out of Jacob; a Scepter shall rise out of Israel." Among scholars there is wide agreement that this is a prophecy about Jesus. Some even believe the wise men who went to Jerusalem and Bethlehem at his birth went there because of this prophecy. At Jerusalem they asked King Herod, "Where is He who has been born King of the Jews? For we have seen His star in the East and have come to worship Him" (Matthew 2:2 NKJV). Balaam also prophesied the destruction of **Moab and Edom**.

Balaam is a man to be remembered. The Bible says:

1. Remember what Balaam said (Numbers 22–25).

2. Remember what Balaam loved—he loved the wages of wickedness and accepted money to do wrong.

3. Remember Balaam's error—he was greedy.

4. Remember what Balaam <u>taught</u>—**idolatry** and sexual immorality.

Balaam said what he saw was "not near." In the future, Israel's ungodly neighbors in southern Jordan will be destroyed and the kingdoms of the world will be subdued. The <u>Bright and Morning Star</u> is one of the names of Jesus. He appeared almost two thousand years ago, and he will appear again near the end of earth's darkest hour (Tribulation Period). His light will overcome the darkness. "Scepter" refers to the rule of Jesus as King of kings and Lord of lords with a rod of iron during the Millennium (Revelation 2:27; 12:5; 19:15–16; Psalm 2:9).

DEUTERONOMY

<u>Israel's History Foretold</u>

taught
Revelation 2:14

Bright and Morning Star
Revelation 22:16

apostasy
rebellion against God

backslide
slip back into sin

DEUTERONOMY 4:26–31 *I call heaven and earth to witness against you this day, that you will soon utterly perish from the land which you cross over the Jordan to possess; you will not prolong your days in it, but will be utterly destroyed. And the LORD will scatter you among the peoples, and you will be left few in number among the nations where the LORD will drive you. And there you will serve gods, the work of men's hands, wood and stone, which neither see nor hear nor eat nor smell. But from there you will seek the LORD your God, and you will find Him if you seek Him with all your heart and with all your soul. When you are in distress, and all these things come upon you in the latter days, when you turn to the LORD your God and obey His voice (for the LORD your God is a merciful God), He will not forsake you nor destroy you, nor forget the covenant of your fathers which He swore to them. (NKJV)*

Moses led the children of Israel out of Egypt, through the wilderness, and to the east bank of the Jordan River. They were ready to enter the Promised Land, but before they did, Moses had some final words of warning. He spoke in the name of the Lord, calling heaven and earth to witness against them. He predicted **apostasy** would grip the new nation, that it would soon **backslide**, that the people would be killed or removed from the land, that the survivors would be few in number, and that they would be compelled to commit idolatry in foreign lands. He also said if the people would repent and seek God, the Lord would forgive them.

For the first time in the Bible, the Tribulation Period is referenced here: "when you are in <u>distress</u>." It will occur in the **"latter days."**

When the Tribulation Period arrives, if people repent, our merciful God will not forsake them; he will not forget the <u>covenant</u> he made with their **fathers**. The same love, mercy, and power that he makes available to others will be available to them.

We know the following about the Israelites in the latter days:

1. God's chosen people will backslide.

2. If backsliders do not repent, God will punish them.

3. If backsliders do repent, God will forgive them.

As long as the nation of Israel remained faithful to God, they would be special to him, he would not forsake them, and he would let them dwell in the Promised Land. If they broke their relationship with him, they would be no different from anyone else, and he would no longer let them dwell in the Promised Land. Removing them would be a judgment designed to bring self-examination and repentance. This will happen during the Tribulation Period—God will remember his covenants and the relationship will be restored.

Israel is notorious for backsliding and because of that, the nation has been destroyed more than once. God's chosen people will once again return to the land, but they will have to flee to the mountains in the future during the Tribulation Period. They will remember this prophecy and repent, and God will remember his covenants and restore them.

go to

distress
Zephaniah 1:14–17

covenant
Deuteronomy 7:9–10

latter days
the days just prior to the end of a period (e.g., Church Age, Tribulation Period)

fathers
in this case, Abraham, Isaac, and Jacob

Prophecy

Chapter Wrap-Up

- Satan's corruption of Adam and Eve brought curses upon the first couple and the serpent. His corruption of the whole earth brought a flood, but as long as the earth exists, there will be crops and seasons. (Genesis 3:14–19; 6:11–13; 8:22)

- God made covenants with Abraham, Isaac, and Jacob promising to give the land of Canaan to them and their descendants, to make them into a great nation, and to bless all the earth through them. (Genesis 12:1–3; 13:14–17; 17:7–8; 17:19; 18:17–18; 22:15–18; 26:3–4; 28:13–15; 35:10–12)

- God promised that the One who will rule the nations will come from the tribe of Jacob. (Genesis 49:10; Numbers 24:14–19)

- If Israel kept the covenants, God promised many blessings, plus he would let Israel stay on the land. If Israel broke the covenants, God promised to chastise the nation, and if the chastisement did not work, he would put the people off the land for a while. (Leviticus 25:1–26:46)

- Moses said Israel would backslide in the latter days (at the end of the age), but God will not forsake them. If the people repent, he will forgive them. (Deuteronomy 4:26–31)

Study Questions

1. Why is knowledge of prophecy so important to understanding the Bible?

2. Does God permit evil?

3. Why is understanding God's covenants so important to understanding the Bible?

4. What do the covenants with Abraham, Isaac, and Jacob have to do with Christians?

5. What clues do we have as to the identity of the Messiah?

Prophecies in the Books of History

Chapter Highlights:
- A Woman's Prayer
- A Covenant for David
- A Warning for Solomon
- A God Who Remembers
- The King Is Coming

Let's Get Started

The second division of the Old Testament, beginning with the book of Joshua and ending with the book of Esther, contains twelve books chronicling the history of Israel. The twelve books do not appear in chronological order in the Bible, so neither will they here. Finally, it should be noted that only four of the books contain prophecies of interest to this study.

go to

anointed
Daniel 9:25–26

King
Jeremiah 23:3–8;
Ezekiel 37:1–28;
John 19:19

kingdom
Luke 1:32–33

Samuel
a Hebrew name
meaning "heard of
God"

1 SAMUEL

A Messiah and King

> **1 SAMUEL 2:10** *The adversaries of the LORD shall be broken in pieces; from heaven He will thunder against them. The LORD will judge the ends of the earth. He will give strength to His king, and exalt the horn of His anointed. (NKJV)*

The first book of Samuel begins with a barren woman named Hannah praying for a child. When her prayer is answered a few months later, she names her newborn son **Samuel**. When he is old enough to be weaned, Hannah takes Samuel to the Lord's house at Shiloh and presents him to Eli the priest for a life of service to God. She begins to pray and ends her prayer with this verse: "He [God] will give strength to His king, and exalt the horn of His anointed" (1 Samuel 2:10 NKJV). The word *anointed* is translated "Messiah" in Hebrew and "Christos" in Greek. This is the first use of the word *Messiah* in the Bible. Hannah rejoices because God's enemies will be shattered. He will move against them from heaven. He will empower his King and exalt his Messiah. God will set up a kingdom, and his Messiah and King will rule over it. This prophecy will be fulfilled at the second coming of Christ.

impostors
false Christs

King David
a great king of Israel
who loved God

David's people
Israel

The Old Testament Jews anointed people for two positions: priest and king. Jesus was anointed to fulfil both roles. He is the believer's High Priest (Hebrews 4:14; 5:5). And he is the King of kings and Lord of lords (Revelation 19:16).

> ### what others say
>
> **Lee Strobel**
>
> Hundreds of years before Jesus was born, prophets foretold the coming of the Messiah, or the Anointed One, who would redeem God's people. In effect, dozens of these Old Testament prophecies created a fingerprint that only the true Messiah could fit. This gave Israel a way to rule out **impostors** and validate the credentials of the authentic Messiah.[1]

2 SAMUEL

God's Covenant with David

> ### the big picture
>
> **2 Samuel 7:4-17**
>
> At a time of peace in Israel, King David wanted to build a house for God. But before he got started, God sent Nathan the prophet to remind David that it was God who made him great. God promised through Nathan: to make David's name great, to provide a place for Israel, to provide a house for David, to raise up one of David's offspring (a son named Solomon) to succeed him, to let Solomon build God's house, to establish Solomon's throne forever, to punish Solomon's sin but never stop loving him, and to establish David's house, kingdom, and throne forever.

God's covenant with **King David** is usually called "the Davidic covenant." It contains seven promises that God made to David:

1. David's name will be revered.

2. **David's people** will have a land forever.

3. David's <u>house</u> will exist forever.

4. David's **son** will succeed him.

5. David's son will build **God's house**.

6. David's son will be punished for his sins.

7. David's <u>kingdom</u> and will last forever.

go to

house
Luke 2:4

kingdom
1 Chronicles
17:11–14

Israel
2 Samuel 7:24–29

temple
1 Kings 5:5

David's house
the dynasty or house
of David, David's
descendants

David's son
Solomon

God's house
the temple

throne
throne authority

---

what others say

Henry H. Halley

Here, in the 7th chapter of 2 Samuel, begins the long line of promises that DAVID'S FAMILY should reign FOREVER over God's people; that is, there should come from David an Eternal Family Line of Kings, culminating in ONE ETERNAL KING.[2]

John F. Walvoord

In these promises God has made clear that the Davidic covenant is not subject to human conditions and that God has vowed on the basis of his own trustworthiness that he will fulfill the covenant. It is also clear that the promise was given to David, not to someone else, though it will be fulfilled by Christ as the descendant of David, and that the fulfillment relates to the people of God, in this context the people of <u>Israel</u>.[3]

King Solomon built the first <u>temple</u>, and the Babylonians destroyed it. The Jews rebuilt it, and the Romans destroyed it. Several prophecies teach that it will be rebuilt again before the second coming of Christ.

The destruction of Israel and Judah does not cancel this covenant. God simply removed the family from the throne to await a suitable, faithful descendant. Some of King David's descendants survived the destruction of Israel and Judah, and the right to reign passed on through them. Then Jesus was born, and it is through him that the **throne** of David will be established forever.

Messianic Expectations

Expectation	Scripture
In you all the families of the earth shall be blessed	Genesis 12:3
All nations shall flow to it [The Lord's house in the latter days]	Isaiah 2:2–4
Unto us a Child is born, unto us a Son is given; and the government shall be upon his shoulder	Isaiah 9:6
The stone [Messiah] that struck the image became a great mountain [kingdom] and filled the whole earth	Daniel 2:35
Behold, your King is coming to you; He is just and having salvation, lowly and riding on a donkey	Zechariah 9:9
The Lord shall be King over all the earth	Zechariah 14:9

two nations
Northern Kingdom, called Israel, and Southern Kingdom, called Judah

David became famous in his lifetime, and even today the Jews revere him as Israel's greatest king. Two cities, Bethlehem and Jerusalem, have become known as "the city of David." David's son Solomon succeeded him as king of Israel. He built the first temple. He also worshiped other gods. Solomon's sin made God angry, so God allowed Israel to be divided into **two nations** following Solomon's death. When Jesus was born, his genealogy was traced back to David through both his legal father, Joseph, and his biological mother, Mary. Thus Jesus is the legal heir to David's throne, and he will sit on the earthly throne of David during the Millennium.

A Sure Thing

2 SAMUEL 23:3–7 The God of Israel said, The Rock of Israel spoke to me: "He who rules over men must be just, ruling in the fear of God. And he shall be like the light of the morning when the sun rises, a morning without clouds, like the tender grass springing out of the earth, by clear shining after rain." Although my house is not so with God, yet He has made with me an everlasting covenant, ordered in all things and secure. For this is all my salvation and all my desire; will He not make it increase? But the sons of rebellion shall all be as thorns thrust away, because they cannot be taken with hands. But the man who touches them must be armed with iron and the shaft of a spear, and they shall be utterly burned with fire in their place. (NKJV)

King David was on his deathbed when God revealed these things. God told David that a **righteous** leader who **fears God** is like sunshine on a cloudy day; God notices him. Such a leader is also a blessing to others. They will prosper and grow under his reign.

David knew that he had not lived up to this. Not many leaders do. But he also knew that he was leaving office in a right relationship with God. He had an everlasting covenant that secured his future. Evil leaders cannot make that same claim. They will be cast aside and burned.

What are your priorities in life? Are you prioritizing first things first? Do righteousness and the fear of God play a part? It is a dangerous thing to come to the end of one's life without a right relationship with God. A covenant with God ensures our salvation.

God's coming King is both Savior and Judge. David will be raised from the dead and enjoy God's blessings at the second coming of Christ. The wicked will be raised and cast into the Lake of Fire after the Millennium. This should motivate us to prepare. We will all appear before one of the judgment seats. There will be no way to avoid it. When we get there, we will need a Savior, but it will be too late for some. It is absolutely necessary to resolve this before we stand in his presence. The Lake of Fire awaits those who do not have a Savior.

go to

burned
John 15:1–8

raised
Daniel 12:1–3

Lake of Fire
Revelation 20:5,
11–14

righteous
just

fears God
has respect for God

1 KINGS

If, and, but . . . Blessings Galore or Judgment

1 KINGS 9:3–9 *And the LORD said to him: "I have heard your prayer and your supplication that you have made before Me; I have consecrated this house which you have built to put My name there forever, and My eyes and My heart will be there perpetually. Now if you walk before Me as your father David walked, in integrity of heart and in uprightness, to do according to all that I have commanded you, and if you keep My statutes and My judgments, then I will establish the throne of your kingdom over Israel forever, as I promised David your father, saying, 'You shall not fail to have a man on the throne of Israel.' But if you or your sons at all turn from following Me, and do not keep My*

go to

fourth
1 Kings 6:1

seven
1 Kings 6:38

thirteen
1 Kings 7:1

turned away
2 Chronicles 7:19–22

Israel
2 Kings 14:27

forsaking
2 Kings 22:15–17

remnant
2 Kings 19:30–31

Judah
2 Kings 17:20

Jerusalem
2 Kings 21:12–15

consecrated
accepted it as a special place

put his name on
agreed to let it be called God's house

his eyes and heart
God's presence

uprightness
a desire to live by God's rules

integrity
faithfulness to God

commandments
all the commandments of God including the Ten Commandments

*commandments and My statutes which I have set before you, but go and serve other gods and worship them, then I will cut off Israel from the land which I have given them; and this house which I have consecrated for My name I will cast out of My sight. Israel will be a proverb and a byword among all peoples. And as for this house, which is exalted, everyone who passes by it will be astonished and will hiss, and say, 'Why has the L*ORD* done thus to this land and to this house?' Then they will answer, 'Because they forsook the L*ORD* their God, who brought their fathers out of the land of Egypt, and have embraced other gods, and worshiped them and served them; therefore the L*ORD* has brought all this calamity on them.'" (NKJV)*

In the <u>fourth</u> year of his reign, King Solomon started construction on the temple (see Illustration #3), and it was completed <u>seven</u> years later. He spent the next <u>thirteen</u> years constructing his palace. Then God appeared to Solomon and assured him that he had heard his prayer, that he had **consecrated** the temple, that he had **put his name on** the temple, and that **his eyes and heart** would be at the temple. God added that if Solomon would have **uprightness** and **integrity** of heart and would keep his **commandments**, the kingdom would be secure and Solomon's descendants would continue to reign. But if Solomon or his descendants <u>turned away</u> from God, and if they worshiped idols, God would put <u>Israel</u> off the land, turn his back on the temple, and cause the Jews to be ridiculed in the world.

God expects rulers to follow him and to be an example for his people. Unfaithful rulers lead people astray. Straying people will be held responsible for their sins. Being faithful to God brings blessings, but <u>forsaking</u> God brings judgment.

God did not say he would cancel his covenant with David. He said he would remove those who rejected him from the land. This was a threat to temporarily set the covenant aside. He could reactivate it with a <u>remnant</u> of faithful people at some point in the future.

Solomon and his descendants turned their backs on God, and the nation was divided into a Northern Kingdom (Israel) and a Southern Kingdom (<u>Judah</u>). Eventually both kingdoms, the temple, and <u>Jerusalem</u> were destroyed, and the Jews have been ridiculed all over the world ever since.

The chart on page 42 depicts the miserable record of those who ruled over Israel and Judah. Out of nineteen kings who ruled in the north, not even one was good in the eyes of God. Out of twenty that ruled in the south, only eight were good according to God's standards. This explains why Judah survived about 136 years longer than Israel, but it also explains why God ultimately allowed his judgment to fall upon the nation. God will bless those who bless him, but he will not forever protect those who turn their backs on him.

go to

Abraham
Genesis 12:1–3

Isaac
Genesis 26:3–4

Jacob
Genesis 28:13–15

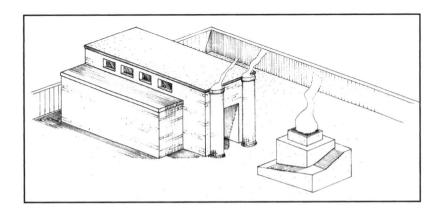

Illustration #3
Solomon's Temple—Solomon's lavish temple would be worth five billion dollars today.

decree
official decision, mandate, or command

everlasting
eternal, forever, never-ending

1 CHRONICLES

God Remembers

> 1 CHRONICLES 16:15–18 *Remember His covenant forever, the word which He commanded, for a thousand generations, the covenant which He made with Abraham, and His oath to Isaac, and confirmed it to Jacob for a statute, to Israel for an everlasting covenant, saying, "To you I will give the land of Canaan as the allotment of your inheritance." (NKJV)*

God does not, will not, and cannot forget his covenants. His covenants are as valid today as they were thousands of years ago. The covenant God made with Abraham and the oath he swore to Isaac were confirmed to Jacob as a **decree** and to Israel as an **everlasting** covenant. Israel will inherit the land of Canaan.

Kings of the Divided Kingdom

The Northern Kingdom (Israel)				The Southern Kingdom (Judah)			
King	Reign (BC)	Character	Scripture	King	Reign (BC)	Character	Scripture
Jeroboam I	931–910	Bad	1 Kings 12–14	Rehoboam	931–913	Bad	1 Kings 12–14
Nadab	910–909	Bad	1 Kings 15	Abijah	913–911	Bad	1 Kings 15
Baasha	909–886	Bad	1 Kings 15–16	Asa	911–870	Good	1 Kings 15
Elah	886–885	Bad	1 Kings 16	Jehoshaphat	870–848	Good	1 Kings 22
Zimri	885	Bad	1 Kings 16	Jehoram	848–841	Bad	2 Kings 8
Omri	885–874	Bad	1 Kings 16	Ahaziah	863–862	Bad	2 Kings 11
Ahab	874–853	Bad	1 Kings 16	Athaliah	841–835	Bad	2 Kings 11
Ahaziah	853–852	Bad	1 Kings 22; 2 Kings 1				
Joram (or Jehoram)	852–841	Bad	2 Kings 3–8	Joash	835–796	Good	2 Kings 12
Jehu	841–814	Bad	2 Kings 9–10	Amaziah	796–767	Good	2 Kings 14
Jehoahaz (or Joahaz)	814–798	Bad	2 Kings 13	Azariah (or Uzziah)	767–740	Good	2 Kings 15
Jehoash (or Joash)	798–782	Bad	2 Kings 13	Jotham	740–732	Good	2 Kings 15
Jeroboam II	782–753	Bad	2 Kings 14	Ahaz	732–716	Bad	2 Kings 16
Zechariah	753–752	Bad	2 Kings 15	Hezekiah	716–687	Good	2 Kings 18–20
Shallum	752	Bad	2 Kings 15	Manasseh	687–642	Bad	2 Kings 21
Menahem	752–742	Bad	2 Kings 15	Amon	642–640	Bad	2 Kings 21
Pekahiah	742–740	Bad	2 Kings 15	Josiah	640–608	Good	2 Kings 22
Pekah	740–732	Bad	2 Kings 15	Jehoahaz	608	Bad	2 Kings 23
Hoshea	732–721	Bad	2 Kings 17	Jehoiakim	608–597	Bad	2 Kings 23
				Jehoiachin	597	Bad	2 Kings 24
				Zedekiah	597–586	Bad	2 Kings 24

Israel Destroyed by Assyria in 722 BC   Judah Destroyed by Babylon in 586 BC

Today, many people make the mistake of thinking the church has replaced Israel because of Israel's sin. The unconditional aspects of God's covenants are not dependent upon the faithfulness of the Jews. They depend upon the faithfulness of God: his character, holiness, truthfulness, memory, power, etc. Since God does not and cannot lie, the covenants are binding upon him forever. For sure, Israel would break the covenants, but God knew that before the foundation of the world and his eternal plan included provision for it. Israel

Prophecies of the Bible

can be forgiven just as surely as a church member can be forgiven. The nation can receive a new heart just as surely as the most evil person on earth can be born again. Instead of replacing Israel, the Scriptures say he will save Israel, keep his covenants, and the Jews will serve him.

God has made some precious promises to Christians (2 Peter 1:4), and all his promises to us will be kept. He promised forgiveness of sins, to raise us from the dead, to give us eternal life. It is good to remember God's promises and, like Israel, we should remain faithful to God.

That God has made distinct promises to Israel isn't the point here. That God remembers his promises to Israel forever isn't the point either. The point is: Israel and the world should know that the Jews will get the land of Canaan. God is always mindful of his covenants; they will be fulfilled.

key point

God's covenants to give Abraham, Isaac, and Jacob many descendants are constantly being fulfilled. His covenants to give them all the land of Canaan will be fulfilled at the Second Coming. And Israel will occupy all their land during the Millennium.

Notice the words "I will." They indicate God's determination to bring these things to pass. Many people don't know about these covenants, many don't think they are important, and many doubt they will be kept, but God never goes back on his word.

There's a Great Day Coming

> 1 CHRONICLES 16:31–33 *Let the heavens rejoice, and let the earth be glad; and let them say among the nations, "The LORD reigns." Let the sea roar, and all its fullness; let the field rejoice, and all that is in it. Then the trees of the woods shall rejoice before the LORD, for He is coming to judge the earth.* (NKJV)

King David had brought the ark of the covenant to Jerusalem, and the Jews were celebrating. It was a great day in Israel, and as the people rejoiced they began to focus on the greater day that is coming. It will be a sad day for the lost, but it will be a great day of celebration for God's people. The Lord will reign and judge the earth. The lost will be purged from the earth, and the saved will enter into the Millennium.

go to

time
John 5:25–29

reap
Galatians 6:7

deed
Ecclesiastes
12:13–14

Something to ponder

The Bible says, "If we would judge ourselves, we would not be judged" (1 Corinthians 11:31 NKJV). Christians believe they will not be judged for their sins because they have practiced a form of self-examination. They have considered their sins, searched their hearts, repented, examined their faith, seen their need for a Savior, and accepted Jesus. Jesus says, "For God so loved the world that He gave His only begotten Son, that whoever believes in Him should not perish but have everlasting life. For God did not send His Son into the world to condemn the world, but that the world through Him might be saved. He who believes in Him is not condemned; but he who does not believe is condemned already, because he has not believed in the name of the only begotten Son of God" (John 3:16–18 NKJV).

Jesus talked about a <u>time</u> when everyone will be judged. There will be no place to run, no place to hide, no way to escape. Every person will <u>reap</u> what they have sown. Every <u>deed</u> will be brought into judgment. The seven groups to be judged are shown in the chart on the next page.

Jesus will judge the nations at his second coming, and he will reign on earth during the Millennium.

A Double Prophecy

1 CHRONICLES 17:11–14 *And it shall be, when your days are fulfilled, when you must go to be with your fathers, that I will set up your seed after you, who will be of your sons; and I will establish his kingdom. He shall build Me a house, and I will establish his throne forever. I will be his Father, and he shall be My son; and I will not take My mercy away from him, as I took it from him who was before you. And I will establish him in My house and in My kingdom forever; and his throne shall be established forever. (NKJV)*

The Seven Judgments of God

Who Judged	What Judged	When Judged	Why Judged	Scripture
Deceased Christians	Works	After the Rapture	For Rewards 10:31;	1 Corinthians 3:11–15; Romans 8:1; 2 Corinthians 5:10; Ephesians 6:7
Deceased O.T.* Saints	Faith in Messiah	Second Coming	For Rewards	Daniel 12:1–3
Deceased T.P.* Saints	Faith in Christ	Second Coming	To Raise Believers	Revelation 20:4–6
Living Jews	Faith in Christ	Second Coming	To Purge Unbelievers	Ezekiel 20:33–38
Living Gentiles	Faith in Christ	Second Coming	To Purge Unbelievers	Joel 3:1–2; 1 Corinthians 11:31–32; Matthew 25:31–46; Revelation 3:21
Satan and Fallen Angels	Rejecting God	After the Millennium	To Destroy Fallen Angels	Matthew 25:41; 2 Peter 2:4; Jude 6; Revelation 20:10; 1 Corinthians 6:3
Unbelievers	Rejecting God Millennium	After the Punishment	Degrees of Luke 12:47–48	Revelation 20:11–15;

* "O.T." stands for Old Testament, and "T.P." stands for Tribulation Period.

David wanted to build a <u>house</u> (temple) for God, but God would not let him because David was a <u>warrior</u> who had shed the blood of men. But God assured David that after his death, one of his "sons" (or "descendants") would succeed him on the <u>throne</u> in Israel. God said <u>David</u>'s son would build him a house, God would establish his kingdom, and David's son would rule over it forever.

Since Old Testament times, scholars have said this is a double prophecy (i.e., it has a double meaning). In one sense, it refers to David's son Solomon, who succeeded David on the throne and built the first earthly temple. But in a greater sense, it refers to David's descendant Jesus, who is building a spiritual <u>temple</u> and kingdom for God. It is his kingdom and reign that will be established forever.

go to

house
2 Samuel 7:4–17

warrior
1 Chronicles 28:3

throne
Acts 2:29–36

David
Jeremiah 23:3–8; Acts 13:34

temple
1 Corinthians 6:19

In the sense that this prophecy refers to Solomon and the earthly temple, it has been fulfilled. Solomon succeeded David on the throne, and he built the first temple. But in the greater and more significant sense that it refers to Jesus, the spiritual temple he is building for God, and the eternal kingdom God is building, this prophecy is yet to be fulfilled. The temple and kingdom that will last forever are the ones that Jesus will rule over.

Chapter Wrap-Up

- Hannah's request for a child was answered by God when Samuel was born. She turned him over to Eli the priest to raise in service to God. Her prayer of thanksgiving ends with a prophecy about the second coming of Christ. He is God's anointed or God's Messiah and King. (1 Samuel 2:10)

- God made a covenant with David to let his descendants succeed him, to make them a dynasty, and to let one of his sons (Jesus) rule over the kingdom forever. While on his deathbed, David said that he had not always been faithful to God, but he knew that God would keep the covenant because it is an everlasting covenant. (1 Samuel 7:4–17; 23:3–7)

- Solomon built the first earthly temple, and God was pleased. He even assured Solomon that his kingdom was secure if he and his descendants remained faithful. But God warned Solomon that if he or his descendants turned away, the kingdom and the temple would be destroyed, and the Jews would be ridiculed all over the world. (1 Kings 9:3–7)

- Those who think God forgets his covenants are wrong. He will

never forget them, so the promises he made to Abraham, Isaac, Jacob, and the others will be fulfilled. A thousand generations can pass, but God's faithfulness will not change.
(1 Chronicles 16:15–18)

• A kingdom requires a king—a King is coming to reign over an earthly kingdom. He will be a descendant of King David, and his kingdom will last forever. (1 Chronicles 16:31–33; 17:11–14)

Study Questions

1. What is so significant about the last verse of Hannah's prayer?

2. What is David's house, and how can it last forever?

3. Why would God allow the temple to be destroyed?

4. When will God's covenants with Abraham, Isaac, and Jacob be forgotten and why?

5. Is the second coming of Christ a reason to celebrate or a reason to weep?

Prophecies in the Books of Poetry

Chapter Highlights:
- The Resurrection of the Dead
- The Coming of Christ, First and Second
- The Tribulation Period
- The Millennium

Let's Get Started

Poetry permeates the Bible. It has been suggested that perhaps as much as one-third of the Old Testament is **Hebrew** poetry. In fact, five of the Old Testament books—Job, Psalms, Proverbs, Ecclesiastes, and Song of Solomon—are almost entirely poetry and are often called the Poetic Books or the Books of Poetry. It's relevant to note that Hebrew poetry is not a series of verses that rhyme. Rather than ending lines with similar-sounding words, Hebrew poetry instead repeats thoughts in varying ways.

Redeemer
1 Peter 1:18–19

Hebrews
another name for the Israelites, the Jews

temporal
worldly or secular

resurrection
the dead coming back to life

knew
was convinced

Redeemer
a deliverer, Jesus

JOB

Job Knows a Thing or Two

JOB 19:25–27 *For I know that my Redeemer lives, and He shall stand at last on the earth; and after my skin is destroyed, this I know, that in my flesh I shall see God, whom I shall see for myself, and my eyes shall behold, and not another. How my heart yearns within me! (NKJV)*

Job lost everything he had. He was very sick, and some of his friends were trying to encourage him by suggesting he concentrate on regaining his wealth and health. But Job was not thinking about **temporal** things. He was thinking about a **resurrection** of the dead, and he reminded his friends of some very important truths. He was full of hope because he **knew** he had a living **Redeemer**, one who at some point in the latter days will stand upon this earth. Job expected to die, to have his soul and spirit leave his body, and to have his flesh turn to dust. But after all that, he expected his soul and spirit to be in his flesh again and to see God with his own eyes. Job longed for this. And Job will be raised from the dead with the Old Testament saints in the resurrection of life. Our bodies will be destroyed, but we will receive new ones.

revelation
a hidden truth that
has been revealed

A remarkable thing about the book of Job is the fact that many scholars believe it is the oldest book in the Bible. Some even suggest it was written before the Flood. Three of the primary reasons for this include:

1. Job never mentions Israel, Moses, the Ten Commandments, etc. leaving some experts to believe he lived before they existed.

2. Job was a priest, but different from the priests of Israel, signifying he lived before the priesthood came into existence.

3. Job was probably getting along in years by the time he had ten children. Then, he lost everything he possessed, regained it all, had ten more children, and lived another 140 years after that (Job 42:16–17). By this time, he was probably several hundred years old, which would place him before the Flood.

This is striking evidence of a pre-Flood belief in the bodily resurrection of the dead. Couple that with the pre-Flood rapture of Enoch (Genesis 5:25; Hebrews 11:5), and it's evident that these doctrines go back to people who lived at the same time as Adam, who was created by God.

what others say

Charles Stanley

Of course, we grieve when someone we love is taken in death. But we grieve differently from the way the world does. We do not grieve as those who have no hope. We can look forward to a wonderful reunion someday with them and with the One who died—and lives—for us!

If He had remained dead, we would have nothing. Nothing. No hope. No faith. No comfort.

But we have a living Savior, who transcended the laws of death and smashed them forever.[1]

How did Job know that he would be raised, that he has a **revelation** from God? If not, it must have been common knowledge among believers in his lifetime.

PSALMS

More Than Just Another Book of Poems

go to

forsaken
Matthew 27:46

Holy One
Jesus

groaning
pain, suffering

> ### the big picture
>
> ### Psalms
>
> The book of Psalms contains 150 different poems covering a variety of subjects, such as the Creation, the history of Israel, the birth of Christ, the Second Coming, the Millennium, praise, thanksgiving, and repentance. Psalms are used in the rituals of both Judaism and Christianity. And they are quoted 186 times in the New Testament.

The book of Psalms is not an ordinary book. It contains a number of verses that are widely recognized by scholars as prophecies relating to the first coming of Christ. Because the verses are scattered throughout the book, a list of prophecies concerning the first coming of Christ and their New Testament fulfillment is provided below.

Prophecy: "You will not leave my soul in Sheol, nor will You allow Your **Holy One** to see corruption" (Psalm 16:10 NKJV).

Fulfillment: "He, foreseeing this, spoke concerning the resurrection of the Christ, that His soul was not left in Hades, nor did His flesh see corruption. This Jesus God has raised up, of which we are all witnesses" (Acts 2:31–32 NKJV).

Prophecy: "My God, My God, why have You forsaken Me? Why are You so far from helping Me, and from the words of My **groaning**?" (Psalm 22:1 NKJV).

Fulfillment: "At the ninth hour Jesus cried out with a loud voice, saying, 'Eloi, Eloi, lama sabachthani?' which is translated, 'My God, My God, why have You forsaken Me?'" (Mark 15:34 NKJV).

Prophecy: "But I am a worm, and no man; a reproach of men, and despised by the people. All those who see Me ridicule Me; they shoot out the lip, they shake the head, saying, 'He trusted in the LORD, let Him rescue Him; let Him deliver Him, since He delights in Him!'" (Psalm 22:6–8 NKJV).

go to

blasphemed
Luke 23:35–37

garments
Luke 23:34–35

spirit
Matthew 27:50

temple
John 2:19

dogs
evil people, like
unclean animals

cast lots
using chance to
determine an out-
come or settle an
issue

Fulfillment: "Those who passed by <u>blasphemed</u> Him, wagging their heads and saying, 'You who destroy the temple and build it in three days, save Yourself! If You are the Son of God, come down from the cross.' Likewise the chief priests also, mocking with the scribes and elders, said, 'He saved others; Himself He cannot save. If He is the King of Israel, let Him now come down from the cross, and we will believe Him. He trusted in God; let Him deliver Him now if He will have Him; for He said, "I am the Son of God."'" (Matthew 27:39–43 NKJV).

Prophecy: "**Dogs** have surrounded Me; the congregation of the wicked has enclosed Me. They pierced My hands and My feet; I can count all My bones. They look and stare at Me. They divide My <u>garments</u> among them, and for My clothing they **cast lots**" (Psalm 22:16–18 NKJV).

Fulfillment: "Another Scripture says, 'They shall look on Him whom they pierced'" (John 19:37 NKJV).

Prophecy: "Into Your hand I commit my spirit; You have redeemed me, O LORD God of truth" (Psalm 31:5 NKJV).

Fulfillment: "When Jesus had cried out with a loud voice, He said, 'Father, "into Your hands I commit My <u>spirit</u>."' Having said this, He breathed His last" (Luke 23:46 NKJV).

Prophecy: "He guards all his bones; not one of them is broken" (Psalm 34:20 NKJV).

Fulfillment: "But when they came to Jesus and saw that He was already dead, they did not break His legs. But one of the soldiers pierced His side with a spear, and immediately blood and water came out. And he who has seen has testified, and his testimony is true; and he knows that he is telling the truth, so that you may believe. For these things were done that the Scripture should be fulfilled, 'Not one of His bones shall be broken'" (John 19:33–36 NKJV).

Prophecy: "Fierce witnesses rise up; they ask me things that I do not know" (Psalm 35:11 NKJV).

Fulfillment: "Then some rose up and bore false witness against Him, saying, 'We heard Him say, "I will destroy this <u>temple</u> made with hands, and within three days I will build another made without hands"'" (Mark 14:57–58 NKJV).

Prophecy: "My loved ones and my friends stand aloof from my plague, and my relatives stand afar off" (Psalm 38:11 NKJV).

Fulfillment: "Many women who followed Jesus from Galilee, ministering to Him, were there looking on from <u>afar</u>, among whom were Mary Magdalene, Mary the mother of James and Joses, and the mother of Zebedee's sons" (Matthew 27:55–56 NKJV).

afar
Mark 15:40

Prophecy: "Even my own familiar friend in whom I trusted, who ate my bread, has lifted up his heel against me" (Psalm 41:9 NKJV).

Fulfillment: "When evening had come, He sat down with the twelve. Now as they were eating, He said, 'Assuredly, I say to you, one of you will betray Me.' And they were exceedingly sorrowful, and each of them began to say to Him, 'Lord, is it I?' He answered and said, 'He who dipped his hand with Me in the dish will betray Me. The Son of Man indeed goes just as it is written of Him, but woe to that man by whom the Son of Man is betrayed! It would have been good for that man if he had not been born.' Then Judas, who was betraying Him, answered and said, 'Rabbi, is it I?' He said to him, 'You have said it'" (Matthew 26:20–25 NKJV).

gall
a bitter juice usually made from herbs

Prophecy: "I am weary with my crying; my throat is dry; my eyes fail while I wait for my God" (Psalm 69:3 NKJV).

"They also gave me **gall** for my food, and for my thirst they gave me vinegar to drink" (Psalm 69:21 NKJV).

Fulfillment: "They gave Him sour wine mingled with gall to drink. But when He had tasted it, He would not drink" (Matthew 27:34 NKJV).

"Immediately one of them ran and took a sponge, filled it with sour wine and put it on a reed, and offered it to Him to drink" (Matthew 27:48 NKJV).

Prophecy: "In return for my love they are my accusers, but I give myself to prayer" (Psalm 109:4 NKJV).

Fulfillment: "He who hates Me hates My Father also. If I had not done among them the works which no one else did, they would have no sin; but now they have seen and also hated both Me and My Father. But this happened that the word might be fulfilled which is written in their law, 'They hated Me without a cause'" (John 15:23–25 NKJV).

go to

blasphemed
Mark 15:29

footstool
Luke 20:42–43

conspire
Acts 4:23–30

anointed
1 Samuel 2:10

Anointed One
Jesus

Prophecy: "My knees are weak through fasting, and my flesh is feeble from lack of fatness. I also have become a reproach to them; when they look at me, they shake their heads" (Psalm 109:24–25 NKJV).

Fulfillment: "Those who passed by <u>blasphemed</u> Him, wagging their heads" (Matthew 27:39 NKJV).

Prophecy: "The LORD said to my Lord, 'Sit at My right hand, till I make Your enemies Your footstool'" (Psalm 110:1 NKJV).

Fulfillment: "The LORD said to my Lord: 'Sit at My right hand, till I make Your enemies Your <u>footstool</u>'" (Matthew 22:44 NKJV).

These were all fulfilled at the first coming of Christ.

what others say

Arno C. Gaebelein

Our Lord used the Psalms in His public ministry. He silenced the tempting Pharisees by asking them a question from the One Hundred and Tenth Psalm. Most likely in the nights spent in prayer He poured out His heart in the language of the Psalms. When He came to Jerusalem He was welcomed by the glad shout, "Hosannah to the Son of David," and when His enemies murmured He referred them to the prediction of the Eighth Psalm. The last word addressed to Jerusalem was a quotation from the Book of Psalms: "Blessed is he that cometh in the name of the Lord" (Psalm 118:26).[2]

Wake Up and Smell the Coffee

the big picture

Psalm 2

This poem divides into four stanzas of three verses each. Verses 1–3 question why the nations, rulers, and peoples of the earth would rebel against God and his Anointed One—Christ. Verses 4–6 picture God laughing, scoffing, rebuking, and terrifying earth's rebels for opposing him and Christ. Verses 7–9 quote Christ as saying he is God's Son and he will crush earth's rebels. Verses 10–12 command the rebels to be wise, be warned, serve the Lord, and kiss the Son or be destroyed.

The question is, "Why would people <u>conspire</u> against God and his **Anointed One**?" The prophecy is that there will be a great worldwide movement to discredit and destroy those who serve God and believe in Christ, that this movement will try to break the **chains and fetters** of Christianity, throw them aside, and set up its own world government. God will laugh at this conspiracy, then he will scoff at it, then he will get <u>angry</u>. Christ will establish a kingdom and rule the <u>world</u> on God's behalf. When the time comes, God will issue a decree, and his Son will come and crush the rebellion. Christ is <u>King</u>; he will establish a <u>kingdom</u> and rule the world with a <u>rod of iron</u>. Society's rebellious unbelievers are going to be destroyed.

go to

angry
Psalm 18:7–15

world
Psalm 24:1–10

King
Psalm 10:15–16;
Jeremiah 30:8–9;
Ezekiel 37:1–28;
Hosea 3:4–5;
Zechariah 14:9,
16–17

kingdom
Psalm 45:6

rod of iron
Numbers 24:14–19;
Revelation 19:15

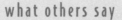
what others say

J. R. Church

God is determined to set His King upon His holy hill of **Zion**. Messiah will establish a worldwide kingdom, be given the nations for His inheritance and the uttermost parts of the earth for His possession. He will come at the end of a series of great wars to *break them with a rod of iron and dash them in pieces like a potter's vessel* (Psalm 2:9).[3]

Thomas Ice and Timothy Demy

The New Testament pictures the condition within the professing church at the end of the age by a system of denials.

- Denial of GOD—Luke 17:26; 2 Timothy 3:4–5
- Denial of CHRIST—1 John 2:18; 4:3; 2 Peter 2:6
- Denial of CHRIST'S RETURN—2 Peter 3:3–4
- Denial of THE FAITH—1 Timothy 4:1–2; Jude 3
- Denial of SOUND DOCTRINE—2 Timothy 4:3–4
- Denial of THE SEPARATED LIFE—2 Timothy 3:1–7
- Denial of CHRISTIAN LIBERTY—1 Timothy 4:3–4
- Denial of MORALS—2 Timothy 3:1–8, 13; Jude 18
- Denial of AUTHORITY—2 Timothy 3:4[4]

David W. Breese

Religious liberalism, which denies the inspiration of the Bible, the deity of Christ, and other precious truths, is continuing to work in our world. Philosophies such as neo-orthodoxy are working their way into many of our churches. When leaders turn from the Gospel to another heretical form of Christianity, it is not long before total deterioration sets in. In America in our time, there are thousands of empty churches where once the Gospel sounded, but now there is a haunting silence. An eerie irresponsibility has settled upon the minds of many who should be giving a loud and forceful presentation of the Gospel.[5]

chains and fetters
laws, truths,
teachings

Zion
a poetic name for
Jerusalem

judge
Psalm 9:7–9

nations
Psalm 22:27–31

**Battle of
Armageddon**
the last and greatest
war before the
Millennium

Apostasy, rebellion, and unbelief anger God, and in due time he will deal with them.

Following are ways world leaders are warring against God and his Son:

1. EU efforts to control "faith groups," and deny the mention of God in its constitution.

2. Efforts to restrict Christian evangelism in China, Egypt, Israel, etc.

3. Removal of prayer, Ten Commandments, and Scriptures from American schools and public buildings.

4. U.N. efforts to eliminate Christian teachings from its global ethic.

The conspiracy of unbelievers against God and Jesus began with the persecution of Jesus and his disciples, and it will lead to a one-world government with a one-world religious system at the end of this age. In short order, the world will experience the Tribulation Period, the **Battle of Armageddon**, and the second coming of Christ. Jesus will judge the nations, the Millennium will begin, the kingdom of righteousness will be established, and Jesus will rule with a rod of iron.

Many of the Psalms contain prophetic references of Jesus doing battle with the wicked on earth during the Tribulation Period. The rebellion of the Antichrist and his followers will be totally crushed. Notice the verses in the following chart.

Fast Facts on the Day of God's Wrath

The Tribulation Period	Scripture
The nations will fall beneath his feet.	Psalm 45:1–6
There will be no mercy for the wicked.	Psalm 59:5–8
The enemies of Christ will cringe.	Psalm 66:3
The wicked will perish.	Psalm 68:1–2
The proud will get what they deserve.	Psalm 94:1–4

When "Peace on Earth" Becomes a Fact

PSALM 46:6–11 *The nations raged, the kingdoms were moved; He uttered His voice, the earth melted. The LORD of hosts is with us; the God of Jacob is our refuge. Come, behold the works of the LORD, who has made desolations in the earth. He makes wars cease to the end of the earth; He breaks the bow and cuts the spear in two; He burns the chariot in the fire. Be still, and know that I am God; I will be exalted among the nations, I will be exalted in the earth! The LORD of hosts is with us; the God of Jacob is our refuge. (NKJV)*

go to

nations
Matthew 24:7

flesh
Zechariah 14:12–15

war
Revelation 19:11–21

remnant
those Jews who are in a right relationship with God

In this poem, the writer looks back on history to the Tribulation Period. He saw the <u>nations</u> in an uproar. War and rumors of war prevailed in many places. Mighty kingdoms fell. All God had to do was lift his voice and the <u>flesh</u> of his enemies dissolved; he won a great victory. Though the world was in turmoil, the God of Jacob (i.e., the God of Israel, Jehovah) protected his people, the **remnant** of Israel. The writer asks us to come and see the works of the Lord and the terrible blow he dealt to the wicked on earth. He used a great battle to bring an end to <u>war</u>, breaking the weapons of his enemies. The writer asks us to be calm and know God, to not fret over the turmoil in the world, to acknowledge what God can do, and to watch him do it. God will be exalted on earth and he will protect his people.

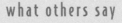

what others say

Ed Hindson

Armageddon! The mere mention of it causes us to tremble. Armageddon is the ultimate biblical symbol for the great war at the end of the age. Its very name conjures up visions of global destruction, worldwide devastation, and indescribable human suffering. It is the war to end all wars![6]

At the Tribulation Period midpoint, a remnant of Israel will flee Jerusalem (Revelation 12:6). Near the end of the Tribulation Period, a great war called the Battle of Armageddon will take place (Revelation 16:12–16). That will trigger the second coming of Jesus—he will win a great victory for God and deliver his people. This prophecy will be fulfilled in the future. Believers will be able to look back on the Tribulation Period and review what happened. We will understand that God used that terrible time to deal with the wicked on earth and to establish his kingdom here.

The return of Jesus as King of kings and Lord of lords is mentioned all through the Psalms. He will come with a great sword to deal with rebellion, and he will also come with grace and mercy to deal with those who love him. The world needs such a man.

It will think it has found him when the Antichrist arrives, but it will be greatly disappointed. Insight into the second coming of Jesus can be gleaned from the following chart.

Fast Facts on the Glorious Appearing of Jesus

The Second Coming	Scripture
The King of glory is coming.	Psalm 24:7–10
Jesus will judge his people.	Psalm 50:3–5
Jesus will judge righteously.	Psalm 96:10–13
Kings and leaders will be crushed.	Psalm 110:1–7

Joy to the World!

PSALM 47 *Oh, clap your hands, all you peoples! Shout to God with the voice of triumph! For the LORD Most High is awesome; He is a great King over all the earth. He will subdue the peoples under us, and the nations under our feet. He will choose our inheritance for us, the excellence of Jacob whom He loves. God has gone up with a shout, the LORD with the sound of a trumpet. Sing praises to God, sing praises! Sing praises to our King, sing praises! For God is the King of all the earth; sing praises with understanding. God reigns over the nations; God sits on His holy throne. The princes of the people have gathered together, the people of the God of Abraham. For the shields of the earth belong to God; He is greatly exalted. (NKJV)*

This psalm presents a prophetic picture of an event that will take place on earth during the Millennium. People on earth are encouraged to show exuberance: to clap, shout, and rejoice. Our King is awesome and great. He has subdued the nations, established his kingdom, and elevated Israel to a place of prominence in the world. He has occupied his holy throne amid shouting and trumpet sounds. Praises are given to him. He is King of all the earth. World leaders are gathered before him. Leaders of his people are there. Control of the earth is in his hands, and he is greatly praised.

Every person on earth belongs to a kingdom: one is God's and the other is Satan's. Ultimately, God's kingdom will prevail, and Satan's kingdom will be destroyed.

Almost two thousand years ago, Jewish leaders conspired against Jesus and had him crucified. Now world leaders conspire against him and try to break his <u>chains</u>. But he is <u>King of the Jews</u> and King of all the earth. God has made him <u>King of kings</u> and Lord of lords, and the day will come when he is established as absolute ruler over all things.

go to

chains
Psalm 2:1–12

King of the Jews
Matthew 2:2;
27:11, 37

King of kings
Revelation 19:16

The God who kept his promises by sending Jesus to the cross, by raising him from the dead, by reuniting Europe, by bringing Israel back into existence, and by causing the city of Jerusalem to be rebuilt will surely bring this to pass too. It will be like a bombshell exploding in the face of an unbelieving world. Jesus will reign, and we will be able to rejoice.

This worship service will take place during the Millennium. Its purpose will be to celebrate the things Jesus has done to accomplish God's will for the world. It will be a time of applause, song, and praise.

The Psalms contain many prophetic snapshots of God's coming kingdom here on earth. Victorious living will be the order of the day. The church will reign and the remnant of Israel will have much to celebrate. Examples are in the following chart.

Fast Facts on Jesus as King

The Millennium	Scripture
Everyone on earth will turn to Christ.	Psalm 22:27–31
Jerusalem will be the city of God.	Psalm 48:1–3
Righteousness will prevail.	Psalm 72:1–20
Jesus will reign.	Psalm 93:1–2
Jesus is God's salvation.	Psalm 98:1–9
God will remember his covenants.	Psalm 105:8–11
The throne of David will be in Israel.	Psalm 132:11–18
The Jews will return to Israel and Jerusalem.	Psalm 147:2–3

THOSE WHO WILL LIVE ON EARTH DURING THE MILLENNIUM

1. The saved Israelites who are alive at the end of the Tribulation Period.

go to

Philistia
Isaiah 14:28–32

Edom
an area in ancient
Jordan

Ishmaelites
descendants of
Ishmael (father of
many Arabs)

Moab
an area in ancient
Jordan

Hagrites
descendants of
Hagar (Sarah's hand-
maid, Egypt)

Gebal
a city in ancient
Lebanon

Ammon
a city in ancient
Jordan

Amalek
descendants of Esau
(Jacob/Israel's
brother, residents
of Sinai Peninsula)

Philistia
Palestinians, PA,
the Gaza Strip

Tyre
a city in ancient
Lebanon

Assyria
an ancient empire
including Syria, Iraq,
and part of Egypt

Lot
a nephew of
Abraham

2. The saved Gentiles who are alive at the end of the Tribulation Period.

3. Children born to saved survivors of the Tribulation Period during the Millennium.

4. The Old Testament saints who trusted God and looked forward to the coming Messiah.

5. Christians who went in the Rapture and return with Jesus at his second coming.

6. Those who accept Christ and are killed between the Rapture and the Second Coming.

THOSE WHO WILL NOT LIVE ON EARTH DURING THE MILLENNIUM

1. All unbelievers who die before the Second Coming.

2. All unbelievers who are alive at the Second Coming. (They will be removed.)

An Evil Alliance

the big picture

Psalm 83

This psalm is a prayer that seems to apply to end-of-the-age events now coming on the scene. It describes how the enemies of God are plotting against the people of God (the nation of Israel). It calls on God to curse and destroy them so he will be recognized and his name will be praised on earth.

In this prayer, God is asked not to be silent, quiet, or still. It is said that his enemies are busy conspiring against his people, that they want to destroy the nation of Israel. The enemies are identified as **Edom**, the **Ishmaelites**, **Moab**, the **Hagrites**, **Gebal**, **Ammon**, **Amalek**, <u>**Philistia**</u>, **Tyre**, **Assyria**, and the descendants of **Lot**. God is asked to make them dust, like a tumbleweed blown by the wind, to make them run as terrified creatures before a fire, to shame and disgrace them. He is asked to do this so they will know that he is God and he alone rules the earth.

Some writers say this prophecy was fulfilled when Assyria destroyed the Northern Kingdom of Israel in 721 BC, but Egypt and Jordan didn't have anything to do with that. This combination of nations has never attacked Israel. But Israel came back into existence in 1948, and this combination of nations is conspiring against her today. They disagree on many issues, but they have attained broad agreement on their common goal to wipe out the state of Israel. The answer to this prayer requires widespread destruction in Lebanon, Syria, Jordan, Egypt, the Gaza Strip, the Sinai Peninsula, and other parts of the Arab world. The clandestine and proxy wars waged against Israel, the terrorist attacks, and the Arab and Palestinian refusals to accept peace will eventually bring on the judgments of God. These peoples will be ashamed and disgraced when that happens (Isaiah 41:8–11).

The underlying causes of this prayer are now coming on the scene. It will be answered because God will defend his people and his name. One purpose of the Tribulation Period is to deal with Israel's enemies.

Chapter Wrap-Up

- Job lost everything, but he was not discouraged. He was full of hope, believed he had a Redeemer, believed he would be raised from the dead, and believed he would have a new body. (Job 19:25–27)

- Rebellion and conspiracy against God and Jesus will be a characteristic of the end of this age. This will anger God. Jesus will return, crush the rebellion, deal harshly with the conspirators, establish a kingdom of righteousness, and reign on earth as King. (Psalm 2:1–21; see also Psalms 24; 50; 96; and 110.)

- The Psalms are quoted 186 times in the New Testament. Many quotes are about Jesus and his crucifixion and resurrection. (See also Psalms 16; 22; 31; 34; 35; 38; 41; 69; 109; and 110.)

- A time of national upset and war is coming. The enemies of Israel will plot to destroy the nation. God will judge them, nations will fall, and the wicked will perish. (Psalms 46:6–11; 83:1–18; see also Psalms 45; 59; 66; 68; and 94.)

- Jesus is King. He will establish a kingdom on earth and sit on the throne of David in Jerusalem. He will be worshiped. Righteousness will prevail. (Psalm 47:1–9; see also Psalms 22; 48; 72; 93; 98; 105; 132; and 147.)

Study Questions

1. How does Hebrew poetry differ from American poetry?

2. What did Job believe about his own resurrection?

3. How does God respond to the conspiracy of unbelievers against him and his Christ?

4. According to the Psalms, how will people react to the first coming of Christ?

5. Who will worship Christ during the Millennium? What city is called the city of God? Where will the throne of David be?

Chapter Highlights:
- Isaiah
- Jeremiah
- Lamentations
- Ezekiel
- Daniel

Prophecies in the Major Prophets

Let's Get Started

The book of Isaiah begins a series of five Old Testament books that are sometimes collectively called the Major Prophets. But they are not major in the sense that their messages are more important than those of the other books in the Bible. They are major in the sense that their messages are long. All of the messages in the Bible are important because they are nothing less than the inspired Word of God. But this section is referred to as major because it is so extensive.

ISAIAH

The Judgment of Judah and Jerusalem

ISAIAH 1:24–31 *Therefore the Lord says, The* LORD *of hosts, the Mighty One of Israel, "Ah, I will rid Myself of My adversaries, and take vengeance on My enemies. I will turn My hand against you, and thoroughly purge away your dross, and take away all your alloy. I will restore your judges as at the first, and your counselors as at the beginning. Afterward you shall be called the city of righteousness, the faithful city." Zion shall be redeemed with justice, and her penitents with righteousness. The destruction of transgressors and of sinners shall be together, and those who forsake the* LORD *shall be consumed. For they shall be ashamed of the terebinth trees which you have desired; and you shall be embarrassed because of the gardens which you have chosen. For you shall be as a terebinth whose leaf fades, and as a garden that has no water. The strong shall be as tinder, and the work of it as a spark; both will burn together, and no one shall quench them. (NKJV)*

God identified himself in three ways: he is the Lord, he is the Lord Almighty, and he is the Mighty One of Israel. He is an all-powerful

redemption
the payment of a
price to free sinners

repent
to turn away from
wrong and toward
God

calamities
war, disasters, etc.

supreme being who is a force not to be trifled with. His judgment will come to Judah and Jerusalem to accomplish two things: to purge the wicked and to restore the nation. Upon completion, Jerusalem will be known as the City of Righteousness and also as the Faithful City. God's judgment will lead to the **redemption** of the godly because they will **repent** of their <u>sins</u>. The ungodly will be destroyed because they have forsaken him. They will reap shame and disgrace because of their false religion. They will deceive themselves into thinking they are strong, but they will perish.

The Jews have returned to the land and Jerusalem has been rebuilt, but the Jews have not accepted Jesus as the Messiah. God is a force to be reckoned with, and he will deal with them. He will send **calamities** during the Tribulation Period to separate the righteous from the unrighteous. Afterward, during the Millennium, Jesus will reign in Jerusalem, and the city will be known as the City of Righteousness, the Faithful City. The important thing here is God's focus on Jerusalem. He lets us know the city will come back into existence at the end of the age, ultimately be redeemed, and be led by men who have turned to God.

The Times, They Are A-Changin'

the big picture

Isaiah 2:1–22

Concerning Judah and Jerusalem in the last days, the temple will be rebuilt. It will be higher than the surrounding area, it will become the religious center of the world, multitudes will go there to learn God's ways, Jesus will rule over the nations, war will end, there will be peace on earth, and all Israel will be encouraged to follow him. God forsook Israel and its temple because the people embraced pagan customs and practiced divination, piled up treasures, and committed idolatry. He forced them out of the country, scattered them among the nations, and set aside a time of judgment. When this happens the proud will be humbled, Jesus will be exalted, idols will be destroyed, men will hide in caves, earthquakes will shake the earth, and Israel will stop trusting in mortal men.

The <u>temple</u> will be rebuilt in the last days. It will be elevated above the surrounding area and transformed into a worldwide religious center, called the house of Israel's God. Jesus will sit on the throne of David, rule the nations, decide national issues, and arbitrate disputes. Weapons will be destroyed and war will cease. Military preparation will end.

God forsook Israel and its former temple because the people forsook him. They took up the customs of **unregenerate** people, customs forbidden in the Bible: they practiced **divination**, <u>coveted</u> wealth, and worshiped <u>idols</u>. Thus, sin is the reason why the Jews were scattered all over the world and why God said there will be a Tribulation Period. The wealthy who suffer from <u>pride</u> and the idolaters who suffer from arrogance will be humbled. Many Jews will abandon their idols and turn back to God.

Many preachers and teachers discard most of the Bible passages about the wrath of God, but they like to use passages like this. God's wonderful plans include a future kingdom with Messianic rule, teachings, and universal peace. Also, one wonders if this is why Muslims like to build their mosques where they can overlook everything in the area. The Millennial Temple will occupy the highest spot in Jerusalem. Gentiles will climb that holy hill to worship and consult with Jesus.

go to

coveted
Exodus 20:17

idols
Exodus 20:4–5

pride
Proverbs 8:13

unregenerate
unsaved

divination
trying to predict the future through omens

what others say

Randall Price

When the Millennium begins, topographical changes will occur that will cause the city itself to be elevated above the surrounding land, which will be flattened into a vast plain (Zechariah 14:10). This will be done so that the Temple Mount will occupy the highest elevation in the region, making Jerusalem the new center of the Land.[1]

There is nothing wrong with acquiring wealth unless it is acquired illegally, used to glorify oneself instead of God, or used as a substitute for trusting in God (see Proverbs 10:4, 22, 28). God's people should not be like everyone else in the world.

The Jews will rebuild their temple by the middle of the Tribulation Period, but that temple (sometimes called the Tribulation Period temple) is not the one that will become the religious center of the world. The glorious temple in this passage that Jesus will rule from

something to ponder

kissed
2 Samuel 20:9

holy kiss
Romans 16:16

is often called the millennial temple. The set time of judgment is the Tribulation Period. Repentance and true worship will be a result.

It's difficult to imagine the extent of Judah's sins before God destroyed the nation and scattered the Jews. But the Jews loved living in darkness. They refused to repent and persuaded themselves that God would take care of them no matter what. The chart below presents a graphic description from God's viewpoint.

Fast Facts on the Dispersion of Israel

The Scattering of the Jews	Scripture
Judah was made desolate, cities were burned, the fields were stripped.	Isaiah 1:7–9
The people spoke against God.	Isaiah 3:8
The land was filled with injustice and unrighteousness.	Isaiah 5:1–10
The people did not understand the Word of God.	Isaiah 6:9–12
The women were complacent about spiritual matters.	Isaiah 32:9–14
The people would not follow God or obey his laws.	Isaiah 42:23–25
All their leaders from the first to the last sinned.	Isaiah 43:26–28
The people failed to respond to God.	Isaiah 50:1–2
Their sleeping, spiritually blind children would not be able to lead them.	Isaiah 51:17–20
Sin separated the people from God.	Isaiah 59:1–2
The people blindly turned their back on God.	Isaiah 59:9–15

The entire Creation will be changed during the Millennium including the heavenly bodies. On earth, Messiah will rule and receive worldwide reverential respect. Several important features of God's new world order are in the chart on the following page.

Wanted: A Few Good Men

ISAIAH 4:1–6 *And in that day seven women shall take hold of one man, saying, "We will eat our own food and wear our own apparel; only let us be called by your name, to take away our reproach." In that day the Branch of the LORD shall be beautiful and glorious; and the fruit of the earth shall be excellent and appealing for those of Israel who have escaped. And it shall come to pass that he who is left in Zion and remains in Jerusalem will be called holy—everyone who is recorded among the living in Jerusalem. When the Lord has washed away the filth of the daughters of Zion, and purged the blood of Jerusalem from her midst, by the spirit of judgment and by the spirit of burning, then the LORD will create above every dwelling place of Mount Zion, and above her assemblies, a cloud and smoke by day and the shining of a flaming fire by night. For over all the glory there will be a covering. And there will be a tabernacle for shade in the daytime from the heat, for a place of refuge, and for a shelter from storm and rain. (NKJV)*

Fast Facts on Jesus as King

The Millennium	Scripture
The government will be upon the shoulders of Jesus.	Isaiah 9:6–7
Righteousness and peace will prevail.	Isaiah 11:1–13
It will be a time of praise, singing, and thanksgiving.	Isaiah 12:1–6
In love, Jesus will sit on the throne of David.	Isaiah 16:5
God will put an end to death and tears.	Isaiah 25:6–9
Judah will be strong and will rejoice.	Isaiah 26:1–17
It will be a time of abundance and restoration in Israel.	Isaiah 27:1–13
The sun and moon will be brighter.	Isaiah 30:23–26
God's people will have spiritual understanding.	Isaiah 32:1–4
There will be no sickness or sin in Jerusalem.	Isaiah 33:20–24
The desert will bloom, the blind will see, the deaf will hear, and the lame will walk.	Isaiah 35:1–10
The Jews will be regathered.	Isaiah 43:5–7
God will pour out his Spirit.	Isaiah 44:3
Gladness and joy will prevail.	Isaiah 51:3–4, 9–16
Everyone will know Jesus.	Isaiah 52:6–10
Israel will be enlarged.	Isaiah 54:1–17
Gentiles will share the blessings.	Isaiah 56:6–8
Gentiles will worship Jesus.	Isaiah 60:1–9
Israel will be blessed.	Isaiah 61:4–11
Jesus will delight in Israel.	Isaiah 62:1–12
There will be a new heaven and a new earth.	Isaiah 65:17–25
God will deal with his enemies.	Isaiah 66:1–24

This passage begins with a verse about the Tribulation Period and moves on to some comments about the Millennium. War will decimate the male population of the earth during the Tribulation Period.

go to

men
Isaiah 3:25

killed
Revelation 6:7–8;
9:15

Branch
Isaiah 4:2; 11:1–5;
Jeremiah 23:5;
Zechariah 3:8; 6:12

cloud
Exodus 33:9

fire
Exodus 40:34–38

survive
Matthew 24:22

So many <u>men</u> will be <u>killed</u> that seven women will be willing to share each male survivor. Women will be so desperate to marry and have children, they will offer to work to support themselves. During the Millennium, the <u>Branch</u> (Jesus) will be the pride and glory of the survivors in Israel. He will be honored by those Jews who make it through the Tribulation Period, and they will be called holy. The city of Jerusalem and women who have sinned will be judged and cleansed by fire. God will be present in a <u>cloud</u> of smoke and flaming <u>fire</u>. He will be the defense, shelter, shade, refuge, and hiding place of the Jews, and they will be safe.

This will be fulfilled during the Tribulation Period and Millennium. Were it not for the second coming of Christ, no one would <u>survive</u> the Tribulation Period. But he will come back, put an end to war, and restore the earth.

There will be worldwide worship of the Antichrist during the Tribulation Period. Many Jews will be led astray, but one-third will escape into the wilderness (probably to Petra) where they will seek the Lord and eventually be forgiven and saved. Suffering will not be limited to the Jews. Many Palestinians and large Arab populations will perish. Terror will spread around the world. Then, Jesus will return, destroy the ungodly, and everything will be made right.

Fast Facts on the Day of God's Wrath

The Tribulation Period	Scripture
A remnant of Jews will rely on the Lord.	Isaiah 10:20–23
Many Palestinians will be destroyed.	Isaiah 14:28–32
The Ethiopian (Cush) army will be destroyed.	Isaiah 18:1–7
Fear will grip the earth.	Isaiah 24:1, 3, 6, 17–22
Jesus will prevail against his enemies.	Isaiah 42:13–16
God's enemies will know his name.	Isaiah 64:1–4

The Virgin Birth

ISAIAH 7:14 *Therefore the Lord Himself will give you a sign: Behold, the virgin shall conceive and bear a Son, and shall call His name Immanuel.*

It was a time of trouble. The nation of Israel had divided (see Illustration #4) into a Northern Kingdom (called Israel) and a Southern Kingdom (called Judah). The Northern Kingdom formed an alliance with a third nation (Syria), and the two <u>besieged</u> Judah along with Jerusalem in an effort to overthrow King Ahaz of Judah. They thought they would prevail, but they did not. When they continued to plot against King Ahaz, God sent the prophet Isaiah to tell King Ahaz not to be afraid. King Ahaz was skeptical, so God sent Isaiah to him with a second message. God would give the king a sign if he would ask for it. King Ahaz refused God's generous offer, so God decided to give one to the whole **house of David** a virgin would give birth to a son, and he would be called Immanuel. The virgin birth of Jesus is a sign.

besieged
2 Kings 16:5

house of David
the Jews

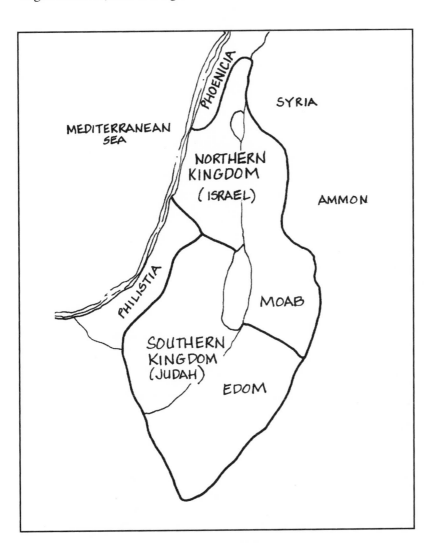

Illustration #4
Northern and Southern Kingdoms—Israel was divided into two kingdoms: Israel in the north and Judah in the south.

Herbert Lockyer

Is it not somewhat remarkable that whenever the birth of the Messiah is spoken of in prophecy, reference is made to His mother, or to the womb, never to a human father, which, of course, Jesus did not have.[2]

Isaiah said, "The Lord Himself will give you a sign" (Isaiah 7:14 NKJV). According to *Webster's*, a sign is something extraordinary. For a young woman to bear a child isn't extraordinary. Young women bear children every day. But it would be extraordinary if a virgin bore a child—that would be a sign. This was fulfilled several hundred years later when the Virgin Mary gave birth to Jesus. When Mary questioned it, an angel said, "With God nothing will be impossible" (Luke 1:37 NKJV).

Those who don't want to believe the Word of God are free to ignore it. The refusal of Ahaz to accept God's offer of a sign was an expression of unbelief. But the unbelief of some doesn't prevent God from revealing miraculous things to those who trust him. As a sign of his love, God would send a Messiah. He would be a light like the Shekinah Glory of God that resided in the Holy of Holies at the tabernacle and like a lamb without blemish and spot that was sacrificed for the sins of the people at the tabernacle. Some of Isaiah's predictions about the first coming of Jesus are found in the chart below. Because they were literally fulfilled many prophecy experts expect everything else Isaiah said to be literally fulfilled.

Fast Facts on Jesus as Messiah

The First Coming	Scripture
The people will see a great light.	Isaiah 9:2
The characteristics of God's servant.	Isaiah 42:1–4
Jesus will be beaten, mocked, and spit upon.	Isaiah 50:6
Jesus will suffer.	Isaiah 52:13–15; 53:1–12
The ministry of Jesus.	Isaiah 61:1–2

Iraq

go to

Sodom and Gomorrah
Genesis 19:1–29

darkened
Matthew 24:29

man
Isaiah 4:1–6

burning
Revelation 18:1–24

the big picture

Isaiah 13:1–22

God will bring many nations with the weapons of his wrath from faraway lands to fight against Babylon. When the Tribulation Period arrives, the land will be made desolate, the universe will experience great cosmic upheavals, multitudes will die, the city of Babylon will be destroyed like Sodom and Gomorrah, and it will never be inhabited by people again.

This prophecy calls for a **banner** to be raised on a bare hilltop (where it can be clearly seen) to summon a great army against Babylon. This army will gather under God's influence and be used to pour out his wrath as he did on <u>Sodom and Gomorrah</u>. Troops from many nations and faraway lands will be assembled during the **day of the Lord** to destroy the whole country. People will become helpless and terrified when they see this awesome force gathered against them. Confusion will grip them. They will realize that they are being punished for their sins. The stars will not shine, the sun will be <u>darkened</u>, and the moon will give no light. The population will be decimated. A <u>man</u> will be worth more than precious commodities. People will scatter. Those who are captured will be killed. Even children will be killed. Houses will be plundered. Women will be raped. There will be no mercy, no compassion, no place to hide. The beautiful city of Babylon will be seen <u>burning</u> to the ground. People will never live there again.

banner
flag

day of the Lord
another name for the Tribulation Period

Prophecy seems to indicate that the land of Babylon (Iraq) and the rebuilt city of Babylon will ultimately come under the control of the Antichrist. There is good reason to believe the city is destined to become the seat of Globalism and global religion during the Tribulation Period. After that, it will be destroyed forever (Zechariah 5:5–11). But an amazing fulfillment of prophecy is seen in the fact that Saddam Hussein started rebuilding the ancient city on its base (Zechariah 5:11). About 2,700 years ago, Zechariah said wickedness (Revelation 17) will build a house in the land of Shinar (Babylon) on its original foundation. Saddam started it and the Antichrist will complete it.

Damascus
the capital of Syria

Aroer
suburbs of Syria

Ephraim
Northern Israel

Aram
part of Syria

Jacob
Israel's name before
he became a
believer

what others say

Noah Hutchings

The subject of Isaiah 13 is total destruction; the object of
destruction is the entire land Babylon (modern Iraq); the time
period is the day of the Lord.[3]

There are those who say this prophecy refers to the capture of
Babylon by the Medes and Persians. But that attack was a two-nation
assault by neighboring countries, while this will be a multination
assault by enemies from faraway places. It is plainly stated that this
prophecy will take place in the day of the Lord.

Syria and Northern Israel

the big picture

Isaiah 17:1–14

Damascus will be destroyed and its suburbs will be abandoned.
Many cities in the northern part of Israel will also be destroyed,
and Israel will be greatly weakened. Jews will go hungry. But a
remnant of Jews will repent and accept Jesus. Meanwhile, many
Syrian cities will be abandoned because they have forgotten
God. A number of nations will rage against Israel, but God will
rebuke them.

It is not hard to find commentators who say this prophecy has
been fulfilled, but because **Damascus** has been destroyed so many
times, there is much doubt about who fulfilled it and when it happened. There are others who believe this has never been fulfilled
because Damascus has always been rebuilt, and it has never ceased to
exist as a city. There may have been an initial partial fulfillment, but
a greater, more complete fulfillment is yet to come.

Thus, we see that Damascus will be permanently destroyed sometime in the future. The cities of **Aroer** will be abandoned. Fortified
cities in **Ephraim** will be destroyed. The power of Damascus will be
broken. The cities of **Aram** will disappear.

When this happens, the glory of **Jacob** will diminish and Israel will
be weakened. Many Jews will have to glean for food, and large cities
will be abandoned because the Jews will have forgotten the God of

their salvation. As a result, some Jews will abandon their idols and false religion, turn from their sins, and accept Jesus.

At that time, nations will rage and threaten Israel, but God will intervene on Israel's behalf and silence the opposing nations.

Today, Damascus headquarters about one dozen terrorist command centers. These deadly organizations receive financing and needed technical support from Syria and Iran. They maintain an estimated 10,000–15,000 missiles that are aimed at Israel and capable of striking the entire northern territory. And they are constantly upgrading their anti-tank weapons and other systems. The threat is so severe that Israeli military experts are predicting weapons of mass destruction will have to be used to stop a terrorist or Syrian attack. The use of nuclear weapons could explain why Damascus will cease from being a city again.

Some people have difficulty believing prophecies like this will be fulfilled. They do not understand that defeating the Muslim terrorists will ultimately lead to salvation for many Arabs, the blessings of God upon many Arabs, and ultimately peace between these two warring nations (Isaiah 19:23–25).

Judah
Genesis 35:21–29

Ephraim
Genesis 41:50–52

what others say

Gary Stearman

This prophecy calls for the complete destruction of Damascus.... Will there be some kind of military exchange between Israel and Syria? Will it destroy parts of both countries? The territory of Ephraim is the heart of Israel, from the River Jordan to the Mediterranean Sea. In the days of Israel's original land grant, it extended from just north of Jerusalem, northward to the region of Shechem. It would encompass all of today's Samaria, plus more land to the west and north. Put in another way, it is the northern half of the contested West Bank Territories.[4]

One of Jacob's sons was named <u>Judah</u>. When the nation of Israel divided into a Northern Kingdom and a Southern Kingdom, the Southern Kingdom called itself Judah. Another one of Jacob's sons was named Joseph. He had two children named Manasseh and <u>Ephraim</u>. When the nation of Israel divided, the Northern Kingdom called itself Israel, but there were times when it was called Ephraim.

Gog and Magog
Ezekiel 38–39

bodies
Matthew 27:52

rise
1 Thessalonians
4:13–18;
John 5:28–29

dust
Daniel 12:2

flee
Matthew 24:15–16

wrath
Zephaniah 1:14–18

Scholars are divided on when this battle will take place. Some, including me, think war between Israel and Syria could break out any moment, while others think this will trigger the Battle of <u>Gog and Magog</u>, and they usually place that in the Tribulation Period.

Some Encouraging Words

ISAIAH 26:19–21 *Your dead shall live; together with my dead body they shall arise. Awake and sing, you who dwell in dust; for your dew is like the dew of herbs, and the earth shall cast out the dead. Come, my people, enter your chambers, and shut your doors behind you; hide yourself, as it were, for a little moment, until the indignation is past. For behold, the LORD comes out of His place to punish the inhabitants of the earth for their iniquity; the earth will also disclose her blood, and will no more cover her slain. (NKJV)*

God's people have much to look forward to. Those who have died will not be put in the grave and forgotten. God will remember his people and restore their bodies. Moreover, wickedness won't consume the earth. Jesus will come from heaven to punish the unrighteous for their sins. Those who have shed the blood of the innocent who cry out to God will be exposed. Isaiah points out several things that will happen:

1. The dead will live (death is not the end of a person).

2. Their <u>bodies</u> will <u>rise</u> (the resurrection will be a resurrection of the body).

3. Those who dwell in the <u>dust</u> will wake up and rejoice (we will be raptured to heaven).

4. God's people on earth are warned to seek shelter ("go" and "hide" or <u>flee</u>).

5. God's <u>wrath</u> will be poured out on the earth (the Tribulation Period).

6. God's wrath will be a punishment for sin (this will be the high cost of low living).

7. The sins of those who have shed blood will be exposed (secret sins will be revealed).

Among Christians there are differences of opinion about when the Rapture will occur in relation to the Tribulation Period, but most believe the church will not go through that terrible time. Notice the sequence of events in this passage. The dead will be raised first (Rapture). God will pour out his wrath on the earth later (Tribulation Period).

There will be a resurrection of life with four phases and a resurrection of condemnation. The resurrection in this passage refers to Phase 2—the resurrection of the church at the Rapture.

The Two Resurrections
(Believers and Unbelievers—John 5:28–29)

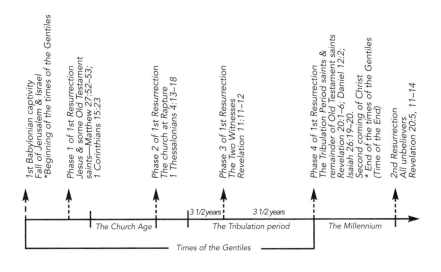

go to

husband
Jeremiah 31:32;
Hosea 2:16–23

shepherds
Psalm 23:1–6

ark
Exodus 25:10–22

adultery
Exodus 20:14;
Leviticus 20:10

faithless
unfaithful

marriage vows
covenant

husband
God

shepherds
here it means rulers

ark of the covenant
a symbol of God's
presence on earth

JEREMIAH

We Will Renew Our Marriage Vows

JEREMIAH 3:14–18 *"Return, O backsliding children," says the LORD; "for I am married to you. I will take you, one from a city and two from a family, and I will bring you to Zion. And I will give you shepherds according to My heart, who will feed you with knowledge and understanding. Then it shall come to pass, when you are multiplied and increased in the land in those days," says the LORD, "that they will say no more, 'The ark of the covenant of the LORD.' It shall not come to mind, nor shall they remember it, nor shall they visit it, nor shall it be made anymore. At that time Jerusalem shall be called The Throne of the LORD, and all the nations shall be gathered to it, to the name of the LORD, to Jerusalem. No more shall they follow the dictates of their evil hearts. In those days the house of Judah shall walk with the house of Israel, and they shall come together out of the land of the north to the land that I have given as an inheritance to your fathers." (NKJV)*

The people in both the Northern Kingdom (Israel) and the Southern Kingdom (Judah) believed they were the people of God, but because they were unfaithful, God compared them to an adulterous wife. This prophecy reminds his **faithless** people that they have broken their **marriage vows**. It calls upon them to return to their **husband**. God assures them that they will be a nation again. He tells them he would prefer to bring them back into the land as a group, but he will choose to bring them back as individuals: "one from a city and two from a family." When they return, he will give them faithful **shepherds**. He will cause them to multiply. They will forget about the **ark** of the covenant and not need it because the Lord will sit on his throne in Jerusalem (Jeremiah 30:8–9; Zechariah 14:9, 16–17). Gentiles from all nations will go there, honor Jesus, and repent of their sins. The Northern Kingdom will be united with the Southern Kingdom, and the two will be one nation again.

God compares unfaithful people to an adulterous or unfaithful wife. Adultery violates the Ten Commandments. It is a sin so serious that God said violators must be dealt with in the harshest of manners. They must be put to death (Deuteronomy 22:22–24).

John called Satan's coming one-world religious system "MYSTERY, BABYLON THE GREAT, THE MOTHER OF HARLOTS AND OF THE ABOMINATIONS OF THE EARTH" (Revelation 17:5 NKJV). He said God will cause world leaders to destroy this prostitute (Revelation 17:16–17).

nations
Psalm 2:1–12;
Revelation 12:5;
19:15

The Jews are currently returning to the land. They are returning not as a nation, but as individuals and families from all over the world. They are returning not to a divided kingdom, but to a united kingdom. But this is just preparation for an ultimate future fulfillment. Not until the Millennium will Jesus sit on the throne in Jerusalem and be worshiped by all people. Notice, this distinction about two returns. A present wave of Jews is returning in unbelief. But there will be a second wave that will return in belief at the beginning of the Millennium.

An Offer That Can't Be Refused

JEREMIAH 12:14–17 *Thus says the LORD: "Against all My evil neighbors who touch the inheritance which I have caused My people Israel to inherit—behold, I will pluck them out of their land and pluck out the house of Judah from among them. Then it shall be, after I have plucked them out, that I will return and have compassion on them and bring them back, everyone to his heritage and everyone to his land. And it shall be, if they will learn carefully the ways of My people, to swear by My name, 'As the LORD lives,' as they taught My people to swear by Baal, then they shall be established in the midst of My people. But if they do not obey, I will utterly pluck up and destroy that nation," says the LORD. (NKJV)*

God has a message for those wicked people who seize the land he gave to his chosen people. What they have done to Israel will be done to them. He will drive them out of their own lands. But then he will have mercy on them and allow them to return home. If they will learn the ways of Israel and accept Jesus as the Messiah, their nations will be restored. But if they refuse, they will be completely destroyed.

The good of the world transcends the right of nations to choose their own government. The time is coming when God will no longer let nations exist if their governments do not honor him. Everything will be done in order. First, God will cause the Jews to repent of their

go to

forgive
Ephesians 4:32

sins and accept Jesus as the Messiah. After that, he will restore the nation. Then, he will offer restoration to Israel's neighbors, and then to all the other nations on earth.

Israel's neighbors will be driven out of their land during the Tribulation Period. They will be given the opportunity to accept Jesus and be restored during the Millennium. Some nations will do that, and they will have a glorious future. Other nations will reject Christ, and they will cease to exist. Just as individuals are responsible for how we respond to Jesus, so are the nations.

God is Sovereign over all the earth. Israel's repentance at the end of the Tribulation Period will bring her blessings during the Millennium. The same is true for all the nations. God's judgments will fall on the wicked, but his blessings will be available to all who will listen and trust him. The following chart indicates this.

Fast Facts on Jesus as King

The Millennium	Scripture
Every Jew will return to Israel.	Jeremiah 16:14–15
The Jews will return to God with all their heart.	Jeremiah 24:4–7
The Jews will pray and seek God.	Jeremiah 29:12–14
Anti-Semitism will end, and the Jews will have a king.	Jeremiah 30:8–9
Israel will prosper, sing, rejoice, build cities, and have their own leaders.	Jeremiah 30:18–22
God will make a new covenant with Israel.	Jeremiah 31:31–34
The new covenant will be an everlasting covenant.	Jeremiah 31:37–41
The Jews will be cleansed, forgiven, and have peace.	Jeremiah 33:8–11
Moab and Ammon (Jordan) will be restored.	Jeremiah 48:46–47; 49:6
Elam (a mountainous area in Iran) will be restored.	Jeremiah 49:39
The Jews will be guiltless and sinless.	Jeremiah 50:19–20

The King Is Coming

JEREMIAH 23:3–8 *"But I will gather the remnant of My flock out of all countries where I have driven them, and bring them back to their folds; and they shall be fruitful and increase. I will set up shepherds over them who will feed them; and they shall fear no more, nor be dismayed, nor shall they be lacking,"* says the LORD. *"Behold, the days are coming,"* says the LORD, *"that I will raise to David a Branch of righteousness; a King shall reign and prosper, and execute judgment and righteousness in the earth. In His days Judah will be saved, and Israel will dwell safely; now this is His name by which He will be called: THE LORD OUR RIGHTEOUSNESS. Therefore, behold, the days are coming," says the LORD, "that they shall no longer say, 'As the LORD lives who brought up the children of Israel from the land of Egypt,' but, 'As the LORD lives who brought up and led the descendants of the house of Israel from the north country and from all the countries where I had driven them.' And they shall dwell in their own land." (NKJV)*

God <u>scattered</u> the Jews all over the world, but that was not permanent. This is his promise to bring every one of them back into the land, to make them fruitful and cause them to increase in number, to give them faithful leaders and make them unafraid. The time will come when God will send a <u>descendant</u> of King <u>David</u>, a righteous <u>branch</u> of the royal family, a wise <u>King</u> who will rule justly. When he comes the Jews will be saved, they will dwell safely in the land, and they will call him the Lord Our <u>Righteousness</u>. One thing is for sure: this return from the north and from the other countries will be so great it will make the Jews forget the exodus from Egypt (see Jeremiah 16:14–15; Exodus 12:31–42).

This is a most amazing prophecy. The Jews recognize the exodus from Egypt as the greatest single event in their history. But God is saying it is a mere shadow of what will happen in the future. Every Jew on earth will return to Israel.

go to

scattered
Ezekiel 34:11–16

descendant
Romans 1:1–4

David
2 Samuel 7:14–17;
Jeremiah 33:14–16;
Ezekiel 34:22–31;
37:1–28;
Hosea 3:4–5;
Luke 1:32–33

branch
Isaiah 4:2; 11:1;
Zechariah 3:8; 6:12

King
Zechariah 14:9,
16–17;
Ezekiel 37:1–28

righteousness
1 Corinthians
1:26–31

what others say

John Hagee

The Jews from the north country (Russia) have returned to Israel by the tens of thousands, as have Jewish people from around the globe. We have seen them on CNN disembarking from planes in Tel Aviv. We have read it in every form of print media. They do live in their own land, just as Jeremiah predicted. Their return to their homeland is another sign of the terminal generation.[6]

Thomas Ice and Timothy Demy

Modern Israel is prophetically significant and is fulfilling Bible prophecy. Readers of God's Word need to be careful to distinguish which verses are being fulfilled in our day and which references await future events. In short, there will be two end-time regatherings—one before the tribulation and one after the tribulation.[7]

The Jewish return to the land of Israel is now under way, but they are not saved and not dwelling safely. That will happen after the second coming of Jesus when he is sitting on the throne in Jerusalem. The ultimate return will occur during the Millennium.

God always intended the scattering of Israel to be corrective, not permanent. He still plans to bring them back and keep all of his covenants. But the chart below gives many reasons why God deemed it necessary to judge his people.

Fast Facts on the Dispersion of Israel

The Scattering of the Jews	Scripture
They brought it on themselves by forsaking God.	Jeremiah 2:14–17
God divorced them for committing spiritual adultery (worshiping false gods).	Jeremiah 3:6–8
They lacked understanding and did not know God.	Jeremiah 4:19–22
They forsook God and served foreign gods.	Jeremiah 5:19
The least to the greatest (people, prophets, leaders) were greedy and deceitful.	Jeremiah 6:11–15
They tried to provoke God, but it backfired.	Jeremiah 7:17–20
They refused to repent.	Jeremiah 8:4–7
They were not ashamed of their sins.	Jeremiah 8:12
They forsook the law of God and their hearts were stubborn.	Jeremiah 9:13–16
Their leaders would not pray.	Jeremiah 10:17–22
They refused to be bound to God.	Jeremiah 13:8–11
They were so accustomed to doing evil they could not do good.	Jeremiah 13:22–27
They rejected God and continued to backslide.	Jeremiah 15:1–9
They were made to serve their enemies.	Jeremiah 17:4
They forgot God.	Jeremiah 18:15–17
Jerusalem was burned, people were captured, many were killed.	Jeremiah 21:8–10

Trouble, Trouble, Trouble

JEREMIAH 30:5–7 *For thus says the LORD: "We have heard a voice of trembling, of fear, and not of peace. Ask now, and see, whether a man is ever in labor with child? So why do I see every man with his hands on his loins like a woman in labor, and all faces turned pale? Alas! For that day is great, so that none is like it; and it is the time of Jacob's trouble, but he shall be saved out of it." (NKJV)*

The Tribulation Period will begin with a <u>covenant</u> of peace, but it will quickly turn into a time of crying, fear, and terror. The impact of humankind's sin and God's judgments will be worse than anything the <u>world</u> has ever experienced. But in spite of everything that happens, Israel will survive as a nation.

covenant
Daniel 9:27

world
Matthew 24:21–22

Isaac
Genesis 25:24–26

Israel
Genesis 32:24–30

> ### what others say
>
> **Charles Halff**
>
> It will involve the Jewish people, the nation Israel and Jews all over the world. Many are in their promised land now, mostly in unbelief. It will also be connected with the horrendous judgments upon Gentile civilization, because of their wickedness, anti-Semitism and rejection of the Gospel.[8]

Many commentators refer to the Tribulation Period as "the time of Jacob's trouble" (Jeremiah 30:7 NKJV). Jacob was one of the twin sons of <u>Isaac</u>. As long as he was an unbeliever, he was called Jacob. But when he became a believer, God changed his name to <u>Israel</u>. "The time of Jacob's trouble" refers to a time of trouble for unbelieving Israel.

Some people teach that the church will go through part of the Tribulation Period. Others teach that the church will go through all of it. But the church is never mentioned in the Bible in connection with that terrible time. That is one reason many authorities believe in a Pre-Tribulation Rapture.

The return of Israel to the land, the rebuilding of Jerusalem, the peace movement, and many other occurrences indicate that this time of trouble is drawing near. But this is a reference to the Tribulation Period.

God's prophets gave some very descriptive names to the Tribulation Period. Some Old Testament names are: his awesome work, the day of their calamity, and the year of recompense for the cause of Zion. Some New Testament names are: the wrath of the Lamb, the hour of trial, and the Great Tribulation. The chart below speaks to some of this.

Fast Facts on the Day of God's Wrath

The Tribulation Period	Scripture
The nations cannot endure God's wrath.	Jeremiah 10:10
God's anger will not cease until his purposes are accomplished.	Jeremiah 23:19–20
The unburied dead will be like garbage lying all over the earth.	Jeremiah 25:29–33
God will completely destroy the nations.	Jeremiah 46:27–28

north
Jeremiah 16:14–15

The Shout in Russia

the big picture

Jeremiah 31:1-11

God says he will be the God of all the families of Israel. He will gather the Jews who were scattered and give them rest in the land. He loves the Jews with an everlasting love and will draw them back to the land of Israel. He will rebuild the nation—they will plant crops and Jerusalem will be rebuilt. God says rejoice, shout among the foremost of the nations, cry out for God to save his people. He will bring them from the land of the north and from the ends of the earth. He will bring the blind and the lame, expectant mothers and women in labor. They will cry and pray. It will be made known all over the world that he who scattered Israel will deliver them.

There are those who say the Northern Kingdom of Israel has been wiped out or lost and only a remnant of Jews from the Southern Kingdom are left in the world. Then there are nations that once refused to release their Jewish citizens. There are skeptics who said most of the Jews will never leave the land of their birth to live in Israel. But God said he is the God of all the Jews. They will be reunited as one nation and regathered back in the land. In spite of their sins, God loves the Jews with a love that will never cease. He will draw them back into the land, rebuild the nation, rebuild Jerusalem, and give them crops.

For several years, Russia was one of those nations that would not release Jews, but God said he would "bring them from the <u>north</u> country, and gather them from the ends of the earth" (Jeremiah 31:8 NKJV). He said he would gather all of them, including the handicapped and pregnant, and they would return with great elation. God wants the nations to notice this because he wants everyone to know him and to know that the same God who scattered the Jews is regathering and protecting them.

Hundreds of thousands of Jews have returned to Israel, causing a population explosion in the Promised Land. The population, which stood at approximately 800,000 in 1948, today exceeds six million. Most have moved from Russia, which lies to the north of Israel, but records show Jews have moved from 120 different nations and speak more than eighty different languages.

Notice who is speaking these words:

- "'At the same time,' says the LORD" (Jeremiah 31:1 NKJV).
- "Thus says the LORD" (v. 2 NKJV).
- "The LORD has appeared of old to me, saying" (v. 3 NKJV).
- "For thus says the LORD" (v. 7 NKJV).
- "Hear the word of the LORD" (v. 10 NKJV).

Now ask two questions: (1) Why is this prophecy so accurate? and (2) How should people respond?

The fulfillment of this prophecy has started, but all the Jews will not be back in the land until the Millennium. In the words of David Ben Gurion, the first prime minister of modern Israel, "The Jews are a miracle of world history. In the course of one generation they have renewed their land, their language and their nationality. The secret of this miracle is found in the Bible."

LAMENTATIONS

The Jews abandoned God and sinned without repentance. Their calamity came in the form of the Babylonian army and they had no God to help them. The destruction of Judah, Jerusalem, and the temple brought great grief and the death wail to the Jewish people. The lamenting of Jeremiah's heart is found in the following chart.

Fast Facts on the Dispersion of Israel

The Scattering of the Jews	Scripture
Jerusalem was deserted, despised, plundered; people were exiled or captured.	Lamentations 1:1–10
The Jews were made desolate.	Lamentations 1:16
God had no pity on them.	Lamentations 2:1–2
God acted like an enemy.	Lamentations 2:5–6
God made the Jews an offscouring and refuse among the nations.	Lamentations 3:45
The Millennium	Scripture
Jerusalem's punishment will come to an end.	Lamentations 4:22

EZEKIEL

The Golden Age

the big picture

Ezekiel 34:22–31

The Lord will save and judge his sheep. They will have one shepherd—his servant David—to tend them. The Lord will be their God and David will be their prince. The Lord will make a new covenant with them; he'll send showers, fruit, and good crops. They will know him and will no longer be prey or be afraid. They will live safely and have plenty to eat.

The Lord had been addressing the **corrupt shepherds** of Israel when his thoughts turned to his own people. Many will die during the Tribulation Period, but he will not let all of them be destroyed. He will rescue a large number of them. The corrupt shepherds favored the rich and powerful, but the Good Shepherd will judge everyone alike. Instead of many corrupt shepherds, Israel will have only one shepherd, his servant David. The Lord will be their God and David will be their prince. The Lord will make a new covenant with them. He will rid the land of wild beasts and will send rain when needed. He will cause the trees to yield fruit and make the crops grow. The people will know him. He will set them free and make them safe. They will know that he is with them and that they are his people.

go to

Shepherd
John 10:11

God
1 Timothy 2:5

Father
John 10:30

free
Luke 4:16–21

judgment
John 5:22

no one
John 10:29

hear
John 10:27

peace
Ezekiel 37:26–28

covenant
Daniel 9:27

what others say

Arnold G. Fruchtenbaum

The absolute monarchy of the Messiah will extend to Israel as well as to the Gentile nations. But directly under Christ, having authority over all Israel, will be the resurrected David, who is given both titles of king and prince. He will be a king because he will rule over Israel, but he will be a prince in that he will be under the authority of Christ.[9]

1. Israel will have a good shepherd.

    Jesus is the Good <u>Shepherd</u>.

2. Israel's shepherd will be their <u>God</u>.

    Jesus is God (the <u>Father</u>).

3. Israel's shepherd will set them free.

    Jesus came to set people <u>free</u>.

4. Israel's shepherd will judge his people.

    God has entrusted all <u>judgment</u> to Jesus.

5. Israel's shepherd will protect his people.

    <u>No one</u> can harm those Jesus protects.

6. Israel will know their shepherd.

    Jesus' sheep <u>hear</u> his voice.

7. Israel will follow their shepherd.

    Jesus' sheep will follow him.

Based on many prophecies, the Jews rightly expect their Messiah to appear and ratify a covenant of <u>peace</u>. But Jesus warns them, "I have come in My Father's name, and you do not receive Me; if another comes in his own name, him you will receive" (John 5:43 NKJV). Before Jesus returns, the Antichrist will appear and produce a worthless <u>covenant</u> of peace. They will accept him, and that will begin the Tribulation Period. They will not have true peace until the Millennium.

Jesus is gathering his sheep back in the land in preparation for this prophecy. But they will have to go through the Tribulation Period before it can be fulfilled. These blessings are reserved for the Millennium.

The restored Israel will be one nation not two. The Messiah will be King over all the world, including Israel, and directly under him will be the newly resurrected King David, who will serve as king of Israel and a prince under the King of kings. The resurrection of the Old Testament saints, including King David, will be after the Tribulation Period, which means the new covenant will go into effect after the Tribulation Period and during the Millennium. It is a future covenant with a literal restored Israel, not the church, and is part of the promises God made to Israel forever. This chart identifies some of the benefits Israel will enjoy at that time.

Fast Facts on Jesus as King

The Millennium	Scripture
God will give the land back to Israel.	Ezekiel 11:17
The Jews will remove all their idols.	Ezekiel 11:18
The Jews will receive the Holy Spirit.	Ezekiel 11:19
The Jews will keep God's laws.	Ezekiel 11:20
God will remember his covenant.	Ezekiel 16:60–63
Jews who do not follow God will be purged.	Ezekiel 20:33–38
God will require the Jews to offer gifts and sacrifices.	Ezekiel 20:40–42
Those who malign Israel will be punished.	Ezekiel 28:25–26

Who Holds the Deed to Israel?

the big picture

Ezekiel 36:1–38

God says Israel's enemies will claim the land of Israel, but because they have harmed and ridiculed the Jews and claimed his land as their possession, he will punish them. He will bring the Jews home, cause the land to produce crops, the towns and cities to be rebuilt, and their enemies to be silenced. God says he is aware that the Jews committed many sins and that is why he scattered them. But many people misunderstand this and do not believe the Jews are his people. So for his name's sake, he will regather them, cleanse them, change their hearts, put his spirit in them, make the land produce, and cause them to know him. When he gets through, the remaining nations will know him.

This is what underlies the Palestinian claim to the land of Israel: Satan wants to keep the Jewish people off the land, and before Jesus can come back and establish his earthly kingdom in Israel, the Jewish nation must be restored. As long as someone else possesses the land, Jesus will not return. God says Israel's enemies will brag that the **ancient heights** belong to them. He says to tell Israel's enemies they have mistreated the Jews, that they have **malice** in their hearts. The land belongs to God and he is upset; he will oppose those who oppose Israel.

God says the Jews rebelled against him so he scattered them, but that does not give Israel's enemies the right to claim the land or criticize him. So he is going to do seven things to protect his name: (1) remove the Jews from foreign countries, (2) cleanse their sins, (3) **regenerate** their hearts and spirits, (4) cause them to keep his laws, (5) put them on the land he gave to their **forefathers**, (6) make the land fertile, and (7) cause them to repent and turn to him. This will be his way of telling the world who he is.

ancient heights
mountains, Temple Mount, holy places

malice
sin (against God and Israel, they do not believe the Bible)

regenerate
remove their rebellion and give them a new nature

forefathers
Abraham, Isaac, and Jacob

what others say

Jimmy DeYoung

Ezekiel 36 refers to the land at least thirty-five times. God's promise to Abraham must be kept. God must give Abraham's descendants the land. Verse 22 says that God will do this, not for the sake of Israel, but for His holy name's sake. Hebrews 6:13 says that, "when God made promise to Abraham, because he could swear no greater, he sware by himself" [KJV]. For His holy name's sake He will give all the land promised to Abraham to his descendants.[10]

Following WWI, the League of Nations gave England control over a large area of the Middle East called Palestine. Both Jews and Arabs lived on the land. The population of neither was very great, and most of the Arabs and Jews who live there today are relative newcomers on the pages of history. Many nations even encouraged the Jews to go back and resettle the land to create a Jewish national home. Immigration was slow at first, but it picked up.

Then, due to Arab claims and complaints, the land of Palestine was partitioned in 1920. The Jews received roughly one-fourth of the territory that had been set aside for them in the British Mandate, and the Arabs received the other three-fourths. The Jewish portion of the territory was called Palestine. And the Arab portion of the territory was called Transjordan. The Jews were told that the land of Palestine would be their national homeland and that they should settle there. They were also told that Transjordan was an Arab homeland and that it was closed to Jewish settlements (but the Jewish territory wasn't closed to Arab settlements). This action was taken by the League of Nations in 1921. Under this formula, Jerusalem and the West Bank were in Palestine, which was Jewish territory.

On May 14, 1948, the United Nations reestablished the Jewish nation on the land that had been called Palestine. However, the Jews called their new homeland Israel instead of Palestine. Since then, almost three million Jews have migrated back to the land. Several Arab nations attacked Israel on May 15, 1948, and Israel quickly defeated them. But this time the United Nations carved Judea and Samaria (the West Bank) out of Israel and placed it under Jordanian rule. Now, the Arabs had close to 90 percent of the British Mandate that had originally been set aside for Israel. In 1964, the PLO came into being, and in 1967 to bolster their claim to the land of Israel the PLO started calling themselves Palestinians. Israel retook Judea and Samaria (the West Bank) in 1967, but the Arabs still claim it to this day. In fact, even though they have been given about 90 percent of what was set aside for Israel, they want more land carved out of Israel to connect Judea and Samaria with Gaza.

key point

To make a long story short, Arab claims to the land never end. There have been the Camp David Accords, the Wye River Accords, Oslo I, II, and III, the Road Map, and other agreements, but none of them have brought peace, and all of them have resulted in the Arabs' asking for more land. However, it's not for the U.S., the Arabs, the Europeans, or even the U.N. to decide who should possess it. To do so is to ignore the sovereignty of God. Who occupies the land of Israel is God's decision. Why is this worth remembering? Because dividing up the land of Israel is one of the reasons God gives for pulling the nations into the Battle of Armageddon. What the nations are doing is satanic. If they could get away with it, they could nullify God's covenants, make the Bible wrong, and stop the second coming of Jesus to rule over the Jewish people. It won't happen. So it's time to prepare for war with the One who can't be defeated.

Prophecies of the Bible

These incredible events are proof positive that prophecy is rapidly being fulfilled and the world is quickly moving toward the Tribulation Period. After going through that, the Jews will repent and be restored. Everyone should pay close attention. God wants to be known and understood. He does not want to be mischaracterized or misrepresented. He is holy, and he will protect his name. Restoring Israel to the land is something he must do. It will cause others to take notice and repent.

Israel wasn't scattered because she was innocent. The nation deserved everything God did to her. And God isn't regathering Israel because she is good. He is regathering Israel because he is good. He will keep the covenants because he promised to do it. That is the only way to protect the reliability of his name. Following are some of the ways God reacted to Israel's sins.

Fast Facts on God's Wrath

The Scattering of the Jews	Scripture
The towns were destroyed, altars devastated, idols smashed, people slain.	Ezekiel 6:6–7
God does not make threats in vain.	Ezekiel 6:10
The Jews were filled with sorrow.	Ezekiel 23:32–34
God would not forgive them until his wrath subsided.	Ezekiel 24:13–14
Survivors were killed by wild animals and plagues.	Ezekiel 33:27–29

Sticks and Bones

the big picture

Ezekiel 37:1–28

The Spirit of God carried Ezekiel to a valley filled with dry bones and told him to prophesy over them. Ezekiel did what God commanded him to do. The bones came together and were covered with sinews, flesh, and skin—in that order. Then Ezekiel was told to prophesy that breath should enter these bodies. He did that and life came into all of them. At that point, God said the bones symbolized the house of Israel. He told Ezekiel to prophesy again and say God will regather the Jews, put his Spirit in them, put them back on the land, and make them his people. He told Ezekiel to take two sticks, write Judah on one and Ephraim on the other, and join them together so they are one stick. God said the joined stick means the Jewish nation would be revived not

> as two nations, but as one single nation. His servant David will be king over it, the Jews will keep his laws, God will make a covenant of peace with them, and he will put his sanctuary in Israel. He will be Israel's God, the Jews will be his people, and the nations will know him.

This is one of the most famous chapters in the Old Testament because it predicts an end-of-the-age return of Israel as a nation, and because Jewish leaders and conservative Christians both apply this prophecy to events taking place in the land of Israel today. The once horrendous scattering of the Jews has been replaced by an amazing regathering. The nation has been resurrected, and multitudes of orthodox Jews expect a Messiah and King to appear at any moment. According to the prediction here, this new life is God's doing, and it precedes a grand conversion. Israel will undergo national restoration and then spiritual restoration. The main points of the passage are as follows:

1. The Spirit of the Lord showed Ezekiel a valley filled with dry bones.

2. God said, "Tell the bones they will live."

3. "Tell them they will come back to life in a gradual step-by-step process."

4. "Tell them God will begin with the bones, attach sinews (tendons), add flesh, cover that with skin, and put breath in the dead bodies."

5. First, there was a rattling noise; second, the bones came together into skeletons; third, sinews appeared; fourth, flesh appeared; and fifth, skin appeared on the dead bodies.

6. The bodies were assembled, but they were not breathing.

7. God commanded breath to enter into the bodies.

8. The bodies came to life and stood on their feet as a great army.

9. God said, "The bones represent the entire nation of Israel."

10. The people say, "Our bones are dried up, our hope is gone, we are cut off from the land."

11. But God said, "I will raise you from the dead, bring you back into the land of Israel, put my <u>Spirit</u> in you, and you will know me."

12. God told Ezekiel to write **Judah** on one stick and **Ephraim** on another.

13. God told Ezekiel to join the sticks together into one stick.

14. God said this means the Jews will be "one nation in the land, on the mountains of Israel."

15. Israel will have one <u>king</u>.

16. Israel will never again be two nations or be divided into two kingdoms.

17. The Jews will stop sinning, be forgiven, be cleansed, serve God, and be his people.

18. <u>David</u> will be Israel's king.

19. Israel will have a <u>shepherd</u>.

20. The Jews will obey God.

21. The Jews will live on the land God gave to Jacob, the land their ancestors lived on.

22. The Jews will live there forever.

23. God will make a <u>covenant</u> of peace with Israel.

24. The covenant of peace will be an everlasting covenant.

25. God will have a dwelling place (temple) in Israel.

26. The Gentiles will know that God has a special relationship with Israel.

go to

Spirit
Zechariah 12:9–10

Judah/Ephraim
Isaiah 17:1–14

king
Psalm 2:1–12;
Jeremiah 23:3–8;
Hosea 3:4–5;
Zephaniah 3:15;
Zechariah 14:9,
16–17

David/shepherd/ covenant
1 Chronicles
17:7–15;
2 Samuel 7:14–17;
Jeremiah 23:3–8;
33:14–16;
Ezekiel 34:21–31;
Luke 1:32–33

Judah
Southern Kingdom

Ephraim
Northern Kingdom

Henry M. Morris with Henry M. Morris III

The "wandering Jews" were without a national home for "many days" (Hosea 3:4–5), and it seemed impossible that such prophecies as these could ever be fulfilled. Even many Bible-believing Christians thought for centuries that God was through with Israel and that all the Old Testament promises to Israel should be spiritualized and applied to the church. But now, with the return of the Jews and the re-establishment of their nation, it is evident in a unique way that God's Word means exactly what it says.[11]

Randall Price

Ezekiel refers to a "covenant of peace" (Ezekiel 34:25; 37:26) made between the Lord and the "sons of Israel" that will have several provisions: (1) it will involve secure occupation of the Land of Israel; (2) it will be everlasting (Ezekiel 37:26b); (3) it will establish and increase the Israeli population in the Land (Ezekiel 37:26c; compare verses 25 and 36:24, 28); and (4) it will secure the rebuilding of the Temple and return the Divine Presence (Ezekiel 37:26d–27; compare chapters 40–48).[12]

Gary Hedrick

With everything that's happening in the world lately many people are wondering what time it is on God's prophetic calendar. How close are we to that midnight hour of world history when Christ will return? Israel is the clock God has given us so we can tell what time it is. In fact, God's prophetic plan revolves around the nation Israel. So when we want to know what time it is on God's prophetic calendar and we want to know where we are on God's prophetic plan all we have to do is look at the clock. Look at Israel.[13]

In this vision, it was the Holy Spirit that assembled the bones, made them into bodies, and gave them life. With this being the case, who or what is causing the Jews to return to Israel? Is this miracle evidence of the existence and power of God?

God's covenant of peace with Israel will be an everlasting covenant, not a seven-year covenant. Israel's seven-year covenant with the Antichrist will begin the Tribulation Period. Their everlasting covenant with God will begin the Millennium.

The Northern Kingdom of Israel fell around 721 BC (more than 2,700 years ago). The Southern Kingdom of Judah fell around 586 BC (more than 2,500 years ago). The nation was rebuilt, but it was destroyed again in AD 70 (more than 1,900 years ago). It is truly incredible that the Jews have been able to keep their identity without a nation of their own. But they have and this is exactly what the Bible says would happen. Fulfillment is well under way, but all of these things will not be completed until the Millennium.

prophecy

Russia Invades Israel

> ### the big picture
>
> ### Ezekiel 38:1–39:16
>
> God told Ezekiel to look at Gog, who lives in Magog and is the leader of Rosh, Meshech, and Tubal. Ezekiel is to tell Gog to prepare because God intends to pull Gog, his army, and the armies of many nations with him to the mountains of Israel. Among these nations will be Persia, Ethiopia, Libya, Gomer, and Togarmah. Their armies will be like a great storm. They will think they are attacking an easy prey and are about to seize valuable booty. Sheba, Dedan, and the nations that have come out of Tarshish will protest their invasion, but offer no help to Israel. Gog will come from his place in the far north, advance against God's people—Israel—and many nations will know God is holy when he takes vengeance against Gog. God will get angry, cause a great earthquake, overturn the mountains, cause Gog's troops to fight among themselves, and attack them with plagues of rain, hail, fire, and brimstone. People in many nations will recognize God's greatness and know him. Gog's army will drop their weapons, die on the mountains, and become a feast for the birds of prey and wild animals. God will put an end to people profaning his name. It will take the Jews seven years to burn Gog's weapons and seven months to bury the remains of his troops.

title
a name like emperor, caesar, pharaoh

Volumes have been written about this prophecy and it is impossible to comment on many of the details. Some of the most significant points are as follows:

1. Most prophetic scholars agree that Gog is a **title** that means "dictator" or "man on top."

go to

Magog
Genesis 10:2

curse
Genesis 12:3

Magog
a grandson of Noah

Rosh
the Hebrew word for
Russia

Meshech
Moscow, a large
Russian city on the
European continent

Tubal
Tobolsk, a large
Russian city on the
Asian continent

2. Gog's territory is the land where **Magog** settled.

3. Gog will be the prince of **Rosh**, **Meshech**, and **Tubal**.

4. Gog will come from his place in the far north.

5. All nations except the four that are north of Israel— Lebanon, Syria, Turkey, and Russia—are ruled out; the one nation in the far north is Russia.

6. God said he is against Russia. He did not say why, but he told Abraham he would <u>curse</u> anyone who curses Israel, and Russia falls into that category.

7. God said he will put hooks in Russia's jaws, which means Russia will lose control of her destiny.

8. Russia's allies will be Persia (Iran), Cush (Ethiopia/Iraq/ Sudan), Put (Libya), Gomer (Germany), and Togarmah (Turkey/Armenia).

9. The time of this attack will be "in the latter years" and "in the latter days" (Ezekiel 38:8, 16 NKJV).

10. One precondition for this attack is the regathering of Jews from many nations. (The current population of Israel exceeds six million.)

11. Another precondition is for Israel to possess silver, gold, livestock, and goods. (She does.)

12. Another precondition is for Israel to be dwelling safely. (The nation has quickly won every war it has been involved in.)

13. Another precondition is for many nations to be living in unbelief.

14. Another precondition is the rebuilding of unwalled villages. They exist.

15. Finally, birds of prey and wild animals will return to the land. (Vultures, buzzards, pelicans, wolves, and jackals are now found in many areas of Israel.)

There is no end to the speculation on what these hooks are, but no one really knows. The most credible possibility may be the fact that Russia has built a nuclear reactor in Iran. The Iranians have declared that they will use a nuclear weapon to wipe Israel off the face of the earth, if they can build one. Israel has said she will bomb the nuclear reactor first. But Russia has a treaty to defend Iran if she is attacked. So one can easily see how Russia could be dragged into a war she doesn't want to be involved in because she has obligated herself to defend a nation that wants to destroy Israel. She has allied herself with nations that are going to run up against the curse (see Genesis 12:3).

Scholars cannot be dogmatic about the identity of all of Russia's allies, but enough is known to say that most or all of them espouse the Islamic religion. Thus, it would appear that Russia is going to be reluctantly sucked into Islam's holy war in the Middle East.

Russia's preparation can be seen in the buildup of her military forces. The preparation of her allies can be seen in her sale and transfer of weapons to Syria, Iran, and the Palestinians. God has a plan for Israel that he must fulfill. If these nations would accept his plan, he would forgive, love, and bless them. As it is, he is showing great patience, but he will eventually be forced to take them out.

go to

temple
Micah 4:1–7

Levi
Ezekiel 43:19

sacrifices
Ezekiel 46:13

offerings
Ezekiel 43:22–27

sinned
Romans 3:23

Temple Mount
the area in
Jerusalem where all
the Jewish temples
were located

The fact that the Antichrist is not mentioned in these verses is viewed by some as a good indication that the Russian invasion occurs before he arrives on the scene. If the Antichrist were a great world leader at this time, it is not likely that he would stand on the sidelines and leave Russia unchallenged. If this were the middle of the Tribulation Period, he would be in control of some of these nations, and they would not be in the Russian coalition. His absence is a good indication of a Pre-Tribulation Period attack.

This combination of nations has never attacked Israel before. When Ezekiel wrote this prophecy, the Northern and Southern Kingdoms had both been destroyed. The nation came back into existence, but we can identify all the powers that controlled Israel until the nation was destroyed again by the Romans in AD 70. We also know that Israel did not come back into existence until 1948. Finally, we are aware of all the nations that have attacked the Jews since then. This prophecy has a future fulfillment, and all the signs indicate that the time is getting close. The end result will be a great defeat for this Russian-Islamic coalition with God being glorified and salvation coming to many.

The Millennial Temple

EZEKIEL 43:10–12 *Son of man, describe the temple to the house of Israel, that they may be ashamed of their iniquities; and let them measure the pattern. And if they are ashamed of all that they have done, make known to them the design of the temple and its arrangement, its exits and its entrances, its entire design and all its ordinances, all its forms and all its laws. Write it down in their sight, so that they may keep its whole design and all its ordinances, and perform them. This is the law of the temple: The whole area surrounding the mountaintop is most holy. Behold, this is the law of the temple. (NKJV)*

The last nine chapters of Ezekiel describe the temple that will be built on earth in Jerusalem and put in use during the Millennium. Both Jews and Gentiles will worship there. The tribe of Levi will serve as priests and handle the daily sacrifices that will be offered. Some sacrifices will be sin offerings and they will be a vivid reminder that all have sinned. The **Temple Mount** will be holy.

Torah
God's instructions

Randall Price

Jerusalem is enlarged and made glorious by the return of the Divine Presence (Jeremiah 3:17; Ezekiel 43:1–7; Zechariah 8:3–8). It is made the center of the world with the Temple Mount as the source of universal religious instruction and worship (Isaiah 2:2–3; 56:7). The Temple is built by Messiah with Gentile assistance (Zechariah 6:12–15; Isaiah 56:5–6), and the Gentile nations learn **Torah** and worship the One True God (Zechariah 14:16–19).[16]

The Old Testament animal sacrifices pointed forward to the future sacrifice of Christ on the cross. New Testament church members do not offer animal sacrifices, but they take part in the Lord's Supper, which, in part, looks back to the sacrifice of Christ. During the Millennium, the animal sacrifices will do the same thing. They will still remind people that Christ died on a cross for their sins.

The adoption of the shekel as a medium of exchange, the manufacture of the vessels for the animal sacrifices, the election of priests from the tribe of Levi, the manufacture of the priests' clothing, the manufacture of the musical instruments for the worship services—these are things that have been done with the millennial temple in mind. Unfortunately, the Jews are being deceived because the Tribulation Period temple will be built first. That temple will be defiled by the Antichrist. Then the millennial temple will be built.

The Jews plan to rebuild the Temple, called the Tribulation Temple by many Christian prophecy experts, but it will be defiled by the Antichrist at the Tribulation Period midpoint and abandoned. What will happen to it after that is not clear, but the Bible does reveal that Jerusalem and the Temple Mount will be elevated when Jesus comes back, and some suggest it will be destroyed by the topographical changes. The bottom line is that Jesus will replace the Tribulation Temple by one that is often called the Millennial Temple. The following chart identifies some of the characteristics of that temple.

Fast Facts on the Millennial Temple

The Millennium Temple	Scripture
It will have several gates.	Ezekiel 40:6–37
It will have a place to prepare the animal sacrifices.	Ezekiel 40:38–43
It will have rooms for the priests.	Ezekiel 40:44–47; 42:1–17
It will be at least three stories high.	Ezekiel 42:1–20
The presence of God will reside at this temple.	Ezekiel 43:1–5; 48:35
The throne of God will be in the temple.	Ezekiel 43:6–7
The system of animal sacrifices will be revived. The shekel will be used for monetary exchanges.	Ezekiel 45:12
The feast of Passover will be observed.	Ezekiel 45:21–24
Worship services will take place on the Sabbaths and the days of the New Moon.	Ezekiel 46:1–10
A river of water will flow from the temple.	Ezekiel 47:1–12
Gentiles will settle in Jerusalem and reproduce.	Ezekiel 47:21–22
The tribe of Dan will be restored.	Ezekiel 48:1–2
The land will be divided among the tribes of Israel.	Ezekiel 48:1–29
Jerusalem will be enlarged.	Ezekiel 48:35

Important Events in the Millennium

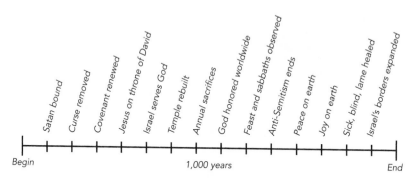

The tabernacle and its replacement temples have long been a critical component in Israel's spiritual experience. The Hebrews used the tabernacle in the wilderness. Solomon built the first Jewish temple, but it was destroyed by the Babylonians when they removed the Jews from the land. After the Jews returned, Zerubbabel built the second Jewish temple, but it was desecrated by Antiochus Epiphanes. Later, it was cleansed, Herod remodeled it, enlarged it, and renamed it after himself, but the Romans soon destroyed it. The third Jewish temple, often called the Tribulation Temple, will be rebuilt in the future by the Jews after the Tribulation Period begins and before the Tribulation Period midpoint. The fourth Jewish temple, often called the Millennial Temple, will be rebuilt by Jesus during the Millennium. There will be no temple in the New Jerusalem because God and his Son will be the temple (Revelation 21:22). More information can be found in the chart below.

Temples in the Bible

Sanctuary	Scripture	Approximate Dates
The Tabernacle	Exodus 26:1–37; 36:8–38; 1 Samuel 4:10–11	Built about 1446 BC Perhaps destroyed (date unknown) or could be hidden in cave under Temple Mount
Solomon's Temple	1 Kings 5–8; Jeremiah 32:28–44; Daniel 1:1–2	Built about 960 BC Destroyed 586 BC
Zerubbabel's Temple	Ezra 3:1–8; 4:1–14; 6:13–15	Built 516 BC Desecrated 169 BC
Herod's Temple (same as Zerubbabel's Temple): Remodeled, enlarged; name changed	John 2:20; Matthew 24:12; Daniel 9:26	Started about 19 BC Destroyed AD 70 Church Age Temple
Church Age Temple	1 Corinthians 6:10–20; 2 Corinthians 6:16–18	Christians indwelt between First Coming and Rapture
Tribulation Period Temple	Daniel 9:27; 11:31; 12:11; Matthew 24:15–16; 2 Thessalonians 2:4; Revelation 11:1–2	Will be defiled at Tribulation Period midpoint
Millennial Temple	Ezekiel 40–48; Isaiah 2:2–3; 56:7	Millennium

DANIEL

A Sign of the Second Coming: World Government

DANIEL 2:38–44 *You are this head of gold. But after you shall arise another kingdom inferior to yours; then another, a third kingdom of bronze, which shall rule over all the earth. And the fourth kingdom shall be as strong as iron, inasmuch as iron breaks in pieces and shatters everything; and like iron that*

Times
Luke 21:24

Jerusalem
Daniel 1:1–2

Medes and Persians
Daniel 5:28; 8:1–21

Gentile
someone who is not
a Jew

**Times of the
Gentiles**
the period of time
Gentiles rule on
earth (the period of
time before the
Second Coming)

crushes, that kingdom will break in pieces and crush all the others. Whereas you saw the feet and toes, partly of potter's clay and partly of iron, the kingdom shall be divided; yet the strength of the iron shall be in it, just as you saw the iron mixed with ceramic clay. And as the toes of the feet were partly of iron and partly of clay, so the kingdom shall be partly strong and partly fragile. As you saw iron mixed with ceramic clay, they will mingle with the seed of men; but they will not adhere to one another, just as iron does not mix with clay. And in the days of these kings the God of heaven will set up a kingdom which shall never be destroyed; and the kingdom shall not be left to other people; it shall break in pieces and consume all these kingdoms, and it shall stand forever. (NKJV)

A **Gentile** named Nebuchadnezzar was king of a world government headquartered in Babylon when he had a distressing dream about a great statue with a head of gold, chest and arms of silver, belly and thighs of brass, legs of iron, and feet of iron mixed with clay. His many advisers could not tell him what the dream meant, but God revealed the dream and its interpretation to a young Jewish captive named Daniel. God told Daniel the head of gold on the statue represented the kingdom of Babylon; the chest and arms of silver represented a second world kingdom that would replace Babylon; the belly and thighs of brass represented a third world kingdom; the legs of iron represented a fourth world kingdom; and the feet of iron mixed with clay represented a fifth world kingdom. While this fifth world kingdom is on earth, Jesus will come back and establish a kingdom that will never be destroyed.

God used this statue in Nebuchadnezzar's dream to give us a broad outline of what the Bible calls the **Times of the Gentiles**. It covers that period of time in history that the city of Jerusalem will be under the influence of Gentile governments. It begins with Babylon's capture of the city of <u>Jerusalem</u> in 586 BC and extends into the future until the second coming of Christ at the end of the Tribulation Period.

History reveals that Babylon's world kingdom (the head of gold on the statue) was replaced by the <u>Medes and Persians</u> (the chest and arms of silver). This kingdom was replaced by the brass kingdom on the statue (the Greek Empire under Alexander the Great). The Greek Empire was followed by the iron kingdom on the statue (the old Roman Empire). This empire was not replaced; it just broke up.

And there has not been a world kingdom since then. But according to Nebuchadnezzar's dream, there will be one more before Jesus returns (the kingdom of iron mixed with clay). It seems this will be the United Nations. If so, the second coming of Jesus is not long off. The second coming of Christ will occur while the fifth world kingdom is in power.

Many very prominent and highly respected scholars say this last Gentile world kingdom will be a Revived Roman Empire, and they specifically say that is the EU today. On the statue in Nebuchadnezzar's dream, the Roman Empire was represented by the legs of iron. If the final Gentile world kingdom was just a reunited Europe, it would have feet and toes of iron. But the statue had feet and toes of iron (EU) plus clay (others). It seems more likely that the final Gentile world government will be a reunited Europe (iron) assisted by others (clay or the United Nations). The iron is just one of the ten toes or just one of the ten horns or kings (Daniel 7:24; Revelation 17:12).

One more thing, pundits have been saying for decades that Jesus can come back at any moment. This is misleading. The Rapture can happen at any moment. But Jesus cannot come back until this last Gentile world government is in existence. The second coming of Jesus cannot take place until seven years after the signing of a seven-year covenant for peace in the Middle East. Jesus cannot come back until after the Antichrist has risen to power, the temple has been rebuilt, the Mark of the Beast has been initiated, and so forth. He cannot come back until there is a one-world government that has been divided into ten divisions and is being dominated by the Antichrist.

Even though the Jews occupied Jerusalem during the life of Jesus, the city was still under the influence of the old Roman Empire. And even though the Jews occupy Jerusalem today, sovereignty over the city—especially East Jerusalem—is questioned and its control is still

prophecy

**trample, and break
in pieces**
be brutal and
destructive

under the influence of the United Nations. Four-fifths of this prophecy (gold, silver, bronze, and iron) has been fulfilled. The feet of iron mixed with clay are now forming. The United Nations is already touting itself as the next one-world government. When that happens the Tribulation Period will arrive; it will end seven years later with the second coming of Christ.

One World Government

DANIEL 7:23–27 *Thus he said: "The fourth beast shall be a fourth kingdom on earth, which shall be different from all other kingdoms, and shall devour the whole earth, trample it and break it in pieces. The ten horns are ten kings who shall arise from this kingdom. And another shall rise after them; he shall be different from the first ones, and shall subdue three kings. He shall speak pompous words against the Most High, shall persecute the saints of the Most High, and shall intend to change times and law. Then the saints shall be given into his hand for a time and times and half a time.*

"But the court shall be seated, and they shall take away his dominion, to consume and destroy it forever. Then the kingdom and dominion, and the greatness of the kingdoms under the whole heaven, shall be given to the people, the saints of the Most High. His kingdom is an everlasting kingdom, and all dominions shall serve and obey Him." (NKJV)

It seems that Daniel was asleep when he had a series of visions about the future. He saw what this writer believes will be demonic forces causing a great disturbance in the Middle East. Four kingdoms will arise. Authorities disagree over their identity, but one of two opinions is widely accepted: (1) these kingdoms are the same as those in Nebuchadnezzar's dream (Babylon, Medo-Persia, Greece, the Roman Empire—old and revived); or (2) these kingdoms are kingdoms that will arise at the end of the age (perhaps England and some allies, Russia and some allies, a coalition of Arab or African nations, and the final Gentile world kingdom).

Daniel told an angel he wanted to know more about the fourth kingdom, and he was informed that it will be an earthly kingdom that will devour, **trample, and break in pieces** the whole earth. In its early existence this fourth world kingdom will have ten kings, which means ten divisions with each one having its own ruler or leader. After the ten divisions appear, an eleventh leader will arise. Other Scriptures teach that this leader will be an evil man who will come straight out of the **bottomless pit** and have satanic <u>power</u>.

According to the angel, this evil man will speak against God and **persecute his saints**. He will be anti-Christian and **anti-Semitic**. This is why Christians call him the **Antichrist**. He "shall intend to change times and law" probably means he will try to change the Christian calendar and all the laws based upon teachings from the Bible. "The saints shall be given into his hand for a time and times and half a time" is a biblical expression that means God will let him get away with persecuting Christians and Jews for three and one-half years (the second half of the Tribulation Period). After that God will judge him and Jesus will return. He will capture him and cast him into the <u>fiery</u> lake, establish his own kingdom, and turn it over to his own people.

The United Nations is currently working on a new charter called the Earth Charter or Earth Ethic, which is expected to be enacted into law at some future time. Although the authors of this charter do not refer to it as a world religion, many prophecy experts believe a world religion will be the outcome. Many prophecy experts believe most of the guiding principles for the charter come from Pantheism.

go to

bottomless pit
Revelation 17:8

power
Revelation 13:2

fiery
Revelation 19:20

something to ponder

bottomless pit
the place where God holds the most vicious demonic spirits

persecute his saints
persecute Christians and Jews

anti-Semitic
against Jews

Antichrist
an enemy of Christ who will come during the Tribulation Period

what others say

J. R. Church

I feel that this beast [the fourth kingdom] represents the New World Order whose power base is built upon the foundation of the United Nations. It is the same beast that John describes in Revelation 13. He writes that it has some of the same features as Daniel's previous three beasts—the body of a leopard, feet of a bear, and mouth of a lion. These three political entities are presently members of the United Nations.[18]

Ed Hindson

Bible prophecies clearly predict the rise of the Antichrist in the end times. Many people believe the great millennial end-game has already begun. As civilization speeds toward its final destiny, the appearance of a powerful world ruler is inevitable. The ultimate question facing our generation is whether he is alive and well and moving into power.[19]

Since the identity of these four kingdoms is questionable, it is difficult to say whether some of this is fulfilled or not. But we do know that the United Nations world government is now forming. Thus, it is not unreasonable to believe that the ten divisions will soon appear. But the Antichrist cannot appear until after the Rapture, and he will not be judged until Jesus returns at the end of the Tribulation Period.

The one-world government will no doubt appear for many reasons, some of which are even commendable (stop the spread of nuclear, biological, and chemical weapons; promote peace; deal with terrorism, and so forth). After it appears and divides into ten regions with a leader over each one (ten horns, kings, toes), an eleventh leader will appear. He will be the world's most dangerous man; a so-called man of peace who will kill without compunction; a lying leader with tainted or poisoned words of deception; Satan's apprentice, whom some call the "counterfeit son" and the second member of the "satanic trinity." He will use his authority over the one-world government to try to impose his pagan mind-set on all the world and will go forth to oppose God and all who follow God. The Almighty has deliberately kept his name a secret, but he has long been given the well-chosen title Antichrist. The good news for the church is that he cannot appear until after the Rapture. The bad news for the world is that he may be alive and waiting in the wings. The following chart reveals much about him.

Fast Facts on the Man of Sin

Daniel's Prophecies About the Antichrist	Scripture
He will have eyes like a man (insight, shrewdness, cunning).	Daniel 7:8
He will have a mouth that speaks pompous words (proud, arrogant).	Daniel 7:8, 11, 20
He will look "greater than his fellows" (impressive, commanding).	Daniel 7:20
He will make war against the saints (God's people) and prevail against them.	Daniel 7:21
He will subdue three kings.	Daniel 7:24
He will speak against the Most High (God).	Daniel 7:25
He will try to change set times and laws.	Daniel 7:25
He will oppress the saints and they will be handed over to him for 3 1/2 years.	Daniel 7:25
His power will be taken away and completely destroyed forever.	Daniel 7:26
He will start small, but grow in power.	Daniel 8:9

Fast Facts on the Man of Sin (cont'd)

Daniel's Prophecies About the Antichrist	Scripture
His power will grow to the south and to the east and toward the Glorious Land.	Daniel 8:9
He will set himself up to be as great as the Prince of the host (Jesus or God).	Daniel 8:11
He will take away the daily sacrifice (at the Jewish temple).	Daniel 8:11
Because of transgression (by those on earth), the saints and sacrifice will be given over to him.	Daniel 8:12–13
He will cast truth to the ground (use deceit and lies).	Daniel 8:12
He will prosper in all he does.	Daniel 8:12
He will understand sinister schemes (occultic or satanic plots).	Daniel 8:23
He will become mighty, but not by his own power (by Satan's power).	Daniel 8:24
He will destroy fearfully but will prosper and thrive.	Daniel 8:24
He will destroy the mighty and also the holy people.	Daniel 8:24
He will cause deceit (lies, corruption) to prosper and he will exalt himself in his heart.	Daniel 8:24
He will destroy many in their prosperity and even rise against the Prince of princes (Jesus).	Daniel 8:25
He will be broken, but not by human means (rather by God's power).	Daniel 8:25
He will confirm a covenant with many for one week (seven years).	Daniel 9:27
In the middle of the week (at the Tribulation Period midpoint), he will bring an end to sacrifice and offering (break the covenant).	Daniel 9:27
He will set up an abomination of desolation (a statue or image of himself).	Daniel 9:27; 12:11
He will do according to his own will (possess great power and authority).	Daniel 11:36
He will exalt and magnify himself above every god (be a braggart).	Daniel 11:36
He will speak blasphemies against the God of gods.	Daniel 11:36
He will prosper until the wrath (Tribulation Period) has been accomplished.	Daniel 11:36
He will show no regard for the God of his fathers.	Daniel 11:37
He will show no regard for the one desired by women (the Messiah).	Daniel 11:37
He will exalt himself above all gods (claim he is greater than every god).	Daniel 11:37
He will honor the god of fortresses (Satan).	Daniel 11:38
He will act against the strongest fortresses with a foreign god (Satan).	Daniel 11:39

rebuild
Nehemiah 2:1–8

seventy "weeks"
70 x 7 years = 490
years

Messiah the Prince
Jesus

cut off
crucified

city
Jerusalem

sanctuary
temple

Fast Facts on the Man of Sin (cont'd)

Daniel's Prophecies About the Antichrist	Scripture
He will make those who honor him rulers over many people.	Daniel 11:39
He will divide the land for gain (swap conquered territory for favors).	Daniel 11:39
He will enter and overwhelm many countries (attack many nations).	Daniel 11:40
He will enter the Glorious Land (Israel).	Daniel 11:41
He will conquer Egypt, Libya, and Ethiopia.	Daniel 11:42–43
He will pitch his royal tents between the seas (Mediterranean Sea and Dead Sea) at the beautiful holy mountain (Jerusalem).	Daniel 11:45
He will come to his end, and no one will help him.	Daniel 11:45

God's Decree

DANIEL 9:27 *Then he shall confirm a covenant with many for one week; but in the middle of the week he shall bring an end to sacrifice and offering. And on the wing of abominations shall be one who makes desolate, even until the consummation, which is determined, is poured out on the desolate.* (NKJV)

One of the most famous prophecies in the entire Bible is found in Daniel 9:24–27. God sent the angel Gabriel to tell Daniel, "Seventy weeks [490 years] are determined for your people and for your holy city, to finish the transgression, to make an end of sins, to make reconciliation for iniquity, to bring in everlasting righteousness, to seal up vision and prophecy, and to anoint the Most Holy" (v. 24 NKJV). He said the **seventy "weeks"** would begin with a decree to restore and <u>rebuild</u> Jerusalem. After the decree is issued, a period of seven "weeks" (49 years) and another period of sixty-two "weeks" (434 years) would pass, and **Messiah the Prince** would come. Then the Messiah would be **cut off**, and the people of the prince who would come would destroy the **city** and the **sanctuary**. It is now widely recognized that he foretold the first coming of Jesus to the exact day, that Jesus would be crucified, that Jerusalem would be destroyed, that the temple would be destroyed, that he foretold these things more than 483 years before they happened, and that all of these things took place exactly as he said they would.

This sum of seven "weeks" (49 years) plus sixty-two "weeks" (434 years) is sixty-nine "weeks" (483 years). It is one "week" (7 years) short of the required seventy "weeks" (490 years) decreed by God. This last week is often called the seventieth week of Daniel. It is also called the Tribulation Period.

Gabriel said, "He [the ruler who will come, the Antichrist] shall confirm a covenant with **many** for one week [7 years]; but in the middle of the week [at the Tribulation Period midpoint] he shall bring an end to sacrifice and offering" (v. 27 NKJV). This foretells the signing of a <u>peace</u> treaty in the Middle East, and it implies the rebuilding of the temple because that is where **sacrifices** and **offerings** were always made. It also implies the existence of priests to conduct the services, tools to sacrifice the animals, furniture for the temple, and clothing for the priests.

Another important point concerns the "ruler who will come." His people are the ones who destroyed Jerusalem and the temple after Jesus was crucified, and history records that it was the Romans who destroyed Jerusalem and the temple. This means the "ruler who will come" will be someone from the group of nations that made up the Roman Empire. Because the Roman Empire broke up before the arrival of this "ruler who will come" came on the scene, the Roman Empire has to come back into existence or be revived in order for this prophecy to be fulfilled. This is why the European Union is so important prophetically—it is the uniting of that group of nations that Gabriel said will produce the "ruler who will come"; he will be the Antichrist.

The last thing Gabriel said was that the Antichrist will set up an abomination that causes desolation on a wing of the <u>temple</u>. This will be something that defiles or contaminates the temple, and most authorities believe it will be an <u>image</u> of the Antichrist. When it happens many of the Jews will abandon everything, including the temple, and <u>flee</u> into the mountains.

A good example in the Bible of one week being equal to seven years is found in the story of Jacob fulfilling Rachel's week. He worked a week, which was seven years, so he could marry her (Genesis 29:21–30; also see Ezekiel 4:4–6; Leviticus 25:8).

Concerning the identity of the "many," know that there have been several attempts to broker a peace treaty between Israel and her enemies. But the Road Map is the first one that has involved the United Nations. It would be difficult to find a "many" that is greater than

go to

peace
1 Thessalonians 5:3

temple
2 Thessalonians 2:4

image
Revelation 13:14–18

flee
Matthew 24:15–16

many
representatives of many nations and groups of nations

sacrifices
animal sacrifices

offerings
gifts, worship

the United States, Europe, Russia, and the United Nations. And it's very intriguing that the EU has been brought in on the negotiations because the Antichrist will arise out of this group and sign the seven-year covenant.

As for the covenant being seven years, Israel has asked for a long-term (could this be seven years?) interim agreement before it signs a permanent treaty. She wants to be sure her enemies are keeping the interim agreement before she signs a permanent one. And as for the Palestinians, they have asked for an agreement for up to ten years (could be seven). The Koran allows a *hudna* (agreement of peace) for up to ten years, but no longer.

Also, notice that all of this requires the existence of Israel, the existence of a reunited Europe, Israel surrounded by enemies, peace negotiations, and efforts to rebuild the Temple. And all of this has to be in place at the same time in history. It hasn't been for almost two thousand years, but it is today.

Daniel's Seventy Weeks

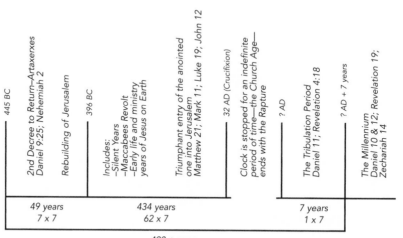

Gary Hedrick

The next event on God's prophetic agenda will be the removal of the Church from planet Earth, an event sometimes called the Rapture, discussed by Paul in 1 Thessalonians 4:13–18. Then, according to Daniel 9, God will call "time in" for Israel. At that point, ". . . the prince that shall come . . ." or the Antichrist, will ". . . confirm the covenant . . ." with Israel for seven years, marking the beginning of the seventieth "week" (verses 26–27 [KJV]), or the Tribulation Period. But at the midpoint of the seventieth week, or three and one-half years into the seven-year Tribulation, Antichrist will break his treaty with Israel, invade the land, enter the newly rebuilt Temple, and demand to be worshiped.[20]

David Jeremiah with C. C. Carlson

More than anything else in the world, the Jews long for the restoration of their temple and the beginning of temple sacrifice. One day there is going to be this great leader who will sit down at a conference table and say, "My dear friends, it's my desire to help you restore your religious heritage. I have the resources and manpower to rebuild your glorious temple."[21]

Charles H. Dyer

The final three-and-a-half years of this period are a time of unparalleled trouble for the nation of Israel. Jesus Christ described this "abomination that causes desolation" (Matthew 24:15 [NIV]) and indicated that its fulfillment was still in the future.[22]

How are we to know the identity of the Antichrist? Here are five clues:

1. He will begin his rise to world power in the European Union (Daniel 9:26).

2. He will rise to power after the world is split into ten regions (Daniel 7:7–8, 24).

3. After rising to power in Europe, he will take over the U.N. (Daniel 2:40–43).

4. He will sign a covenant with many, promising to protect Israel for seven years (Daniel 9:27).

5. He will desecrate the temple in Jerusalem at the Tribulation Period midpoint (Daniel 9:27).

Daniel calls the Antichrist

- another horn (Daniel 7:8, 24)
- a little horn (Daniel 7:8; 8:9)
- a king with fierce features (Daniel 8:23)
- the prince who is to come (Daniel 9:26)

Some people wrongly believe that the Tribulation Period begins with the Rapture, but it actually begins with the signing of a well-publicized covenant. It will be signed by representatives of many nations, and it will be a covenant to protect Israel for seven years. The signature of the Antichrist on the seven-year covenant begins the Tribulation Period. The second coming of Jesus ends the seven-year Tribulation Period.

Things are shaping up for the fulfillment of this prophecy: the U.N. is being transformed into a world government, the Roman Empire is being revived in the form of the European Union, Israel is back in the land, the quest for a peace treaty in the Middle East is going strong, and preparations for rebuilding the temple are well under way. But the stage for the seventieth "week" will not be completely set until after the Rapture and the rise of the Antichrist.

Chapter Wrap-Up

- Isaiah predicted the defeat of Judah, the destruction of Jerusalem, the regathering of Israel, the building of a millennial temple, the reign of Christ on earth during the Millennium, peace on earth during the Millennium, the Tribulation Period, the virgin birth of Christ, the destruction of Babylon (Iraq), the destruction of Damascus (Syria), and the resurrection of the dead. (Isaiah 1:24–31; 2:1–22; 4:1–6; 7:14; 13:1–22; 17:1–14; 26:19–21)

- Jeremiah predicted the restoration of Israel as a nation, the destruction of those nations that seize Jewish land, the second coming of Christ, the Millennium, and the Tribulation Period. (Jeremiah 3:14–18; 12:14–17; 23:3–8; 30:5–7; 31:1–11)

- The writer of Lamentations predicted the scattering of the Jews and the Millennium. (Lamentations 1–4)

- Ezekiel predicted that many Jews will survive the Tribulation Period and have a new covenant with God, that Israel will be regathered, that the Jews will repent of their sins and return to God, and that Russia and her allies will invade Israel. He also gave a detailed description of the millennial temple. (Ezekiel 34:22–31; 36:1–38; 37:1–28; 38:1–39:16; 40–48)

- Daniel predicted a coming world government at the end of this age, that it will be divided into ten divisions, that it will be ruled by a satanic person Christians call the Antichrist, and that the Tribulation Period will be in response to a decree from God. (Daniel 2:38–40; 7:23–27; 9:27)

Study Questions

1. Why will Israel be a testimony to the nations during the Millennium, and what two things will the city of Jerusalem be called?

2. What do Christians call the time of trouble for Jacob, and what will mark its beginning and midpoint?

3. What is the new covenant, what will God do, and when will it expire?

4. In Ezekiel's visions, what did the valley of dry bones and the joined sticks symbolize?

5. What powerful group of nations will attack Israel and be destroyed at the end of the age? What other nations will be destroyed?

Prophecies in the Minor Prophets

Chapter Highlights:
- God Loves Israel
- The Worst Is Yet to Come
- God Will Intervene
- Anti-Semitism Will Boomerang

Let's Get Started

The Old Testament ends with twelve short books that, because of their length, are often called the Minor Prophets. These twelve prophets lived from about 840 BC to 420 BC, and they were the main moral and spiritual leaders of their time. They spoke to the needs of the people, informing them about God, obedience, faith, love, patience, sin, and judgment, but there were times when they predicted future events, and that is where we will concentrate. The messages are widely recognized as being inspired by God, yet critics are surprisingly quiet about the content of these books.

harlotry
spiritual adultery (they took up false religions)

what others say

Irving L. Jensen

The books are "minor" only in the sense of being much shorter than such prophecies as Isaiah and Jeremiah (called "major prophets"). Their message is surely not less important today, nor was it when first delivered in Old Testament times. They were minor prophets preaching a major message.[1]

HOSEA

Hope for the Jews

HOSEA 1:10–11 *Yet the number of the children of Israel shall be as the sand of the sea, which cannot be measured or numbered. And it shall come to pass in the place where it was said to them, "You are not My people," there it shall be said to them, "You are sons of the living God." Then the children of Judah and the children of Israel shall be gathered together, and appoint for themselves one head; and they shall come up out of the land, for great will be the day of Jezreel!* (NKJV)

God told the prophet Hosea to marry an adulterous woman and have children by her to illustrate the fact that the Israelites had "committed great **harlotry** by departing from the LORD" (Hosea

go to

covenants
Genesis 17:7–8

sand
Genesis 22:17

one
Ezekiel 37:15–22

1:2 NKJV). Hosea's heart would break, and that would illustrate that Israel's sin was breaking the heart of God. Hosea's home would be torn apart, and that would illustrate that Israel's sin was tearing apart the house of God.

Hosea married an adulterous woman named Gomer. They had three children, and God named all of them. The first was a boy named Jezreel, which means "God sows" or "God scatters," and his name illustrated the fact that God planned to judge Israel's sin and scatter the people. The second was a girl named Lo-Ruhamah, which means "not pitied," and her name illustrated the fact that God was going to stop pitying and forgiving the sinful people. The third was a boy named Lo-Ammi, which means "not my people," and his name illustrated the fact that Israel's sins meant that the Jews were no longer God's people.

These analogies meant that God planned to destroy the nation of Israel. Some even want to believe that he planned to put an end to the nation forever. But that goes against the <u>covenants</u>, which must be fulfilled, and it ignores the prophecies in Hosea 1:10–11. In these verses, God promises that "the children of Israel shall be as the <u>sand</u> of the sea, which cannot be measured or numbered" (v. 10 NKJV). Although the Jews were no longer his people, the time will come when they will be called "sons of the living God" (v. 10 NKJV). And although Israel was divided into a Northern Kingdom and a Southern Kingdom, the time will come when they will be <u>one</u> nation. Finally, instead of having separate kings for the two kingdoms, the time will come when they will have one leader.

Think of Israel as a great ballplayer who was recruited by a coach (God), but he wouldn't do what his coach said. His coach tried to get his attention, but he wouldn't listen. Finally, his coach took him out of the game, set him on the sidelines, and put in another player (the church). After two quarters, and in the third quarter of the game, the great ballplayer realizes he has been sitting on the sidelines because he wouldn't listen. He tells his coach he will do what he is asked to do. Then, and only then, is he allowed to re-enter the game. And when he plays by the rules he becomes a great star. This is the point: Israel is simply sitting on the sidelines until she repents. Then, she will re-enter the game and prosper.

Israel and Judah were both destroyed. Many of the Jews were killed, something that has happened again and again. But the Jewish people have never been completely wiped out. They are now a rapidly growing nation again, and they are just one nation, not two. But they will not be called "sons of the living God" until the Millennium, and the one leader mentioned here is a reference to their acceptance of Jesus as the Messiah. That will occur at his second coming.

You Are My People

HOSEA 2:18–23 *"In that day I will make a covenant for them with the beasts of the field, with the birds of the air, and with the creeping things of the ground. Bow and sword of battle I will shatter from the earth, to make them lie down safely. I will betroth you to Me forever; yes, I will betroth you to Me in righteousness and justice, in lovingkindness and mercy; I will betroth you to Me in faithfulness, and you shall know the LORD. It shall come to pass in that day that I will answer," says the LORD; "I will answer the heavens, and they shall answer the earth. The earth shall answer with grain, with new wine, and with oil; they shall answer Jezreel. Then I will sow her for Myself in the earth, and I will have mercy on her who had not obtained mercy; then I will say to those who were not My people, 'You are My people!' And they shall say, 'You are my God!'" (NKJV)*

God's <u>covenant</u> will include the animals, the birds, the creatures that move along the ground, and the nations. It will establish a period of security and peace for every living thing on earth. All weapons will be destroyed. Israel, the land that has committed <u>harlotry</u>, will be forgiven, taken back, and **betrothed** to God forever. As Israel's <u>husband</u>, the Almighty will establish a new relationship with the nation based upon his **righteousness**, **justice**, **lovingkindness**, and **mercy**. This wonderful relationship will not be the result of Israel's merits. Rather, it will come about because of God's faithfulness—his unwavering commitment to keep the promises he has made. He will bless Israel and cause the land to be fruitful and the people to prosper. They will have the best of everything in abundance. He will be their God, and they will be his people.

go to

covenant
2 Samuel 7:4–17;
1 Chronicles
16:15–18;
Jeremiah 31:31–34

harlotry
Hosea 1:2

husband
Jeremiah 3:14–18;
31:32

betrothed
engaged to be
married

righteousness
his ability to do right

justice
his ability to give
each person their
due

lovingkindness
his ability to be
gracious, tender,
affectionate

mercy
his ability to be
compassionate

go to

ephod
Exodus 28:1–43

sacred pillar
pillars of stone
erected in honor of
pagan gods

ephod
sacred garment
worn by a priest

teraphim
statue or image
used to represent a
god (false god)

key point

what others say

Duane A. Garrett

It would seem, in fact, that faithfulness sums up the other four qualities in a single word. Because God is consistently good ("righteousness and justice"), one can rely upon him to do good consistently to his people. And because God is consistently merciful ("love and compassion"), one can rely upon him to show mercy consistently to his people. The consistent goodness of God, his faithfulness (in contrast to the capriciousness of Baal), is the basis for Israel's salvation.[2]

Some do not believe the Jews are God's chosen people, but to deny that fact is to deny the faithfulness of God. And to deny his faithfulness is to misunderstand his nature.

Nature will turn against humanity during the Tribulation Period, war will be a common thing, and the Jews will be despised. But this will be reversed during the Millennium. Nature will turn the earth into a paradise, peace will prevail, and the Jews will be respected.

The current restoration of Israel is taking the nation toward the fulfillment of these things. The Jews are not more righteous than other people, but by the time the Millennium arrives, the faithfulness of God will prevail. On the cross, Jesus died for the sins of the world. This includes the Jews who accept Christ at the end of the Tribulation Period. Forgiveness, salvation, and national restoration will be theirs in the future because God's blessings are for all who repent.

Give Us a King

HOSEA 3:4–5 *For the children of Israel shall abide many days without king or prince, without sacrifice or sacred pillar, without ephod or teraphim. Afterward the children of Israel shall return and seek the LORD their God and David their king. They shall fear the LORD and His goodness in the latter days. (NKJV)*

Because they committed spiritual adultery (Hosea 1:1–11) by departing from the Lord, he decreed that the Jews would live many days without a king or prince to rule over them, without priests to offer sacrifices or erect **sacred pillar**, and without spiritual symbols such as an **ephod** or **teraphim**. After the many days have ended, the

Jews will abandon their spiritual adultery, seek the Lord their God (Jehovah) and David their king (a <u>king</u> in the line of <u>David</u>—Jesus). They will do this in the **latter days** (that period of time that will end with the second coming of Jesus).

king
Psalm 2:1–12;
10:15–16;
Jeremiah 23:3–8;
Zephaniah 3:15;
Zechariah 14:9,
16–17

David
1 Chronicles
17:7–15;
2 Samuel 7:14–17;
Jeremiah 23:3–8;
33:14–16;
Ezekiel 34:22–31;
37:1–28;
Luke 1:32–33

---

what others say

Robert T. Boyd

After the worldwide dispersion under Titus and Hadrian, the Jews had no place to worship and offer sacrifices. They built synagogues and observed some feasts, had Rabbis, and offered chickens on the Day of Atonement. But they were a wandering, scattered people until Israel became a nation in 1948. They still have no king, no temple, no scriptural sacrifices, and no priests. And Hosea predicted this over 2,700 years ago.[3]

Arnold G. Fruchtenbaum

When the restoration of Israel comes, it will no longer be in the form of two kingdoms with each one having their own king. They will be a reunited nation with only one head, and that head will be the resurrected David, who will serve as their prince. So while Jehovah will serve as their God and absolute King, David will serve under Him as God's prince over Israel.[4]

---

latter days
the last days of the "times of the Gentiles"

Messiah
Jesus

It is important to notice that this prophecy was uttered about 2,700 years ago, which was before Israel split into two kingdoms (Northern and Southern) and before the temple was destroyed. In other words, it was given at a time when Israel had a king, priests, and many spiritual symbols. Apart from a revelation from God, how else could anyone foretell these things? But not only have the Jews been without a king, temple, and sacrifice for almost two thousand years, now that they have returned they are seeking to change their political system, reestablish the throne of David, identify one of his descendants to be king, build a palace, a throne, a temple, and resume the sacrifices.

God put the Jews off the land. Then he restored the nation and sent the **Messiah**. But the Jews rejected him. So God put them off the land a second time. He is now restoring the nation again and the Jews are returning, but they are not returning to accept Jesus. According to the Bible, they will not do that until after the Tribulation Period when Jesus comes a second time. The

Millennium will start, he will rule as their King, and they will worship him.

Can We Be Sure?

Israel
Ezekiel 37:1–28

thousand
Psalm 90:4;
2 Peter 3:8

last days
2 Peter 3:3–4

repentance
turning toward God,
away from wrong

> HOSEA 6:1–3 *Come, and let us return to the LORD; for He has torn, but He will heal us; He has stricken, but He will bind us up. After two days He will revive us; on the third day He will raise us up, that we may live in His sight. Let us know, let us pursue the knowledge of the LORD. His going forth is established as the morning; He will come to us like the rain, like the latter and former rain to the earth. (NKJV)*

Hosea acknowledges the fact that the Jews left the Lord and called on them to join him in **repentance**. He predicted God's deathlike destruction of Israel and the fact that God will eventually revive and raise up the nation. This resurrection of Israel begs for a date, which Hosea said would be after two days and on the third day. As God counts time, one day to him is a thousand years to us. Thus, it is revealed that the revival of Israel as a nation would come after two thousand years of our time had passed and before three thousand years of our time was gone. Hosea calls on the Jews again, asking them to repent. He tells them that the return of Christ is as certain as the rising of the sun and the coming of the seasonal rains.

Time is an essential element in the lives of most people, but God is not subject to time as we are. When he said he would revive Israel after two days and raise her up in the third day, he was speaking in terms of his own view of time. He was saying two thousand years would pass before he revived Israel, and it would take place within the next one thousand years.

Looking back on history, the Northern Kingdom of Israel fell around 721 BC, more than 2,700 years ago, and the Southern Kingdom of Judah fell around 586 BC, more than 2,500 years ago. Two "God days" have passed, and we are now in the third "God day" for both kingdoms, as God reckons time.

The Bible predicts that the last days will be characterized by moral decay, with scoffers ridiculing the Second Coming. Evildoers will ask, "Where is the promise of His coming?" And they will say, "Since the fathers fell asleep, all things continue as they were from the beginning of creation" (2 Peter 3:4 NKJV). But God doesn't break his promises, and the second coming of Christ is as sure as the rising of the sun.

The resurrection and national restoration of Israel have begun, but the Jews will not abandon their <u>sin</u> until the Tribulation Period (seventieth week of Daniel). The Tribulation Period will trigger repentance and the second coming of Christ. Several things will happen to trigger the repentance:

sin
Daniel 9:24

1. The gospel will be preached to all nations including Israel (Matthew 24:14).

2. Elijah the prophet will appear in Israel and change the hearts of many (Malachi 4:5–6).

3. The 144,000 Jewish evangelists will preach (Revelation 7:2–8).

4. The two witnesses will appear and preach (Revelation 11:3–13).

5. The Jews will realize their mistake when the Antichrist breaks the covenant and begins to kill them (Daniel 9:24–27; Revelation 12:13–17).

Repentance in the third day will trigger the Second Coming and the restoration of Israel.

Instead of listening to God's prophets and laying aside the sins that separated them from God, the Jews readily followed the prophets of their own choosing and did things to make Satan rejoice. Her failures to heed the warnings of God were many, and they will endure until the time of the end. The good news is the day will come when they will realize their mistake, repent, and be restored. The following chart shows some of the bad news and why they will suffer for some time to come.

locust
Revelation 9:3–11

Fast Facts on the Dispersion of Israel

The Scattering of the Jews	Scripture
God will stop showing mercy to Israel.	Hosea 1:6
God will stop their celebrations and ruin their crops.	Hosea 2:11–12
The Jews will reject knowledge and forget the law of God.	Hosea 4:6
The Jews will be prideful.	Hosea 5:5
God will be like a moth and a lion to Israel; like rottenness and a young lion to Judah.	Hosea 5:12–14
Israel will be swallowed up among the Gentiles.	Hosea 8:8
The Jews will have to eat unclean (defiled) food in a foreign land.	Hosea 9:3
Many Jews will die in foreign lands.	Hosea 9:6
Israel's glory (God) will abandon them.	Hosea 9:11
God will cast away the Jews for their disobedience.	Hosea 9:17
Because the Jews planted wickedness, they will reap iniquity.	Hosea 10:13
The Jews will be punished according to their ways.	Hosea 12:2
The Jews will be like a cloud, dew, chaff, and smoke that disappears.	Hosea 13:3
Because of rebellion, Jewish children and pregnant women will die.	Hosea 13:16

JOEL

A Snapshot of Things to Come

> JOEL 1:15–20 *Alas for the day! For the day of the LORD is at hand; it shall come as destruction from the Almighty. Is not the food cut off before our eyes, joy and gladness from the house of our God? The seed shrivels under the clods, storehouses are in shambles; barns are broken down, for the grain has withered. How the animals groan! The herds of cattle are restless, because they have no pasture; even the flocks of sheep suffer punishment. O LORD, to You I cry out; for fire has devoured the open pastures, and a flame has burned all the trees of the field. The beasts of the field also cry out to You, for the water brooks are dried up, and fire has devoured the open pastures. (NKJV)*

When Joel wrote his prophecy, Israel was in the midst of the greatest <u>locust</u> plague the nation had ever experienced. Dark clouds of locusts covered the land, causing the prophet to say, "What the chewing locust left, the swarming locust has eaten; what the swarming locust left, the crawling locust has eaten; and what the crawling locust left, the consuming locust has eaten" (Joel 1:4 NKJV). The vineyards were destroyed; the bark and leaves were stripped off the trees; there was no pasture for the animals, no crops to harvest, no sacrifices for the priests to offer, no ground that was not barren, no farmer that was not in poverty and despair, and no joy in the land.

The devastating effects of this unprecedented plague caused Joel's mind to skip far into the future to another desperate time the Bible calls the **day of the Lord**. Trouble will come like a judgment from the Almighty. Food will vanish; <u>famine</u> will grip the land; the absence of <u>sacrifice and offering</u> will leave nothing for the priests in the house of God to rejoice about; seeds will rot in the ground; barns will ruin because they will not be needed; granaries will break down because they will not be used; cattle and sheep will cry because they will have nothing to eat or drink; even the wild animals will suffer. The devastation wrought by the swarms of locusts in Joel's time is just a glimmer of the greater destruction to come in the day of the Lord. This is something that will take place during the Tribulation Period.

Jesus said there will be famines, pestilences, and earthquakes in various places (Matthew 24:7). John said the fourth horseman of the Apocalypse will be given power over a fourth of the earth, to kill with sword, with hunger, with death, and by the beasts of the earth (Revelation 6:8). It will be unprecedented, but it will lure people away from trusting in themselves and cause multitudes to look to God.

famine
Revelation 6:5–8

sacrifice and offering
Daniel 9:27

day of the Lord
another name for the Tribulation Period

what others say

Irving L. Jensen

Five times in Joel the phrase "the day of the Lord" appears. As we shall see in the next lesson, Joel is looking with his prophetic telescope to the end of time. Even when the New Testament writers referred to that day, it was still in the future.[5]

Duane A. Garrett

This portrayal of starvation and drought gives the reader a sense that creation itself is dying. The "good" order of seedtime and harvest (Genesis 1:14–18; 8:22) has been disrupted; and the variety of plants, creeping things, and beasts is receding into a chaos of dust and death.[6]

go to

locusts
Joel 1:15–20

quake
Revelation 11:13;
12:16; 16:18

sun and moon
Amos 8:9;
Matthew 24:29

great
Matthew 24:21–22

symbolic
words that represent
something else

dogmatic
positive or assertive

Zion
another name for
Jerusalem

A Call to Arms

the big picture

Joel 2:1-11

These verses call for an alarm to be sounded announcing the arrival of the day of the Lord. It will be a time of darkness, gloom, clouds, and thick darkness. A great and strong people will march on the fertile land of Israel, destroying everything in its path. It will be like the plague of locusts described in Joel 1. The locusts looked like horses, ran like swift steeds, leaped over mountaintops, and devoured everything. The sight of this great army will make people afraid and sick. Troops will charge like brave soldiers—scaling walls, marching in line, staying on course, breaking through defenses, rushing into cities, and breaking into houses. The earth will quake, the heavens will tremble, and the heavenly bodies will diminish and grow dark. God will issue a command to his great army. The day of the Lord will be terrible, and we are asked, "Who can endure it?"

The word *like* appears eleven times in these eleven verses, which means the language is **symbolic**. It would be unwise to be **dogmatic** about this event. Joel is using his memories of the plague of <u>locusts</u> to illustrate what a coming military invasion of Israel will be like during the day of the Lord. He calls for the trumpet to be blown in **Zion** to signal the coming Tribulation Period—a time of cloudiness and thick darkness like the time when great swarms of locusts filled the skies over Israel. A large and mighty army will spread across the mountains of Israel like the millions of locusts in Joel's day. In front of this army, Israel will be like the garden of Eden; behind it Israel will be like a desert. There has never been anything like it before and will never be anything like it again. Everything this army encounters will be destroyed. The troops will move like galloping cavalry. They will produce a noise like chariots leaping over the mountaintops, like a crackling fire burning everything in its path. The sight of this great army will make people afraid and sick. It will be a well-trained force—charging, scaling walls, marching in line, focused on the target, and plunging through defenses without pulling back. Troops will rush into Jerusalem, breaking into houses and seizing whatever they want. The earth will <u>quake</u>, the <u>sun and moon</u> will be darkened, and the stars will not shine. If God doesn't cut this <u>great</u> and terrible time short, no one will survive.

Some critics contend that these verses deal with a past plague of locusts instead of a future military invasion of Israel. But swarms of locusts move in a disorganized, haphazard manner. Joel calls this force "a people . . . great and strong" (v. 2 NKJV), and he paints a picture of a well-trained, efficient military force marching in line, not breaking rank or pushing one another. It is unreasonable to believe locusts have moved like this in the past.

Joel gives us an important clue when he refers to this great army as "the northern army" (2:20 NKJV). We know that there will be a future invasion of Israel by a group of nations from the <u>far north</u> (Russia and her allies); that the <u>king of the North</u> will attack the Antichrist in the Middle East; and that there will be a war between Israel and Syria resulting in the destruction of <u>Damascus</u> and northern Israel. Incidentally, Russia, the king of the North, and Syria will all be defeated and so will this northern army.

This passage makes a good case for the Pre-Trib Rapture. Joel said, "The day of the LORD [Tribulation Period] is coming, for it is at hand: A day of darkness and gloominess" (Joel 2:1–2 NKJV). Amos said it will be "darkness, and not light" (Amos 5: 18, 20 NKJV). And Zephaniah said, "That day is a day of wrath . . . A day of darkness and gloominess" (Zephaniah 1:15 NKJV). But Paul said, "You, brethren [Christians], are not in darkness, so that this Day [day of the Lord] should overtake you as a thief. You are all sons of light and sons of the day. We are not of the night nor of darkness" (1 Thessalonians 5:4–5 NKJV). Believers shouldn't be concerned about going through the Tribulation Period. But we should be concerned for our loved ones and those we know who haven't accepted Jesus.

This invasion of Israel is associated with the day of the Lord. That ties it to the coming Tribulation Period. The Jews who are alive at that time should be concerned about it because they haven't accepted Jesus and they will be the object of this attack.

<u>A Bountiful Supply</u>

JOEL 2:28–29 *And it shall come to pass afterward that I will pour out My Spirit on all flesh; your sons and your daughters shall prophesy, your old men shall dream dreams, your young men shall see visions. And also on My menservants and on My maidservants I will pour out My Spirit in those days.* (NKJV)

far north
Ezekiel 38:1–39:16

king of the North
Daniel 11:40

Damascus
Isaiah 17:1–14

key point

go to

northern army
Joel 2:1–11, 20

praise
Joel 2:26

Spirit
Ezekiel 36:27; 39:29

false prophets
Matthew 24:24–25

dreams
Deuteronomy
13:1–5;
Jeremiah 23:25

visions
Jeremiah 14:14

Pentecost
Acts 2:1–18

his Spirit
the Holy Spirit

prophesy
foretell events

dreams
images that occur
while one is asleep

visions
images that occur
while one is in a
trance

"Afterward" reveals when this prophecy will be completely fulfilled: it will be after what Joel just said about the defeat of the <u>northern army</u> and after what he said about Israel beginning to <u>praise</u> the name of the Lord. After these things, God will pour out **his Spirit** on all people. "Pour out" means give his Spirit with great abundance, and "all flesh" means all those who praise him regardless of their age, gender, race, nationality, or status in life. And God's reason for doing this will be so that people will be able to: (1) **prophesy**, (2) receive revelations in **dreams**, and (3) receive messages in **visions**. In short, the time is coming when an abundant supply of God's <u>Spirit</u> will be given to all of his people, and it will not matter if they are young or old, male or female, Gentile or Jew, rich or poor. These gifts will verify the presence of the Holy Spirit and identify those who possess them as God's people. Although Joel said God will give these prophetic gifts to his people, the Bible warns us to beware of <u>false prophets</u> who use <u>dreams</u> and false <u>visions</u> to pull people away from God.

The apostle Peter made it plain that God began fulfilling this on the day of <u>Pentecost</u>. But that was just a hint of things to come. The northern army had not yet attacked Israel, and the Jews as a nation were not praising the name of the Lord. This prophecy will not be completely fulfilled until the Millennium.

It will begin with the Jews confessing their sins at Petra (or wherever they flee to in the wilderness) and carry over into the Millennial kingdom. It will be a great demonstration of God's grace. The Jews who have rebelled against God for so long and did so much to contribute to the death of his Son will be among those who receive the outpouring of the Holy Spirit.

<u>D-Day (Or Should It Be "A-Day" for Armageddon)</u>

JOEL 3:9–16 *Proclaim this among the nations: "Prepare for war! Wake up the mighty men, let all the men of war draw near, let them come up. Beat your plowshares into swords and your pruning hooks into spears; let the weak say, 'I am strong.'" Assemble and come, all you nations, and gather together all around. Cause Your mighty ones to go down there, O LORD. "Let the nations be wakened, and come up to the Valley of Jehoshaphat; for there I will sit to judge all the surrounding nations. Put in the sickle, for the harvest is ripe. Come, go down; for the winepress is full, the vats overflow—for their wickedness is great." Multitudes, multitudes in the valley of decision! For the day of the LORD is near in the valley of decision. The sun and moon will grow dark, and the stars will diminish their brightness. The LORD also will roar from Zion, and utter His voice from Jerusalem; the heavens and earth will shake; but the LORD will be a shelter for His people, and the strength of the children of Israel. (NKJV)*

This passage calls for unnamed messengers to fan out all over the world to advise the <u>nations</u> to prepare for war. The text does not say so, but these messengers are probably the three <u>unclean spirits</u> mentioned in the book of Revelation. They are told to wake up the "mighty men" and to assemble the "men of war" (Joel 3:9 NKJV). This war will exempt no one. Those who would normally be excused from military service will not be excused from this great battle. Troops will be mobilized from all over the world. They will gather to attack <u>Jerusalem</u> and to challenge the <u>armies</u> of the <u>Lord</u>. They will assemble in a place called the **Valley of <u>Jehoshaphat</u>**. The heavenly hosts will be told to put in the **sickle** because the earth is ripe for harvest. They will be told to trample the armies because the world is overflowing with wickedness. Multitudes, great multitudes will be there. They will have to face their Maker. It will be the day of the Lord. The <u>sun and moon</u> will grow dark and the stars will diminish in brightness—darkness will cover the land. Jesus will rush out of Jerusalem to meet this great army. There will be a terrible earthquake and vibrations in the sky. The Messiah will **deliver** his people. The text does not tell us what will happen to the troops, but elsewhere we learn that their dead bodies will provide a great feast for the <u>birds</u> of prey.

go to

nations
Psalm 2:1–12;
Micah 4:11–13;
Obadiah 1:15–16

unclean spirits
Revelation 16:13–14

Jerusalem
Zechariah 14:1–21;
Luke 21:20–22

armies
Revelation 19:11–16

Lord
Zechariah 14:5

Jehoshaphat
Joel 3:1–2

sun and moon
Joel 2:30–31;
Amos 8:9;
Matthew 24:29

birds
Revelation 19:17–18

Valley of Jehoshaphat
It means "the valley of God's judgment."

sickle
a large knife used for harvesting crops

deliver
save the Jews from this great army

what others say

Thomas Ice and Timothy Demy

According to the Bible, great armies from the east and the west will gather and assemble on this plain. There will be threats to the power of the Antichrist from the south, and he will also move to destroy a revived Babylon in the east before finally turning his forces toward Jerusalem to subdue and destroy it. As he and his armies move on Jerusalem, God will intervene and Jesus Christ will return to rescue His chosen people, Israel.[7]

swords
Isaiah 2:4

Micah 4:3 says the people will "beat their <u>swords</u> into plowshares, and their spears into pruning hooks" (NKJV). But we must remember that that is something to be done during the Millennium when Christ reigns on earth and the nations are at peace. Until then, the nations should do the opposite so they can be prepared to defend themselves. Why? Because we live in a time of "wars and rumors of wars" (Matthew 24:6 NKJV).

There is wide agreement among prophetic scholars that this prophecy refers to the Battle of Armageddon, which will take place during the Tribulation Period. God appears to be taunting Satan, the Antichrist, and their supporters here. He is saying you are weak but you think you are strong. You think your tanks, missiles and multitudes of troops will make quick work of the outnumbered and outgunned Jews. I will show you what real power is. Imagine the look on their faces when they go out to kill a few helpless Jews and they suddenly see the Son of God coming in the clouds with the heavenly armies. Who can imagine the terror?

Most of the crops and farmland will be destroyed during the Tribulation Period. Farmers and farm workers will be few and far between. Poverty will be the rule of the day. But the situation will be completely reversed during the Millennium as the next chart shows.

Fast Facts on Jesus as King

The Millennium	Scripture
Israel will have crops, rain, and food in abundance.	Joel 2:21–27
Because of God's presence, Israel will prosper.	Joel 3:17–21

AMOS

Out of the Frying Pan and into the Fire

go to

lament
2 Chronicles 35:25

wail
Jeremiah 9:17

tribulation
Matthew 24:21–22

AMOS 5:16–20 Therefore the LORD God of hosts, the Lord, says this: "There shall be wailing in all streets, and they shall say in all the highways, 'Alas! Alas!' They shall call the farmer to mourning, and skillful lamenters to wailing. In all vineyards there shall be wailing, for I will pass through you," says the LORD. Woe to you who desire the day of the LORD! For what good is the day of the LORD to you? It will be darkness, and not light! It will be as though a man fled from a lion, and a bear met him! Or as though he went into the house, leaned his hand on the wall, and a serpent bit him! Is not the day of the LORD darkness, and not light? Is it not very dark, with no brightness in it? (NKJV)

wail
a loud, painful cry
(the death wail)

Some say there won't be a Tribulation Period, but the Lord says people everywhere—people in all the streets and public places (cities, towns), the farmers (those in the country), the hired mourners (those paid to cry or <u>lament</u>), and those in the vineyards (laborers)—will **wail**. There will be bitter weeping when God passes through their midst in judgment.

Many do not understand the seriousness or severity of the day of the Lord. Some very piously wish that it would arrive. But that is a mistake. The Tribulation Period will be a day of darkness, not light; a period of <u>tribulation</u>, not joy; it will be a time when danger will surround every person, encircle every human being, and there will be no way for anyone to escape. People will flee one danger and encounter another greater peril. Everyplace on earth will be under siege. It will be like running from a hungry lion and falling into the clutches of a ferocious bear, like leaning upon a wall to rest and putting your hand upon a poisonous snake.

When hurricanes Katrina and Wilma struck the United States large numbers of people tried to ride out the winds and rain. A few didn't survive, but many who did faced floods, polluted drinking water, snakes, looting and such. Then, before the floods were gone, many ran out of food. But the stores and gas stations were closed. The roads were blocked. The electricity didn't work. The telephones and cell phones didn't work. Emergency workers didn't know where

go to

darkness
Genesis 1:14–18;
Exodus 10:21–23

Millennium
the thousand-year
reign of Christ on
earth

they were, couldn't get to them even if they found out, and the hospitals were cut off or out of supplies. It was one problem after another. That's the way it will be during the Tribulation Period only much worse. And instead of a small number of deaths, it will be two-thirds to three-fourths of the population of the earth in just seven years. The good news is disasters sometimes cause people to change their life and that's what will happen during the Tribulation Period when multitudes will get saved.

what others say

Thomas Ice

Armageddon is the last major event on the prophetic timeline before the establishment of the Millennial Kingdom, Christ's 1,000-year reign on Earth. Armageddon isn't an event people should desire or anticipate with joy because it will bring death and destruction. It is, however, a definite future military conflict that will not, and cannot, be avoided by any amount of negotiation.[9]

Among prophetic scholars there is no disagreement on the timing of this prophecy. It is plainly stated that this is a reference to the day of the Lord.

A Short Day

AMOS 8:9 *"And it shall come to pass in that day,"* says the Lord GOD, *"that I will make the sun go down at noon, and I will darken the earth in broad daylight."* (NKJV)

"In that day" (Amos 8:9 NKJV) is a phrase often used in the Bible to refer to the day of the Lord or to the **Millennium**. The day of the Lord will be a time of unusual events. One of those unusual events will be a noon sunset. The earth will go from broad daylight to total darkness at midday.

1. God is the One who separated light from darkness (Genesis 1:3–4).

2. God covered the land of Egypt with total darkness for three days (Exodus 10:21–23).

3. God made the sun and the moon stand still in the middle of the sky for nearly a whole day (Joshua 10:12–14).

4. God covered the <u>land</u> of Israel with darkness for three hours when Jesus was crucified (Matthew 27:45).

When the fifth angel pours out his vial during the Tribulation Period, darkness will cover the kingdom of the Antichrist, causing his followers to gnaw their tongues in pain. This will be appropriate punishment for those who use their tongues to blaspheme God (Revelation 16:9–11). We should not delude ourselves about the Tribulation Period, because it will be a time of unparalleled and inescapable danger.

Critics offer many different interpretations of this verse. Some say this darkness is just a **metaphor**. Some say it refers to an eclipse during the lifetime of Amos. One writer says smoke will darken the sun. Another thinks this is a reference to the darkness of sin coming into young lives. Still another thinks this refers to the untimely death of the ungodly. But all of these interpreters overlook the plain truth of what Jesus and several of the prophets said: "The <u>sun</u> will be darkened, and the moon will not give its light" (Matthew 24:29 NKJV). Where is the explanation for the moon not giving its light in all of these different interpretations?

Jesus placed the darkened sun at the end of the Tribulation Period when he said, "Immediately after the tribulation of those days the sun will be darkened, and the moon will not give its light; the stars will fall from heaven, and the powers of the heavens will be shaken" (Matthew 24:29 NKJV).

Hope for the Future

AMOS 9:11–15 *"On that day I will raise up the tabernacle of David, which has fallen down, and repair its damages; I will raise up its ruins, and rebuild it as in the days of old; that they may possess the remnant of Edom, and all the Gentiles who are called by My name," says the LORD who does this thing. "Behold, the days are coming," says the LORD, "when the plowman shall overtake the reaper, and the treader of grapes him who sows seed; the mountains shall drip with sweet wine, and all the hills shall flow with it. I will bring back the captives of My people Israel;*

sun
Isaiah 13:9–10;
Joel 2:30–31; 3:15;
Revelation 8:12

metaphor
a literary device, when one thing stands for something else

house of David
2 Samuel 7:4–17;
Luke 2:4–7

they shall build the waste cities and inhabit them; they shall plant vineyards and drink wine from them; they shall also make gardens and eat fruit from them. I will plant them in their land, and no longer shall they be pulled up from the land I have given them," says the LORD your God. (NKJV)

Here, "on that day" (Amos 9:11 NKJV) refers to the Millennium. God will do four things at that time: (1) he will restore David's fallen tent, which means he will restore the <u>house of David</u> (a reference to the reign of Christ on earth); (2) he will repair its broken places, which means he will correct the mistakes the leaders of Israel have made while ruling the nation; (3) he will restore its ruins, which means he will rebuild the towns and cities; and (4) he will build it as it used to be, which means he will rebuild Israel according to the instructions he gave to David when he reigned.

"Possess the remnant of Edom, and all the Gentiles who are called by My name" (Amos 9:12 NKJV) is usually interpreted to mean God will elevate Israel to the head of the nations. To emphasize the certainty of this, the writer adds that this is a declaration of the Lord. It will be a time of bountiful crops and abundant harvests. The Jews will return to the land—they will rebuild the cities, live in them, and never be put off again.

what others say

Billy K. Smith and Frank S. Page

God's forgiveness of Israel will be permanent. His blessing will be constant. Restoration of covenant blessings is an unconditional promise. Once and for all time God promised to plant Israel on their ground, never to be uprooted again. The land would be theirs as a gift from God. "Says the Lord your God" is the closing messenger formula, guaranteeing the promises based on the sure word of Israel's covenant God.[10]

God says, "I will bring back the captives of My people Israel," and he says, "I will plant [Israel] in their land, and no longer shall they be pulled up from the land I have given them" (Amos 9:14–15 NKJV). If the return of the Jews is God's doing, and if he has declared that the land belongs to them, what should happen to those nations that oppose him? If the nations choose to be willingly ignorant of God's will, is a Tribulation Period justified?

Such famous Bible cities as Ashdod, Ashkelon, Beersheba, Jaffa (now Tel Aviv), and Jerusalem have already been rebuilt. Flowers, grain, cotton, tomatoes, peppers, and more are now growing on rich farmland that was barren just a few years ago. Trees loaded with lemons, limes, oranges, grapefruit, tangerines, and other fruit now cover the once-bleak hills. The stage is being set for the fulfillment of this prophecy.

go to

judge
Matthew 7:2

nation
Psalm 2:1–12;
Joel 3:2, 9–16;
Micah 4:11–13;
Zechariah 14:1–21;
Luke 21:20–22

killed
Revelation 13:10

cup
Matthew 10:40–42;
26:39

drink
Matthew 25:31–46

principles
fundamental truths

OBADIAH

All Nations Will Reap What They Sow

OBADIAH 1:15–16 *For the day of the LORD upon all the nations is near; as you have done, it shall be done to you; your reprisal shall return upon your own head. For as you drank on My holy mountain, so shall all the nations drink continually; yes, they shall drink, and swallow, and they shall be as though they had never been. (NKJV)*

These verses identify three **principles** about God's judgment of the nations during the Tribulation Period. First, "the day of the LORD . . . is near" (Obadiah 1:15 NKJV) means the time when God will judge the nations is approaching. Nations will go too far in their mistreatment of Israel, causing God to intervene in the affairs of the world. Second, "upon all the nations" (1:15 NKJV) means no nation will be spared. When his wrath is kindled it will fall upon every nation on earth. And third, "as you have done, it shall be done to you" (1:15 NKJV) means that God will take into account how the nations have treated his people. Those who kill will be killed. Those who make Israel drink a cup of suffering will be made to drink from that same cup. They will perish from the earth and be remembered no more.

One purpose of the Tribulation Period is to punish all nations for their mistreatment of the Jews. Those who are particularly cruel (goat nations) will be destroyed before the Millennium.

MICAH

The Future Kingdom

go to

Jerusalem
Zechariah 14:10

mountains
Zechariah 14:4–5

temple
Isaiah 2:1–22;
Ezekiel 43:10–12

Jacob
Genesis 28:13–15

latter days
the last days of
"the times of the
Gentiles"

God of Jacob
Israel's God

disarmament
the destruction of
weapons

MICAH 4:1–7 Now it shall come to pass in the latter days that the mountain of the LORD's house shall be established on the top of the mountains, and shall be exalted above the hills; and peoples shall flow to it. Many nations shall come and say, "Come, and let us go up to the mountain of the LORD, to the house of the God of Jacob; He will teach us His ways, and we shall walk in His paths." For out of Zion the law shall go forth, and the word of the LORD from Jerusalem. He shall judge between many peoples, and rebuke strong nations afar off; they shall beat their swords into plowshares, and their spears into pruning hooks; nation shall not lift up sword against nation, neither shall they learn war anymore. But everyone shall sit under his vine and under his fig tree, and no one shall make them afraid; for the mouth of the LORD of hosts has spoken. For all people walk each in the name of his god, but we will walk in the name of the LORD our God forever and ever. "In that day," says the LORD, "I will assemble the lame, I will gather the outcast and those whom I have afflicted; I will make the lame a remnant, and the outcast a strong nation; so the LORD will reign over them in Mount Zion from now on, even forever." (NKJV)

"In the latter days" (Micah 4:1 NKJV) is a Bible term referring to that period of time that ends with the second coming of Christ. In the **latter days**, Jesus will return. The topography of <u>Jerusalem</u> will change. The Temple Mount will be elevated above the surrounding <u>mountains</u>. The Millennial <u>Temple</u> will be built and become the most sacred place on earth. Multitudes will stream to that place like a mighty rushing river.

Even people from foreign countries will go there. They will visit the house of the **God of <u>Jacob</u>** (Israel). The Word of God will be taught there, and people will live by those teachings. God's law and God's Word will come out of Jerusalem. This will be the millennial kingdom.

Jesus will sit as a judge, and he will settle disputes among the nations. His reign will produce world peace, **disarmament**, and the end of military training. It will also produce safety and prosperity. This is what God himself says.

Today, all people walk in the name of their own God, but in the future their devotion will be given to Israel's God. He will gather the lame, the exiled, and the afflicted and rule over them from the temple in Jerusalem. And his kingdom will never end.

During the Millennium there will be no need for the United Nations and the World Court because nations and leaders will place themselves under the rule of Christ. There will be no poverty, no theft, no war, only one God, and pure worship. With Jesus on the throne, this world will be the wonderful place God always intended.

We are already in the last days of "the times of the Gentiles" (see Acts 2:14–21), but the events described in this passage are still future. They will begin with the second coming of Christ and carry over into the Millennium.

Don't Count Your Chickens Before They Hatch

> **MICAH 4:11–13** *Now also many nations have gathered against you, who say, "Let her be defiled, and let our eye look upon Zion." But they do not know the thoughts of the LORD, nor do they understand His counsel; for He will gather them like sheaves to the threshing floor. "Arise and thresh, O daughter of Zion; for I will make your horn iron, and I will make your hooves bronze; you shall beat in pieces many peoples; I will consecrate their gain to the LORD, and their substance to the LORD of the whole earth." (NKJV)*

In Micah 4:1–7 we learned about the future kingdom. But the establishment of that kingdom will be preceded by a planned attack on <u>Jerusalem</u>. Many <u>nations</u> will gather against the chosen city. The great number of attackers will be gloating about what they think will happen to the Jews and will plan to **defile** the Holy City. But they will be unaware of the thoughts and plans of God. They won't know that he has <u>gathered</u> them there to be destroyed. The whole area will be like a giant **threshing floor**, the enemy troops like freshly cut grain, and Jerusalem like a powerful animal with horns of iron and hooves of bronze. The foreign armies will be pulverized. Israel will gather their ill-gotten wealth and give it to God. Everything will be done for his glory.

Jerusalem
Joel 3:1–2, 9–16;
Zechariah 14:1–21;
Luke 21:20–22

nations
Psalm 2:1–12;
Obadiah 1:15–16;
Revelation 19:11–16

gathered
Revelation 16:13–14

defile
to corrupt

threshing floor
a place where grain was beaten or pounded to separate the kernels from the chaff

Charles L. Feinberg

The besiegers will look with delight on the calamities of the Jews.... They do not comprehend the love, wisdom, and grace of God which will overrule Israel's calamities for good. In their venomous hatred against Zion the nations will believe that they have hit upon a plan which will successfully deliver to Israel a death-dealing blow.[11]

Kenneth L. Barker and Waylon Bailey

The nations that are enemies of both God and his people do not know or understand that he is in complete control of everything that is happening, carrying out his own sovereign purpose, plan, and will—including even the siege of Jerusalem. They also do not realize what he has in store for them, to gather them "like sheaves to the threshing floor" to be threshed.[12]

Some critics say these verses refer to the Assyrian army attacking the Northern Kingdom of Israel. Others say they refer to the Babylonian army attacking the Southern Kingdom of Judah. Still others say they refer to the Roman army attacking Jerusalem after the death of Jesus. But this is a prophecy about "many nations" (Micah 4:11 NKJV) attacking Jerusalem, not just one nation. And these "many nations" are not victorious—they lose.

Here we have more information about the Battle of Armageddon. The troops will gather late in the Tribulation Period. And they will be destroyed at the second coming of Christ.

Demonic beings will gather the nations against Jerusalem for the purpose of wiping her off the face of the earth. The Jews will fight valiantly, but begin to lose. The Antichrist and his forces will enter the city, loot, plunder, and rape. But before the victory is won and while the celebrations are going on, the sky will light up with the return of Christ to establish his kingdom on earth. The following chart lists some of the highlights of that kingdom.

Fast Facts on Jesus as King

The Millennium	Scripture
The future Ruler of Israel will come out of Bethlehem Ephrathah.	Micah 5:2–4
The Jews will be a source of blessing for many people.	Micah 5:7
Israel's weapons, fortresses, witches, idols, and sacred stones will be destroyed.	Micah 5:10–15
God will forgive Israel because he made covenants with Jacob and Abraham.	Micah 7:18–20

sun and moon
Amos 8:9;
Matthew 24:29

calamities
famine, pestilence,
earthquakes, war

ZEPHANIAH

There's Nothing on TV but a Lot of Bad News

ZEPHANIAH 1:14–18 *The great day of the LORD is near; it is near and hastens quickly. The noise of the day of the LORD is bitter; there the mighty men shall cry out. That day is a day of wrath, a day of trouble and distress, a day of devastation and desolation, a day of darkness and gloominess, a day of clouds and thick darkness, a day of trumpet and alarm against the fortified cities and against the high towers. "I will bring distress upon men, and they shall walk like blind men, because they have sinned against the LORD; their blood shall be poured out like dust, and their flesh like refuse." Neither their silver nor their gold shall be able to deliver them in the day of the LORD's wrath; but the whole land shall be devoured by the fire of His jealousy, for He will make speedy riddance of all those who dwell in the land.* (NKJV)

The time for God's judgment of the earth is approaching, and it will arrive quicker than most people realize. Zephaniah describes what it will be like. It will be a time of bitter crying. Even battle-hardened warriors will weep uncontrollably. During this time, God will loose his fierce anger on the world. The **calamities** that follow will produce distress and anguish such as the world has never seen. People will be surrounded by trouble and ruin—loved ones will be killed, houses will be destroyed, jobs will be lost. Even the heavenly bodies—the <u>sun and moon</u>—will be affected, and the earth will be covered with thick clouds and intense darkness. The sound of the trumpet and the battle cry will be heard everywhere, signaling the beginning of war. The strongest places will be attacked, great cities

blind
Deuteronomy 28:29

nation
Haggai 2:6–7

will be captured, and fortified places will fall. The distress will be so great people will appear to be <u>blind</u>, feeling their way around wherever they go. God will do this because the people have sinned against him. He will show them no mercy. Their blood will be poured out like unwanted dust. Their insides will be poured out like something dirty and worthless. Every <u>nation</u> will be affected, not just Israel. All who have angered him will come to a sudden end.

The day of the Lord will be an actual event of tragic proportions. It's no wonder that people call it the Tribulation Period. Christians should pray that they will be accounted worthy to escape all these things (Luke 21:36). And be thankful God has not appointed us to wrath, but to obtain salvation by our Lord Jesus Christ (1 Thessalonians 5:9).

what others say

J. A. Motyer

The day of the Lord is not arbitrary; it is the logical outgrowth of what humankind is (1:17b); it will bring what humankind deserves (1:17), and it will expose the uselessness of what humans trust (1:16, 18).[13]

David Reagan

The Bible clearly teaches that society will degenerate in the end times, becoming as evil as it was in the days of Noah (Matthew 24:37–39). The Apostle Paul, speaking as a prophet, says that society will descend into a black pit of immorality, violence, and paganism (2 Timothy 3:1–5). He asserts that men will be "lovers of self, lovers of money, and lovers of pleasure." People will be "boastful, arrogant, and unholy," and children will be "disobedient to parents." Sounds like the evening news, doesn't it? In short, we have arrived.[14]

ZECHARIAH

<u>A National Hot Potato</u>

the big picture

Zechariah 12:1–14

In this passage, God reminds the people that he created the heavens, the earth, and the spirit of man, and that he intends to use Jerusalem to make the nations stagger and fall. Judah and Jerusalem will come under siege by all nations, but God will strengthen the Jews and cause their enemies to injure themselves. He will smite the attackers with fear, madness, and blindness. The Jewish leaders will know that God has strengthened them. Those who attack Israel will be playing with fire. Jerusalem will not be destroyed, but God will save the people of Judah first, so the leaders and inhabitants of Jerusalem will not gloat. God will help the Jews who live in Jerusalem by giving them supernatural courage and strength. He will destroy all nations that attack Jerusalem, but he will pour out a spirit of grace and supplication upon the Jews, and they will recognize the One they pierced. All Israel will weep.

go to

Jerusalem
Zechariah 14:1–21;
Luke 21:20–22

nations
Psalm 2:1–12;
Micah 4:11–13;
Obadiah 1:15–16

pierced
Isaiah 53:1–12;
John 19:28–37

Judah
the West Bank,
Judea

Gentile
non-Jewish

grace
a desire to follow
the Holy Spirit

supplication
prayer

followed
obeyed

This passage begins with a reminder that the following prophecy comes from an all-powerful God, the Creator of all things. Out of love, God offers the nations a warning before they make a terrible mistake—they should not doubt that he can do, or will do, these things. God will cause **Judah** and <u>Jerusalem</u> to occupy center stage at the end of the age. He will use that area to judge the nations and deal a staggering blow to his enemies. It will be the entire world's problem. **Gentile** <u>nations</u> will respond by gathering a great army to attack the West Bank and the Holy City. But God will strengthen the Jews. Attacking them will be the same as attacking God. He will strike the enemy with fear, insanity, and blindness. Afflicted with terror, confusion, ignorance, and stupidity, they will injure themselves and seal their own doom.

In order to reach Jerusalem, the enemy will have to pass through Judah. That is where the first great victory will come. A victory in the outlying settlements before Jerusalem is delivered will prevent the inhabitants of Jerusalem from becoming proud.

God will help the Jews by infusing the Israeli army with supernatural abilities. Jewish soldiers will be exceptionally courageous and strong. They will eventually overcome those who attack them. Then God will instill a spirit of **grace** and **supplication** in the Jewish people. They will realize that they have not **followed** him. They will understand what they have not understood before: their Messiah is the One who was <u>pierced</u>. They will go through a time of national mourning and intense sorrow. Every person will go into seclusion to be alone with God, to grieve over their own sins, and to mourn their past rejection of Jesus.

Since the God who created all things—including the heavens, the earth, and humans—also destroyed armies, wouldn't it be a terrible mistake to make him angry? An attack on the tiny nation of Israel would be a big gamble. Is that really the best way to find out if God exists?

Some people believe that there is a God who created all things, but they also believe that he does not intervene in what goes on here on earth. This chapter refutes that. It reminds us that there is a Creator, that he is involved in the affairs of the world, and that he is going to have the final say on matters concerning Israel.

Jerusalem is already a cup of trembling and a burdensome stone for the whole world. The Jews claim all of Jerusalem as the eternal capital of the Jewish nation. The Palestinians claim East Jerusalem as the capital of its future Palestinian state. Muslims believe they will incur the wrath of Allah if they cede control of Jerusalem to the Jews. They wrongly believe they can drive the Jews out, seize the

Temple Mount, and get away with it, but God won't allow it. The struggle for Jerusalem will unleash the Four Horsemen of the Apocalypse, and the holy city will be in the line of fire right up until the Battle of Armageddon.

The beginning of this battle will be in the Tribulation Period, just before the second coming of Christ. After it starts, Christ will return, he will destroy Israel's enemies, and the Jews will recognize him by his wounds.

false prophets
Matthew 7:15; 24:4, 11, 24

There Is a Fountain Filled with Blood

ZECHARIAH 13:1–5 *"In that day a fountain shall be opened for the house of David and for the inhabitants of Jerusalem, for sin and for uncleanness. It shall be in that day," says the LORD of hosts, "that I will cut off the names of the idols from the land, and they shall no longer be remembered. I will also cause the prophets and the unclean spirit to depart from the land. It shall come to pass that if anyone still prophesies, then his father and mother who begot him will say to him, 'You shall not live, because you have spoken lies in the name of the LORD.' And his father and mother who begot him shall thrust him through when he prophesies. And it shall be in that day that every prophet will be ashamed of his vision when he prophesies; they will not wear a robe of coarse hair to deceive. But he will say, 'I am no prophet, I am a farmer; for a man taught me to keep cattle from my youth.'"(NKJV)*

These verses pick up where chapter 12 left off. Following a brief period of national mourning and repentance, a fountain will be opened to all Jews, and God will forgive their sins including the rejection of Jesus as their Messiah. This forgiveness will be followed by the abolition of false worship, the destruction of idols, and the elimination of false prophets. In many cases, false prophets will be killed by their own parents. Some false prophets will be ashamed of what they have done. And some will try to disguise themselves and deceive people by pretending they are farmers.

what others say

Charles L. Feinberg

Israel now enters into the provision of God at Calvary. . . . The provision of God will avail for both sin and uncleanness.

image
Revelation 13:14–15

evil spirits
Revelation 16:13–14

> Zechariah has in mind moral not ceremonial uncleanness. Justification is here and sanctification as well. Judicial guilt and moral impurity will be removed at the same time.[18]
>
> ### Ed Hindson
>
> A true prophet—
>
> 1. must speak in the name of the Lord, not some other god.
> 2. must have a message that is in accord with God's revealed truth in Scripture.
> 3. must give predictions of future events that come true exactly as stated.[19]

There will be a multiplication of false prophets and a surge in idolatry during the Tribulation Period. Multitudes will worship the image of the beast (the Antichrist); and evil spirits from the mouth of Satan, the mouth of the Antichrist, and the mouth of the False Prophet will gather the nations for the Battle of Armageddon.

The forgiveness will take place at the second coming of Christ. The abolition of false worship and the destruction of idols will begin immediately and carry over into the Millennium.

During the Millennium, Jerusalem will become the religious center of the world. All of the Jews and multitudes of Gentiles will go on pilgrimages to worship there. But they won't worship Allah or any other false god. They will worship Jehovah and his Son, Jesus. The next chart provides several facts about his reign.

Fast Facts on Jesus as King

The Millennium	Scripture
God will have mercy on Israel and build his house in Jerusalem.	Zechariah 1:16–17
Jerusalem will be a great city protected by God.	Zechariah 2:1–5
When God lives in Jerusalem many nations will accept Christ.	Zechariah 2:10–13
Christ will rule with wisdom and remove Israel's sin in one day.	Zechariah 3:8–9
Israel will succeed and the temple will be built by the power of the Holy Spirit.	Zechariah 4:1–14
Christ will build the temple and sit upon the throne in Israel.	Zechariah 6:11–12
God will live in Jerusalem, bless it, and cause the Jews to return.	Zechariah 8:1–8
Many Gentiles will visit Jerusalem and join the Jews in worshiping God.	Zechariah 8:20–23
Israel's borders will be expanded to encompass all the returning Jews.	Zechariah 10:8–11

 Prophecies of the Bible

ZECHARIAH 13:7–9
"Awake, O sword, against My Shepherd,
Against the Man who is My Companion,"
Says the LORD of hosts.
"Strike the Shepherd,
And the sheep will be scattered;
Then I will turn My hand against the little ones.
And it shall come to pass in all the land,"
Says the LORD,
"That two-thirds in it shall be cut off and die,
But one-third shall be left in it:
I will bring the one-third through the fire,
Will refine them as silver is refined,
And test them as gold is tested.
They will call on My name,
And I will answer them.
I will say, 'This is My people';
And each one will say, 'The LORD is my God.'" (NKJV)

go to

shepherd
Psalm 23:1;
John 10:11, 14

scattering
Matthew 26:31

striking
crucifixion

shepherd
Jesus

calamity
the Tribulation
Period

call
pray

A Purifying Holocaust

Zechariah looked into Israel's future and saw the **striking** of God's shepherd. The death of the <u>shepherd</u> would be followed by the <u>scattering</u> of Israel. A long period of time would pass, and Israel would return to the land. This much has happened in history, but the rest is yet future. A great **calamity** will come upon the land, says Zechariah, and two-thirds of Israel's people will be killed. The other third will be purified. The result of this national calamity will be that the purified will **call** upon the name of God, and they will be heard by him. He will accept them and they will accept Jesus as their Messiah.

> **what others say**
>
> ### Jimmy DeYoung
> This will mark the beginning of the most horrible time for God's chosen people in Jewish history. Satan and Antichrist will unleash unprecedented persecution on Israel. This period, known as the Great Tribulation, will see two of every three Jews killed (Zechariah 13:8). Jesus warned Israel to flee to the wilderness for protection during this time.[20]

Notice that the returning Jews need to be purified. This is because they are making the same mistake as those who struck the shepherd. They are returning in unbelief. Out of his mercy God will send great tribulation to change this.

The shepherd was struck in AD 30 when Jesus was crucified. Israel was scattered in AD 70 when the Romans destroyed the nation. The return is now under way. Two-thirds of Israel's Jews will die during the Tribulation Period. The remainder will accept Jesus at his second coming.

This is two-thirds of those who live in the land, not two-thirds of those who live in Jerusalem. Most of those who survive will do so only because they will be among those who flee into the wilderness when the Antichrist defiles the temple at the Tribulation Period mid-point. Death will stalk the Jews all through the Tribulation Period, but the greatest number of deaths will occur late in the Tribulation Period when the nations decide to attack Jerusalem.

Never Bite Off More Than You Can Chew

the big picture

Zechariah 14:1–21

The day of the Lord is approaching. When it arrives the nations will unite, gather an army, attack Jerusalem, capture the city, plunder the houses, rape the women, and cause half the Jews to flee into exile. Those who escape will not be prevented from reentering the city. Then the Lord will enter the battle on Israel's side. He will return to the Mount of Olives, a great earthquake will cause it to split in half, a valley will be created, and many Jews will escape through it. The Lord will have his saints with him; the heavenly bodies will be darkened; Jesus will reign as king over all the earth; the land of Palestine will be leveled out; Jerusalem will be elevated, inhabited, and made secure. Jesus will use a terrible plague to defeat those who attack Jerusalem. He will cause his enemies to fight among themselves, and Jews in the surrounding area will also fight against them. The attackers will be defeated, their valuables will be collected and taken to Jerusalem, their animals will die, and the whole world will turn to Christ. Those who disobey him will be punished, and the Jews will dedicate everything they have to the Lord.

Here Zechariah presents more information about the Tribulation Period and the Battle of Armageddon. A world army will capture the city, but it will not be destroyed, and half the Israeli citizens will <u>flee</u> to safety in the city. A world army will capture the city, but it will not be destroyed, and half the Israeli citizens in the city will flee to safety. Enemy soldiers will enter the city, seize valuables, and rape the women, but they will not prevent Jews who escape from returning to the city.

These events will trigger the second coming of Jesus. He will return to fight on Israel's side and he will make his first appearance at the **Mount of Olives**. He will temporarily stand on the mountain, there will be a tremendous earthquake, and the mountain will split from east to west. Half of the mountain will shift toward the north and half toward the south, leaving a great valley in between for the Jews to escape through. This valley will extend to **Azel**.

Jesus will bring the <u>armies</u> of heaven with him and the very Creation will be affected. There will be no light, but its absence, which normally causes a temperature drop, will not cause the weather to turn cold or frost to appear. At night, when it should be dark, the light will return. **Living water** will begin to flow from Jerusalem in two directions—half toward the **eastern sea** and half toward the **western sea**—and it will flow year-round.

The attitude toward Jesus will change. He will be <u>King</u> over all the earth. He will have worldwide recognition, and he alone will be called God.

The topography in that area will also change. All the land from **Geba** to **Rimmon south** (as opposed to the city by the same name in the north) will become a plain, but Jerusalem itself will be elevated. The Jews will return to the city and finally have peace and safety.

Concerning the defeat of Israel's enemies, Jesus will smite them with a plague. Their flesh, eyes, and tongues will immediately rot away. They will panic and fight each other, and a similar plague will strike their animals. Because they plundered Jerusalem, their wealth will be collected and taken there.

Survivors living in the nations that attack Jerusalem will visit the Holy City to worship Jesus and celebrate the **Feast of Tabernacles**. If a nation withholds its worship, God will withhold its rain (their

flee
Matthew 24:15–16

armies
Revelation 19:11–21

King
Jeremiah 30:8–9;
Hosea 3:4–5;
Zephaniah 3:15

Feast of Tabernacles
Leviticus 23:33–36

Mount of Olives
a mile-long ridge on the east side of Jerusalem

Azel
a village lying just east of the Mount of Olives

living water
fresh, pure running water

eastern sea
Dead Sea

western sea
Mediterranean Sea

Geba
modern Jeba, a town about six miles north of Jerusalem

Rimmon south
a town about thirty-five miles southwest of Jerusalem

Feast of Tabernacles
a feast of praise, rest, and thanksgiving

spiritual drought will be answered with a physical drought). Everything in Jerusalem will be dedicated to the Lord. And only those who are true believers will be allowed to serve at the temple.

For the real Battle of Armageddon to take place:

key point

1. Israel must be a nation.

2. Jerusalem must be a city.

3. Jerusalem must be controlled by the Jews.

4. The nations must decide to forcefully take Jerusalem away from the Jews

5. Jesus must return to defeat the nations.

God's promises to Israel and the world have to be fulfilled. The Tribulation Period and Armageddon don't have to happen, but they will happen because the nations of the world refuse to go by what the Bible says. In essence, the world will bring these tragedies on itself because of its ignorance, rebellion, and unbelief.

The war against Israel and Jerusalem is a spiritual war. It started in the Garden of Eden when Satan tempted Adam and Eve, and God told that old serpent Eve's Seed would bruise his head (Genesis 3:15). During Old Testament times, Satan did everything he could to corrupt and destroy the Jewish people in an effort to prevent the first coming of Jesus. He even tried to destroy Jesus, get him to sin, get him to come down off the cross and more. He wanted to prevent the Messiah from dying on the cross.

Israel and Jerusalem are in Satan's crosshairs today because he is trying to prevent the second coming of Jesus. Lucifer doesn't want to be cast out of heaven, be bound and chained for 1,000 years, be cast into the bottomless pit, or be cast into the Lake of Fire. He doesn't want Jesus to return to Jerusalem or rule on earth for 1,000 years. The underlying cause of the world's anti-Semitism is satanic because the evil one wants to replace God and be worshiped. However, Israel and Jerusalem will survive.

This prophecy does not refer to the attack on Jerusalem by the Romans in AD 70. They literally wiped the city off the face of the earth and killed or carried off all the Jews. In this case, the city will not be destroyed, not all of the Jews will be killed, and some will be allowed to reenter the city.

The vast majority of prophetic scholars agree that this is a prophecy about the Battle of Armageddon and the second coming of Christ. And it will be fulfilled late in the Tribulation Period.

Chapter Wrap-Up

- Hosea had an adulterous wife, but he loved her very much. Her unfaithfulness pictured Israel's attitude toward God. And Hosea's love mirrored God's attitude toward Israel. He will forgive the unfaithful nation, the people will abandon their spiritual adultery, and Jesus will be their King. (Hosea 1:16; 2:18–23; 3:4–5; 6:1–3)

- The great locust plague that laid waste to Israel during Joel's life pictured a much greater destruction that is coming during the Tribulation Period. The millions of locusts that stripped the land are just a glimmer of what a great army will do when it invades Israel and Jerusalem during the day of the Lord. But this great army will be destroyed at what is commonly called the Battle of Armageddon. (Joel 1:15–20; 2:28–29; 3:9–16)

- When the Tribulation Period arrives, God will pass through Israel with great wrath to punish the Jews for their sins. But that does not mean he has stopped loving Israel. He will send Jesus to reign on earth there, correct the mistakes of Israel's leaders, rebuild Israeli towns and cities, restore the nation, cause the crops to flourish, and see that the Jews are never put off the land again. (Amos 5:16–20; 8:9; 9:11–15)

- Those who harm Israel during the Tribulation Period will find that their sins will come back to haunt them. Those who attack Israel will be destroyed. Because of sin, God will send great distress upon the world. When he is through, Jesus will reign in Israel and the nation will prosper. (Obadiah 1:15–16; Micah 4:1–7, 11–13; Zephaniah 1:14–18)

- God will deal a staggering blow to Israel's enemies during the Tribulation Period. They will harm and kill many Jews, but God will use Israel's calamities to bring repentance and salvation to the nation. When it is surrounded, Jesus will return and deliver his people. He will pour out his spirit upon the Jews and forgive their sins. They will accept Jesus as their Messiah, and God will accept them as his people. (Zechariah 12:1–14; 13:1–5, 7–9; 14:1–21)

Study Questions

1. Can a wicked nation be redeemed and restored to the Lord? Explain.

2. What are some of God's judgments mentioned in the book of Joel?

3. What is wrong with wishing the day of the Lord would arrive?

4. According to the prophets Obadiah and Zephaniah, what nations will be affected by the judgments of God during the Tribulation Period?

5. What prophecies refer to Christ in the book of Zechariah?

Part Two
Prophecies in the
New Testament

Silently Looking Forward

After God gave the prophecies found in the Old Testament books, most scholars believe he went silent for about four hundred years. This period of silence is often referred to as the **Intertestamental Period**. During this time, the Old Testament books were collected, copied, and **validated** by Jewish authorities as meeting the standard of divine inspiration. They were assembled into a single collection, accepted as the Word of God, and kept in a safe place.

Shortly after the Old Testament was written, the Greeks took over the world and their language became the common language on earth. Tradition says a man called Ptolemy Philadelphus assembled seventy scholars who were experts in both Hebrew and Greek and commissioned them to translate the Old Testament writings into the Greek language. This translation, which is called the **Septuagint**, meaning "seventy," was in use when God began to speak again and the New Testament came into being.

Intertestamental Period
the four hundred–year period between the Old and New Testaments

validated
officially confirmed, found to be accurate or true

Septuagint
Greek translation of the Bible written third century BC

what others say

Irving L. Jensen

The thirty-nine books of the Old Testament . . . were God's total written revelation during that time. God was preparing his world for the coming of his Son, the Messiah, the central promise of the Old Testament. Then it happened, Jesus actually came, to live and die for the sins of the world. After that, God inspired new writers to complete the Bible by telling the New Testament story of Jesus and what his coming means for us.[1]

Jesus often quoted from the books found in the Old Testament, but he never quoted from the Apocrypha. The same can be said of the New Testament writers. They quoted from the Old Testament over and over again, but there is only one questionable instance of the Apocrypha being quoted. This seems to be evidence that Jesus and the New Testament writers accepted the authority of the Old Testament writings but not the authority of the Apocrypha.

Some will argue that several prominent early church leaders, including Irenaeus and Tertullian, accepted the Apocrypha as scripture. That's true, but others can compile a long list of prominent early church leaders, including Jerome and Origen, who rejected it.

Some will argue that the Roman Catholic Church includes the Apocrypha in their Bible so Protestants should include it in theirs. The Roman Catholic Church does include it, but did not for about 1,500 years. Which is right: the early Roman Catholic Church or the modern Roman Catholic Church?

Some will argue that the Russian Orthodox and the Greek Orthodox Churches include the Apocrypha in their Bible. That's true, but they disagree with each other and with the Roman Catholic Church over which books to include so they each have a different Apocrypha.

Finally, some will argue that a few good seminaries teach the Apocrypha. That's true too, but they don't teach it as God-inspired Scripture. They teach it because it contains valuable information about the Jewish nation, its history and customs, which is helpful in understanding the sixty-six books that are recognized as Scripture.

These seminaries deny salvation by works, which is taught in the book of Tobit (12:19), and prayers for the dead, which is taught in the book of 2 Maccabees (12:45–46). They also denounce adding to or taking away from the Bible, which agrees with what is taught in the book of Revelation (22:18–19). If they are aware of it, they will probably admit that many of Mohammad's ideas came from the Apocrypha and that at least some of them have been a disaster for the world and especially for the Islamic people (The rationale for suicide bombers and jihad is rooted in salvation by works).

Prophecies in the Gospels and Acts

Chapter Highlights:
- Matthew
- Mark
- Luke
- John
- Acts

Let's Get Started

The first segment in the New Testament is a group of four books called the Gospels. The word *gospel* comes from the Greek language and it means "good news" or "glad tidings." These books present the "good news" about Jesus: his death, burial, resurrection, ascension, and second coming. They also contain several prophecies, of which many were given by Jesus, and some are recorded more than once by the different Gospel writers.

The second segment in the New Testament is a single book commonly called Acts. Some refer to Acts as the fifth Gospel because it picks up where the four Gospels leave off and takes us to the next book—one of the many letters written by the apostle Paul. Without this transition we wouldn't understand many things about the early church, including its beginning, doctrines, power, and phenomenal growth.

The Gospels teach many important truths about man and his relationship with God. Some of the most important truths include:

go to

gospel
1 Corinthians
15:1–58

sin
John 1:29

world
John 3:14–18

will
Matthew 6:5–13

end of the age
Matthew 24:1–51

gospel
"good news"

1. Man is a sinner.

2. Jesus' death is payment for man's <u>sin</u>.

3. Apart from Jesus the human race is fallen and without hope.

4. Jesus' death offers hope to the whole <u>world</u>.

5. God wants us to live our lives according to his <u>will</u>.

6. Prophecies reveal that histroy is moving toward the <u>end of the age</u>, to a time when Jesus will sit on a throne and rule over a kingdom here on earth.

Sermon on the Mount
a famous sermon preached by Jesus on a high hill near Capernaum

Beatitudes
a declaration of blessedness in the Sermon on the Mount

The first five truths are very important, especially if one wants to know who God is and how to have a personal relationship with him, but for this study, we are chiefly concerned with the sixth truth.

MATTHEW

MATTHEW 5:3–12
Blessed are the poor in spirit,
    For theirs is the kingdom of heaven.
Blessed are those who mourn,
    For they shall be comforted.
Blessed are the meek,
    For they shall inherit the earth.
Blessed are those who hunger and thirst for righteousness,
    For they shall be filled.
Blessed are the merciful,
    For they shall obtain mercy.
Blessed are the pure in heart,
    For they shall see God.
Blessed are the peacemakers,
    For they shall be called sons of God.
Blessed are those who are persecuted for righteousness' sake,
    For theirs is the kingdom of heaven.
Blessed are you when they revile and persecute you, and say all kinds of evil against you falsely for My sake. Rejoice and be exceedingly glad, for great is your reward in heaven, for so they persecuted the prophets who were before you. (NKJV)

Prophecy on the Mount

This section of Scripture is part of the **Sermon on the Mount** preached by Jesus. It is commonly called the **Beatitudes** and it is one of the most popular passages in the Bible. It contains high **ethical** standards and is a favorite of many preachers. Some who never deliver a prophetic sermon preach from these verses over and over again. But these Beatitudes are more than an amazing set of principles to live by. They also have a prophetic nature.

The <u>poor</u> in spirit are people who know they are sinners and are convinced they have no way to pay for the sins they have committed. Because they are unable to settle their own sin debt, they humble themselves and seek a Savior to pay in their place. Those who do this are made members of the kingdom of heaven. Their membership becomes effective as soon as they sincerely profess their faith in Jesus, but they will not realize the full benefits of it until the Millennium begins.

The meek are people who profess faith and have received the nature of Jesus. They are <u>gentle</u> people who practice self-control and tolerance, a <u>fruit of the Spirit</u>. They are <u>God's children</u> and, as such, will possess the earth when the Millennium arrives.

Those who are persecuted because of **righteousness** are the ones who try to live right and seek to spread right living around the world. They have accepted Christ as their Savior, are God's children, and want others to be God's children too. Because of this they are ridiculed, shunned, and in some cases physically harmed. God has made them members of the kingdom of heaven.

go to

poor
2 Corinthians 6:10

gentle
Matthew 11:29

fruit of the Spirit
Galatians 5:22–23

God's children
Romans 8:16–17

ethical
moral

righteousness
justice, peace, right doing

what others say

John F. Walvoord

A careful reading of the Sermon on the Mount supports the conclusion that what Christ was dealing with were the ethical principles of the kingdom which will come into play in the future millennial kingdom but to some extent are applicable now. Accordingly, in the Sermon on the Mount there are frequent references to the present and how the principles He is annunciating should be applied. At the same time there is the distant view of the realization of these ethical principles when Christ will be reigning on earth.[2]

Being a Christian in this life will cost a person. Those who try to do the will of God will be insulted, persecuted, and falsely accused. But God will give them a great reward in heaven.

The Parable of the Weeds
Matthew 13:24–30

Son of Man
Matthew 13:37

sons of the kingdom
Matthew 13:38

world
Matthew 13:39

parables
stories about familiar things that teach or illustrate unfamiliar things

Son of Man
Jesus

children of God
the saved

children of the devil
the lost

These are ethical principles that spell out the way God wants us to live now, but they will have a greater application in the Millennium and beyond. Those who try to live by them now will receive great rewards in the future.

From the First Coming to the Second Coming

MATTHEW 13:24–30 *Another parable He put forth to them, saying: "The kingdom of heaven is like a man who sowed good seed in his field; but while men slept, his enemy came and sowed tares among the wheat and went his way. But when the grain had sprouted and produced a crop, then the tares also appeared. So the servants of the owner came and said to him, 'Sir, did you not sow good seed in your field? How then does it have tares?' He said to them, 'An enemy has done this.' The servants said to him, 'Do you want us then to go and gather them up?' But he said, 'No, lest while you gather up the tares you also uproot the wheat with them. Let both grow together until the harvest, and at the time of harvest I will say to the reapers, "First gather together the tares and bind them in bundles to burn them, but gather the wheat into my barn."'"* (NKJV)

Matthew 13 is a well-known chapter in the Bible because it contains a series of **parables** about the kingdom of heaven. These parables give insight into the course of events in the kingdom of heaven between the first and second comings of Jesus. One of them is called The Parable of the Weeds.

The kingdom of heaven can be compared to a man (the **Son of Man**) who sowed good seed (sons of the kingdom, or the **children of God**) in his field (the world). But while everyone was sleeping, his enemy (the devil) came and sowed weeds (sons of the evil one, or the **children of the devil**) among the wheat (children of God), and went away. When the wheat (children of God) sprouted and formed heads (when they began to grow and produce), then the weeds (children of the devil) also appeared. When that happened, servants of the owner (Jesus) asked if they should remove the weeds (children of the devil) from the field (world). The owner said no. To do so might harm some of the wheat (children of God). He said to let them grow together until the harvest (end of the age). Then he will send the harvesters (angels); they will collect the weeds (children

of the devil), tie them in bundles, and they will be burned (in the
<u>fiery</u> furnace).

Jesus is revealing the fact that there are two sowings going on in
the kingdom of heaven—one is of God, and the other is of the devil.
The children of God and the children of the devil are growing along-
side each other in the world. Some would like to have the children
of the devil removed, but God does not want that to happen until
the end of the age. When the time arrives, God's angels will remove
them. They will be restrained until the judgment and then burned.

fiery
Revelation 21:8

what others say

Thomas Ice and Timothy Demy

Actually, since Matthew 13 surveys this present age in relation
to the kingdom, the parables cover the period of time
between Christ's two advents—His first and second comings.
This includes the tribulation, Second Coming, and final judgment after the rapture.[3]

Life Application Bible Commentary

[The weeds] may be people in the church who appear to be
believers but who never truly believe. The apostles later bat-
tled the problem of false teachers who came from within
the ranks of the believers (see, for example, 2 Peter 2:1–3,
13–22). . . . God will not eliminate all opposition until the end
of the age.[4]

Comparisons have been drawn between the seven parables
of Matthew 13 and the seven letters of Revelation 2 and 3. Jesus
spoke the parables and Jesus dictated the letters. Both are about
the Church Age. The Parable of the Sower has the Church Age
beginning with the sowing of the Word, but some members are not
producing fruit or are declining in fruit-bearing because of Satan's
interference. The Letter to the Church at Ephesus compares by
showing the Church Age getting off to a good start, but some members are declining by leaving their first love. The Parable of the
Wheat and Tares has Jesus sowing the Word, but Satan is following
with a false sowing. The Letter to the Church at Smyrna compares
by showing people entering the church who are from the Synagogue
of Satan. The Parable of the Mustard Seed shows unusual expansion
of the church during the Church Age because Satan nests in its

branches. The Letter to the Church at Pergamos compares somewhat by revealing that false teachers will enter into the church. Skipping forward, the last parable, the Parable of the Dragnet, shows Jesus coming back at the end of the Church Age with his angels to separate the good fish from the bad fish and to cast the bad fish away. The Letter to the Church at Laodicea compares by having Jesus spew out lukewarm members. The entire picture is a prophecy about the church going through phases or stages with the overall result being the church growing numerically while declining spiritually. Corruption in the church will be a major problem for true believers at the end of the age. Jesus is patient and loving, but he will ultimately and severely deal with it.

The Church Age and the Kingdom of Heaven

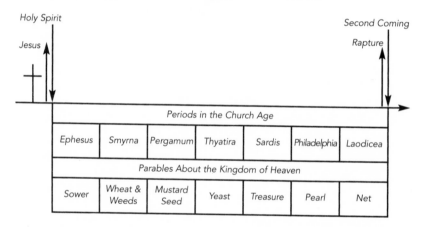

Holy Spirit					Second Coming
Jesus					Rapture

Periods in the Church Age						
Ephesus	Smyrna	Pergamum	Thyatira	Sardis	Philadelphia	Laodicea

Parables About the Kingdom of Heaven						
Sower	Wheat & Weeds	Mustard Seed	Yeast	Treasure	Pearl	Net

what others say

Mike Gendron

- *What is apostasy?*

  The falling away from the faith.

- *Where will apostates come from?*

  The Church. Even from your own number men will arise and distort the truth in order to draw away disciples after them (Acts 20:29).

- *What will apostates look like?*

  Servants of righteousness (2 Corinthians 11:15).

- *Where will apostates fall away "to"?*

  Not to atheism but to a false Christianity (Matthew 7).[5]

Many people make the mistake of thinking this harvest is the Rapture. But the Rapture removes the church from the earth and takes it to heaven. This harvest removes the children of the devil from the earth and binds them for burning. The Rapture occurs before the Tribulation Period. This harvest occurs after the Tribulation Period.

The wheat and the weeds represent people in the kingdom of heaven. The wheat represents saved Gentiles and Jews. The weeds represent lost Gentiles and Jews, but many of them will claim to be saved. Christians are sowing the gospel today, but after the Rapture the <u>144,000</u> Jews, the <u>two witnesses</u>, and an angel will sow the <u>gospel</u> for God. And the Antichrist and <u>False Prophet</u> will sow for the devil. The harvest is the Second Coming.

go to

144,000
Revelation 7:4–8

two witnesses
Revelation 11:3–12

gospel
Revelation 14:6

False Prophet
Revelation 16:13

birds
Matthew 13:4, 19

The Parable of the Sower
Matthew 13:1–23

The Parable of the Weeds
Matthew 13:24–30

What Happened to the Shrub I Planted?

MATTHEW 13:31–32 *Another parable He put forth to them, saying: "The kingdom of heaven is like a mustard seed, which a man took and sowed in his field, which indeed is the least of all the seeds; but when it is grown it is greater than the herbs and becomes a tree, so that the birds of the air come and nest in its branches." (NKJV)*

The kingdom of heaven can be compared to a tiny mustard seed that grows into a tree and becomes the resting place for <u>birds</u>. Ordinarily, the mustard seed would grow into a large shrub. It should never grow into a tree. So there is something unusual here. And birds represent the wicked in <u>The Parable of the Sower</u>.

Jesus is saying the kingdom of heaven will experience abnormal growth. It will begin small like a tiny mustard seed and grow much larger than it should. And wicked people will flock to it. This is consistent with <u>The Parable of the Weeds</u> where Jesus taught that there are two sowings—one of God and one of the devil. If the kingdom of heaven had only true believers, it would be like a shrub, but because of the corruption introduced by the devil, it is more like a tree. In fact, it will be like a tree that has become the resting place of many unbelievers.

There is only one gospel. It tells people everything they need to know. God's true servants preach and teach this gospel. They speak the truth. They may make a few mistakes, but they never knowingly contradict what it says. They strive hard to stay with the fundamentals of the faith: the deity of Jesus, the virgin birth of Jesus, the death, burial, and resurrection of Jesus, and so on.

But Jesus wants us to know that many lost people join the church. Some attend seminary. Some teach in seminaries and preach in church. They are of the devil, but they have made the church their nesting place. To say they are Christians and contradict what Jesus said is a sure sign that something is wrong. Those who constantly do this are false teachers and their doctrines are false. They should not be believed.

People should study the Bible and compare what they hear to what the Bible says. They should determine who is telling the truth and who should not be believed. To follow someone who stands behind a pulpit and contradicts what the Bible says is to invite disaster. They may say it doesn't matter what the Bible says, but Jesus taught that it does. He even taught that it will become a great problem in the church and grow worse at the end of the age. That's the clear implication of the mustard shrub growing into a tree with the birds of the air on all its branches.

Prophecies of the Bible

Some scholars refer to the kingdom of heaven as professing Christendom or the organized church. Those who use these terms believe there are true Christians and false Christians, a true church and a false church, true believers and make believers. They believe it is the false church or make believers that turn the kingdom of heaven into a monstrosity, a perch for the wicked, etc. This is partly true. The kingdom of heaven does include professing Christendom, but it also includes all those (good and bad, Christians and Jews) who will claim to be people of faith after the church is raptured.

The kingdom of heaven began small with just one person—Jesus. Twelve were added when the disciples joined him. More were added when crowds began to follow and believe. Many true believers (Christians and Jews) will be added after the Rapture, but most of them will be killed. The false church will add large numbers of New Agers, Satan worshipers, cults, and the like. This is why some will be weeded out at the Second Coming and cast into the <u>fiery</u> furnace.

go to

fiery
Matthew 13:40–42

yeast
Exodus 13:3;
Matthew 16:6–12;
Mark 8:15;
1 Corinthians 5:6–8;
Galatians 5:7–10

woman
Revelation 2:20–21;
17:1–8

seed
Matthew 13:38

weeds
Matthew 13:24–30

birds
Matthew 13:4, 19

small
Matthew 13:31–32

A Perplexing Parable

> **MATTHEW 13:33** *Another parable He spoke to them: "The kingdom of heaven is like leaven, which a woman took and hid in three measures of meal till it was all leavened." (NKJV)*

Commentators are divided over the interpretation of this parable. The **premillennial** view is that Jesus was saying the kingdom of heaven is like <u>yeast</u> (false teachings) that a <u>woman</u> (the false church) took and mixed into a large amount of flour (processed grain or <u>seed</u>, sons of the kingdom, the children of God) until it all worked through the dough (until the kingdom was corrupted). The **postmillennial** view is that Jesus was saying the kingdom of heaven is like yeast (the **gospel**) that a woman took and mixed into a large amount of flour until it all worked through the dough (until the gospel had impacted the whole world). The premillennial view is compatible with the teaching that Satan is sowing <u>weeds</u> in the kingdom and that <u>birds</u> (wicked people) will flock to it. And the postmillennial view is compatible with the teaching that the kingdom of heaven will start <u>small</u> and become great.

The idea that the church will preach the gospel and convert the world simply does not mesh with other Bible teachings. In the Olivet Discourse, Jesus deemed it necessary to warn the world about

premillennial
the view that Christ will return before the Millennium

postmillennial
the view that Christ will return after the Millennium

gospel
good news of Jesus Christ

end-of-the-age deception four times (Matthew 24:4–5, 11, 24). Paul clearly taught that there will be a great falling away and a persecution of true believers at the end of the age (2 Thessalonians 2:3; 2 Timothy 3:12). He clearly said impostors will grow worse and worse, deceiving and being deceived (2 Timothy 3:13). He even added that people will not endure sound doctrine and will turn from the truth to fables (2 Timothy 4:3–4). The church is not bringing in a converted world. It's facing a wicked world. It's not bringing in a world that loves Jesus. It's facing a dangerous world that is hostile to Jesus. Our Lord didn't say the church will win the world. He said the world will wind up like it was in the days of Noah and Lot when wickedness was rampant. It would be more accurate to believe God is bringing Israel back on the scene because the church is failing.

Jesus was speaking to some religious leaders when he said, "Hypocrites! Well did Isaiah prophesy about you, saying: 'These people draw near to Me with their mouth, and honor Me with their lips, but their heart is far from Me. And in vain they worship Me, teaching as doctrines the commandments of men'" (Matthew 15:7–9 NKJV). Could it be said that modern religious leaders who teach "Political Correctness" instead of Bible doctrine are teaching the rules of men?

The prophecies in Scripture do not have their origin in the <u>will</u> of man. Since they come from God, it is always right to let the Bible interpret them and never right to impose our own interpretations. The word *yeast* appears in the Bible almost a hundred times. Over and over again it is identified as a symbol of evil, but it is never identified as a symbol of the gospel. For this reason, we should choose the Premillennial view.

False doctrines are being introduced into the church and the kingdom is being corrupted. More than once Jesus warned the disciples about this. The true church will be raptured and the false church will be left behind to enter the Tribulation Period. The kingdom will continue to grow with God's servants taking in more believers and Satan's servants taking in more pretenders. At the Second Coming what's left of the false church will be removed by the angels of God and bound for burning.

Amazing Grace

> **MATTHEW 13:44** *Again, the kingdom of heaven is like treasure hidden in a field, which a man found and hid; and for joy over it he goes and sells all that he has and buys that field.* (NKJV)

Here Jesus says the kingdom of heaven is like a <u>treasure</u> (Israel) hidden in a <u>field</u> (the <u>world</u>). When a <u>man</u> (Jesus) found it (Israel), he hid it again (<u>scattered</u> Israel around the world) and then in his joy went and sold all he had (Jesus left the glories and riches of heaven) and bought (**<u>redeemed</u>**) that field.

Premillennialists say this means the kingdom of heaven is like a valuable treasure found in a field. It is so valuable we should be willing to give up everything we possess to purchase it. The problem with this is that the kingdom of heaven cannot be bought.

go to

will
2 Peter 1:20–21

treasure
Exodus 19:5–6

field
Matthew 13:38

world
John 3:16

man
Matthew 13:37

scattered
John 11:49–52

redeemed
1 Peter 1:18–19

redeemed
bought, purchased

what others say

J. Dwight Pentecost

The purpose of this parable is to depict the relationship of Israel to this present age. Although set aside by God until this age is completed, yet Israel is not forgotten and this age does have reference to that program.[10]

part
Romans 11:25–29

what others say

Arno Froese

Never must we be so naive to think that God has rejected Israel and replaced her with the Church. The erroneous conclusion is being made that all the promises given in the Old Testament now belong to the Church. Unfortunately, this teaching is widely accepted among established Protestant denominations and reinforced under the leadership of the Roman Catholic Church. This false doctrine, however, is easily refuted because the prophets clearly write about the return of the Jewish people from the dispersion to the land of Israel, giving an abundance of literal geographic references.[11]

God has transferred stewardship over his kingdom to the church, but that stewardship is temporary. The Church Age will end with the Rapture and the stewardship will return to Israel.

Why the Church Has Not Replaced Israel

Reason	Scripture
God made an everlasting covenant to be Israel's God.	Genesis 17:7–8
God promised to save Israel.	Zechariah 12:10; Romans 11:26–29
The kingdom will be restored to Israel.	Acts 1:6–7
Israel's blindness is only until the Times of the Gentiles is complete.	Romans 10:25
Jesus must still reign as King of the Jews.	Luke 1:33
Everything the prophets said has to be fulfilled.	Matthew 5:17–18

The Jews have been blinded in <u>part</u> and scattered around the world, but they have not been forgotten by God. Jesus redeemed them when he died on the cross for the sins of the world. They are lost and blind, but by the grace of God they will be saved at the end of the Tribulation Period when they accept Jesus at his second coming.

From Heav'n He Came and Sought Her

MATTHEW 13:45–46 *Again, the kingdom of heaven is like a merchant seeking beautiful pearls, who, when he had found one pearl of great price, went and sold all that he had and bought it.* (NKJV)

This parable is similar to others in this chapter in that Premillennialists and Postmillennialists differ on how it should be interpreted. According to Premillennialists, Jesus is saying the kingdom of heaven is like a merchant man (Jesus) seeking beautiful pearls, who, when he had found one pearl of great price (the church), went and sold all that he had (gave up everything in heaven) and bought (redeemed) it. But according to Postmillennialists, Jesus was saying the kingdom of heaven is like a merchant (the sinner) seeking beautiful pearls, who, when he had found one pearl of great price (Jesus, or the kingdom, or salvation), went and sold all that he had (wanted that pearl more than anything else) and bought it. The church was born through injury (the crucifixion of Jesus), and a pearl begins when foreign matter irritates an oyster.

Gentiles
Matthew 12:15–21;
Acts 15:13–18

> ### what others say
>
> #### Arnold G. Fruchtenbaum
>
> The pearl comes from the sea, and the sea symbolizes the Gentile world (Daniel 7:2–3; Revelation 17:1, 15) . . . This teaches the concept that the Gentiles in the Church are being formulated by gradual accretion. One of the primary purposes of the Church Age is to call out from among the gentiles a people for His name (Acts 15:14), and this is to continue until the fullness of the Gentiles be come in (Romans 11:25).[12]

Here is really "good news." The kingdom of heaven is for <u>Gentiles</u> as well as Jews. Jesus treasures the church, and he gave up everything at his first coming to purchase it. It is continually growing.

Good Fish In, Bad Fish Out

MATTHEW 13:47–50 *Again, the kingdom of heaven is like a dragnet that was cast into the sea and gathered some of every kind, which, when it was full, they drew to shore; and they sat down and gathered the good into vessels, but threw the bad away. So it will be at the end of the age. The angels will come forth, separate the wicked from among the just, and cast them into the furnace of fire. There will be wailing and gnashing of teeth. (NKJV)*

More than just a few commentaries say this parable means the kingdom of heaven is like a net (the church) that is cast into the sea

end of the age
Matthew 13:39

angels
Matthew 13:41;
2 Thessalonians 1:7;
Matthew 25:31–46

fire
Revelation 20:11–15

gnashing
Matthew 13:42

(the world) where it catches or gathers in all kinds of fish (Christians and pretend Christians). They say it means Jesus will return at the end of the Church Age with his angels, and they will separate the good fish (true Christians) from the bad fish (pretend Christians).

But this cannot be. The net is not the fish. It is what pulls in the fish. The church (true Christians) will not be separated from the wicked (pretend Christians) at the judgment. The church will be removed in the Rapture before the judgment. Moreover, the Jews have been ignored in this explanation and excluded from the kingdom of heaven.

It makes more sense to say the kingdom of heaven is like a net (the Word of God) that is cast into the sea (from heaven to the world) where it catches or gathers in all kinds of fish (people). When the net is full (has gathered in all it can), Jesus will come with his angels and they will separate the good from the bad (the saved from the lost). This is how it will be at the <u>end of the age</u> (at the end of the Tribulation Period). The <u>angels</u> will separate the bad fish from the good fish and cast the bad into the Lake of <u>Fire</u> where there will be weeping and <u>gnashing</u> of teeth.

what others say

Billy Graham

So angels will not only accompany Christ when He returns, but will be assigned the responsibility of gathering out of His kingdom all things that offend and work iniquity, that they might be judged.[13]

J. Dwight Pentecost

We may summarize the teaching as to the course of the age by saying: (1) there will be a sowing of the Word throughout the age, which (2) will be imitated by a false counter sowing; (3) the kingdom will assume huge outer proportions, but (4) be marked by inner doctrinal corruption; yet, the Lord will gain for Himself (5) a peculiar treasure from among Israel, and (6) from the church; (7) the age will end in judgment with the unrighteous excluded from the kingdom to be inaugurated and the righteous taken in to enjoy the blessing of Messiah's reign.[14]

This parable does not teach that Satan has been bound during the Church Age as the Amillennialist believes. And it does not teach that the world will be totally Christianized before the Second Coming as the Postmillennialist believes. It teaches just the opposite of these two views.

The loving Jesus is warning us in this parable that there will be weeping and gnashing of teeth in hell. He is clearly letting us know that the lost person is making a terrible mistake—hell is forever.

The age described in this parable is that period of time between Christ's birth and the Second Coming. Between these two great events, Jesus will add multitudes to his kingdom and Satan will infiltrate it with multitudes more. The age will end with Satan's people being removed and cast into the Lake of Fire.

Two Bad Boys

MATTHEW 21:28–32 *"But what do you think? A man had two sons, and he came to the first and said, 'Son, go, work today in my vineyard.' He answered and said, 'I will not,' but afterward he regretted it and went. Then he came to the second and said likewise. And he answered and said, 'I go, sir,' but he did not go. Which of the two did the will of his father?" They said to Him, "The first." Jesus said to them, "Assuredly, I say to you that tax collectors and harlots enter the kingdom of God before you. For John came to you in the way of righteousness, and you did not believe him; but tax collectors and harlots believed him; and when you saw it, you did not afterward relent and believe him." (NKJV)*

Jesus said there was a man (the Father, God) who had two sons (two groups of Jewish citizens). He (God) went to the first (the common people—tax collectors, prostitutes) and said, "Son, go, work today in my vineyard" (Israel). "I will not," he answered, but later he changed his mind (**repented**) and went. Then the father (God) went to the other son (Jewish religious leaders) and made the same request. He answered, "I go, sir," but he did not go. Jesus asked, "Which of the two (the common people or the religious leaders) did the will of his father (God)?" "The first" (the common people), they answered. Jesus explained that this was why the common people would enter the kingdom of God instead of the Jewish religious leaders. __John__ preached the __way__ of **righteousness** and the common people repented and believed, but the religious leaders did not.

go to

John
Matthew 3:1–2

way
John 14:6

repented
turned toward God, away from sin

John
John the Baptist, a cousin of Jesus

righteousness
justice, peace, right doing

hundred
Acts 1:15

thousand
Acts 2:41; 4:1–4

temple
main religious center
of the Jews

disciples
the chosen twelve

Good people may not make it to heaven because they did not repent and confess a faith in Jesus. Bad people may make it because they did. But it's important to remember that when people truly repent they change their behavior. The inner change of heart and mind is accompanied by an outward change of obedience to God. The inner reception of the Holy Spirit is accompanied by an outward demonstration of faith in Jesus.

what others say

William Barclay

This parable teaches us that promises can never take the place of performance, and fine words are never a substitute for fine deeds.[15]

The false prophets of Israel were religious, but lost. The Antichrist will be religious, but lost. This is also true of cults and false religions. Doing religious things is not necessarily synonymous with serving God.

The church began with Jewish common people: the twelve disciples, more than a <u>hundred</u> followers, and several <u>thousand</u> who were saved early in their ministry. The Romans destroyed Israel in AD 70 including most of the religious leaders.

A House of Cards

MATTHEW 24:1–2 *Then Jesus went out and departed from the temple, and His disciples came up to show Him the buildings of the temple. And Jesus said to them, "Do you not see all these things? Assuredly, I say to you, not one stone shall be left here upon another, that shall not be thrown down." (NKJV)*

While Jesus was leaving the **temple** for the last time before being crucified, his **disciples** approached him to point out its buildings. They were built with extremely large stones of granite weighing several tons each. Together they made a massive structure that appeared to be indestructible. But Jesus said the temple would be so thoroughly destroyed that not one stone would be left on top of another.

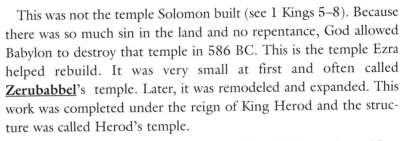

what others say

The Nelson Study Bible

The devastation of the temple by the Romans in AD 70 was so thorough that the precise location of the sanctuary is still unknown today.[16]

This was not the temple Solomon built (see 1 Kings 5–8). Because there was so much sin in the land and no repentance, God allowed Babylon to destroy that temple in 586 BC. This is the temple Ezra helped rebuild. It was very small at first and often called **Zerubbabel**'s temple. Later, it was remodeled and expanded. This work was completed under the reign of King Herod and the structure was called Herod's temple.

Many people are not interested in studying Bible prophecy. Most don't realize that 23 of the 27 New Testament books refer to the Second Coming (all except Galatians, and the one-chapter books of Philemon, and 2 and 3 John). The following chart shows that more than one-fourth of the Bible is prophecy. People cannot ignore more than one-fourth of the Bible and have a good understanding of what it teaches.

Prophetic Verses in the Bible

	Regular Verses	Prophetic Verses	Percentage
Old Testament	23,210	6,641	28.6
New Testament	7,914	1,711	21.6
Entire Bible	31,124	8,352	26.8

Note: Seven out of every 10 chapters in the New Testament and 1 out of every 12 verses in Paul's writings mention the Second Coming.[17]

In AD 70 a powerful Roman general named Titus captured Jerusalem and set it on fire. He planned to save the temple, but his troops harbored such great hatred for the Jews they set it on fire too. Gold decorations on the building melted and the hot liquid flowed into cracks between the temple stones. After the stones cooled, soldiers pried them apart to get the gold out. Not one stone was left unfettered.

go to

heaven
Acts 1:10–12

stand
Zechariah 14:4

buildings
Matthew 24:1–2

beginning
Matthew 24:8

Gabriel
Daniel 9:21–27

white horse
Revelation 6:2

beast
Revelation 13:1–10

Mount of Olives
a very high hill
about 3/4 mile east
of Jerusalem

**the ruler who will
come**
a title referring to
the Antichrist

many
probably the United
Nations or leaders
of many nations

Antichrist
against the Christ,
the anti-Messiah

False Christs

MATTHEW **24:3–5** *Now as He sat on the Mount of Olives, the disciples came to Him privately, saying, "Tell us, when will these things be? And what will be the sign of Your coming, and of the end of the age?" And Jesus answered and said to them: "Take heed that no one deceives you. For many will come in My name, saying, 'I am the Christ,' and will deceive many."* (NKJV)

Now we come to some of the most famous prophecies in the Bible. They were given on the **Mount of Olives** and for this reason they have been given a special name: the Olivet Discourse. This is the place from which Jesus ascended into <u>heaven</u> when he left the earth after his first coming, and it is also the place where he will <u>stand</u> when he returns at his second coming.

He went to the Mount of Olives and sat down. Four of his disciples approached him, wanting to know when the temple <u>buildings</u> would be destroyed and what would be the signs of his second coming and the end of the age. He began his answer by identifying several that he compared to "the <u>beginning</u> of birth pains." It is well known that an expectant mother's birth pains get closer together, harder, and more painful as the birth of her child nears. By analogy, Jesus was saying that these signs are things that always occur, but they will get closer together, harder and more destructive as my second coming draws near.

The first sign mentioned is false Christs. This sign is significant because the angel <u>Gabriel</u> told Daniel that the Tribulation Period will begin when **the ruler who will come** confirms a covenant with **many** to protect Israel for seven years. This ruler will be the ultimate false Christ and he is the one Christians call the **Antichrist**. He is the first rider on the <u>white horse</u> mentioned in the book of Revelation. He's called a <u>beast</u> because he will be so evil; he will be possessed by Satan. And Jesus is saying that the Antichrist is a false Christ who will come during the Tribulation Period, but there will be many false Christs before he arrives and none of them will be as wicked. The fact that the Temple buildings were literally destroyed causes many to believe everything Jesus said in this Olivet Discourse will be literally fulfilled.

Many people are critical of those who study or ask questions about Bible prophecy, but notice that the disciples asked Jesus questions about it and he did not condemn them. He even answered their questions.

These signs (false Christs, wars, famine, pestilence, earthquakes) have a twofold nature. First, they are pre-Rapture signs. And second, they are post-Rapture or Tribulation Period signs. These five signs will occur in a lesser degree before the rapture of the church. And they will occur in a greater degree after the rapture of the church.

Jim Jones, Sun Myung Moon, and David Koresh are just a few of the people who claimed to be Christ in the latter half of the twentieth century. It has even been estimated that there are now more than ten thousand false Christs in the U.S. alone. And there will be many more as we approach the end of the age and the arrival of the Antichrist at the beginning of the Tribulation Period.

It's more than a Christian problem, and it's even a worldwide problem. In the late 1990s the Lubavitcher Jews said Rabbi Menachem Mendel Schneerson was the Messiah. Rabbi Schneerson died, and some Christians thought that would be the end of it, but the Lubavitchers said it only means that he will be raised from the dead before he resumes his role as Messiah. Now the Jews have reestablished the Sanhedrin so Elijah can appear before them and announce the identity of the Messiah. And within Islam, the Saudi Royal family supports the Sunni sect, which is prominent in their country. This sect calls the Messiah the Mahdi. They have even had several people, including Osama bin Laden, who claim to be the Mahdi. In Iraq, the United States has had problems with a firebrand cleric named Muqtada al-Sadr who poses as the Mahdi and calls his followers the Mahdi army. In Iran, the Shiite Muslims are expecting the second coming of a different Mahdi, which they sometimes call the twelfth Imam or the hidden Madhi. This devotion to false messiahs explains the commitment of some terrorists: they think they are following the Mahdi.

Anointed One
Daniel 9:26

red horse
Revelation 6:3–4

nations
Joel 3:9–16;
Zechariah 14:1–21

birth pains
Matthew 24:8

Battle of Armageddon
the last and greatest war

God gave so many details in the Old Testament about the Christ that only one person could fulfill them all. The following chart gives a little insight into this.

Recognizing the Messiah from Old Testament Scriptures

Characteristic	Scripture
The Messiah would be a man.	Genesis 3:15
The Messiah would be a descendant of Abraham.	Genesis 12:1–3
The Messiah would be an Israelite.	Numbers 24:17–19
The Messiah would be from the Tribe of Judah.	Genesis 49:10
The Messiah would be a descendant of Jesse.	Isaiah 11:1–2, 10
The Messiah would be a descendant of David.	2 Samuel 7:12–13
The Messiah would be born in Bethlehem Ephrathah.	Micah 5:2
The Messiah would be born of a virgin.	Isaiah 7:14
The Messiah would appear while the Temple was present.	Malachi 3:1
The Messiah would appear 483 years after the command to rebuild Jerusalem.	Daniel 9:24–27

Wars and Rumors of Wars

MATTHEW 24:6–7a *And you will hear of wars and rumors of wars. See that you are not troubled; for all these things must come to pass, but the end is not yet. For nation will rise against nation, and kingdom against kingdom.* (NKJV)

This is not only a prophecy given by Jesus, it is also part of a previously mentioned prophecy that the angel Gabriel gave to Daniel (Daniel 9). Gabriel predicted the death of the Anointed One (crucifixion of Jesus), the destruction of the city and the sanctuary (Jerusalem and the temple), and even that war will continue to the end. The war to end all wars will be when the fiery red horse is released, peace is removed from the earth, and the nations gather against Jerusalem for the **Battle of Armageddon**.

But a close reading of what Jesus said here reveals that it is actually a loving warning. He is saying there will be many wars and rumors of wars before the end arrives. Those who thought WWI, WWII, or the Vietnam War was the end of the world had a right to be concerned, but the beginning of a war is not sufficient reason to think the end has come. Keep in mind that wars will be like birth pains. They will get closer together and more destructive as the end of the age approaches.

The Antichrist will present himself as a man of peace. He will falsely claim to be the Prince of Peace (Jesus). But God will expose this fake to the world by causing his phony peace programs to fail. World leaders who follow him will be rejecting the true Christ and the only solutions to world problems.

According to the April 1999 issue of the *Prophetic Observer*, "In the course of human history, man has fought 4,535 wars, up to the last count, and 600 million men have been killed in these conflicts... and compare this statistic with the fact that half of these—300 million casualties—have been in wars which occurred in the twentieth century. In other words, there have been as many people killed in war since 1914 as in the previous 5,500 years."[19]

And world leaders don't expect things to get better in the near future. They keep warning everyone that the nations of the world are arming themselves at an alarming rate. Its not new, but these weapons of war are designed to kill.

Famine

MATTHEW 24:7b *And there will be famines . . . in various places.* (NKJV)

The Antichrist will come on the scene predicting an era of economic growth for the world. His promises will include plenty of food and an abundance of goods for all people. But he will be a false **Bread of Life** and God will not let his false claims succeed. The rider on the <u>black horse</u> will be loosed bringing economic collapse and causing the price of wheat and barley (food) to soar. Multitudes will not be able to afford the excessive prices. And **the two witnesses** will come on the scene with power to shut up the sky so that it will not <u>rain</u> during their 3 1/2 year presence on earth.

> ### what others say
>
> **Jack Van Impe**
> <u>Warfare</u> from earliest times has also been a primary contributor to the destruction of crops and animals, and subsequent blockades and attacks on cities and ports have been responsible for countless famines.[20]

go to

Bread of Life
John 6:35

black horse
Revelation 6:5–6

rain
Revelation 11:1–6

warfare
Matthew 24:6–7

Bread of Life
Jesus

the two witnesses
two powerful men of God who will preach during the Tribulation Period

plague
Zechariah 14:12–15

pale horse
Revelation 6:7–8

strike the earth
Revelation 11:3–6

Jesus is coming back to put an end to the Antichrist, to false worship, to war, to those who will use their control of food and water to subjugate people, to the wicked who persecute and kill Christians, and to failed policies that starve people and enslave.

Famine is an enormous problem in the world today, especially in many African countries. And with thousands dying every day, some nations including the United States are cutting back on food contributions to starving people. But as bad as it is, things will be much worse during the Tribulation Period.

Pestilences

MATTHEW 24:7a *There will be . . . pestilences . . . in various places. (NKJV)*

diseases
pestilence or plague

mutating
changing, taking on
a new form

biological weapons
weapons containing
harmful diseases
and organisms

The prophet Zechariah said God will strike all those nations that fight against Jerusalem during the Tribulation Period with a <u>plague</u>. The apostle John said the rider on the <u>pale horse</u> will be loosed with power to kill one-fourth of the earth with war, famine, **diseases**, and wild animals. The two witnesses will have power to stop the rain and <u>strike the earth</u> with every kind of plague as often as they want.

But what about today? Scientists and doctors are constantly reporting outbreaks of new, unknown, and more deadly diseases. Drug use, sexual activity, natural disasters, and other problems are causing explosive and dangerous outbreaks. In some African countries, as much as one-fourth of the population is now HIV positive. The disease is **mutating**, and many types and subtypes are now spreading among both homosexuals and heterosexuals. The production of **biological weapons** is given top priority in several nations. And some producers are selling to anyone who has the money.

Some military experts are even predicting that bio-terrorism could become a major battle front in the future. Several nations and terrorist organizations are known to maintain secret germ banks and germ warfare programs. The suicide bomber who can't get through a metal detector at the airport may think he is doing Allah a favor by inoculating himself with a deadly disease, getting on an airplane, and breathing on as many people as he can while flying to as many nations as he can before he keels over. He may be someone who mixes a deadly concoction and sends it through the mail; someone who inoculates himself, crosses our border, and goes to a football game where 100,000 people are gathered; someone who gets a job on an oil tanker and enters the country legally. The possibilities are endless, and nations that support terrorism like it because it's easy for them to escape the blame.

Just fifty years ago, scientists and doctors were confidently predicting the soon eradication of terrible diseases from the earth, but things changed and they now say the spread of diseases is a major problem in the world. Medical experts, health agencies, the CIA, and others are trying to warn the world about possible outbreaks of pestilences on a massive worldwide scale. This problem will become more serious as the Tribulation Period approaches. Then it will reach a horrifying peak.

go to

Mount of Olives
Zechariah 14:3–5

shake
Isaiah 13:13

tremble
Joel 3:16

earthquake
Revelation 16:18

Mount of Olives
a very high hill about 3/4 mile east of Jerusalem

> **what others say**
>
> ### Prophetic Observer
>
> What if 100 million people in just India alone die of starvation? This would be equal to all the people in the United States west of the Mississippi River starving to death. We cannot begin to imagine the carnage, the filth, the contamination, and the spread of deadly diseases that would result. There would not be enough doctors or vaccination serum in the world to fight it.[21]

Earthquakes

MATTHEW 24:7b *And there will be . . . earthquakes in various places. (NKJV)*

The prophet Zechariah predicted that a massive earthquake will split the **Mount of Olives** in two when Jesus returns; the prophet Isaiah said the earth will shake from its place at that time; the prophet Joel said the earth and sky will tremble; and the book of Revelation says there will be a tremendous earthquake such as "had not occurred since men were on the earth" (Revelation 16:18 NKJV). Skyscrapers and bridges will fall, islands will sink into the sea, entire mountains will drop into the earth, and houses will splinter and collapse.

But what about today? At the beginning of the twentieth century, between 1900 and 1910, there was only one earthquake measuring

7.2 or higher on the Richter scale. Between 1950 and 1960, there were nine. There were 125 in just five years, between 1990 and 1995. And every year scientists tell us a "big one" is on the way.

go to

nations
Zechariah 12:1–3

two-thirds
Zechariah 13:8

> what others say
>
> **Billy Graham**
>
> There have been famines, plagues, and earthquakes for thousands of years, but seldom so many all at once and seldom so concentrated in time and space.[22]

Various signs are vivid reminders that the Tribulation Period is drawing near. And the fact that these signs are occurring simultaneously makes it even more sure.

There is overwhelming evidence on the occurrence of these things—false Christs, wars, famine, pestilence, and earthquakes—that would be hard for anyone to deny. This evidence demands the most serious consideration possible.

God is sending the world a message every time an earthquake rattles the earth. He is using their increased frequency and intensity to tell us the Tribulation Period is approaching and we need to be prepared for eternity.

Persecution

MATTHEW 24:9 *Then they will deliver you up to tribulation and kill you, and you will be hated by all nations for My name's sake.* (NKJV)

Verses 1 and 2 in Matthew 24 deal with fulfilled prophecy: the destruction of the temple in AD 70. Verses 3 through 8 deal with prophecy that is continuously being fulfilled: birth pain–type false Christs, war, famine, pestilence, and earthquakes. Here, the word *then* signals a change in the Olivet Discourse. Verses 9 through 51 deal with future events: the Tribulation Period, Second Coming, judgment. Although those who accept Christ after the Rapture will be affected by these things, the events described in these verses refer primarily to Israel and the Jews.

During the Tribulation Period, the <u>nations</u> will hate Israel and lay siege to Jerusalem. In the whole land <u>two-thirds</u> of the Jews will be killed. Concerning both Christians and Jews, those who refuse to take the **Mark of the Beast** will be <u>killed</u>. The Antichrist and his corrupt followers will try to wipe out God's true people before Jesus returns to establish his earthly kingdom.

World leaders professed amazement in 2005 when Iran's conservative President Mahmood Ahmadinejad called for a global Islamic revolution, said he wanted to export it to every nation on earth, and said he wanted to wipe Israel off the face of the earth. Then, after several criticisms that produced a mild apology, he came right back a few days later and called for a world without America. The problem is a misguided religious fervor that cannot tolerate Christians and Jews. While it must be admitted that many Muslims do not think like Ahmadinejad, and even that many will be saved at the end of the age, Christians need to spread the word that hatred of Christians and Jews is the way it will be during the Tribulation Period.

When conservative Christians express biblical views that oppose politically correct ones, they are criticized as mean-spirited extremists and enemies of world peace. When this occurs, who is spreading the hate?

go to

killed
Revelation 6:11; 13:15

Mark of the Beast
the mark, number or name of the Antichrist

something to ponder

---

what others say

David Hocking

These signs will actually occur—exactly as Christ foretold—only during the Tribulation. And though we believe we will escape the great sufferings of the Tribulation by being with Christ in heaven, this is very serious stuff.[23]

J. Vernon McGee

The affliction He is talking about is anti-Semitism on a worldwide scale.[24]

Randall Price

Once Israel asserts her independence from the rule of Antichrist, anti-Semitism will explode on a worldwide scale, and Israel will truly be "hated by all nations."[25]

Israel has been restored as a nation, but the people have not been restored spiritually. Unfortunately, preparing them will require a great deal of persecution. During the Tribulation Period, the Jews will be seen as a threat to world government, world religion, and

prophecy

go to

buying or selling
Revelation 13:16–17

hatred
Mark 13:12–13

betray
Luke 21:15–19

Holocaust
mass destruction of
the Jews during
World War II

world peace. The world's desire for ethnic cleansing will produce another **Holocaust**. Hatred of Christians and Jews will greatly accelerate and include terrible acts of betrayal and violence during the Tribulation Period.

Betrayal

MATTHEW **24:10** *And then many will be offended, will betray one another, and will hate one another.* (NKJV)

What Jesus said here can be applied to Christians, but his primary reference is to Jews living during the Tribulation Period. Doing the will of God will be more than frowned upon, it will be dangerous, and it will even get many killed. When <u>buying or selling</u> basic necessities such as food, water, medicine, and electricity becomes illegal for all who refuse to take the Mark of the Beast, dissension and <u>hatred</u> will develop not only with the civil and religious authorities, but also with those who are normally one's most faithful allies. To curry the favor of the authorities, to secure safety for themselves, and to acquire goods and services, people will <u>betray</u> their parents, brothers, relatives, and friends to death.

In recent years, merchants have stirred up a controversy by telling their employees to say "Happy Holidays" instead of "Merry Christmas." Reports say one of the largest retailers in the world even told its employees they would be fired for saying "Merry Christmas." Christians should not be surprised that unbelievers would do this. But the startling thing about this is that some churches decided to call their Christmas tree a holiday tree. How can a congregation call itself the Body of Christ, call itself Ambassadors for Christ, say its first love is Christ, or try to win the world to Christ when it is reluctant to use the word *Christ*? It can't unless it has left its original calling in favor of a political correctness that denies the truth of Scripture.

These are signs of the predicted turning away from the faith. And in some cases, it's even worse than that. Many of these apostates and lukewarm believers take the next step of betrayal by offering strong opposition to those who call for a return to true Christianity. They are not content to oppose Christ. They add to what they have done by opposing those who call for repentance.

go to

Union Gospel Press

As persecution increases, believers and unbelievers will be separated. There will be some who, like **Judas**, will be fellow travelers for a while. When things do not go as they expect, however, these people will turn on friends and family.[26]

Judas
Matthew 26:47–50

people
Matthew 25:31–46

Judas
a disciple who betrayed Jesus

disciples
Jesus' followers

false prophets
people God did not send who claim to have a message from God

Concerning anti-Semitism, Christians should remember that the **disciples** were Jewish, the apostle Paul was Jewish, and the Old and New Testaments were written by Jews. Most importantly, a Jew named Jesus died for our sins. He will return to Israel in the near future, judge the nations, and separate <u>people</u> in accordance with their treatment of his followers.

something to ponder

When God's people abandon him, ignore the Bible, and worship false gods, they must repent, or he will eventually withdraw his protection. Without his help, they will face disease, fear, injustice, oppression, poverty, tyranny, violence, and a host of other problems. He is patient, but eventually it will come down to this: repent or perish.

More Christians and Jews have been persecuted and killed this century than in all of history. Some want to deny the death of six million Jews in Germany during WWII. Current apathy will explode into bitter hatred during the Tribulation Period.

False Prophets

MATTHEW 24:11a *Then many false prophets will rise up.* (*NKJV*)

There have been many **false prophets** in the history of the world, but the rapture of the church will leave a vacuum the false church will rapidly try to fill and explain. This vacuum will produce an explosion of pretenders who will claim to speak for God. But their God will not be the God described in the Bible; the salvation they proclaim will not be the death of Jesus on the cross; many of the moral standards they espouse will contradict what the Bible says, and their "feel good" predictions of love, justice, peace, and prosperity will turn into rubbish.

translation
the Rapture

False Prophet
the second beast of
Revelation, he seeks
devotees for the
Antichrist

It seems reasonable to expect many of these false prophets to show strong opposition to Israel. Many will deny that the regathering of millions of Jews in Israel and the creation of the modern Jewish state are a fulfillment of prophecy. They will refuse to accept the fact that God intends for Jerusalem to belong to the Jews, thus making Jerusalem the burdensome stone predicted in Scripture. They will declare that Israel and Jerusalem do not occupy a special place in the heart of God and set themselves against the One who can release the Four Horsemen of the Apocalypse. The Scriptures are clear on these matters, but rather than belief and acceptance, Jesus and the prophets predicted a strong wave of anti-Semitism.

what others say

Thomas Ice and Timothy Demy

While the next event for the true church—the body of Christ—is **translation** from earth to heaven at the rapture, those unbelievers left in the organized church as an institution will pass into the tribulation and form the base of an apostate super-church that the **False Prophet** will use to aid the world-wide rule of the Antichrist (Revelation 13; 17–18).[27]

Charles Halff

A true prophet magnifies Christ. A false prophet doesn't. A true preacher will always point you to the Word of God. A false preacher will point you to visions, dreams, maybe rituals or ceremonies. Some will point you to mind reading, astrology, and a thousand and one other things.[28]

Mike Gendron

Satan's Devices for Apostasy

- Counterfeit gods—2 Thessalonians 2:3–4
- Counterfeit Jesus(es)—2 Corinthians 11:4
- Counterfeit Christs—Matthew 24:24
- Counterfeit spirits—1 John 4:1; 1 Timothy 4:1
- Counterfeit apostles—2 Corinthians 11:13; Revelation 2:2
- Counterfeit prophets—2 Peter 2:1; 1 John 4:1
- Counterfeit ministers—2 Corinthians 11:15
- Counterfeit gospels—Galatians 1:6–9
- Counterfeit miracles—2 Thessalonians 2:9; Revelation 16:13
- Counterfeit worship—John 4:24[29]

Astrologers, fortune tellers, psychics, and witches have been predicting a new age of peace and prosperity for several years, but Bible signs indicate the world is on the brink of the Tribulation Period and that it will be accompanied by an economic collapse. President Clinton predicted there will be no more armies, just peacekeeping forces. But the United States wound up in the war on terrorism, and the Bible predicts a two hundred million–man army will invade the Middle East. Clinton predicted no more wars, just peacekeeping operations, but the Bible predicts a Russian-Islamic invasion of Israel and a Battle of Armageddon. Clinton predicted the era of big government is over, but Globalism is expanding, and the Bible predicts a coming world government led by the Antichrist. President Bush predicted a comprehensive peace in the Middle East by the end of his second term. He later backed off, but the Bible teaches that there will be no peace until Christ returns. Who or what should people believe?

There is nothing wrong with wanting to know the future, but we should realize that there are many false prophets in the world and there will be a myriad more when the Tribulation Period arrives, especially in the false church and in Israel.

Religious Deception

MATTHEW 24:11 *Then many false prophets will rise up and deceive many.* (NKJV)

It was a priest named Aaron who sinned against God by building a golden <u>calf</u> in the wilderness; corrupt priests and elders who plotted to <u>kill</u> Jesus; one of the <u>twelve</u> disciples who betrayed Jesus; a United Methodist theologian who said, "God is dead"; a Presbyterian bishop who said, "The virgin birth is a myth"; an Anglican bishop who said, "Hell does not exist"; and an Episcopal bishop who said, "There is no God." Good people making mistakes and unbelievers teaching error for truth are not new. This is why Jesus said, "Take heed that no one deceives you" (Matthew 24:4 NKJV). He knew that the winds of deceit will reach gale force during the Tribulation Period.

calf
Exodus 32:1–35
kill
Matthew 26:3–5
twelve
Matthew 26:14–16

deception
Revelation 23:3, 8

Joe Chambers

Satan's chief attack against the church has always been to produce a counterfeit. After Satan has produced his counterfeit preachers and prophets, he uses the world to talk about how crazy all Christians are by pointing out the false crowd. How clever and double-tongued the devil and his spirits are in their evil design.[30]

Church leaders who have abandoned the faith are not new, but it seems like they are cropping up in ever-increasing numbers. In complete disregard of what the Bible says, one church bishop now teaches that everyone will go to heaven even if they do not believe in Jesus. And despite the fact that the Bible says Satan will be cast into the Lake of Fire, this bishop declares that even Satan may go to heaven. During the Tribulation Period, the Antichrist and his corrupt religious followers will try to reinvent Christianity and Judaism. Powerful and very popular religious figures will make a strong effort to dilute and redefine the long-held beliefs of conservative Christians and Jews. It will be their goal to shift people from the scriptural teachings of true Christianity and Judaism to the false teachings of a global secular society.

Political correctness appears to be an effort to bend the Word of God, an effort to substitute a form of godliness for true Christianity and Judaism, an effort to produce an unscriptural set of government-approved religious and social values. Could this kind of religious deception be the underlying cause of the coming persecution of Christians and Jews?

Religious <u>deception</u> can prosper only in the presence of religious ignorance. It is one of Satan's favorite tools. People use it for gain when the truth is an obstacle. The Antichrist and his corrupt religious leaders will use it during the Tribulation Period to gain religious support and secure peace treaties, and so forth. It will be difficult to be a Christian during the Tribulation Period.

A Falling Away

MATTHEW 24:12 *"And because lawlessness will abound, the love of many will grow cold."* (NKJV)

184   **Prophecies of the Bible**

The effect of religious deception will be **sin** in the religious community and a turning away from God. In some cases, it will be the Antichrist and his corrupt religious leaders instigating the persecution of true believers causing those on the fringe to abandon the faith for fear of their lives. In other cases, it will be weak morals stemming from false teachings that will cause people to go astray. But the end result will be the same: during the Tribulation Period widespread sin will drive many from God.

Tolerance of false doctrines leads to moral confusion. Out of that comes immoral decisions, the eroding of society, and the eventual collapse of social order. And, without God, this is exactly what will happen during the Tribulation Period.

Preaching the Gospel

MATTHEW 24:14 *And this gospel of the kingdom will be preached in all the world as a witness to all the nations, and then the end will come.* (NKJV)

False Christs, false prophets, betrayal, and persecution will take a toll, but they will not prevent the **gospel** from going all over the world during the Tribulation Period. Wicked men have never been allowed to stop the spread of God's Word, and they will not be permitted to do it in the future. After God raptures the church, he will do three things:

1. <u>Seal</u> 144,000 Jews to preach the gospel to the world
2. Send <u>two witnesses</u> to prophesy to the world
3. Send an <u>angel</u> to preach to every nation, tribe, language, and people on earth

go to

seal
Revelation 7:1–8

two witnesses
Revelation 11:3–12

angel
Revelation 14:6–7

sin
missing the mark, wrongdoing

gospel
good news of Jesus Christ

seal
a mark or symbol to identify and protect

---

what others say

Dave Breese

The message of the gospel of the grace of God is to be preached in the Gentile world. On the occasion of the Rapture, however, it is the gospel of the kingdom that shall be the message from God. This is the announcement that "the kingdom of heaven is at hand."[31]

Grant Jeffrey

The Bible has now been translated in more than 3,850 languages in every nation, tribe and dialect on this planet. Electronic communication transmits the message of hope in Jesus Christ through the air waves worldwide.[32]

Christians are also now sending the gospel of grace all over the world electronically via the Internet. Some of the larger Christian ministries are reporting more than one million hits a month on their Web site. Clear evidence supports that the gospel of the kingdom can go all over the world in our time.

- In 1993, the gospel of grace was being broadcast worldwide, twenty-four hours a day and in ninety different languages.

- In 1995, Dr. Billy Graham preached to the entire world over television, 70 percent of the world's population had the opportunity to hear him, interpreters were used, and it is estimated that as many as one billion people listened in their own language.

- In 1996, with the assistance of one million pastors and churches on every continent, Billy Graham preached to the entire world again, and it is estimated that approximately 2 billion people listened this time.

- In 1997, Princess Diana was killed in a car wreck, and it was estimated that one-fourth of the earth's population watched her funeral on television.

- In 2001, President George W. Bush spoke at a memorial service for victims of the World Trade Center collapse, and it was reported that one-fourth of the earth's population and the heads of every nation on earth watched the service on television.

- In 2005, Pope John Paul II died, and an estimated one-third of the earth's population watched his funeral on television.

Defilement of Temple

MATTHEW 24:15 *Therefore when you see the "abomination of desolation," spoken of by Daniel the prophet, standing in the holy place . . . (NKJV)*

The "holy place" will be the future Jewish temple. "The abomination that causes desolation" will be the Antichrist who will rise to power over a reunited Europe. He will visit the temple, declare that he is God, and set up an idol on the wing of that holy building. This will happen 3 1/2 years after he has signed a seven-year covenant with many to protect Israel. Hence, this prophecy is implying several future events:

- The existence of Israel as a nation
- The rebuilding of the Jewish temple
- Jewish control over the **Temple Mount** (partial, if not complete)
- The reuniting of Europe
- The existence of the Antichrist as a world leader
- The existence of a seven-year **covenant** to protect Israel as a nation
- A visit by the Antichrist to Israel and the temple at the Tribulation Period midpoint

Many Christians believe the Tribulation Period begins with the Rapture. God outlined the Tribulation Period in terms of the Antichrist. The following chart is helpful.

The Tribulation Period

Antichrist Revealed	Antichrist Exalts Himself	Antichrist Captured
Tribulation begins when Antichrist signs the 7-Year Covenant	Tribulation midpoint occurs when Antichrist defiles the Temple	Tribulation ends when Antichrist is captured
3 1/2 years		3 1/2 years

The existence of Israel and Jerusalem is as undeniable fact. The existence of a united Europe in the form of the European Union is also a fact. There will be some changes, but Europe is now united. The existence of the Antichrist can neither be confirmed nor denied because the Holy Spirit will not permit him to be revealed until after the Rapture, but many authorities believe he is alive today. The existence of a comprehensive Middle East peace treaty is not a fact, but there are signs that a treaty will be signed by many (UN, EU, Russia, U.S., Arabs, Israel). The existence of the Temple is not a fact, but most of the preliminary work has been done, and the Sanhedrin

go to

abomination
Daniel 9:27; 11:31; 12:11

God
2 Thessalonians 2:1–4

temple
main religious center of the Jews

Temple Mount
the hill where all of the Jewish temples have been built

covenant
a comprehensive Middle East peace agreement

wants to prefabricate it so it can be put up in as little as six weeks. It will be constructed and defiled by the middle of the Tribulation Period. It is time for people to wake up.

The stage is rapidly being set for the fulfillment of this prophecy. And the rapture of the church will occur before we get there.

Many Will Run for Their Lives

MATTHEW 24:16–20 *Then let those who are in Judea flee to the mountains. Let him who is on the housetop not go down to take anything out of his house. And let him who is in the field not go back to get his clothes. But woe to those who are pregnant and to those who are nursing babies in those days! And pray that your flight may not be in winter or on the Sabbath. (NKJV)*

Here Jesus is warning the Jews about when the Antichrist defiles the Temple at the Tribulation Period midpoint. They are the ones who live in Judea, the ones who observe the Sabbath. The Antichrist will begin a major persecution of the Jews immediately after he defiles the Temple. They will have very little time to escape, and many who try to take their possessions will be killed. This extreme persecution will continue for three and one-half years. It will culminate at the Battle of Armageddon when the nations of the earth gather against Judah and Jerusalem, capture the city, ransack the houses, and rape the women.

Defilement of the Temple at the Tribulation Period midpoint should be seen as a sign to the Jews to flee as fast as they can.

Most prophetic scholars believe the Jews will flee to the ancient city of Petra. It is located in a mountainous area of Jordan about twenty miles south of the Dead Sea. About twenty-five hundred years ago, the Edomites carved a large city with business buildings, houses, and caves out of the white and red sandstone there. They eventually deserted the city, but it is an ideal place to hide—it would be easy to defend because of the narrow passages leading to it, and it can be quickly reached by the residents of Judea. Isn't it interesting that a new road to Petra is under construction today, that utilities are being installed there, and that Israel is even storing supplies there?

Prophecies of the Bible

what others say

Sol Scharfstein

Before the [1967 War] began Israel promised King Hussein of Jordan that no harm would come to his country if he stayed out of the fighting. Hussein ignored the peace overture and attacked Jerusalem. Israel counterattacked, and within a few days had defeated the Jordanians. Israeli forces were now in control of the West Bank (Judea and Samaria), and had captured the Old City of Jerusalem. The Temple Mount was under Jewish rule for the first time in almost 2,000 years.[33]

Jewish priests have been identified using DNA and everything needed for conducting animal sacrifices and worship services at the temple has been prepared. This includes a meeting place for the Sanhedrin (the highest legal and religious authority of the ancient Jewish nation), clothing for the priests, furniture for the temple, and musical instruments for the services. The priests are not permitted to make a mistake when they perform animal sacrifices so schools have been established near the Temple Mount for them to train by sacrificing real animals. Some reports say archaeologists have uncovered an exact full-scale replica of the Temple on **Mount Gerizim**, so all the building materials for a new Temple can now be precut and fabricated for rapid assembly when the proper time comes. Since the Temple only has to be present by the middle of the Tribulation Period, for all practical purposes everything is now ready. The Sanhedrin has been re-established so Elijah can appear before the group and announce the identity of the Messiah. Jews believe Messiah will give them permission to rebuild the Temple.

Christians believe the Sanhedrin will produce a hand-picked Elijah, and the man he identifies will be the Antichrist. The stage is set for this, but don't expect to see it. The church will be raptured first.

Great Distress (Tribulation)

MATTHEW 24:21 *For then there will be great tribulation, such as has not been since the beginning of the world until this time, no, nor never shall be. (NKJV)*

It is important to remember that the **Holy Spirit** will be removed from the earth when the church is **raptured** before the Tribulation

evil
2 Thessalonians
2:1–12

hurled
Revelation 12:8–9

seal/trumpet/bowl
Revelation 6–16

survive
Matthew 24:22

Period. Evil will no longer be restrained and the Antichrist will go on a violent rampage. Then at the Tribulation Period midpoint, Satan will lose his place in heaven and be hurled down to the earth. As if that isn't bad enough, there will be an outpouring of God's seal, trumpet, and bowl judgments upon the Antichrist and his followers. Crisis will follow crisis like a raging storm that cannot be stopped. Except for the intervention of God, no one would survive.

The Tribulation Period gets its name from the fact that Jesus talked about "great tribulation" and "the tribulation of those days" (Matthew 24:21, 29 NKJV). This terrible time is referred to by more than three dozen different names in the Bible. Some are shown in the following chart.

Names of the Tribulation Period

Name	Scripture
The time of Jacob's (unbelieving Israel's) trouble	Jeremiah 30:7
The great day of the Lord, a day of wrath, a day of trouble and distress, a day of wasteness and desolation, a day of darkness and gloominess, a day of clouds and thick darkness, a day of trumpet and alarm	Zephaniah 1:14–16
The indignation	Isaiah 26:20
The day of the Lord's vengeance	Isaiah 34:8
The seventieth week	Daniel 9:24–27
The day of the Lord's anger	Zephaniah 2:2–3
The wrath of the Lamb	Revelation 6:16

what others say

Dave Breese

It will be the time of the worst carnage and the most despicable situations and the most overwhelming impact of the judgment of God that the world will ever see. If you think that God doesn't see, that He doesn't notice, that He won't judge the world one day, think again. The judgment of God during the Great Tribulation will be absolutely indescribable.[34]

The group of people called Preterists teaches that Matthew chapter 24 was fulfilled in AD 70 when the Romans destroyed Jerusalem and the temple. But Jesus said, "There will be great tribulation, such as has not been since the beginning of the world until this time, no, nor ever shall be" (Matthew 24:21 NKJV). The destruction of Jerusalem was terrible, but there have been other destructions as bad or worse.

The <u>tribulation</u> in this passage is a reference to the coming Tribulation Period. "Great tribulaton" refers to the second half or the last 3 1/2 years of the Tribulation Period, that period of time immediately after the Antichrist defiles the temple.

Signs and Miracles

> MATTHEW 24:24 *For false christs and false prophets will rise and show great signs and wonders to deceive, if possible, even the elect.* (NKJV)

Some ask, Why would anyone follow the Antichrist, false Messiahs, or false prophets? When Jesus walked this earth, he performed great <u>miracles</u> and what he did attracted great <u>crowds</u>. John said, "Many <u>believed</u> in His name when they saw the signs which He did" (John 2:23 NKJV). This is one reason why so many people will make such a terrible mistake. They will fall prey to religious deception backed up by signs and miracles.

The Bible contains many warnings about corruption in the church at the end of the age. Many seminaries will grow weeds and the truth will be choked out. They will graduate spiritually bankrupt pastors with seductive ideas more dangerous than poisoned stew. The following list identifies six characteristics of false prophets:

1. Instead of affirming what the Bible says, they will ignore or condemn it.

2. Instead of meticulously quoting what the Bible says, they will use nonbiblical sources for their message or deliberately misquote it.

3. Instead of denouncing sin as found in the Bible, they will redefine sin to espouse the politically correct or popular view.

4. Instead of saying the way is narrow or Jesus is the only way, they will say there are other ways or many ways.

5. Instead of being motivated by serving God with character and personal integrity, they will often be motivated by serving a system for money, applause, or worldly success.

6. During the Tribulation Period, they will disagree with the 144,000 Jewish evangelists and the Two Witnesses.

go to

tribulation
Daniel 12:1–3;
Luke 21:20–23

miracles
John 2:1–11; 3:2

crowds
John 6:1–15

believed
John 2:23

Without question God can perform signs and miracles. But Satan and his crowd of false Christs, witches, and mystics can do some pretty amazing things too and they will be out in full force during the Tribulation Period.

key point

During the Tribulation Period the Antichrist will display "all power, <u>signs</u>, and lying wonders" (2 Thessalonians 2:9 NKJV). The False Prophet will perform great and miraculous signs, and the spirits of <u>demons</u> will perform miraculous signs to gather the leaders of the world for the Battle of Armageddon.

<u>Birds of Prey</u>

MATTHEW 24:28 *For wherever the carcass is, there the eagles will be gathered together. (NKJV)*

This is an ancient proverb that Jesus applied to the Battle of Armageddon. A carcass is a dead body. Job noted that the **eagles** gather where the slain are. The main idea of this sign is that the death of many people will cause a gathering of the birds of prey in Israel.

what others say

Charles Capps

This plainly reveals it to be the same event as described in Revelation 19:17–18. When the angel will cry with a loud voice for all of the fowls of the earth to come and feast on kings and great men of the earth. The carcass to which Jesus gives reference is of the Antichrist, as well as the armies that follow him. These will all be slain when Christ comes back with His saints at the end of the Tribulation.[35]

go to

signs
Revelation 13:13

demons
Revelation 16:12–14

eagles
the Palestinian eagles are actually vultures or birds of prey

Before the Jews started returning to Israel in great numbers, the land was barren and wild animals and birds of prey avoided the area. Along with the returning Jews came the greening of the land, the blossoming of the desert, the reforestation of the hills, the return of wild animals, and the arrival of the birds. During the migration season, birds of prey now fly over Israel by the hundreds of thousands. Thus, they will be there when this great feast is prepared at the Battle of Armageddon.

When Jesus returns at the end of the Tribulation Period, he will find that two-thirds to three-fourths of those on earth have been killed. By far, the largest percentage of those who are alive will be unbelievers who followed the Antichrist. The remainder will include a small number of believers who have survived, the remnant of Jews in Israel and other nations who have survived, and those Jews who escaped into the wilderness at the Tribulation Period midpoint. People do not like to think of judgment, but everyone needs to realize that the earth will be purged of unbelievers at the Second Coming. Unbelievers will immediately die in their sins and be cast into hell. The chart below provides more information.

Fast Facts on the Glorious Appearing of Jesus

Second Coming	Scripture
The wheat (the saved) will be separated from the chaff (the lost).	Matthew 3:12
The lost will not be allowed to enter the kingdom.	Matthew 7:21–23
Those who did not receive or listen to God's people will suffer terribly.	Matthew 10:14–15
Those who confess or deny Jesus will be acknowledged or denied before God.	Matthew 10:32–33
Those who help God's people in the name of Jesus will be rewarded.	Matthew 10:40–42
Jesus will return with his angels and reward the faithful.	Matthew 16:27
Only those who are prepared (the saved) will enter the kingdom.	Matthew 25:1–13
People will be judged for their faithfulness to Jesus.	Matthew 25:14–30
Good nations will enter the Millennium, but wicked nations will be destroyed.	Matthew 25:31–46

Heavenly Signs

MATTHEW 24:29 *Immediately after the tribulation of those days the sun will be darkened, and the moon will not give its light; the stars will fall from heaven, and the powers of the heavens will be shaken. (NKJV)*

At the very end of the tribulation there will be great disturbances in the heavenly bodies. The <u>sun</u> will turn black, there will be no light for the <u>moon</u> to reflect, the stars fall like <u>figs</u> dropping from a fig tree, and the heavenly bodies will shake like they are being rolled up inside a great <u>scroll</u>. Luke adds that there will be <u>anguish</u> and perplexity on earth, and people will faint from terror and apprehension over what is happening to the world.

sun
Joel 2:30–31;
Amos 8:9

moon
Isaiah 13:9–13

figs
Revelation 6:12–13

scroll
Revelation 6:14

anguish
Luke 21:25–26

The Bible speaks of the world that was (2 Peter 3:6), this present world (Titus 2:12; 2 Timothy 4:10), and the world to come (Ephesians 1:21; Hebrews 2:5). Peter clearly teaches that the world that was refers to the pre-flood world (2 Peter 3:5–7). When the fountains of the deep broke up and the windows of heaven opened, the world that was (this planet) went through a geophysical change (Genesis 7:11). It was a literal catastrophic change. Jesus is clearly saying this present world will go through another catastrophic change when he returns. He does not lie, deceive, or exaggerate.

If you are here when this happens, what will you do? How will you protect yourself when there is no place to hide? The stress, anxiety, and terror will be so great that people will have heart attacks and fall in their tracks. Those who put their trust in Jesus Christ now won't have to worry about it.

It is impossible to say just what will happen, but this appears to be a Nova, or a partial Nova, of the sun. Scientists see about thirty of these in our galaxy each year. When a star does this it gets very bright, it collapses, and then its light fades somewhat. This would account for both the sun and the moon going dark, and something like this will happen at the end of the Tribulation Period.

The Second Coming

MATTHEW 24:30 *Then the sign of the Son of Man will appear in heaven, and then all the tribes of the earth will mourn, and they will see the Son of Man coming on the clouds of heaven with power and great glory. (NKJV)*

"Then" refers to Matthew 24:29. When the sun is darkened, the moon fails to shine, and hundreds of stars start falling out of the sky, then the sign of Jesus will appear in the sky; and people all over the earth will see it and experience great distress. They will be people who mocked, <u>scoffed</u>, and refused to believe in the Second Coming. But when this sign appears, reality will set in and the tears will flow as Jesus returns in the <u>clouds</u> with power and great glory.

go to

scoffed
2 Peter 3:3–7

clouds
Matthew 26:64;
Mark 14:62;
Acts 1:9–11

face
Revelation 1:16

shekinah glory
glory brighter than
the noonday sun

> ### what others say
>
> #### Billy Graham
> The good news for Christians who have remained faithful through trials and persecution will be bad news indeed for everyone who has denied Christ, slandered His people, and followed after false gods.[37]
>
> #### Charles Capps
> Not many years ago, people were saying, "This couldn't happen! It's impossible for everyone to see Him!" But with satellite news coverage as competitive as it is today, I believe CNN as well as many other TV networks will be there to broadcast Christ's Second Advent live via satellite and it will be seen around the world.[38]

What is the sign of Jesus? The Bible does not say, but some commentators think it is something called the **shekinah glory**. When John saw Jesus on the Isle of Patmos, our Lord's <u>face</u> "was like the sun shining in its strength" (Revelation 1:16 NKJV). It will be so bright everyone everywhere will see it. People who scoffed at the Second Coming will suddenly realize their sin and weep. But it will be too late to repent.

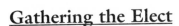

This is not the Rapture, which will remove the church from the earth and catch the unbelieving world by surprise. This is the second coming of Christ in power to put down evil on earth and to establish justice, peace, and righteousness. It will happen at the end of the Tribulation Period, not before.

Gathering the Elect

MATTHEW 24:31 *And He will send His angels with a great sound of a trumpet, and they will gather together His elect from the four winds, from one end of heaven to the other.* (*NKJV*)

angels
Hebrews 1:14

trumpet
Numbers 10:1–7;
Leviticus 23:23–24

God often uses <u>angels</u> to do great things, and he often uses <u>trumpet</u> blasts to assemble his people. Here we are told that Jesus will use angels and trumpet blasts to gather his people. The "four winds" and "from one end of heaven to the other" simply means from wherever they are on earth or in heaven. No one will be ignored or forgotten.

A key point to pick up on here concerns the fact that some authorities wrongly teach that the seventh trumpet in Revelation 11:15 is the last trump of 1 Corinthians 15:52. Neither one is the last to blow. This trumpet will sound after both of those. The seventh trumpet is the last in the series of seven trumpets, and it will probably sound near the Tribulation Period midpoint. The last trump is the last blast of the trumpet on the day of the Rapture, and it will sound before the Tribulation Period. This trumpet will sound at the end of the Tribulation Period. It doesn't announce one of the seven trumpet judgments or signal the Rapture. It fulfills Isaiah 27:12–13 by gathering the Jews from the land of Assyria, the land of Egypt, and the uttermost parts of the earth.

what others say

Arnold G. Fruchtenbaum

Since the Jewish prophets had predicted in great detail the worldwide regathering of Israel, Jesus did not spend much time with this, but only pointed out that it will occur after His Second Coming.[39]

John F. Walvoord

At that time Old Testament saints will be resurrected and believers from the tribulation will be raised from the dead. Living Christians will also be gathered. The millennial kingdom will extend to all believers, and at its beginning all the saved will be resurrected.[40]

The angels of heaven will scour the earth immediately after the second coming of Christ. This will be one of the first events to take place in the Millennium.

The followers of Jesus who do not experience death before the Millennium and are privileged to live on into that period will be in their old bodies and therefore will give birth to children. These children will be born with a sin nature just like children who are born now. Most will serve Jesus, but not all. Christian service will not go unnoticed by our Lord as the following chart shows.

Fast Facts on Jesus as King

The Millennium	Scripture
Those following Jesus will be rewarded in the Millennium.	Matthew 19:27–30
God is preparing rewards for the faithful.	Matthew 20:20–23

figs
Jeremiah 24:1–10

early fruit
Hosea 9:10

sign
Matthew 24:30

The Nation of Israel

MATTHEW 24:32–33 *Now learn this parable from the fig tree: When its branch has already become tender and puts forth leaves, you know that summer is near. So you also, when you see all these things, know that it is near—at the doors! (NKJV)*

The prophet Jeremiah used good <u>figs</u> to represent good Jews who had been taken captive to Babylon, and he used bad figs to represent bad Jews who had escaped the captivity. The prophet Hosea compared Israel's fathers (Abraham, Isaac, and Jacob) to the <u>early fruit</u> of a fig tree. So Israel is the Bible "fig tree." And Jesus, in effect, was saying, "Watch Israel, and when you see all these things happening, understand that the end of the age is near."

> ## what others say
>
> ### Gary Hedrick
>
> In fact, all the events in Matthew 24 center around Jerusalem. Jerusalem and Israel are the point of reference for anyone who wants to know what time it is on God's prophetic calendar. In Matthew 24, our Lord is saying, "Keep your eyes on Israel. Israel is your point of reference. Israel is the indicator. Watch the fig tree and when you see the branches begin to blossom, when you see the nation begin to come to life again, then you will know the end is approaching."[41]

The disciples asked, "What will be the <u>sign</u> of Your coming, and of the end of the age?" (Matthew 24:3 NKJV). Jesus said the sign of his coming will appear in the sky, and he said we will know the end of the age is near, right at the door, when we see the rebirth of Israel and all these other things happening.

There is much criticism of those who try to relate current events to Bible prophecy. If this practice is wrong, why did Jesus give the signs and have the Holy Spirit record them, and why did he indicate that we can watch and know when the end of the age is near? Who would not want us to watch?

Jesus said, "When you see ALL THESE THINGS" (Matthew 24:33 NKJV, emphasis mine). This tells us that we should look at the whole picture. Those who think just one earthquake, one war, one terrible disease is a sign are not looking at the complete picture. It is the increase in earthquakes, plus the increase in wars, plus the increase in terrible diseases, plus everything else that is an indicator. And the super-indicator is the fact that God would resurrect the nation of Israel just before he is ready to close out the age. Prophetically speaking, wars, earthquakes, and pestilence mean nothing without Israel. The Tribulation Period cannot begin without a seven-year treaty guaranteeing peace for Israel. The Tribulation midpoint cannot arrive without a rebuilt Jewish Temple. There will be false Christs, but not the Antichrist until Israel is in place. But the return of Israel, its sprouting and early growth after almost two thousand years, is something Jesus said God would do to give a sure sign that these things will soon be fulfilled.

Jesus gave us these signs. He wants us to understand them and to know what all of them happening at the same time means. The end of the age could not have happened until Israel came back into existence. But the rebirth of that nation has occurred and it has occurred at a time when all the other signs are on the scene. There is only one way to interpret it.

prophecy

One Generation

MATTHEW 24:34 *Assuredly, I say to you, this generation will by no means pass away till all these things take place. (NKJV)*

The end will come within one generation. But how long is that? The following are a few opinions one can expect to find when studying this bewildering subject:

1. The word *generation* comes from the Greek word *genea*, meaning "race, family, or breed"; so this prophecy means the Jews will be preserved as a distinct race until everything is fulfilled.

Prophecies of the Bible

2. The generation living on earth when Israel became a nation in 1948 will not all pass away before everything is fulfilled.

3. A generation lasts approximately twenty years because young people get married and start a new generation at about that age.

4. A generation lasts thirty-five years because Job lived <u>140 years</u> or four generations after he recovered everything.

5. A generation lasts <u>forty</u> years because one generation of Jews died during forty years of wandering in the wilderness.

6. A generation lasts <u>seventy</u> years because the normal length of life is seventy years.

7. A generation lasts anywhere from thirty to seventy years because it was <u>fourteen</u> generations (almost a thousand years) from Abraham to David, fourteen generations (a little more than four hundred years) from David to the exile in Babylon, and fourteen generations (about six hundred years) from the Babylonian exile to the birth of Jesus.

8. A generation lasts 100 years because the Hebrews spent <u>400 years</u> or four generations in Egypt.

go to

140 years
Job 42:16

forty
Numbers 32:11–13

seventy
Psalm 90:10

fourteen
Matthew 1:17

400 years
Genesis 15:13–16

If anyone can figure out how long a generation is, they will still need to figure out when the terminal generation begins. Some say May 1948 when Israel became a nation. Others say June 1967 when Israel captured the Temple Mount. There are a variety of unprovable opinions.

Everyone wants to know "How long is a generation?" There have been many efforts to figure this out, but the answer appears as elusive as the identity of the Antichrist (he cannot be identified until after the Rapture). Could it be that God deliberately made this vague to prevent us from figuring out when the Second Coming will be? We are not supposed to know the day or hour of that. The fact is, a generation depends on when it was measured. It changed depending upon where the Jews were in history and which covenant God was working under. It's best to do what Jesus said: Watch and be ready all the time.

something to ponder

There is good reason to believe that this present generation is the generation that will see the complete fulfillment of all these prophecies, but it is impossible to be dogmatic about this belief.

Like the Days of Noah

MATTHEW 24:37–39 *But as the days of Noah were, so also will the coming of the Son of Man be. For as in the days before the flood, they were eating and drinking, marrying and giving in marriage, until the day that Noah entered the ark, and did not know until the flood came and took them all away, so also will the coming of the Son of Man be. (NKJV)*

Noah was a <u>preacher</u> of **righteousness** at a time when people **scoffed** at messages from God. When Noah foretold the <u>Flood</u>, the people refused to listen. Because of this lack of interest in **spiritual things**, they lived as they pleased right up until the very day the great Flood started. That awesome day began just like every other day, but it wasn't long until it started to rain, and the floodwaters began to rise, and in a matter of days, except for Noah and his family, everyone perished.

Jesus is saying, "This is the way it will be at the end of the age. People will scoff at messages about the Tribulation Period, refuse to listen to prophecies about the Second Coming, and do as they please right up until the very last day. That day will begin like every other day with people eating, drinking, attending weddings, etc. But it will be the day their doom is sealed."

Noah and his family entered the ark, survived the Flood, and returned to the earth after the waters receded. While they were in the ark, those who were left behind on the outside were taken away by the Flood (they drowned or perished). The Rapture will occur at a time known only to God. Those who have prepared will enter the ark of heaven and survive. They will return to the earth when the Tribulation Period is over. But those who have heard the signs and ignored them will suffer a fate similar to those in Noah's day (be taken away by death or perish on or before the Second Coming). The decisions people make are very important.

preacher
2 Peter 2:5

Flood
Genesis 6:1–7:24

righteousness
justice, peace,
right doing

scoffed
ridiculed

spiritual things
things about God

go to

evil
Genesis 6:5

what others say

John Hagee

If you open your morning paper at breakfast tomorrow, you're likely to lose your appetite. Murders, rapes, kidnapping, assault, child abuse, spouse abuse, parental abuse—these are common headlines for even small town newspapers. [People] are thinking evil all the time. And just as the floodwaters caught them unaware, so the end of the earth will catch these deceived sleepers. The Messiah will come, the thread of history will snap, and those who were unprepared will be caught up in the Tribulation which is to follow.[42]

Charles Capps

In Matthew 24, Jesus refers to "Noah's day," because Noah and his family represented all of the righteous on the earth at that time. They were taken into the safety of the ark before the judgment of God was released on the earth. Notice that His emphasis is really on the fact that the wicked didn't know what was coming until after Noah had escaped to safety. Then the flood came and took the wicked away.[43]

Our generation has witnessed unparalleled spiritual apathy and ignorance. Most people are ambivalent toward what is happening on the prophetic front. This may well be the group of people that is caught completely off guard.

The Great Separation

MATTHEW 24:40–41 ***Then two men will be in the field: one will be taken and the other left. Two women will be grinding at the mill: one will be taken and the other left.*** *(NKJV)*

Many people make the mistake of thinking this is the Rapture, but it has nothing to do with that mysterious event. It is a continuation of what Jesus was saying about the Days of Noah and all those who were removed from the earth by drowning in the great Flood. Here he is telling us two men will be in the field; one will be removed for judgment and the other left. It will be that way for women also: two women will be grinding with a hand mill; one will be removed for judgment and the other left. Those who are left will help repopulate the earth during the Millennium.

Parable
Matthew 13:24–43

field
Matthew 13:38

weeds
Matthew 13:38

Throne
Revelation 20:11–15

what others say

John F. Walvoord

The context indicates that the one who is taken is taken in judgment, much like the people who perished outside the ark, as illustrated in the previous context (Matthew 24:39). Also, according to Luke 17:37, those who are taken are killed, and vultures eat their bodies. This is exactly the opposite of the Rapture.[44]

In the <u>Parable</u> of the Weeds, the <u>field</u> is the world. That parable teaches that Jesus will send his angels out at the end of the age to collect the <u>weeds</u> (wicked people) and throw them into the fiery furnace, where there will be weeping and gnashing of teeth.

God intends to remove the wicked from the earth at the end of the age so they cannot enter the Millennium. At the Second Coming they will be taken away and held for judgment before the Great White <u>Throne</u> of God.

MARK

A Sobering Word

MARK 9:42–48 *But whoever causes one of these little ones who believe in Me to stumble, it would be better for him if a millstone were hung around his neck, and he were thrown into the sea. If your hand causes you to sin, cut it off. It is better for you to enter into life maimed, rather than having two hands, to go to hell, into the fire that shall never be quenched—where*
"Their worm does not die
And the fire is not quenched."
And if your foot causes you to sin, cut it off. It is better for you to enter life lame, rather than having two feet, to be cast into hell, into the fire that shall never be quenched—where
"Their worm does not die,
And the fire is not quenched."
And if your eye causes you to sin, pluck it out. It is better for you to enter the kingdom of God with one eye, rather than having two eyes, to be cast into hell fire—where
"Their worm does not die,
And the fire is not quenched." (NKJV)

After explaining to his disciples the fact that every act of kindness toward his people will be greatly rewarded, Jesus focused on children and taught that anyone causing them to sin will be severely punished. The punishment will be so harsh, those who experience it would be better off if they had a large **millstone** tied around their neck and were cast into the sea where they would surely drown. He then taught that we should be willing to go to extremes to avoid sinning because it will be a terrible thing to be cast into the eternal <u>fire</u> of <u>hell</u> where the worms never die.

Think about who it is that is saying this. It is Jesus, the Son of God, the **Omniscient One**, the One who loves us so much he literally left heaven and willingly died a cruel death. Why do you think he warned us about the horrors of hell? Could it be that he knows what hell is like? Is it wise to ignore this?

The word *hell* is a translation of the word *Gehenna*, a form of a Hebrew word that means "Valley of <u>Hinnom</u>." This is a valley southeast of Jerusalem where, at one time, wicked Jews burned their children as sacrifices to the false gods they were worshiping. When the good king Josiah took the throne, he declared that place unclean and would not let anyone <u>sacrifice</u> their children there anymore. Then the residents of Jerusalem started dumping their garbage there, the place became infested with worms, and fires burned there day and night. In effect, Jesus is saying, "Stop sinning because you do not want to spend eternity in a place like that."

This is a warning to unbelievers about their judgment before the Great White Throne of God. All who have not accepted Jesus as their Savior will be cast into the Lake of Fire.

go to

fire
Revelation 20:11–15

hell
Matthew 5:22; 10:38

Hinnom
2 Chronicles 28:3;
Jeremiah 7:31;
32:35

sacrifice
2 Kings 23:10

millstone
a large round, flat stone (doughnut-shaped) used for grinding corn, wheat, or other grains

Omniscient One
the One who knows everything

virgin
she had never had sexual relations with a man

favor
obtained God's approval

LUKE

A King Forever

Luke 1:32–33 *He will be great, and will be called the Son of the Highest; and the Lord God will give Him the throne of His father David. And He will reign over the house of Jacob forever, and of His kingdom there will be no end.* (NKJV)

God sent the angel Gabriel to visit a **virgin** named Mary, to tell her that she had found **favor** with God, and that she had been chosen

King
1 Samuel 2:10;
Jeremiah 23:3–8;
Ezekiel 37:1–28;
Hosea 3:4–5;
Zechariah 14:9–17

**Son of the Most
High**
Son of the Supreme
God

given a throne
become a king

Jacob
the nation of Israel

to bear a very special child. The angel told her to name this special child Jesus. He said Jesus would be called the **Son of the Most High**. Jesus would be **given a throne** and would rule over the house of **Jacob**; he would rule forever.

The angel is quite clear: Jesus will have a very special Father-Son relationship with God. He will someday sit on the throne of Israel. And his rule will never end. Other kings have come and gone, but this <u>King</u> will not.

Dozens of verses of Scripture teach that Jesus is a King of kings and Lord of lords who will return to sit upon the throne of David and rule over all the earth. Christians often hear these Scriptures without realizing the full impact of what they are saying. For example:

1. Isaiah said, "For unto us a Child is born, unto us a Son is given [the first coming]; and the government will be upon His shoulder [the Second Coming]" (Isaiah 9:6–7 NKJV). He said this Son would sit upon the throne of David.

2. Micah said, "But you, Bethlehem Ephrathah, though you are little among the thousands of Judah, yet out of you shall come forth to Me the One to be Ruler in Israel" (Micah 5:2 NKJV). Like Isaiah's prophecy above, this is a double-reference prophecy referring to both the first and second comings of Jesus.

3. Zechariah said, "Rejoice greatly, O daughter of Zion! Shout, O daughter of Jerusalem! Behold, your King is coming to you; lowly and riding on a donkey, a colt, the foal of a donkey. He is just and having salvation" (Zechariah 9:9 NKJV). He said, "The Lord shall be King over all the earth" (Zechariah 14:9 NKJV).

4. The wise men asked, "Where is He who has been born King of the Jews?" (Matthew 2:2 NKJV).

5. Pilate put a sign on the cross that read "THIS IS JESUS THE KING OF THE JEWS" (Matthew 27:37 NKJV).

Legion
Mark 5:1–20

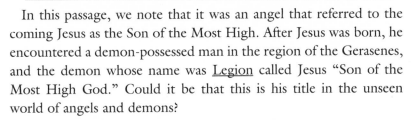

John F. Walvoord

The throne of David was a political throne, the house of Jacob encompassed the literal descendants of Jacob, and the prediction that Jesus' kingdom would never end was a repetition of the perpetuity of the Davidic kingdom.[45]

David Hocking

In 2 Samuel 7, God told David that Messiah would come out of his "body," and that God would establish his throne forever. In Psalm 132:10–11, God confirmed that He would set on David's throne the fruit of his "body." So when we say that Jesus is of the house of David, we are saying that He is the One who fulfills all the hopes of the Jewish people.[46]

In this passage, we note that it was an angel that referred to the coming Jesus as the Son of the Most High. After Jesus was born, he encountered a demon-possessed man in the region of the Gerasenes, and the demon whose name was <u>Legion</u> called Jesus "Son of the Most High God." Could it be that this is his title in the unseen world of angels and demons?

It is almost certain that Mary expected great things of Jesus, but, as great as he was, he did not completely fulfill this prophecy at his first coming. The Jews rejected him as their king and managed to have him crucified. Therefore, this must be fulfilled in the future. Almost two thousand years have passed since the angel Gabriel told Mary that Jesus would rule in Israel. For most of this time the nation did not exist and no earthly king was needed. But things have changed. Everyone knows the nation has been restored. It only remains for the King to return and take his throne.

God's church, those Gentiles who get saved after the Rapture, and those Jews who turn to Christ at the end of the Tribulation Period will enter God's kingdom here on earth. Jesus will literally rule on this earth for one thousand years. The following chart gives some insight into God's wonderful plan for his people.

Fast Facts on Jesus as King

The Millennium	Scripture
Those who practice humility and tenderness toward the weak will be great.	Luke 9:48
Those who seek the kingdom will receive it.	Luke 12:31–32

Fast Facts on Jesus as King (cont'd)

The Millennium	Scripture
Those who are faithful until the end will be rulers in the kingdom.	Luke 12:42–44
Those wanting to enter the kingdom will have to completely trust God.	Luke 18:17
Those willing to give up everything for God will receive great rewards.	Luke 18:29–30
The original disciples will occupy a special place in the kingdom.	Luke 22:29–30

Live Like His Return Is Soon

LUKE 12:45–48 *But if that servant says in his heart, "My master is delaying his coming," and begins to beat the male and female servants, and to eat and drink and be drunk, the master of that servant will come on a day when he is not looking for him, and at an hour when he is not aware, and will cut him in two and appoint him his portion with the unbelievers. And that servant who knew his master's will, and did not prepare himself or do according to his will, shall be beaten with many stripes. But he who did not know, yet committed things deserving of stripes, shall be beaten with few. For everyone to whom much is given, from him much will be required; and to whom much has been committed, of him they will ask the more. (NKJV)*

This parable deals with the attitudes of two groups of people who know the will of God, but do not believe Jesus will return anytime soon, and a third group that does not know the will of God and, therefore, is not looking for the return of Jesus. The first group is warned about abusing their authority—those who fail to look for the Lord's return and start abusing their weaker fellowmen will be caught by surprise when he returns and suffer the most terrible of fates. The second group is warned about being lazy—those who know the will of God and ignore the opportunity to serve him will be subjected to a series of harsh punishments in the life to come. The third group is composed of those who do not know the will of God—if they use the little knowledge they have to do things worthy of punishment, they will be punished and it will be a series of minor punishments in the life to come.

what others say

William Barclay

Knowledge and privilege always bring responsibility. Sin is doubly sinful to the man who knew better; failure is doubly blameworthy in the man who had every chance to do well.[47]

There are degrees or grades of punishment in the life to come. Notice that the first group will be cut in pieces and assigned a place with the unbelievers (<u>Lake of Fire</u>); the second group will be beaten with many blows; and the third group will be beaten with few blows.

Some live like they think the Second Coming will never arrive. Without question it has taken longer than most people thought, but that does not mean it will never happen. Jesus will come again and the skeptics will find themselves standing before the Great White Throne.

The soul and spirit of the believer who dies go to be with God, but the soul and spirit of the unbeliever are a different matter. He rejected Jesus, so his soul and spirit will immediately enter hell. He will be raised from the dead after the Millennium and appear for judgment before the very One he rejected. Following are three facts about that judgment.

Lake of Fire
Revelation 20:11–15

distress
Matthew 24:21–22

false Christs
Matthew 24:23

Fast Facts on the Judgment of Unbelievers

The Great White Throne	Scripture
People will be held responsible for hearing and rejecting God's Word.	Luke 8:16–18
Cities will be held responsible for hearing and rejecting God's Word.	Luke 10:10–16
Every secret sin will be exposed.	Luke 12:2–3

With Lightning Speed

LUKE 17:22–24 *Then He said to the disciples, "The days will come when you will desire to see one of the days of the Son of Man, and you will not see it. And they will say to you, 'Look here!' or 'Look there!' Do not go after them or follow them. For as the lightning that flashes out of one part under heaven shines to the other part under heaven, so also the Son of Man will be in His day." (NKJV)*

This is something Jesus said to his disciples, but the text shows that it not only applied to them, but also to those followers who will be alive at the end of the age. There will be great <u>distress</u> on earth during the Tribulation Period with people longing for the second coming of Jesus to make things better. But he will not return until the time is right. In the meantime, there will be false sightings and the appearance of <u>false Christs</u>, but they will not be credible. When

lightning
Matthew 24:27

Sodom and Gomorrah
Genesis 19:1–29

Jesus returns, it won't be to visit different sites on earth. It will be like a flash of <u>lightning</u> streaking across the sky. The return of Jesus will be without warning and the overwhelming judgments will begin in the blink of an eye. What changes can one make in the blink of an eye? Wouldn't it be wise to make things right with God beforehand and not be caught off guard? There will be no need to go here or there because the Second Coming will be as sudden as a bolt of lightning.

The first time Jesus came he spent about thirty-three years on earth. Even that was not enough time for some to recognize him and repent of their sins. He will return at the end of the Tribulation Period, and it will be so fast that there will be no need to go looking for him and no time to change anything.

Like the Days of Lot

> LUKE 17:28–30 *Likewise as it was also in the days of Lot: They ate, they drank, they bought, they sold, they planted, they built; but on the day that Lot went out of Sodom it rained fire and brimstone from heaven and destroyed them all. Even so will it be in the day when the Son of Man is revealed.* (NKJV)

When Jesus returns things on earth will be very much like they were in the days of Lot. The cities of <u>Sodom and Gomorrah</u> stood on the brink of a fiery destruction from heaven, but the people went about their daily pursuits as though nothing bad would ever happen to them. They partied, bought and sold, built houses, etc., right up to the last day of their existence, the day Lot left Sodom. On that day, fire and brimstone fell from heaven and destroyed them all.

what others say

The Pulpit Commentary

The cities are trading and feasting, and lo! the fires of heaven come down and consume them. They who trifle with the most sacred things are sure to find that, suddenly, in such an hour as they think not, the end arrives. The business plans are broken off; the brilliant career is concluded; the flow of pleasures is arrested. Death suddenly appears, and deals his fatal blow. . . . The soul awakes from its long lethargy to see that its powers have been wasted and that its chance is gone![48]

Many people act like nothing bad will ever happen to them. They refuse to let world events open their eyes. During the Tribulation Period there will be some who fancy themselves safe right up to the last day of their existence on earth. But just as surely as fire fell from heaven to destroy Sodom and Gomorrah, Jesus will return to deal with them.

Lot's wife
Genesis 19:17–26

She Needed an Attitude Adjustment

LUKE 17:32–33 *Remember Lot's wife. Whoever seeks to save his life will lose it, and whoever loses his life will preserve it. (NKJV)*

Jesus said, "No one can serve two masters; for either he will hate the one and love the other, or else he will be loyal to the one and despise the other" (Matthew 6:24 NKJV). The point is that people should develop the right attitude about God and the things of this world; to put off doing so is foolish.

Lot's wife is an example. God sent angels to get her out of Sodom before he destroyed that city with fire and brimstone. The angels told her to flee and not look back, but she did not listen; she disobeyed and lost her life when she was turned into a pillar of salt. Apparently she loved Sodom, did not want to leave it, did not want to give up her worldly goods, and did not believe God would destroy that loathsome place. So while fleeing, she hesitated, looked back, and perished—she ended up losing everything anyway.

This goes to the heart of people's attitude toward worldly things. We should always be ready to give up our possessions for the things of God. Those who seek to save their life (refuse to turn it over to Jesus) will lose it, and those who are willing to lose their life (give it up for Jesus) will save it.

what others say

Henry M. Morris with Henry M. Morris III

Christ accepted the historicity of Adam and Eve (Matthew 19:4–5), of Abel (Matthew 29:35), of Noah (Luke 17:26), of Abraham (John 8:56–58), and Lot (Luke 17:28).... He believed in the supernatural destruction of Sodom and Gomorrah (Luke 17:29) and the calamity of Lot's wife.[49]

wars
Matthew 24:6

Jerusalem
Zechariah 14:1–21;
Joel 3:9–16

Judea
the southernmost
part of Israel, it was
occupied by the
tribes of Judah and
Benjamin Petra: an
ancient city in the
mountains of Jordan

Can you give up your vehicles, your house, and all your other possessions for Jesus? During the Tribulation Period, those who want to keep everything will lose; and those who are willing to lose everything will gain. The decision should not be tough and a person should not hesitate, but many will. What will you do?

We all know that we can die on a moment's notice, but most people think they have plenty of time to prepare for that. It will not be that way during the Tribulation Period when approximately three-fourths of the world's population will die, and most of the others will be caught by the surprising return of Jesus.

There are many important doctrines in the Bible, and it is difficult to say one is more important than another because all are given by God, but the Second Coming appears to be one of the most important because it is mentioned so often and because it is tied to other teachings. For example, the return of Jesus will prevent mankind from destroying itself, Satan will be bound and chained when Jesus returns, many Jews will be saved, and many people will be raised from the dead. The chart shows that we should not take the Second Coming lightly.

Fast Facts on the Glorious Appearing of Jesus

The Second Coming	Scripture
If anyone is ashamed of Jesus, he will be ashamed of them at his coming.	Mark 8:38
Be prepared because the Second Coming will catch the lost by surprise.	Luke 12:35–40

The End Is Near

> **LUKE 21:20–22** *But when you see Jerusalem surrounded by armies, then know that its desolation is near. Then let those who are in Judea flee to the mountains, let those who are in the midst of her depart, and let not those who are in the country enter her. For these are the days of vengeance, that all things which are written may be fulfilled. (NKJV)*

Jesus talked about <u>wars</u> and rumors of wars and he said, "But the end is not yet" (Matthew 24:6 NKJV). Here he speaks of a war that will signal the approach of the end. He warned that hostile armies will encircle <u>Jerusalem</u>, that when it happens the people of **Judea** should immediately flee to the mountains (probably Petra), that the people in Jerusalem should evacuate the city, and that those in the surrounding area should stay away from there. Terrible events will follow and most of the area will be made <u>desolate</u>.

go to

desolate
Daniel 9:26

punish
Isaiah 26:19–21

nations
Ezekiel 36:1–38

Zion's
Isaiah 34:8

wrath
Micah 7:9

prophecy
Daniel 9:24

turn to Jesus
Zechariah 12:10–14

scattered
Joel 3:2

seized
Jeremiah 12:14–17

divided
Joel 3:2

Israel
Amos 9:13–15

what others say

Irvin Baxter Jr.

The pressure will build on Israel to either share Jerusalem or place it under international control. Israel will refuse. International condemnation will come against Israel because of her actions concerning Jerusalem. Finally, a resolution will be passed on the UN Security Council demanding that Israel comply to the directives of the International Community. Israel will refuse.[50]

The Tribulation Period serves several purposes:

1. To <u>punish</u> the people of the earth for their sins, for the blood shed upon the earth (war, murder, abortion, etc.)

2. To restore to Israel their land which other <u>nations</u> lay claim to

3. To uphold <u>Zion's</u> (Jerusalem's) cause, a recompense to the nations for their mistreatment of Israel

4. To allow Jews to bear the Lord's <u>wrath</u> for sinning against him

5. To fulfill <u>prophecy</u>.

6. To cause Israel to <u>turn to Jesus</u>.

The Battle of Armageddon will occur because the nations have <u>scattered</u> the Jews, <u>seized</u> land belonging to the Jews, and <u>divided</u> up the land of Israel.

God is returning the Jews to the land of <u>Israel</u>, and any nation that tries to put the Jews off the land is going against what he is doing. The Jews and the land go together. God will punish those nations that oppose what he is doing by drawing them into the Battle of Armageddon. Isn't it clear what side the United States should be on?

Israel will not be able to stand up against the superior forces of the Antichrist and his UN or world army at first. But attacking Jerusalem is a step toward the Battle of Armageddon. Just when it appears that everything is hopeless for Israel Jesus will return, the Jews will accept him as their Messiah, and you can tell the world army good-bye.

JOHN

Father
John 5:17–19

sent
John 5:30

false Christs
Matthew 24:24

How Could You Do That?

> **JOHN 5:43** *I have come in My Father's name, and you do not receive Me; if another comes in his own name, him you will receive.* (NKJV)

Jesus was talking to a group of Jews and he reminded them that, as a nation, they had rejected him. He was the Messiah and he came to them in the name of God, but they wanted to get rid of him. Someday there will be someone else who will come to them as a great leader in his own name, and the Jews as a nation will eagerly accept him. This verse does not identify that person, but virtually all prophetic writers agree that he will be the Antichrist.

The Jews have reestablished their Sanhedrin for many reasons, but one very important reason is the fact that they believe Elijah will appear before them and announce the identity of their Messiah. Christians believe this Elijah will be their own hand-picked Elijah, not the real one, and this phony will identify the wrong man.

what others say

David Reagan

But the Bible does not teach that the Jews will receive the Antichrist as their Messiah. It teaches they will accept him as a great political leader and diplomat and that they will put their trust in him as the guarantor of peace in the Middle East.[51]

Jesus came in his Father's name. He called God his <u>Father</u> and said he could do what he saw the Father do, that the Father <u>sent</u> him, and that his works were testimony to that. But the Antichrist will come to honor his own name and to boast of his own works.

Jesus warned that <u>false Christs</u> will appear and perform great signs and miracles to deceive even the very elect. The Antichrist cannot come on the scene until after the Rapture, but when he arrives the Jewish nation will love him. They will accept him as the great leader they have been looking for.

Most unbelievers do not know that Christians and non-Christians will be raised from the dead and judged at different times. Christians will be raised and judged before the Judgment Seat of Christ, and non-Christians will be raised and judged before the Great White Throne of God. The chart below provides information about the judgment of those who do not receive Jesus as their Savior.

go to

dead
Ephesians 2:1–7

death
Revelation 1:18;
2:11; 20:14–15

Fast Facts on the Judgment of Unbelievers

The Great White Throne	Scripture
Unbelievers are already under the condemnation of God.	John 3:18
The wrath of God abides on those who reject Jesus.	John 3:36
The lost will be raised from the dead and condemned forever.	John 5:28–29
Those who reject Jesus will be judged by the words he spoke.	John 12:48

second death
spiritual death,
being cast into the
Lake of Fire

The Dead Will Be Raised

JOHN 11:25–26 *Jesus said to her, "I am the resurrection and the life. He who believes in Me, though he may die, he shall live. And whoever lives and believes in Me shall never die. Do you believe this?" (NKJV)*

When a man named Lazarus became seriously ill his two sisters sent for Jesus, but he did not go immediately and Lazarus died.

Jesus finally arrived four days after Lazarus was buried, Lazarus's sister Martha was distressed. Jesus told Martha that her brother would rise again. She thought he was talking about a future resurrection. Jesus explained that she was right to believe in a future resurrection, but that was not what he was talking about. He called himself "the resurrection and the life" (John 11:25 NKJV), which means he is the One who raises the <u>dead</u>, the One who gives spiritual life and physical life. He also said the living who believe in him will never die, meaning they will never die the **second <u>death</u>**. Jesus then raised Lazarus from the dead.

> ### what others say
>
> **W. Herschel Ford**
> He was saying that those who believed in Him, even if they were dead like Lazarus, would again be brought to life.[52]

Is it possible that Jesus was also revealing the **Rapture** in these verses? In essence he said those who are dead will live again and those who are alive will never die. When Paul revealed the Rapture he said, "The dead in Christ will rise first" (1 Thessalonians 4:16 NKJV). In other words, the dead will live. Then Paul said, "We who are alive and remain shall be <u>caught up</u> together with them in the clouds to meet the Lord in the air" (1 Thessalonians 4:17 NKJV). Believers who are alive when Jesus comes for his church will go directly to heaven and not die.

There will be two future resurrections (John 5:28–29): a resurrection of life, and a resurrection of damnation. This passage not only refers to the resurrection of Lazarus, but it also refers to one phase of the resurrection of life known as the Rapture.

God's plan for the future includes a time when Satan will be bound and Jesus will reign on the earth for a thousand years. Some of what John said is in the following chart.

Fast Facts on Jesus as King

The Millennium	Scripture
There will be just one group of believers in the future.	John 10:16
Jesus was born to be a king.	John 18:37

It's the Rapture

caught up
1 Thessalonians
4:13–18

angels
Luke 16:22

alive
1 Thessalonians
4:13–18

Rapture
when the church is
removed from the
earth

JOHN 14:2–3 *In My Father's house are many mansions; if it were not so, I would have told you. I go to prepare a place for you. And if I go and prepare a place for you, I will come again and receive you to Myself; that where I am, there you may be also. (NKJV).*

Frequently read at funerals, this is one of the most beloved passages in the entire Bible. Few people associate it with the Rapture, but that is what it actually refers to.

Jesus was going away, but he promised to return to take us back with him. He is not talking about collecting us when we die. His <u>angels</u> take care of that. Rather, he is talking about returning to raise the dead in Christ and to gather those who are <u>alive</u>. This is what Christians call the Rapture.

saints
believers

Hal Lindsey

We are snatched away before we even know what hit us. We are then taken to His Father's House where He has already prepared a place for us (John 14:1–4). So the Rapture literally could occur at any moment.[53]

There is a difference between Jesus' coming for his **saints** and Jesus' coming with his saints. His coming for his saints is the Rapture (see 1 Thessalonians 4:17), and his coming with his saints is the Second Coming (see Revelation 19:11–14).

Jesus comes for his saints before the Tribulation Period, and Jesus comes with his saints at the end of the Tribulation Period. When Jesus comes for his saints (for those alive on earth) they go up to meet him in the air. When Jesus comes with his saints they come down with him to the earth.

Without question, the soul and spirit of a believer go to be with God when the Christian dies. But the day will soon come when Jesus will bring that soul and spirit back so he can raise the believer from the dead with a new body. He will receive the resurrected believer unto himself and take him or her back to heaven with him.

When Jesus comes for his saints, he will take them to heaven where they will remain until the Tribulation Period is over. While there they will appear before the Judgment Seat. The following chart indicates some of what John said about this.

Fast Facts on the Evacuation of the Saints

The Rapture	Scripture
Those who win souls for Jesus will be rewarded.	John 4:36
The saved will be raised from the dead to live forever.	John 5:28–29
Jesus will not lose any of his, and all will be raised from the dead.	John 6:39, 44, 54

ACTS

You Don't Need to Know

ACTS 1:6–7 *Therefore, when they had come together, they asked Him, saying, "Lord, will You at this time restore the kingdom*

kingdom
Luke 1:32–33

king
Jeremiah 23:3–8;
Hosea 3:4–5;
Zephaniah 3:15;
Zechariah 14:9,
16–17

watch
Matthew 24:42

Messiah
the Christ, the
coming King and
Deliverer (Jesus)

to Israel?" And He said to them, "It is not for you to know times or seasons which the Father has put in His own authority." (NKJV)

The disciples grew up with the Old Testament Scriptures. They were rightly taught that **Messiah** will return to establish a <u>kingdom</u>, that the kingdom will be centered in Israel, that Messiah will be the <u>king</u>, and that he will sit on the throne of David in Jerusalem.

The event in this passage took place after Jesus was raised from the dead. He had returned to visit his disciples and teach them, but they seemed to think he had returned to establish his earthly kingdom. They wanted to know if the time for him to do that had arrived. Jesus did not deny that the kingdom will be restored. He simply pointed out that God did not want him to reveal the time to them.

Some people criticize those who are interested in Bible prophecy. But the disciples were interested in it and Jesus did not rebuke them for that. He said, in fact, we should <u>watch</u> for his coming.

The question the disciples asked Jesus has nothing to do with signs of the Rapture, with the time of the Rapture, or with anything else about the Rapture. They asked about the earthly kingdom of Jesus. But many mistakenly think they asked about the Rapture. Actually, they probably didn't even know what the Rapture is.

We now know that God decided to establish his church and call out a people before he restores the kingdom to Israel. But after the church is raptured, and after the Tribulation Period, Jesus will return to restore a kingdom that will exist through the Millennium.

He'll Be Back

ACTS 1:9–11 *Now when He had spoken these things, while they watched, He was taken up, and a cloud received Him out of their sight. And while they looked steadfastly toward heaven as He went up, behold, two men stood by them in white apparel, who also said, "Men of Galilee, why do you stand gazing up into heaven? This same Jesus, who was taken up from you into heaven, will so come in like manner as you saw Him go into heaven." (NKJV)*

This event took place when Jesus appeared to his disciples for the last time. He walked around on earth talking to them and then suddenly he began to rise into the <u>clouds</u>. He went up and disappeared from sight. The disciples were still looking at the clouds when two **angels** said Jesus had gone to heaven. He is now seated at the right hand of God and will one day return in the same way he left. His departure was literal, bodily, and visibly. To return the same way he will have to come back literally, bodily, and visibly.

clouds
Daniel 7:13–14;
Matthew 24:30;
Revelation 1:7

> what others say
>
> **John Hagee**
> Jesus Christ, the Prince of Glory, will appear suddenly in the heavens, brilliantly, in a way that no one will be able to miss.[54]

angels
heavenly beings that
serve God, usually
messengers

Mount of Olives
a very high hill
about 3/4 mile east
of Jerusalem

Jesus was taken up into heaven in a body that his disciples could see and talk to, which means he will return in a body that people can see and talk to. This is important because some people do not believe in a bodily resurrection of the dead and some people wonder what Jesus will be like when he sits on his throne in Jerusalem. Just remember that Jesus was raised with a body, he went away with a body, and he will return with a body.

The return being referred to here is the Second Coming, not the Rapture.

Jesus was on the **Mount of Olives** (Acts 1:12; Zechariah 14:4; Matthew 24:3) with his disciples when he ascended into heaven and he will return there at his second coming. This also happens to be the same place where he taught his disciples about his second coming and the end of the age.

God's Threefold Program

ACTS 15:14–17 *Simon has declared how God at the first visited the Gentiles to take out of them a people for His name. And with this the words of the prophets agree, just as it is written:*
"After this I will return
And will rebuild the tabernacle of David, which has
*   fallen down;*
I will rebuild its ruins,
And I will set it up;
So that the rest of mankind may seek the LORD,
Even all the Gentiles who are called by My name,
Says the LORD who does all these things." (NKJV)

go to

house of David
Amos 9:11–12; 2
Samuel 7:14–17;
Luke 2:4–7

Gentiles
non-Jews

house of David
the family, lineage,
or descendants of
King David, a great
Jewish king

Church leaders had gathered in Jerusalem for a very important meeting. After much discussion, a man named James began to speak. What he said reveals God's threefold program for the future beginning almost two thousand years ago: (1) James agreed with Simon (Peter) that God is currently working among the **Gentiles** to select a group of people for himself. This select group is called the church; (2) after God has taken out his church, Jesus will return to reestablish the **house of David**. This means Jesus, a descendant of David, will come back to restore the nation of Israel and rule over it; and (3) then the remnant of Jews that is left, and all the Gentiles who call themselves Christians, will serve Christ.

> **what others say**
>
> ## J. R. Church
>
> James said Cornelius, the Roman centurion, was the first convert among Gentiles—the first of millions to come. He proclaimed that God was calling out of the Gentiles a people who would be called by His name. Then he quoted the Amos passage, which predicted the raising up of the tabernacle of David, at which time a remnant of Jews would seek after the Lord, along with all the Gentiles who are called by His name.[55]

It is important to notice that James pointed out that what Peter had said conformed to the words of the prophets. The claims of religious people should always be compared to the Scriptures. This will be especially critical when the Antichrist and his false prophets are in control.

Step one: the establishment of the church has been under way for almost two thousand years. Step two: the return of Jesus to rule over Israel is future, but it appears to be getting close because of the reestablishment of that nation. Step three: a remnant of Jews and Gentile believers will survive the Tribulation Period and repopulate the earth during the Millennium.

Some people are not interested in the Rapture, but that is when church members will be raised with a new body. It is also a prelude to the judgment of believers and the dispensing of heavenly rewards. Some of what Luke said is in the following chart.

Fast Facts on the Evacuation of the Saints

The Rapture	Scripture
Jesus will judge the living and the dead.	Acts 10:42
The resurrection of Jesus is assurance that God will judge believers.	Acts 17:31
There will be a resurrection of the just (believers).	Acts 24:15
Christians have forgiveness and an inheritance.	Acts 26:15–18

The Bible speaks of a judgment of self, a judgment of nations, a judgment of believers, a judgment of fallen angels, and a judgment of unbelievers. Two things Luke said about that are listed in the chart below.

Fast Facts on the Judgment of Unbelievers

The Great White Throne	Scripture
The resurrection of Jesus is assurance that God will judge unbelievers.	Acts 17:31
There will be a resurrection of the unjust (unbelievers).	Acts 24:15

Chapter Wrap-Up

- Matthew recorded a series of prophecies Jesus gave about the kingdom of heaven. He taught that the kingdom of heaven contains a mixture of saved and unsaved, but angels will remove the unsaved at the end of the age. He revealed many signs that can be interpreted to mean the end of the age is near if these signs are being simultaneously fulfilled. (Matthew 5:3–12; 13:24–50; 21:28–32; 24:3–41)

- Mark recorded a warning Jesus gave about causing children to sin and an exhortation he gave to go to extremes to avoid sinning. Jesus taught that it will be a terrible thing to be cast into hell. (Mark 9:42–48)

- Luke recorded what the angel Gabriel told Mary—that Jesus would be a King with a kingdom. Luke also recorded: (1) a parable Jesus told that taught we should live like the Second Coming is near; (2) a revelation of Jesus that predicts things will eventually get so bad, many will long for the Second Coming; (3) another revelation that others will live like nothing bad will ever happen to them; (4) a teaching that we should be ready to give up everything for God; and (5) a revelation that armies surrounding Jerusalem suggest all the prophecies are about to be fulfilled. (Luke 1:32–33; 12:45–48; 17:28–33; 21:20–22)

- John records Jesus' prediction that many Jews will eagerly accept the Antichrist and believers will be raised from the dead. John also tells us that Jesus is preparing places in heaven for believers. (John 5:43; 11:25–26; 14:2–3)

- In the book of Acts we learn that God wants to keep secret the time and date he has chosen for restoring the kingdom to Israel. We are also given details of Jesus' ascension into heaven and told that he will return in the same way. And we learn that God plans to include the church in the kingdom, restore the nation of Israel under Jesus, and include a remnant of Jews and Gentiles who survive the Tribulation Period. (Acts 1:6–7, 9–11; 15:14–17)

Study Questions

1. Whom does Jesus call blessed?

2. What is the name of the famous sermon Jesus preached about the end of the age and why is it called that? What does it have to do with his ascension into heaven and his second coming?

3. What connection did Jesus make between sin and hell? Name two things that will never cease to exist in hell.

4. Will there be different degrees of punishment in hell? Explain.

5. Who raises the dead, and when will Christians be raised?

Chapter Highlights:
- A Time to Reap Rewards
- A Time to Confess
- A Time of Wrath
- A Time of Trouble
- A Time for Great Things

Prophecies in the Letters

Written by the Apostle Paul

Let's Get Started

The New Testament contains twenty-seven books and there is wide agreement that the apostle Paul authored thirteen of them. Many scholars also believe Paul wrote a fourteenth, the book of Hebrews. But since this cannot be proven, the prophecies in Hebrews will be treated in the next chapter. Nine of the thirteen books accepted as Paul's are addressed to churches and four to individuals. The nine addressed to churches are placed in the Bible before the four addressed to individuals and all are organized according to length—the longest appear first in each category and the shortest appear last. The only book that seems out of order is the book of Galatians and for that we have no explanation.

The nine books addressed to churches are: Romans, 1 and 2 Corinthians, Galatians, Ephesians, Philippians, Colossians, and 1 and 2 Thessalonians. The four books addressed to individuals are: 1 and 2 Timothy, Titus, and Philemon.

go to

kindness
Romans 3:4

ROMANS

A Treasure You Don't Want

ROMANS 2:5–6 *But in accordance with your hardness and your impenitent heart you are treasuring up for yourself wrath in the day of wrath and revelation of the righteous judgment of God, who "will render to each one according to his deeds."* (NKJV)

Paul was talking about the coming judgment of God when his thoughts turned to those who reject the treasures of God: his <u>kindness</u>, tolerance, and patience. People ought to recognize the goodness of God and repent of their sins, but many will not do that. They receive his blessings daily, but will not change their wicked ways.

wrath
John 3:36;
Romans 1:18–20;
Ephesians 5:3–7;
Colossians 3:5–6

books
Revelation 20:11–15

wrath
God's firm intent to
punish sin and
sinners

When the record books are opened, they will receive a different kind of treasure. It will coincide with the evil they have done and come out of the **wrath** of God.

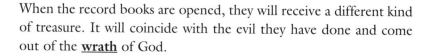

what others say

Noah Hutchings

In 1 Corinthians 3 we are informed about the treasures of the children of God which have been laid up in Heaven, but here in Romans 2:5 Paul says that the ungodly are likewise laying up treasures to be revealed in the day of wrath at the "revelation of the righteous judgment of God." From verse six we know the latter refers to the Great White Throne judgment.[1]

Dave Breese

So the fund of human iniquity and consequent divine judgment is building in a kind of cosmic bank. While this is the day of grace and God is not moving in devastating judgment, it is also the time that iniquity is being recorded in a book that will one day be opened.[2]

Those who respond to the goodness of God, repent of their sins, and accept Jesus as their Savior are storing up treasure also: rewards in heaven. What kind of treasure do you want in your account?

Judgment of Believers and Unbelievers

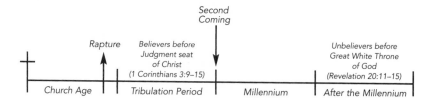

After the Millennium those who have died without accepting Jesus as their Savior will be raised from the dead and made to appear before the Great White Throne of God. The <u>books</u> will be opened and they will be judged according to what they have done. And all of them will wind up in the Lake of Fire.

The Bible clearly teaches that there is a judgment after death, but most people give little consideration to what that will be like (Hebrews 9:27). The following chart shows some of what Paul said concerning those who have not accepted Jesus as their Savior.

Fast Facts on the Judgment of Unbelievers

The Great White Throne	Scripture
People will be judged even if they do not know what the Bible says, but those who have heard the Word will be judged more severely.	Romans 2:12–13
The judgment will include secret thoughts, motivations, and intentions.	Romans 2:16

go to

wrath
Zephaniah 1:14–15

trouble and distress
Zephaniah 1:14–18;
Matthew 24:21, 29

<u>Those Who Don't Learn from History Are Doomed to Repeat It</u>

ROMANS 2:8–9 *But to those who are self-seeking and do not obey the truth, but obey unrighteousness—indignation and wrath, tribulation and anguish, on every soul of man who does evil, of the Jew first and also of the Greek. (NKJV)*

Those individuals and nations that have the wrong attitude toward God, the self-seeking ones who live to glorify themselves, and those who reject the truth of God's Word—the ones who follow sin instead of Jesus—will receive <u>wrath</u> and anger. There will be a time of <u>**trouble and distress**</u> for every human being who sins. It will begin with the Jews, but it will include the Gentiles.

trouble and distress
suffering and afflic-
tion, the Tribulation
Period

> **what others say**
>
> **Woodrow Kroll**
>
> As the gospel was promised to the Jew first and also to the Greek, so likewise the fruit of unrighteousness is of the Jew first and also of the Gentile.[3]

The power of God to save people is found in the gospel. It was given to the Jews (nation of Israel) first and then it was given to the Gentiles. And that is the way the judgment of God will fall. The nation of Israel will be first in line, but the Gentile nations will be right behind them.

The Gentile world seems to have forgotten that God allowed the Northern Kingdom of Israel to fall to the Assyrians in the eighth century BC, that he allowed the Southern Kingdom of Judah to fall to the Babylonians in the sixth century BC, and that he allowed the Romans to defeat Israel in 70 AD. Gentile nations have failed to learn lessons about how God deals with wayward countries from

go to

Isaiah
Isaiah 10:22–23

Lord Almighty
Isaiah 1:9

remnant
the few within Israel
who trust God

these historical events, so we are doomed to go through what Israel went through.

Something to Cry About

ROMANS 9:27–29 *Isaiah also cries out concerning Israel:*
"Though the number of the children of Israel be as the
sand of the sea,
The remnant will be saved.
For He will finish the work and cut it short in righteousness,
Because the LORD will make a short work upon the earth."
And as Isaiah said before:
"Unless the LORD of Sabaoth had left us a seed,
We would have become like Sodom,
And we would have been made like Gomorrah." (NKJV)

Here we have three verses and three different thoughts about Israel and the Tribulation Period:

1. In verse 27, Paul is saying that the prophet Isaiah was crying over Israel when he said even though there will be a great number of Jews, only a **remnant** will be saved. It grieved Isaiah to know that out of a very large number of Jews only a small percentage will be saved.

2. In verse 28, Paul is expressing the certainty or the determination of God to execute his judgments swiftly and completely.

3. In verse 29, Paul is saying that it will be like the prophet Isaiah said once before: "If the Lord Almighty does not intervene to save a remnant the nation will be like Sodom and Gomorrah." The startling truth here is that God will be forced to intervene to keep the entire nation from being corrupted and destroyed.

what others say

The Pulpit Commentary

Hence the relevance of the passage, not only as showing God's way of dealing with his people in times of old, but also as an intimation of how it should be when the Messiah should come.[4]

what others say

Noah Hutchings

The work will be finished during a very short time of great tribulation, and those Jews during the tribulation who come to a knowledge of the truth that Jesus Christ is the Messiah who is coming back, will be saved to enter the kingdom age. All others will be killed.[5]

Some ask, Why would God allow the world to go through the Tribulation Period? But look at what will happen if he doesn't. All Israel will be corrupted and destroyed. Is it not an act of love and grace that he refuses to let that happen?

mystery
hidden truth

The things the Bible predicts will happen to all the earth during the Tribulation Period are horrible indeed. But the awesome truth is that even worse things will happen if the world should somehow escape that terrible time. Even though the Tribulation Period will only last seven years, the percentage of Jewish survivors will be small. This will include the 144,000 sealed <u>servants</u> of God plus those who <u>flee</u> to the mountains when the Antichrist defiles the temple.

Don't Get a Big Head

ROMANS 11:25–27 *For I do not desire, brethren, that you should be ignorant of this mystery, lest you should be wise in your own opinion, that blindness in part has happened to Israel until the fullness of the Gentiles has come in. And so all Israel will be saved, as it is written:*
"The Deliverer will come out of Zion,
And He will turn away ungodliness from Jacob;
For this is My covenant with them,
When I take away their sins." (NKJV)

It is clear to Christians that Jesus is the Messiah, but unclear why most Jews—not all because the early Christians were Jews—will not accept him as their Messiah. It was a **mystery** in Paul's lifetime, but it is not one now because Paul chose to explain it. The main points are as follows:

1. "Blindness in part has happened to Israel" means part of the nation has been blinded by ignorance. The "blindness in part" is

seal
Revelation 7:3–8

two witnesses
Revelation 11:3–12

angels
Revelation 14:6

perish
Zechariah 13:7–9

flee
Matthew 24:15–22

Zion
Isaiah 59:20;
Joel 3:16–17

covenant
Isaiah 59:21;
Jeremiah 31:31–34

people
Ezekiel 36:24

remnant
the few within Israel
who trust God

Gentiles
non-Jews

not a partial or incomplete blindness in ignorance of every Jew. It is a definite blinding of most of the Jews, but no blinding of some of them. This explains why a few in every generation accept Jesus as their Messiah and how there is always a **remnant** in existence.

2. "Until the fullness of the Gentiles has come in" means the "blindness in part" is not permanent. The end of the blindness depends upon when God receives all the **Gentiles**. In other words, the "blindness in part" will continue until the church is raptured. At that point, God will <u>seal</u> the 144,000, call the <u>two witnesses</u>, and use his <u>angels</u> to evangelize the nation.

3. "All Israel will be saved" does not mean everyone who calls himself a Jew will be saved. It means everyone that God recognizes as a Jew will be saved. Think of it like this: not everyone who calls himself a Christian is a Christian by God's reckoning and, in like manner, not everyone who calls himself a Jew is a Jew by God's standards. With God it is a matter of faith and not ancestry. During the Tribulation Period most of the Jews will <u>perish</u> in the wars against Israel. But 144,000 sealed Jews, all those who obey Jesus and <u>flee</u> into the mountains when the Antichrist defiles the temple, and a few out in the country, will be saved. But obedience to Jesus is the key.

4. Verse 26 can be linked to several Old Testament passages. The deliverer is Jesus and <u>Zion</u> is Jerusalem. This means Jesus will establish his throne in Jerusalem and issue his decrees concerning Israel and the world from there.

5. Verse 27 tells us that God will remove the hardening because he made a <u>covenant</u> to take away Israel's sins. He promised to make the Jews his <u>people</u> and to be their God, and that will happen.

what others say

John F. Walvoord

The answer to the question of whether God rejects His people (v. 1) is answered by the fact that God has not rejected them but will carry out His purposes as indicated in prophecy.[6]

go to

judgment
2 Corinthians 5:10;
Matthew 12:36

bow
Isaiah 45:23

Great White Throne
Revelation 20:11–15

second advent
Second Coming

genuflect
to bend the knee in obedience or worship

God is not through with Israel. The nation and the people have a definite role to play in the future. After the Rapture, God will begin to remove the hardening. Those Jews who survive the Tribulation Period will turn to Christ at his second coming.

It's More Than a Genuflect

ROMANS 14:10–12 *But why do you judge your brother? Or why do you show contempt for your brother? For we shall all stand before the judgment seat of Christ. For it is written:*
"As I live, says the LORD,
Every knee shall bow to Me,
And every tongue shall confess to God."
So then each of us shall give account of himself to God. (NKJV)

Paul is asking why one Christian would judge or look down on another. He reminds us that we will all appear before the judgment seat of God and be required to bow down and make confession. Instead of passing judgments on others and condemning them for their failures, he is suggesting that we instead concentrate on cleaning up our own lives. This means each one of us. The judgment of Christians is not the same as the judgment of non-Christians. Christians will appear before the judgment seat of Christ. Our eternal destiny will be secure because of our faith in Christ, but our works will be judged to determine what heavenly rewards we will receive. Non-Christians will appear before the Great White Throne of God. Their eternal destiny will not be secure because they have

Lamb's Book of Life
Revelation 21:27

missionary
a person called by
God and sent by a
church to serve God

not had their name recorded in the <u>Lamb's Book of Life</u> for accepting Jesus.

Many Christians never go to the altar at church to bow in the presence of God. But when we get to heaven, we will be compelled to do so and to account for such lapses. It would be much better to start now and avoid the excuses.

God is good. He asks us to serve him and he wants us to know that he will not overlook what we do. One reason for the Rapture is to protect the church from the Tribulation Period. Another is for church members to receive the treasures they have laid up in heaven. Some of Paul's thoughts are in the following chart.

Fast Facts on the Evacuation of the Saints

The Rapture	Scripture
Following Jesus (doing good) will be rewarded with eternal life.	Romans 2:7
Glory, honor, and peace will be given to all who do good (follow Jesus).	Romans 2:10
The blood of Jesus will deliver the saved from God's wrath.	Romans 5:9
Believers who suffer for Christ will share in the glory of Christ.	Romans 8:17–18

1 CORINTHIANS

<u>The Right Stuff</u>

> 1 CORINTHIANS 3:10–13 *According to the grace of God which was given to me, as a wise master builder I have laid the foundation, and another builds on it. But let each one take heed how he builds on it. For no other foundation can anyone lay than that which is laid, which is Jesus Christ. Now if anyone builds on this foundation with gold, silver, precious stones, wood, hay, straw, each one's work will become clear; for the Day will declare it, because it will be revealed by fire; and the fire will test each one's work, of what sort it is. (NKJV)*

Paul was a **missionary** and an expert at starting and building churches. He compared what he did to building a building and warned that all buildings should be built with great care, especially spiritual buildings like the church. God laid the foundation for his church when he sent his Son, Jesus. Anyone who tries to build on any other foundation is rejecting the one God has already laid, and that will not work with God.

Anyone who builds a building must choose the kind of materials to build with—steel, brick, wood, straw—and some materials are better than others (brick is better than straw, etc.). Those who want to build a spiritual building (the church, their life) must choose between indestructible high-quality materials like gold, silver, and costly stones (sound Bible doctrines like the death, burial, and resurrection of Jesus, holy living) and destructible low-quality materials like wood, hay, and straw (unsound, feel-good, no-demand doctrines). All structures face the test of high winds, hard rains, heat, or cold. And all spiritual buildings face the day of <u>judgment</u>. These will test the quality of the builder's work.

Builders who want their buildings to stand should use the best materials. Builders of spiritual buildings who have used indestructible high-quality materials will receive a reward in heaven because what they did will survive the day of judgment. Builders of spiritual buildings who have used destructible low-quality materials will survive, but suffer great loss and have no reward.

go to

judgment
2 Corinthians 5:10

house
Luke 6:46–49

rock
1 Corinthians 10:4

what others say

Arnold G. Fruchtenbaum

If a believer is doing the will of the Lord, obeys His commandments, and fulfills the ministry for which he received his spiritual gifts, then he is building on the foundation with gold, silver, and precious stones. But where he falls short of these things, he is building wood, hay, and stubble.[9]

Jesus told a story about two men who built themselves a <u>house</u>. One man dug deep and built his house upon a <u>rock</u>. But the other man built his house on top of the ground. Later, a storm came, it rained, the river got out of its banks, and floodwaters beat vehemently upon both houses. The house built upon the rock stood. But the house built upon the ground collapsed. A giant flood cannot do much to a large rock, but it can turn the ground into mud and wash it away. Building materials are very important from the foundation to the top of the building.

Notice that the main issue is the quality of the building materials, not the quantity. A small amount of gold, silver, and costly stones will survive a fire, but a huge mansion of wood and straw will not. Some believers will receive a reward in heaven, even though they didn't build very much, because they used the right materials. Other believers will receive no reward in heaven, even though they built all their life, because they didn't use the right materials. What kind of building materials are you using?

Many people give no thought to their heavenly reward, but God wants us to build the biblical way so we can be <u>rewarded</u> fully. That which honors Jesus is worthy of a full reward; that which doesn't honor him is worthless. This principle will be very important when the believer stands before the throne on the day of judgment.

I Can't Believe You Didn't Know That

1 CORINTHIANS 6:1–4 Dare any of you, having a matter against another, go to law before the unrighteous, and not before the saints? Do you not know that the saints will judge the world? And if the world will be judged by you, are you unworthy to judge the smallest matters? Do you not know that we shall judge angels? How much more, things that pertain to this life? If then you have judgments concerning things pertaining to this life, do you appoint those who are least esteemed by the church to judge? (NKJV)

Believers are told to settle their <u>disputes</u> with each other within the church. Those who go to court against each other are often asking unbelievers to rule on their problems. More often than not, this shames the church. Knowing that some may think church members are not qualified to settle the disputes of others, Paul asks, "Don't you know that believers will judge the world, and if God trusts us to do a great task like that, don't you think believers are qualified to judge trivial matters? Don't you know that believers will judge <u>angels</u>?"

rewarded
2 John 1:8

disputes
1 Corinthians 6:1

angels
Jude 6;
2 Peter 2:4

what others say

Dave Breese

The devil, as you know, is an angel. Therefore, the devil will be a part of this group that is judged by you, and by me. . . . We will be a part of that tribunal that makes right everything that is wrong in the world.[10]

go to

authority
Revelation 2:26

reign
2 Timothy 2:12;
Revelation 20:4

what others say

Billy Graham

Is it not stranger still that angels themselves will be judged by believers who were once sinners? Such judgment, however, apparently applies only to those fallen angels who followed **Lucifer**.[11]

Believers are going to be given <u>authority</u> over the nations during the Millennium. We will <u>reign</u> with Christ, solve problems, and pass judgment on fallen angels. This may seem like an impossible task to some, but the **Holy Spirit** will help us with it.

Everyone should know that God is all-powerful, he is in control, and he intervenes in history. His judgment of Israel in the past should be clear evidence that he will judge all nations in the future. One of Paul's comments is shown in the following chart.

Fast Fact on God's Intervention in History

The Second Coming	Scripture
The tragic events in Israel's history are given to prevent others from making the same mistakes.	1 Corinthians 10:11

I Want a Real One

1 CORINTHIANS 9:24–25 *Do you not know that those who run in a race all run, but one receives the prize? Run in such a way that you may obtain it. And everyone who competes for the prize is temperate in all things. Now they do it to obtain a perishable crown, but we for an imperishable crown.* (NKJV)

Most scholars think Paul loved sporting events because he often used them to illustrate the things of God. This illustration refers to the fact that many contestants entered the Greek races, but only one came in first; also, that even though the contestants trained very hard for those races, the winner's crown of laurel leaves soon dried out. Then Paul plainly states that Christians are striving for crowns that will last forever.

go to

Rejoicing
2 Corinthians 1:14

Incorruptible Crown
a crown that lasts forever

temptation
an inward pull to do wrong

soul winners:
those who win others to Christ

Theodore H. Epp

The word "crown" implies a kingdom. A crown is not just something beautiful to look at; it speaks of a reward in connection with a kingdom. A crown is placed upon a king because he has dominion over a certain area. Christ's rewards have to do with sharing the rulership of His kingdom.[12]

Believers can win five crowns:

1. **Incorruptible Crown** for those who overcome **temptation** (1 Corinthians 9:25)

2. Crown of Rejoicing for **soul winners** (1 Thessalonians 2:19–20)

3. Crown of Life for those who give up their life for Christ (James 1:12; Revelation 2:10)

4. Crown of Righteousness for those who have longed for the Second Coming (2 Timothy 4:8)

5. Crown of Glory for faithful teachers and preachers (1 Peter 5:2–4)

apply it

Considering that believers will be given valuable rewards in heaven, isn't it wise to discipline ourselves and to use our lives to honor Jesus? Isn't it foolish to aimlessly drift through life doing things that dishonor him?

Those Christians who use their lives to serve Christ are storing up treasure in heaven. Their treasure will be given to them shortly after the rapture of the church.

Some expositors say God may have more than five crowns for his people. That may be true, but he mentions only five in the Scriptures. But the point is not how many crowns will be given out. The point is that obedience in this life will pay off in the next. More of what Paul said about God's plans is found in the following chart.

Fast Facts on the Evacuation of the Saints

go to

The Rapture	Scripture
The faithful will not be found lacking at the Rapture.	1 Corinthians 1:6–8
Rewards beyond our imagination await the faithful.	1 Corinthians 2:9
Every believer will be judged fairly and receive praise from God.	1 Corinthians 4:5
Satan can harm the flesh, but not the spirit of an unfaithful believer.	1 Corinthians 5:5
God raised Jesus from the dead and he will raise his people also.	1 Corinthians 6:14
The Lord's Supper looks to the death of Jesus and the rapture of his church.	1 Corinthians 11:26
Death entered the world by a man (Adam) and it will be removed by a man (Jesus).	1 Corinthians 15:21–22
Not everyone will die, but everyone will receive a new body.	1 Corinthians 15:51
The Rapture will take place in a split second.	1 Corinthians 15:52
Our new bodies will be immortal.	1 Corinthians 15:53

Adam
1 Corinthians 15:22

die
Genesis 3:1–19

Lord
Revelation 19:11–21

reign
Revelation 20:1–6

thousand
Revelation 20:7

Lake
Revelation 20:10

death
Revelation 20:14;
21:4

The End

1 CORINTHIANS 15:24–26 *Then comes the end, when He delivers the kingdom to God the Father, when He puts an end to all rule and all authority and power. For He must reign till He has put all enemies under His feet. The last enemy that will be destroyed is death. (NKJV)*

Because <u>Adam</u> and Eve sinned, people <u>die</u> and their bodies return to the dust. But the dead will be raised in the Rapture and taken to heaven with those believers who are alive at that time. That will be followed by the seven-year Tribulation Period and the second coming of our <u>Lord</u>. We will <u>reign</u> with him while Satan is bound for a <u>thousand</u> years during the Millennium. After the thousand years have passed, Satan will be released for a short time, but he will eventually be cast into the <u>Lake</u> of Fire. Finally, even <u>death</u> will be destroyed and it will exist no more.

The end of things on earth will come after Jesus turns the kingdom over to his Father. But that will not happen until after Jesus puts down all of our enemies. He must reign until that happens. And the last enemy to be destroyed will be death, not Satan.

go to

Damascus
Acts 9:1–19

God
Colossians 1:19–22

what others say

William Barclay

As God sent forth His Son to redeem the world so in the end God will receive back a world redeemed, and then there will be nothing in heaven or in earth outside the love and power of God.[13]

Anytime Satan is free there will be sin and death on earth. But Jesus will put an end to them all: Satan, sin, and death. Then he will turn this creation back over to God and subordinate himself to the Father.

2 CORINTHIANS

We Go, Too

2 CORINTHIANS 4:14 *Knowing that He who raised up the Lord Jesus will also raise us up with Jesus, and will present us with you. (NKJV)*

Paul knew that death was not the end of Jesus. Our Lord had been raised from the dead when he talked to Paul on the road to Damascus. So Paul was absolutely sure that the resurrection of Jesus was an accomplished fact. And because of this he was persuaded that we will be raised from the dead too and that we will be taken into the very presence of God.

what others say

The Nelson Study Bible

Paul's belief was focused upon the God of resurrection power, which motivated him to face difficulties, danger, and death for Christ's sake. Paul rested in what he knew about God, not how he felt.[14]

Multitudes are going to beat death and the grave. Following the Rapture, we will be presented holy in the sight of God, without blemish and free from accusation.

Having seen the resurrected Jesus, Paul was convinced of the resurrection of believers. He knew that life on this earth is temporary, but immortality and rewards await those who believe the gospel and receive Jesus as their Savior. The following chart is a partial list of what Paul told the Corinthian church.

Fast Facts on the Evacuation of the Saints

The Rapture	Scripture
The things on earth are temporary, but the things in heaven last forever.	2 Corinthians 4:17–18
If a believer's earthly body is destroyed, he will receive a heavenly body.	2 Corinthians 5:1–4
If a believer's spirit leaves its body, it goes to be with Jesus.	2 Corinthians 5:6–8
Every believer must go before Jesus to receive or lose rewards.	2 Corinthians 5:10
Sorrow that causes repentance leads to salvation; otherwise to judgment.	2 Corinthians 7:10
The church will be presented to Jesus as the bride of Christ.	2 Corinthians 11:2

GALATIANS

The Law of the Harvest

GALATIANS 6:7–9 *Do not be deceived, God is not mocked; for whatever a man sows, that he will also reap. For he who sows to his flesh will of the flesh reap corruption, but he who sows to the Spirit will of the Spirit reap everlasting life. And let us not grow weary while doing good, for in due season we shall reap if we do not lose heart. (NKJV)*

Every farmer knows if he sows corn, he will harvest corn; if he sows wheat, he will harvest wheat. The crop is determined by the kind of seed sown. This is an immutable law of nature. We should not deceive ourselves about life because we are unable to deceive God. If a person's life doesn't please God, then he will die without pleasing God—his harvest will be destruction. But if a person's life pleases God, then he will die pleasing God—his harvest will be eternal life. So it is with the Law of the Harvest: the one who uses all of his time, talent, and resources to satisfy himself will be destroyed;

way
John 14:6

but the one who uses some of it to do things for God will reap eternal life. Hence, we should keep sowing and be patient because there will be a harvest.

what others say

Theodore H. Epp

Galatians 6:7–9 tells us that to sow to the flesh, to use our resources to fulfill selfish personal desires, will result in spiritual decay. But to yield ourselves to the Holy Spirit in our thinking, planning, praying and believing will result in abundant living.[15]

Paul is not teaching salvation by works. The only <u>way</u> to please God with your life is to serve Christ.

A farmer cannot sow seed one day and harvest a crop the next. And the size of the harvest depends on the amount of seed sown. A good harvest takes time and lots of seed. The judgment may not be as soon as we think, and it may seem like we will never be rewarded, but it is a law that cannot be broken. Wait patiently for the Rapture and keep on sowing.

God voluntarily sent his Son, and Jesus willingly went to the cross to make it possible for sinners to find acceptance with God. The greatness of what they did has benefits in both this life and the life to come. Believers have become citizens of heaven. One of Paul's comments to the Galatians is in the following chart.

Fast Fact on the Evacuation of the Saints

The Rapture	Scripture
It is the will of God that Jesus deliver us from this world.	Galatians 1:4

Those who have truly committed their lives to Jesus discipline themselves in this life, and that shows that they have been brought into God's kingdom. Those who fail to discipline themselves in this life are just as immortal as believers, but their lives show that they will not spend immortality in God's kingdom. The following chart is a very brief list of sins that will ruin eternity for a person.

Fast Facts on the Judgment of Unbelievers

The Great White Throne	Scripture
Those who teach false doctrines will pay a terrible penalty.	Galatians 5:10
The list of sins that will send a person to hell is long.	Galatians 5:19–21

EPHESIANS

EPHESIANS 5:5–6 For this you know, that no fornicator, unclean person, nor covetous man, who is an idolater, has any inheritance in the kingdom of Christ and God. Let no one deceive you with empty words, for because of these things the wrath of God comes upon the sons of disobedience. (NKJV)

go to

hell
Matthew 5:27–30

wrath
John 3:36

judgment
Matthew 5:21–22

sin
missing the mark, wrongdoing

hell
a place of eternal punishment

empty
meaningless

A Sure Thing

Some rightly argue that **sin** in this life has its own rewards. The alcoholic often loses his job, health, and family. The drug addict often loses his money, property, health, and life. Premarital sex results in more than one million teenage American girls getting pregnant out of wedlock each year. Divorce results in 35–40 percent of America's children living in single parent homes. Crime results in American taxpayers having to shell out $10–20 billion per year. No one can deny the terrible consequences of sin in this life.

But the problem is that some wrongly say the tragic price of immorality ends for each person when they die. There are many in the world, and even many in the church, who say there is no such thing as a place called **hell**, and no such thing as the <u>wrath</u> or <u>judgment</u> of God. Their words are **empty** and should not be believed. Sin upsets God, and we can be sure that morally impure people will be excluded from the kingdom of heaven.

> ### what others say
>
> **William Barclay**
>
> The gravest disservice that any man can do to a fellow man is to make him think lightly of sin. Any teaching which belittles the horror and the terror of sin is poisonous teaching. Paul besought his converts not to be led away and deceived with those empty words which took the terror and the sting from the idea of sin.[16]
>
> **The Pulpit Commentary**
>
> Scripture tells us plainly that sins of impurity entail exclusion from "the kingdom of Christ and of God" (Ephesians 5:5); that he will judge whoremongers and adulterers (Hebrews 8:5), and that "the abominable, and murderers, and whoremongers, and sorcerers, and idolaters, and all liars, shall have their part in the lake that burneth with fire and brimstone" (Revelation 21:8).[17]

deceive
Matthew 24:11, 24

comes
Matthew 25:31–46

gave
Ephesians 2:1–2

crucified
Matthew 27:32–56

Word
John 15:3; 17:17

This does not mean a person can enter the kingdom by living a morally pure life. But it does mean that those who have truly accepted Jesus as their Savior will give up their greed and idolatry. When Christ is Lord of a person's life, it shows.

Jesus warned that false prophets will arise and <u>deceive</u> many. Those who listen to them will come under the wrath of God, be excluded from the kingdom when Jesus <u>comes</u> back, and be made to stand before the Great White Throne of God.

Anyone who takes the Bible literally and knows much about it is aware that there are some dark days ahead. But that's just a blip on God's radar, and the future is full of hope as the following chart shows.

crucified
nailed to a cross

holy
separated or set apart

Fast Fact on Jesus as King

The Millennium	Scripture
History is moving toward the reign of Jesus over all things in heaven and on earth.	Ephesians 1:10

<u>Your Past, Present, and Future</u>

EPHESIANS 5:25–27 *Husbands, love your wives, just as Christ also loved the church and gave Himself for her, that He might sanctify and cleanse her with the washing of water by the word, that He might present her to Himself a glorious church, not having spot or wrinkle or any such thing, but that she should be holy and without blemish.* (NKJV)

This passage is really a teaching about what God wants in the relationship between a husband and wife, but it also contains great truths about the past, present, and future of the church. The past event: Jesus died for the church. His life was not taken from him, he <u>gave</u> it up because he loves us. It was an unselfish sacrifice for our benefit and it was accomplished when he was **crucified**.

The present event: his **holy** church is being cleansed by the "washing of water by the word" (Ephesians 5:26 NKJV). True church members are constantly undergoing change for the better and the agent of that change is the Bible. The <u>Word</u> of God is read or proclaimed and people respond by abandoning their sins, worshiping God, and doing acts of charity.

The future event: the church will be presented to Jesus radiant—without **stain**, **wrinkle**, or **blemish**—holy and blameless. On earth the church has many flaws, but in heaven the flaws will be eliminated, the church will take on the glory of Christ, and it will be accounted blameless before God.

stain
sign of sin

wrinkle
sign of old age

blemish
scars, wounds, or imperfections

what others say

John F. Walvoord

The cleansing "by the washing with water through the Word" refers to the cleansing power of the Word of God, not to the baptismal ceremony as some have taken it. This is the basic reason for expository preaching and the study of Scripture. The goal is not simply to comprehend the truth but to apply it in its sanctifying power to the individual life.[18]

Jesus is not acting haphazardly. His ultimate goal is to redeem a people, help them change their ways, and have them presented to himself in heaven in such a way that no harm can ever come to them.

The Bible mentions many exciting events, but the Rapture may be the most exciting of all. In the blink of an eye, every believer who has died since the church began will be raised with a new body, and the body of every believer who is alive will be changed into a new immortal body. Christians have already received evidence of God's power, and there is more to come as the following chart shows.

Fast Facts on the Evacuation of the Saints

The Rapture	Scripture
The Holy Spirit is the beginning of what Christians will receive and a sign of more to come.	Ephesians 1:14
Christians have a great inheritance in the Lord.	Ephesians 1:18
Christians will be exhibits of God's grace in the ages to come.	Ephesians 2:7
The Holy Spirit is evidence of our salvation until we are presented to Jesus.	Ephesians 4:30

PHILIPPIANS

PHILIPPIANS 2:9–11 *Therefore God also has highly exalted Him and given Him the name which is above every name, that at the name of Jesus every knee should bow, of those in heaven, and of those on earth, and of those under the earth, and that every tongue should confess that Jesus Christ is Lord, to the glory of God the Father. (NKJV)*

go to

right hand
Romans 8:34;
Colossians 3:1;
Hebrews 10:12;
1 Peter 3:22

name
Matthew 1:21

Lord
Matthew 7:22–23

Lord
the One who is over
everything

The Real CEO

Paul is saying that because Jesus humbled himself and died on a cross, God honored him by giving him the highest place in the kingdom. Other Scriptures say Jesus is seated at the <u>right hand</u> of God. God has also given him a <u>name</u> greater than the name of any other being who ever lived. In fact, the time will come when every knee will bow at the mention of his name. This includes everyone in heaven (Christians, angels), everyone on earth (the Jews, others), and everyone under the earth (Satan, demons, the lost). Everyone will also confess that Jesus is **Lord**.

what others say

Oliver B. Greene

The tongue of the atheist, the tongue of the pagan, the tongue of the blasphemer, the tongue of the ungodly—ALL will one day confess that Jesus is God's Christ—to the glory of God.[19]

Billy Graham

The wicked angels would never want to call God "Father," though they may call Lucifer "father," as many Satan worshipers do. They are in revolt against God and will never voluntarily accept His sovereign lordship, except in that Day of Judgment when every knee will bow and every tongue confess that Jesus Christ is Lord.[20]

David Hocking

The greatest thing we can do as believers is praise Jesus Christ as Lord to the glory of God the Father. And when we proclaim Him as Lord, let no one misunderstand—we are proclaiming Him as the Lord Jehovah of the Old Testament, the Almighty God in human flesh![21]

Those sincere believers who confess Jesus is Lord here on earth will do it again in heaven shortly after the Rapture. Those pretenders who call him <u>Lord</u> and all those who have never called him Lord will be forced to do so at the Great White Throne judgment following the Millennium.

Believers from every generation have found hope and comfort in the teaching that death cannot hold or thwart God's plan for his people. As shown in the following chart, Paul revealed some of this to the Christians at Philippi.

Fast Facts on the Evacuation of the Saints

The Rapture	Scripture
God will complete his purpose in the life of every believer.	Philippians 1:6
Christians who spread the Word of God will not lose their reward.	Philippians 2:16
Being raised from the dead in the Rapture should be more important than anything in life.	Philippians 3:11
Christians are citizens of heaven who should wait for Jesus to return, to give them a new body, and to subdue all things.	Philippians 3:20–21

inheritance
Ephesians 1:13–14;
Colossians 1:12

God
Galatians 6:7–10

Judgment Seat of Christ
2 Corinthians 5:10

Great White Throne
Revelation 20:11–15

COLOSSIANS

You Have Inherited a Great Fortune

COLOSSIANS 3:23–25 *And whatever you do, do it heartily, as to the Lord and not to men, knowing that from the Lord you will receive the reward of the inheritance; for you serve the Lord Christ. But he who does wrong will be repaid for what he has done, and there is no partiality. (NKJV)*

This passage was addressed to Christians who were slaves in Paul's lifetime, but the teachings are still applicable to all Christians. Slaves worked long and hard for little or no pay. Inheriting anything was out of the question. Yet Paul advised them to work without grumbling or complaining, to work enthusiastically and cheerfully, to do it like they were working for the Lord instead of people. Christians know they will receive an <u>inheritance</u> from Jesus in heaven. They are his representatives here on earth, and any good is done for him. Those who wrong Christians will be repaid by <u>God</u>. They are in his hands and he will show no partiality or favoritism when he judges them.

> *what others say*
>
> **Life Application Bible Commentary**
>
> Christians work first for the Lord Jesus Christ and second for the companies that write their paychecks. No matter what the job, our first goal is serving Jesus.[22]

Christians will appear before the <u>Judgment Seat of Christ</u> and receive or lose rewards shortly after the Rapture. Non-Christians will go before the <u>Great White Throne</u> of God after the Millennium.

There are many benefits in this life for those who accept Jesus as their Savior, but some of the most important benefits include the Rapture and what follows soon after that. Christians will appear before the Judgment Seat of Christ to receive rewards in proportion to their service and faithfulness (Luke 19:11–27). Some of what Paul revealed to the Colossians can be found in the following chart.

Fast Facts on the Evacuation of the Saints

The Rapture	Scripture
The Christian's hope (rewards, eternal life) is in heaven.	Colossians 1:5
Christians are partakers in the inheritance of all who belong to Jesus.	Colossians 1:12
Christians will go before Jesus holy and free of blame.	Colossians 1:22
When Jesus returns, Christians will be raised and appear with him in glory.	Colossians 3:4

The prophecies are clear about the destinies of nations and people. They will move farther and farther from God, thus angering him and causing him to react violently. At some future point, he will rapture his church and unleash his divine judgments. Some of the sins that will trigger his judgments are shown in the following chart.

Fast Fact on the Day of God's Wrath

The Tribulation Period	Scripture
Because of sexual sins, impurity, lust, and idolatry God will send tribulation.	Colossians 3:5–6

1 THESSALONIANS

The Rapture

1 THESSALONIANS 4:13–17 *But I do not want you to be ignorant, brethren, concerning those who have fallen asleep, lest you sorrow as others who have no hope. For if we believe that Jesus died and rose again, even so God will bring with Him those who sleep in Jesus. For this we say to you by the word of the Lord, that we who are alive and remain until the coming of the Lord will by no means precede those who are asleep. For the Lord Himself will descend from heaven with a shout, with the voice of an archangel, and with the trumpet of God. And the dead in Christ will rise first. Then we who are alive and remain shall*

be caught up together with them in the clouds to meet the Lord in the air. And thus we shall always be with the Lord. (NKJV)

The Thessalonian believers seemed to think that Christians who died before the Rapture should somehow be separated from Christians alive during the Rapture. They were worried that they might not see their deceased loved ones again. This was a misunderstanding that Paul sought to clear up. He did not want them worrying about those who had died (or those who had "fallen <u>asleep</u>"); and he did not want them grieving over their loved ones like "others which have no <u>hope</u>" (the lost). He pointed out that we <u>believe</u> Jesus died and rose again, and we believe that when he returns he will bring with him the souls and spirits of believers who have died. Paul assured the Thessalonian believers that he had a direct promise from Jesus that those who are living when Jesus returns will not displace or hinder the resurrection of those who have died.

After addressing the misunderstanding, Paul gave an explanation of what will happen. He said the **Lord** will descend from heaven and give a very loud command. His voice will sound like the voice of an **archangel**. The <u>trumpet</u> of God will sound and the dead in Christ will rise first. This will include every Christian that has died since the beginning of Christianity. After that, all Christians who have not yet died, the ones who are alive at the time the dead are raised—will be **caught up** with the resurrected believers to join Jesus in the air.

go to

asleep
John 11:1–16

hope
Ephesians 2:12

believe
Romans 10:9–13

trumpet
1 Corinthians 15:52

Lord
Jesus

archangel
a leader or angel of the highest rank

caught up
raptured

Resurrection/Rapture Timeline

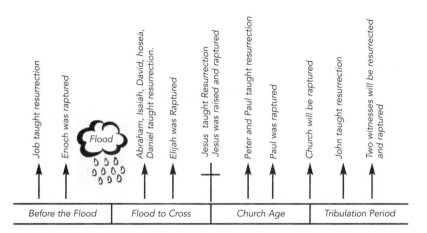

| Before the Flood | Flood to Cross | Church Age | Tribulation Period |

Job taught resurrection · Enoch was raptured · Flood · Abraham, Isaiah, David, hosea, Daniel taught resurrection. · Elijah was Raptured · Jesus taught Resurrection / Jesus was raised and raptured · Peter and Paul taught resurrection · Paul was raptured · Church will be raptured · John taught resurrection · Two witnesses will be resurrected and raptured

what others say

Charles Capps

The "trump of God" in 1 Thessalonians 4:16 and Revelation 4:1 is not the same as the seventh angelic trumpet mentioned in Revelation 11:15. The trumpet of the seventh angel signals a series of events which will take place over several days. The trump of God signals an event which will take place in the twinkling of an eye. So they can't be the same.[23]

Norbert Lieth

[This passage] isn't referring to a general resurrection. Only the dead in Christ and those who are alive in Christ will be raised or transformed. All the other dead will remain in their graves until the day of judgment.[24]

Dave Breese

The Rapture is important for many things, but its chief importance is that it marks the end of the epoch of grace and the beginning of the dispensation of the Tribulation.[25]

key point

Do not confuse the Rapture with the Second Coming. Jesus comes FOR his church at the Rapture. He comes WITH his church at the Second Coming. The Rapture will take place BEFORE the Tribulation Period. And the Second Coming will take place AFTER the Tribulation Period.

The word *Rapture* is not in the English translations of the Bible, but the concept is. The original New Testament text was written in the Greek language and it used the Greek word *harpazo*. When the Greek was translated into Latin, *harpazo* became *rapere*. When the Latin was translated into English, *rapere* could not be translated into just one word. The combination of words used was "caught up." But the word *rapere* has been Anglicized into the word *Rapture* and this is the word most Christians now use. People shouldn't expect to find foreign words in the English translation of the Bible. Also, they shouldn't expect to find words in the Bible that didn't exist in 1611 when the King James Version was printed. Furthermore, the fact that a word is not in the Bible doesn't mean something doesn't exist. The word *Bible* is not in the Bible, but the Bible exists. The word *Iran* is not in the Bible, but Iran exists. One simply needs to look under Persia to find out what the Bible says about Iran. That is because Persia changed its name in 1935.

Apart from the grace of God none of us would make it to heaven. But the age of grace will be over when the Rapture occurs. Wouldn't it be wise to accept the grace of God before he completes his church and turns back to Israel and the Law?

There are no specific signs of the Rapture. The Bible teaches that it can happen at any time and without any advance notice. However, we do know about many things that will happen after the Rapture and there are signs that all those things are approaching. Therefore, we know that the Rapture is getting close.

Keep Your Eyes Peeled

1 THESSALONIANS 5:1–9 *But concerning the times and the seasons, brethren, you have no need that I should write to you. For you yourselves know perfectly that the day of the Lord so comes as a thief in the night. For when they say, "Peace and safety!" then sudden destruction comes upon them, as labor pains upon a pregnant woman. And they shall not escape. But you, brethren, are not in darkness, so that this Day should overtake you as a thief. You are all sons of light and sons of the day. We are not of the night nor of darkness. Therefore let us not sleep, as others do, but let us watch and be sober. For those who sleep, sleep at night, and those who get drunk are drunk at night. But let us who are of the day be sober, putting on the breastplate of faith and love, and as a helmet the hope of salvation. For God did not appoint us to wrath, but to obtain salvation through our Lord Jesus Christ. (NKJV)*

This passage addresses the question, When will the **day of the Lord** take place? We are told that we do not need an answer because we already have it. "The day of the Lord will come like a thief in the night." This means it will come unexpectedly.

Notice what the people will be saying when the day of the Lord arrives: "Peace and safety!" (1 Thessalonians 5:3 NKJV). The peace movement will be very strong and the seven-year <u>covenant</u> signed by the Antichrist with many to protect Israel will create a false sense of peace and safety in the world. It will be like it was in Jeremiah's day when people said they had peace, but there was no <u>peace</u>.

Notice also two things about what will happen to unbelievers when the day of the Lord arrives: (1) destruction will come suddenly

covenant
Daniel 9:24–27

peace
Jeremiah 6:14; 8:11

day of the Lord
the Tribulation
Period

go to

darkness
Joel 2:2;
Amos 5:18–20

light
John 12:36

wrath
Zephaniah 1:14–16;
1 Thessalonians 1:10

blood
Romans 5:8–9

asleep
Matthew 25:1–13

awake
Revelation 16:15

watching
Luke 12:37

approaching
Hebrews 10:25

coming
2 Peter 3:3–4

hope
Titus 2:13

upon them, the unbelievers who are proclaiming peace and safety; and (2) they, the unbelievers, will not escape.

Notice four things about believers: (1) believers will not be caught by surprise. They know the signs. They are watching and will not be caught off guard; (2) believers do not belong to the darkness. The day of the Lord is a day of darkness. Believers are children of light; (3) believers are not appointed to suffer wrath. Not one drop of floodwater fell on Noah. Not one spark of fire and brimstone fell on Lot. And not one iota of wrath will fall on believers; and (4) believers are appointed to receive salvation. The blood of Jesus does this.

Finally, notice four things about how believers should react: (1) believers should not fall asleep. All of our life many of us have heard the Second Coming is near. We have heard it so much it would be easy for us to fall asleep. But we should stay awake; (2) believers should watch. Some are critical of Christians who study the prophetic signs, but Jesus wants us to be watching. The Bible says we can see the day approaching; (3) believers should be alert and self-controlled. Some go overboard one way, selling everything, and sitting down to wait on his coming. Others go overboard the other way and scoff at the idea of his coming again. Both attitudes are errant. We should stay busy and never scoff because it will happen when God is ready; and (4) believers should put on faith, love, and hope. Faith comes from hearing the Word. Lovingly anticipating his appearing will be rewarded with a crown of righteousness. And the Second Coming is our hope.

Many Christians know absolutely nothing about Bible prophecy. Others who are faithful study it, but they come to different conclusions. Some reasons to believe in the Pre-Trib Rapture appear in the following chart.

Should We Believe in the Pre-Trib Rapture?

Characteristics of Pre-Trib Rapture	Scripture
The Tribulation Period comes as a thief in the night, but it will not catch the brethren as a thief in the night.	2 Peter 3:10
The Tribulation Period is a day of darkness, but the brethren are not in darkness.	Zephaniah 1:15
The Tribulation Period is a day of wrath, but the brethren are not appointed unto wrath.	Zephaniah 1:15
The Tribulation Period is a day of destruction, but destruction comes upon them (not us).	Joel 1:15

Because peace negotiations have been going on for many years, some do not realize the significance of what is happening. This is because they do not understand that the negotiations are going through stages. Most of the current agreements are just steps toward a final settlement. The important thing now is the fact that negotiations have now reached the final stage and a comprehensive agreement is on the horizon.

Peace negotiations in the Middle East have now reached a fever pitch. Experts say it is just a matter of time until a comprehensive agreement is signed. This is the kind of situation that will prevail when the Tribulation Period arrives. But the Rapture will occur first.

A very small minority of Christians believe in a partial Rapture. They say the most spiritual Christians will be taken first, and the lukewarm or shallow Christians will be left behind to grow and become more mature or spiritually prepared. Pre-Tribulation believers reject this as works salvation and a division of the body of Christ. More of what Paul told the Church at Thessalonica about the Rapture is shown in the following chart.

killed
Revelation 13:10

angels
Mark 8:38

Lake of Fire
Revelation 20:11–15

Fast Facts on the Evacuation of the Saints

The Rapture	Scripture
Jesus rescues Christians from God's forthcoming wrath.	1 Thessalonians 1:10
Saved souls are the joy of Christains.	1 Thessalonians 2:19–20

2 THESSALONIANS

Trouble for Trouble

2 THESSALONIANS 1:6–10 Since it is a righteous thing with God to repay with tribulation those who trouble you, and to give you who are troubled rest with us when the Lord Jesus is revealed from heaven with His mighty angels, in flaming fire taking vengeance on those who do not know God, and on those who do not obey the gospel of our Lord Jesus Christ. These shall be punished with everlasting destruction from the presence of the Lord and from the glory of His power, when He comes, in that Day, to be glorified in His saints and to be admired among all those who believe, because our testimony among you was believed. (NKJV)

The wicked understand practically nothing about the nature of God. He is a God who judges sin and all his judgments are just. If he acted unjustly in any way, he would sin, but he is holy and cannot do that. So his very nature requires him to send trouble upon those who trouble his people. If someone enslaves his people during the Tribulation Period, they will be enslaved. If someone kills his people, they will be <u>killed</u>.

It is also the nature of God to give relief to his people. He will do this when he comes in judgment at the end of the Tribulation Period. His powerful <u>angels</u> will be with him to gather those who have afflicted his people and bind them for judgment. Jesus will pour out his divine anger upon them: (1) because they did not take the opportunity to know God, and (2) because they refused to obey the gospel. These will be people who heard the gospel but refused to respond.

The result of the Lord's divine anger will be horrible for the lost: "These shall be punished with everlasting destruction" (2 Thessalonians 1:9 NKJV), which means they will be cast into the <u>Lake of Fire</u>. They will also be shut out "from the presence of the Lord"

(1:9 NKJV), which means they will be expelled from his kingdom. And they will be shut out "from the glory of His power" (1:9 NKJV), which means they will be banished from the source of all good things.

Victory will come when he returns to display his church at the end of the Tribulation Period. Then people will marvel at what he has done for his followers.

Some Christians teach that the church will convert the world and then Jesus will come back, but the Bible teaches that the Second Coming is necessary before most of the evil is done away with. The following chart provides insight into this.

Reasons for the Second Coming of Christ

Reason	Reference
To prevent from destroying everyone.	Matthew 24:22
To capture the Antichrist and False Prophet.	Revelation 19:20–21
To gather and return all believing Jews to Israel.	Matthew 24:31
To remove unbelievers from the earth.	Matthew 25:31–46
To capture, bind, and chain Satan.	Revelation 20:1–3
To raise Old Testament and Tribulation Period Saints.	Daniel 12:2; Revelation 20:4
To establish his kingdom on earth.	Revelation 20:4–6

what others say

Billy Graham

For the Christian believer, the return of Christ is comforting, for at last men and women of faith will be exonerated. They will be avenged. The nonbeliever will see and understand why true Christians marched to the sound of another drum. But for the sinful unbeliever, the triumphant return of Christ will prove disastrous, because Christ's return ensures final judgment.[29]

Everlasting destruction does not mean total annihilation or ceasing to exist. It means being cast into the Lake of Fire and being cut off from the goodness of God forever.

Terrible calamities await all who harm those who turn to God after the Rapture. The wicked will receive affliction for affliction, misery for misery, woe for woe. Those who harm God's people will be repaid at the Second Coming.

Do Not Be Deceived

rebellion
apostasy

man doomed to destruction
the Antichrist

2 THESSALONIANS 2:1–12 *Now, brethren, concerning the coming of our Lord Jesus Christ and our gathering together to Him, we ask you, not to be soon shaken in mind or troubled, either by spirit or by word or by letter, as if from us, as though the day of Christ had come. Let no one deceive you by any means; for that Day will not come unless the falling away comes first, and the man of sin is revealed, the son of perdition, who opposes and exalts himself above all that is called God or that is worshiped, so that he sits as God in the temple of God, showing himself that he is God. Do you not remember that when I was still with you I told you these things? And now you know what is restraining, that he may be revealed in his own time. For the mystery of lawlessness is already at work; only He who now restrains will do so until He is taken out of the way. And then the lawless one will be revealed, whom the Lord will consume with the breath of His mouth and destroy with the brightness of His coming. The coming of the lawless one is according to the working of Satan, with all power, signs, and lying wonders, and with all unrighteous deception among those who perish, because they did not receive the love of the truth, that they might be saved. And for this reason God will send them strong delusion, that they should believe the lie, that they all may be condemned who did not believe the truth but had pleasure in unrighteousness.* (NKJV)

This passage was written to correct several mistaken beliefs that cropped up in the early Thessalonian church. Apparently someone created an erroneous document or report, falsely attributed it to Paul, and circulated it among the believers there. Some church members thought it was true and wrongly believed Jesus had already come to rapture his church, that they had somehow missed this great gathering in the sky, that the Antichrist had already arrived, and that they had entered the Tribulation Period.

Paul warned them not to become alarmed and not to let anyone deceive them about these things. He pointed out that there will be a great rebellion against God before the Tribulation Period arrives. This **rebellion** will precede the Tribulation Period and pave the way for the appearance of the **man doomed to destruction**.

One of the things this wicked man (the Antichrist) will do is to think he is greater than everything that is worshiped. He will go to the temple and announce that he is God. Daniel called this terrible act "<u>the abomination of desolation</u>" and Jesus himself spoke of it. From what they said it is obvious that this will take place at the Tribulation Period midpoint and it implies that the temple in Jerusalem will be rebuilt. When the Jews see this, many of them will <u>flee</u> into the mountains.

Paul reminded the Thessalonians that he told them all these things when he was with them. He rebuked them because they had been taught and should not have allowed themselves to be so easily led astray. He reminded them that they knew what is holding the Antichrist back, and that it is being done to prevent this wicked man from being revealed before God's appointed time.

Paul assured the Thessalonians that the **secret power of lawlessness** was already with them and working among them, but that the Antichrist himself will continue to be held back. Hence the power of rebellion is working in the world, but it is partially restrained and it will remain partially restrained until the Holy Spirit is taken out of the way. This will happen when the church is raptured. The indwelling presence of the Holy Spirit in the church is helping to check the great rebellion and also preventing the appearance of the Antichrist.

After the church is raptured, and the Holy Spirit is removed with it, God will let the Antichrist be revealed. He will rule until Jesus returns at his second coming to <u>capture</u> and destroy him. Jesus will do this to the Antichrist because the Antichrist's reign will be brought about by the work of Satan. The Antichrist will use the power of Satan to perform many kinds of counterfeit miracles, signs, and wonders, and to do all kinds of evil things to deceive people. Multitudes will perish because they will not listen to the Word of God when they are exposed to it, and they refuse to be saved while they have the opportunity. God will make sure they are deceived by the Antichrist to punish them for not listening and being saved. He will judge them for rejecting the truth about his Son and for enjoying their life of sin.

Most Christians have loved ones who are not saved and it troubles them to hear that their loved ones will be deceived after the Rapture. But the Jews were blinded because they refused to believe the Scriptures about the first coming of Jesus (Luke 19:41–44), the Lord spoke in parables so those who rejected the gospel would not understand what he was saying (Matthew 13:10–17), he refused to

the abomination of desolation
Daniel 9:27;
Matthew 24:15

flee
Matthew 24:16

capture
Revelation 19:19–20

secret power of lawlessness
power of rebellion, the spirit of the Antichrist

Prophecies in the Letters Written by the Apostle Paul — 253

give a sign to the unbelieving Pharisees and Sadducees except for the sign of Jonah (Matthew 16:1–4), he said the way is narrow and difficult (Matthew 7:13–14), he said the lukewarm will be vomited out (Revelation 3:14–22), and Paul said he spoke God's wisdom in a mystery so only those in a right relationship with God could understand it (1 Corinthians 2:7).

Some expositors disagree with the statement that this "falling away" (v. 3) is rebellion against God. The first seven English translations of the Bible (Wickliffe, Tyndale, Coverdale, Cranmer, Breeches, Beza, and Geneva) read that there will be a "departing" before the Tribulation Period arrives. For many years, most authorities believed Paul was talking about a physical departure or Pre-Trib Rapture, but a minority believed he was talking about a spiritual departure or a departing from the faith. When the King James Version came out it read "falling away," and most authorities started saying it means falling away from the faith or rebellion against God. It really doesn't change much. Both views are consistent with the other teachings of the Bible.

what others say

Dave Hunt

These apostates, however, will not leave the church and announce themselves as atheists. They will not convert to Buddhism or Hinduism. While there are always some exceptions, it is important to understand that the apostasy doesn't represent a massive defection from Christianity but a turning away from the truth within the professing church.[30]

Dave Breese

Here Paul introduces a character that will be of consequence during the days of the Tribulation. And what does he call him? The great benefactor of mankind? No. The "man of sin" will be revealed, the man whose fundamental nature is sin. He is the embodiment of sin.[31]

Bill Perkins

God currently allows a delicate balance of good and evil in the universe. . . . For every depraved act, there is a righteous deed. As evil builds upon evil, Christianity builds on the Rock. Both evil and good are increasing proportionately on the scales until the day when God removes the counterweight, leaving evil no restraint.[32]

The great rebellion has begun and the Rapture will soon follow. Then there will be two supernatural comings: the first will be the Antichrist and the second will be Jesus. The Antichrist will appear at the beginning of the Tribulation Period and Jesus will appear at the end. In between these two comings will be a seven-year period of great evil, great deception, and great death. When the temple will be rebuilt is unknown, but most scholars think it will be after the Rapture and all agree that it will be before the Tribulation Period midpoint.

1 TIMOTHY

The Dark Side

1 TIMOTHY 4:1–4 Now the Spirit expressly says that in latter times some will depart from the faith, giving heed to deceiving spirits and doctrines of demons, speaking lies in hypocrisy, having their own conscience seared with a hot iron, forbidding to marry, and commanding to abstain from foods which God created to be received with thanksgiving by those who believe and know the truth. For every creature of God is good, and nothing is to be refused if it is received with thanksgiving. (NKJV)

There is general agreement that these verses refer to the **Church Age** and especially to the latter part of it leading up to the Rapture. <u>Rebellion</u> against God will increase as the Rapture nears.

<u>Persecution</u> and deceit will also increase. The <u>love</u> of many will grow cold. Some will depart from what they once professed to believe and follow other religions. They will be in touch with wandering evil <u>spirits</u> from the sanctuaries of Satan and they will be listening to doctrines taught by demons. These demonic doctrines will come through hypocritical liars, religious pretenders, false preachers, counterfeit Christians, and the like who will not be grieved by what they do. They will be able to speak demonic doctrines and lies without remorse. Marriage is ordained by God and he created meat to feed his people, but these deluded people will forbid marriage and the <u>eating</u> of animals.

rebellion
2 Thessalonians 2:3

persecution
Matthew 24:9–11

love
Matthew 24:12

spirits
1 John 4:1–3

eating
Colossians 2:16

Church Age
the time the true church is on earth before the Rapture

go to

spiritual forces of evil
Ephesians 6:12

latter times
the last days of the
"times of the
Gentiles"

what others say

Billy Graham

Demonic activity and Satan worship are on the increase in all parts of the world.[33]

Noah Hutchings

We look over the world today and see the rise of spiritualism, astrology, ESP, mediums talking with the dead, ministers holding seances, devil worship, witchcraft, etc., and we know that we must be living in the **latter times**. Never has there been such a worldwide revival of spiritualism, even in the Dark Ages.[34]

Mike Gendron

Our Marching Orders:

- Keep away from every brother who does not live according to apostolic teaching. (2 Thessalonians 3:6)

- Do not associate with anyone who does not obey Paul's instruction (so they will be ashamed). (2 Thessalonians 3:14–15)

- Avoid those who oppose sound doctrine. (Romans 16:17)

- Withdraw from those who advocate a different doctrine. (1 Timothy 6:3–5)

- Be sanctified (set apart) by the truth. (John 17:17)

- Do not be yoked with unbelievers. (1 Corinthians 6:14–17)

- Expose false teachers. (Ephesians 5:11; Revelation 2:2)[35]

When the Sadducees asked Jesus a ridiculous question about marriage, he told them the angels do not marry. And here we have a teaching that demonic spirits will lure people into forbidding marriage in the latter times. Is it possible that the <u>spiritual forces of evil</u> in the heavenly realm are trying to enforce their laws on human beings?

Interest in the occult is at an all-time high around the world. Pagan religions are promoted under the guise of protecting the environment. Contacting spirits of the dead is no longer taboo and in some circles it is viewed as an act of enlightenment. Cohabitation is common and there are many who wrongly advocate and practice vegetarianism in the name of Christianity. Many of those involved in these things are religious people and some are associated with the church.

The Bible speaks of sins of omission, sins of commission, and sins of ignorance (Leviticus 4:2). Some people may not know they sin, but they are still responsible. God is just, and he may consider their sin less heinous, but his holiness still requires him to deal with it. When people discover that they have sinned they need to deal with it. See the following chart for more information.

Fast Facts on the Judgment of Unbelievers

The Great White Throne	Scripture
Some sins are obvious; others become evident only with time.	1 Timothy 5:24

God calls and empowers his people to do works of faith. Those who obey will be greatly rewarded after the Rapture. Some of the things revealed in Paul's two letters to Timothy are shown in the following chart.

Fast Facts on the Evacuation of the Saints

The Rapture	Scripture
Good deeds are obvious, but those that are not cannot be hidden.	1 Timothy 5:25
Christians have a command that must be kept until the Rapture.	1 Timothy 6:11–14
Living or dead, Christians will be judged by Jesus at the Rapture.	2 Timothy 4:1
A crown of righteousness will be given to those who long for his appearing.	2 Timothy 4:8
Christians will be delivered from evil in this world and transferred safely to heaven.	2 Timothy 4:18
The hope of Christians is the appearance of Jesus in glory to rapture his church.	Titus 2:13

2 TIMOTHY

Rough Times

2 TIMOTHY 3:1–5 *But know this, that in the last days perilous times will come: For men will be lovers of themselves, lovers of money, boasters, proud, blasphemers, disobedient to parents,*

go to

proclaim
2 Thessalonians 2:4

great wealth
Revelation 18:17

boastfully
Daniel 7:8

proud
Daniel 13:5

blasphemers
Revelation 13:5–6

children
Mark 13:12

stand
Daniel 8:25

holy
Daniel 8:24;
Matthew 24:15

forbid marriage
1 Timothy 4:3

love
Matthew 24:12

conqueror
Revelation 6:2

slander
Revelation 13:5–6

desires
2 Timothy 3:6

unthankful, unholy, unloving, unforgiving, slanderers, without self-control, brutal, despisers of good, traitors, headstrong, haughty, lovers of pleasure rather than lovers of God, having a form of godliness but denying its power. And from such people turn away! (NKJV)

Here Paul offers a partial list of things we can expect in the last days of the Church Age. Evil will prevail and characteristics of the Antichrist will be apparent. Those influenced by the Antichrist will be:

1. Lovers of themselves—the Antichrist will <u>proclaim</u> himself to be God.

2. Lovers of money—world leaders will weep over the loss of their <u>great wealth</u> during the Tribulation Period.

3. Boasters—the Antichrist will speak <u>boastfully</u>.

4. Proud—the Antichrist will utter <u>proud</u> words.

5. <u>Blasphemers</u>—the Antichrist will blaspheme God, God's name, God's church, and all those in heaven.

6. Disobedient to their parents—<u>children</u> will rebel against their parents and have them put to death.

7. Unthankful—Jesus died for the sins of the world, but the Antichrist will take his <u>stand</u> against Christ.

8. Unholy—the Antichrist will kill <u>holy</u> people and defile the holy place with his image.

9. Unloving—the false church will <u>forbid marriage</u>, and the <u>love</u> of many will grow cold.

10. Unforgiving—the Antichrist will be a <u>conqueror</u> bent on conquest.

11. Slanderers—the Antichrist will <u>slander</u> the name of God.

12. Without self-control—people will be swayed by evil <u>desires</u> especially sexual desires.

13. Brutal—the Antichrist will have believers <u>beheaded</u> during the Tribulation Period.

14. Despisers of good—church leaders should love what is <u>good</u>, hold fast to the message of God and teach sound doctrine, but it will not be so in the last days of the Church Age.

15. Traitors—the Antichrist will be a liar, breaking his <u>covenant</u> to protect Israel.

16. Headstrong—the Antichrist will change <u>set times</u> and laws.

17. Haughty—the Antichrist will <u>magnify</u> himself.

18. Lovers of pleasure more than lovers of God—<u>sexual immorality</u> will be a major Tribulation Period sin.

19. Having a form of godliness but denying its power—the Antichrist will be a <u>false Christ</u>.

The **spirit of antichrist** is to be against the things of Christ. Notice how this "spirit" and the things the Antichrist himself will do break the Ten Commandments:

1. No other god should be placed before God, but the Antichrist will exalt himself above every god.

2. Idols are forbidden, but the Antichrist will place an image of himself at the temple.

3. God's name should not be taken in vain, but the Antichrist will call himself God and pretend to be the Christ.

4. The Sabbath day should be kept holy, but the Antichrist will try to change times (the Sabbath) and seasons.

5. People should honor their father and mother, but children will be disobedient to parents, and the Antichrist will show no regard for the gods of his fathers.

6. People should not murder, but the Antichrist will kill the saints.

beheaded
Revelation 20:4

good
Titus 1:6–9

covenant
Daniel 9:27

set times
Daniel 7:25

magnify
Daniel 11:36

sexual immorality
Revelation 9:21

false Christ
Matthew 24:5, 23–24

spirit of antichrist
any inclination to oppose Christ or be against the things of Christ

theft
Revelation 9:21

7. People should not commit adultery, but sexual immorality will be a major sin when the Antichrist reigns.

8. People should not steal, but <u>theft</u> will be a major sin when the Antichrist reigns.

9. False testimony is forbidden, but the Antichrist will be a slanderer.

10. Coveting is forbidden, but people will be lovers of money.

Some say there is no need for church members to watch for signs because none have been given to the church. This is not true. The church has been told that the spirit of antichrist will prevail and actually pave the way for the arrival of the "man of sin." The current disrespect for the Ten Commandments is a good indication that this is happening.

The Church Age began with the first Pentecost following the death of Jesus, and it will end with the rapture of the church. During this time multitudes will be saved, but apostasy will be a major problem as the end of the age draws near. This is shown in the following chart.

Fast Fact on the Present Age

The Church Age	Scripture
The time will come when church members will not listen to sound doctrine.	2 Timothy 4:3–4

The time is coming when the reign of Jesus will be universal and the governments of this world will submit to him. It will be a time of justice, peace, and righteousness. Some of what Paul revealed to Timothy is in the following chart.

Fast Facts on Jesus as King

The Millennium	Scripture
If we endure we will reign with him, but if we disown him, he will disown us.	2 Timothy 2:12
When the Millennium begins, Jesus will judge those who turned to him during the Tribulation Period.	2 Timothy 4:1

Chapter Wrap-Up

- Paul advised the Galatians to please the Holy Spirit because "whatever a man sows, that he will also reap" (Galatians 6:7 NKJV). He advised the Corinthians to build on Jesus with sound doctrines and holy living, etc., because the believers' works will be tested and rewards will be passed out for works that last. He also advised the Corinthians to run life's race to win because believers who win will be rewarded with a crown. He advised the Colossians to work with all their heart because believers will receive an inheritance from Jesus as a reward. (Galatians 6:7–9; 1 Corinthians 3:10–15; 1 Corinthians 9:24–25; Colossians 3:23–25)

- Paul advised the Romans not to judge others because they too will be judged and they will have to account to God. He told the Philippians that God has exalted Jesus—every knee will bow and every tongue will confess that he is Lord. (Romans 14:10–12; Philippians 2:9–11)

- Paul said those who reject God's goodness are storing up wrath. All who are self-seeking, who reject the truth and follow evil will receive wrath and anger. The Day of Wrath will come like a thief in the night for those who are not watching for the return of Jesus. When he comes back those who do not know God and do not obey the Gospel will be punished. (Romans 2:5–6, 8–9; 1 Thessalonians 5:1–9; 2 Thessalonians 1:6–10)

- Paul said many who falsely claim to be Christians will abandon the faith and follow deceiving spirits near the end of the Church Age. Terrible times will come and the spirit of antichrist will prevail. This great rebellion will pave the way for the wicked Antichrist, who will visit the temple in Jerusalem and claim to be God. Many will be deceived by his miracles and signs, and they will perish because they refused to love the truth and be saved. We can be sure that the immoral, the impure, and the greedy will not inherit the kingdom of Christ. (1 Timothy 4:1–3; 2 Timothy 3:1–5; 2 Thessalonians 2:1–12; Ephesians 5:5–6)

- A time will come when the dead in Christ will be raised and all living believers will be raptured; when the church will be presented to Christ and be found holy and blameless; when the hearts of the Jews will no longer be hardened and the nation will be saved; when Christians will judge the world and angels; when all of God's enemies will be destroyed, including death. (1 Thessalonians 4:13–18; Ephesians 5:25–27; Romans 11:25–27; 1 Corinthians 15:24–26; 1 Corinthians 15:24–26)

Study Questions

1. When God judges the lost what will he go by?

2. When will the partial blinding of Jewish hearts cease? What part of Israel will be saved?

3. How is building in the church with gold, silver, and costly stones different from building with wood, hay, and straw?

4. Name five things that will take place at the Rapture.

5. Will the day of the Lord catch everyone as a thief in the night? Explain.

Prophecies in the Letters
Written by Other Apostles

Chapter Highlights:
- The New Covenant
- Hoarding Wealth
- Eyewitnesses
- Scoffers and Fallen Angels

Let's Get Started

Following the thirteen New Testament books written by the **apostle** Paul is a series of eight books written by other apostles. These books are sometimes called general **epistles** because they are not directed to a particular person, such as Timothy or Titus, and they are not directed to a particular congregation, such as the one at Corinth or the one at Ephesus. The book of Hebrews is addressed to all Jews who convert to Christianity regardless of where they attend church. And the other seven books are addressed to the **church** as a whole, not to specific individuals or congregations.

The subject matter is primarily Christian doctrine, but the authors make many appeals for obedience and faithful service. And they include tidbits of prophetic information not found anywhere else in the Bible. God wanted these things included so we dare not neglect them.

apostle
one who is sent out, specifically applied to the twelve disciples, Paul, and other New Testament missionaries

epistles
New Testament letters written by apostles

church
the followers of Jesus Christ, as opposed to a building where people meet to worship

what others say

Larry Richards

Others wrote letters to some of the first century churches, and these are usually called the "general epistles." They include writings of Peter and John, who were apostles, and Jesus' half-brothers James and Jude, who were leaders in the church. They also include the book of Hebrews.[1]

HEBREWS

Out with the Old and In with the New

HEBREWS 8:7–13 *For if that first covenant had been faultless, then no place would have been sought for a second. Because finding fault with them, He says: "Behold, the days are coming, says the LORD, when I will make a new covenant with the house of Israel and with the house of Judah—not according to the*

go to

new covenant
Jeremiah 31:31–34

Hebrews
another name for
the Israelites, the
Jews

Law
all the rules God
gave to Moses

grace
the undeserved
favor of God

key point

covenant that I made with their fathers in the day when I took them by the hand to lead them out of the land of Egypt; because they did not continue in My covenant, and I disregarded them, says the LORD. For this is the covenant that I will make with the house of Israel after those days, says the LORD: I will put My laws in their mind and write them on their hearts; and I will be their God, and they shall be My people. None of them shall teach his neighbor, and none his brother, saying, 'Know the LORD,' for all shall know Me, from the least of them to the greatest of them. For I will be merciful to their unrighteousness, and their sins and their lawless deeds I will remember no more." In that He says, "A new covenant," He has made the first obsolete. Now what is becoming obsolete and growing old is ready to vanish away. (NKJV)

There were problems with the old covenant God made with Israel when Moses led the **Hebrews** out of Egypt. That covenant was temporary in the sense that it did not permanently deal with sin. It required people to keep the **Law**, but they kept breaking it, causing God to find fault with them. So he promised a new covenant with Israel and Judah. This new covenant will not be like the old covenant, the covenant of Law, because the Jews' ancestors failed to keep that one and God finally canceled it. It will be a new covenant, the covenant of **grace**, written not on tablets of stone like the Ten Commandments, but placed in the minds and written on the hearts of people, giving them a new intimate relationship with God. This inward relationship will mean the Jews will not need priests, such as Aaron was in the wilderness, to teach them because everyone will have a built-in knowledge of God. And this new covenant will be better because God will permanently forgive the people's sins. By calling this a new covenant, God is saying the old covenant made with the Jews is obsolete. Those Jews who accept Christ should go by the new one, not the old one.

what others say

John F. Walvoord

The details of the covenant relate primarily to Israel's future in the millennial kingdom. At that time Israel will experience spiritual revival. The knowledge of Christ will be universal, as Christ will be dwelling bodily on earth.[2]

Irving L. Jensen

These promises were better in two respects. First, while the promises of the old covenant pertained mainly to the present life, being promises of length of days, prosperity and national privileges, the promises of the new covenant are principally for spiritual blessings, and they pertain not only to this life but also to the life to come. Second, the promises of the new covenant are not conditional upon man's works, but upon Christ's death. In the old covenant God said, "If ye will." In the new covenant He says, "I will."[3]

People who do not follow God's laws need to have their hearts changed. The indwelling presence of Christ does that. The person who receives Christ has a built-in desire to obey God. Could it be that the reason the Jews failed so often is that they did not have a desire to obey in their heart?

This will be exactly what the writer to the Hebrews says it will be: a new covenant with Israel. The Jews who accept Christ now are under the same covenant of grace the church is under. And, in the future, the entire nation will be brought under this covenant. The Law of Moses has been superseded by grace.

At the Second Coming, the church will return to earth with Jesus, the deceased Jewish saints and Tribulation saints will be raised from the dead, the saved Jews and Gentiles on earth will enter the Millennium with them, Satan will be bound, and Jesus will begin his Millennial reign on earth as King of kings and Lord of lords. Other facts are shown in the following chart.

Fast Facts on Jesus as King

The Millennium	Reference
Jesus is God and he will rule in righteousness forever.	Hebrews 1:8
The Jews who accept Jesus will enter the Millennium.	Hebrews 4:6
There will be a Sabbath-rest for the people of God.	Hebrews 4:9
God will make a new covenant with Israel.	Hebrews 10:16–17

It's easy to find people who do not believe in a literal resurrection and Rapture. Not watching is as old as the Pharisees and Sadducees, who paid more attention to the weather than they did to the signs of the times in Jesus' day. The following chart shows that those who watch will be rewarded.

Fast Fact on the Evacuation of the Saints

The Rapture	Scripture
Those who look for Jesus will see him in the Rapture.	Hebrews 9:28

Large numbers of people mistakenly believe they will have the opportunity to be saved after the Rapture and all through the Tribulation Period. They don't realize that their rejection of Jesus now means they will be counted with the enemies of God when our Lord returns. Notice the Scripture in the following chart.

Fast Fact on the Glorious Appearing of Jesus

The Second Coming	Scripture
God will destroy all the enemies of Jesus.	Hebrews 11:13

At his last Passover, which Jesus turned into the Lord's Supper, he took the cup and said it is the New Testament (or New Covenant) in his blood that is shed for others. The New Covenant clearly includes the church, but some expositors wrongly believe it excludes Israel. However, it was made with Israel first (Jeremiah 31:31–33; Ezekiel 20:37; 37:26), and the following chart shows that saved Israel will be brought back under it during the Millennium.

Fast Facts on the Inclusion of Israel in God's Covenants

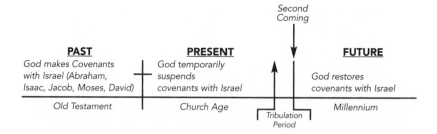

JAMES

<u>Raise Your Right Hand and Repeat After Me</u>

JAMES 5:1–3 *Come now, you rich, weep and howl for your miseries that are coming upon you! Your riches are corrupted, and* *your garments are moth-eaten. Your gold and silver are corroded, and their corrosion will be a witness against you and will eat your flesh like fire. You have heaped up treasure in the last days.* (NKJV)

rich
Revelation 18:1–24

gains
Matthew 16:26

Everyone who has money would do well to listen to this scathing rebuke of the rich. God is not against people having money, but he is against people permitting money to interfere with their relationship with him. Here he tells the <u>rich</u> who hoard wealth for the last days to cry because misery awaits them. When he says, "Your riches are corrupted" (James 5:2 NKJV), he means the time will come when it will be worthless. Even good clothes and precious metals will be worthless. When the Tribulation Period arrives one's riches will be worthless, and when the judgment comes one's riches could very well be evidence that they did not give to the poor, evidence of greed and selfishness, evidence that will cause the awesome judgment of God to fall on them.

what others say

William Barclay

Now the point is that gold and silver do not actually rust; so James in the most vivid way is warning men that even the most precious and even the most apparently indestructible things are doomed to decay and to dissolution. The rust is a proof of the impermanence and the ultimate valuelessness of all earthly things.[4]

Life Application Bible Commentary

Their hoarding will not only demonstrate their wrong priorities, it will also show how their actions deprived the needy of help and resources that could have been given. James has already pointed out that "judgment without mercy will be shown to anyone who has not been merciful" (2:13).[5]

In the last days, people will hoard gold and silver, stocks and bonds, food, and other things in an effort to provide a safety net for themselves during hard times. But the riches they so dearly trust in will become a snare because ultimately only those who trust in God will be safe. Jesus asked, "What good will it be for a man if he <u>gains</u> the whole world, yet forfeits his soul?"

something to ponder

go to

treasures
Matthew 6:19

theft
Revelation 9:21

gold
Revelation 18:11–14

wages
Revelation 6:5–6

It will be useless to hoard <u>treasures</u> during the Tribulation Period. <u>Theft</u> will be a major problem. People will stop buying <u>gold</u>, silver, and fine clothes. A day's <u>wages</u> will not buy enough food. And one's works, not wealth, will be the basis of judgment when the books are opened at the Great White Throne. With the Second Coming looming on the horizon, one would be wise to use his wealth to help the poor and to give to those doing the work of God. The comforts of this world will be short-lived, but the rewards for sharing will last forever.

The decisions people make are very important. Those who don't ask Christ to be their sin bearer will be raised in the resurrection of the lost and have their sins fully exposed. Some of what James said is in the following chart.

Fast Facts on the Judgment of Unbelievers

The Great White Throne	Scripture
Evil desires produce sin, and sin will lead to the second death.	James 1:15
The person who breaks just one Commandment is guilty of breaking all the laws of God.	James 2:10
God will not be merciful to those who have not shown mercy.	James 2:12–13

God wants his people to serve and worship him in spirit and in truth. Those who do will participate in his coming kingdom on earth as the following chart shows.

Fast Fact on Jesus as King

The Millennium	Scripture
Believers who have humbled themselves before God, shown faith, and loved him will inherit the kingdom.	James 2:5

<u>Waiting for a Harvest</u>

JAMES 5:7–9 *Therefore be patient, brethren, until the coming of the Lord. See how the farmer waits for the precious fruit of the earth, waiting patiently for it until it receives the early and latter rain. You also be patient. Establish your hearts, for the coming of the Lord is at hand. Do not grumble against one another, brethren, lest you be condemned. Behold, the Judge is standing at the door!* (NKJV)

Every Christian should have patience. When the Bible talks about patience, it usually refers to being patient with people. But here it means being patient about the Rapture. James asks us to consider how the Jewish farmer waits on the land to produce a valuable crop. He sows his crop in the fall and waits for the autumn rain to make the seed sprout. He works long and hard to tend the crop and waits for the spring rain to provide moisture for the grain to fill out. James says this is the kind of patience and endurance that is needed for the Rapture, and he advises Christians to settle their differences because Jesus will return and we will be judged. It takes a long time for seed to sprout and produce a crop, but it happens. Likewise, Jesus will return.

what others say

Theodore H. Epp

On my desk at work I have a sign which reminds me of this. It says, "Perhaps today." On my desk at home I have a sign which reminds me of this. It says, "Watch and pray." We need reminders to keep our attention focused on the possibility that Christ can come back at any time. Concentrating on this blessed hope will do many things for our attitudes, faithfulness, actions and reactions.[6]

The Pulpit Commentary

Think, he says, of the long-suffering of the farmer. His is a life of arduous toils and of anxious delays. He must wait for the "early rain" in the late autumn before he can sow his seed; and for the "latter rain" in April, upon which his crops depend for the filling of the ear before the harvest ripens. This patience is necessary. Although sometimes sorely tried, it is reasonable. The "fruit" which the farmer desires is "precious"; it is worth waiting for.[7]

The concept of the imminent return of Christ should impact our lives. It should motivate those who are living in sin to abandon their sin. It should motivate Christians to settle disputes, pray, and do good works. Is the nearness of his return and the approaching judgment affecting you?

The farmer cannot plant a crop one day and harvest it the next. He must be patient, allowing nature to do its work. Then he receives a valuable reward. In like manner, Christians cannot expect to be

go to

Father
2 Corinthians 1:3;
Ephesians 1:3

Son
Luke 1:26–38

Trinity
a word not found in
the Bible, refers to
the idea that God
exists in three ways:
as God the Father,
as God the Son,
and as God the
Holy Spirit

saved today and raptured to heaven tomorrow. We must be patient, have hope, and let Jesus prepare the way. Then he will return and we will receive the treasures we have hoped for.

Jesus said over and over again to watch for his any-moment return. Some people have been watching all their lives, and a few are ready to give up. The following chart shows that the faithful will be rewarded.

Fast Facts on the Evacuation of the Saints

The Rapture	Scripture
The Christian who perseveres under trial will receive a crown of life.	James 1:12
The person who chooses to keep God's commandments will be blessed.	James 1:25

1 PETER

Something to Rejoice About

1 PETER 1:3–7 *Blessed be the God and Father of our Lord Jesus Christ, who according to His abundant mercy has begotten us again to a living hope through the resurrection of Jesus Christ from the dead, to an inheritance incorruptible and undefiled and that does not fade away, reserved in heaven for you, who are kept by the power of God through faith for salvation ready to be revealed in the last time. In this you greatly rejoice, though now for a little while, if need be, you have been grieved by various trials, that the genuineness of your faith, being much more precious than gold that perishes, though it is tested by fire, may be found to praise, honor, and glory at the revelation of Jesus Christ. (NKJV)*

Peter prepares Jewish and Gentile believers for triumph over suffering by emphasizing seven key truths of Christianity:

1. *"The God and __Father__ of our Lord Jesus Christ"* (1 Peter 1:3 NKJV) is a phrase the apostle Paul used also. It reveals that God holds the position of Father in the **Trinity** and Jesus holds the position of Son.

2. *"According to His abundant mercy"* (1 Peter 1:3 NKJV) refers to

the fact that we cannot save ourselves, raise ourselves from the dead, take ourselves to heaven, but these things will happen because God decided to have mercy on us.

go to

born again
John 3:1–21

temporary
2 Corinthians
4:16–18

3. *"Has begotten us again to a living hope"* (1 Peter 1:3 NKJV) is something Jesus taught when he told Nicodemus he must be <u>born again</u> if he wanted to see the kingdom of God. Among other things it means God changes lives and allows people to start over again.

4. *"Hope through the resurrection of Jesus"* (1 Peter 1:3 NKJV) means we have proof that God can raise the dead and reason to believe he will raise us.

rescued
raptured

5. *"Inheritance"* (1 Peter 1:4 NKJV) refers to eternal life in heaven, a place that can never be defiled, damaged, or destroyed.

6. *"Kept by the power of God"* (1 Peter 1:5 NKJV) means no matter what happens to us in this life, God has provided a way to protect us in the future.

7. *"Salvation ready to be revealed in the last time"* (1 Peter 1:5 NKJV) means he has provided a way to rescue Christians from the time of judgment. We will be **rescued** before the Tribulation Period and protected from judgment at the Great White Throne.

According to Peter, Christians should rejoice for three main reasons: (1) the grief in our trials of life is only <u>temporary</u>. The hardships will be done away with, giving us much to look forward to; (2) the trials of life are God's way of testing us. He does not permit them out of a desire to hurt us. He permits them because they will help us grow as Christians and bring more praise to him; and (3) the trials of life will make us stronger, equip us to endure even greater hardships, and prepare us to meet Christ at his coming.

key point

The new birth is something God does for everyone who sincerely accepts Jesus as their Savior. The Holy Spirit works in people's lives to bring about changes according to the will of God. The "born again" person develops a new character, a desire to please God, a new set of priorities and values, and hope for the future. Experience the new birth and you will be brought into the kingdom of God.

Death delivers all Christians from the hardships and dangers of this world. And the Rapture will deliver living Christians from the great-

distress
Matthew 24:21–22

est period of <u>distress</u> the world has ever known. All the signs indicate that this deliverance is near.

When Jesus "catches up" his church, it will move from earth to heaven, and each member will appear before the Judgment seat of Christ. Believers should maximize their commitment and prepare for rewards. Some of what Peter said is in the following chart.

Fast Facts on the Evacuation of the Saints

The Rapture	Scripture
Believers should prepare for the grace to be given when Christ raptures the church.	1 Peter 1:13
All believers will be judged.	1 Peter 4:5
Jesus can return at any moment so believers should be self-controlled and clear-minded and should pray.	1 Peter 4:7
The Holy Spirit rests on believers who suffer for Christ; they will receive a future inheritance.	1 Peter 4:13–14
Believers will be judged first, but unbelievers will suffer more.	1 Peter 4:17
Believers will share in the glory of Christ at the Rapture.	1 Peter 5:1
Believers who remain faithful under trial will receive a crown of glory when Christ returns.	1 Peter 5:4

After the Millennium, all those who have refused to accept Jesus as their Savior, dead or alive, small or great, in hell, on earth, or under the earth will appear before the Great White Throne of God for a judgment of their works. There will be degrees of punishment, but no salvation for any of these. The following chart below that Peter confirmed this.

Fast Fact on the Judgment of Unbelievers

The Great White Throne	Scripture
All unbelievers will be judged.	1 Peter 4:5

2 PETER

We Saw It with Our Own Eyes

2 PETER 1:16–19 *For we did not follow cunningly devised fables when we made known to you the power and coming of our Lord Jesus Christ, but were eyewitnesses of His majesty. For He received from God the Father honor and glory when such a voice came to Him from the Excellent Glory: "This is My beloved Son,*

in whom I am well pleased." And we heard this voice which came from heaven when we were with Him on the holy mountain. And so we have the prophetic word confirmed, which you do well to heed as a light that shines in a dark place, until the day dawns and the morning star rises in your hearts. (NKJV)

Here Peter declares that he and the apostles did not invent stories about the second coming of Jesus. He states that he and the apostles were eyewitnesses to what Jesus will be like when he returns in glory. He was referring to the appearance of Jesus when he was **transfigured** on the mountain. But they not only saw this, they heard God honor and glorify Jesus by speaking from heaven about his love for his Son. Peter continued by reminding us that we not only have the **apostolic** assurances of the Second Coming, we also have the assurances of the prophets. In fact, we have so much evidence, we would be wise to heed these things until the day Jesus returns. He is the <u>Light</u> of the world, the bright Morning Star (Revelation 2:28; 22:16).

go to

transfigured
Matthew 17:1–13

Light
John 8:12

transfigured
his appearance was drastically changed

apostolic
from the apostles

what others say

Life Application Bible Commentary

Thus all that the apostles taught and wrote, even regarding the awesome power of Christ and the promise of his second coming, was grounded in experience and fact, without embellishment or speculation. The believers must always remember that the truth they received was truth indeed, passed on by those who had lived with and learned from Jesus.[8]

The transfiguration of Jesus gave the disciples a brief glimpse into the future. It was God's way of providing them with information about the Second Coming so they could pass it on to the world and assure us it will happen. It is evidence that what the prophets said is true. People would be wise to pay attention. Those who live for God will receive a rich welcome into his kingdom (2 Peter 1:11).

"Where Is He?"

2 PETER 3:3–4 *Knowing this first: that scoffers will come in the last days, walking according to their own lusts, and saying, "Where is the promise of His coming? For since the fathers fell asleep, all things continue as they were from the beginning of creation."* (NKJV)

go to

scoffing
Jude 18

"Knowing this first" (2 Peter 3:3 NKJV) means this is a high-priority item. It may not seem very important, but it is. The last days of the Church Age will be characterized by people mocking the doctrine of the second coming of Christ. Their apostasy will generate from evil desires and come in the form of a <u>scoffing</u> question: Why hasn't Jesus returned like he promised? Then they will pretend to prove that he will not return with a ridiculous argument. Nothing, they will say, has changed since the beginning of the earth.

> **what others say**
>
> **Dave Hunt**
>
> The apostasy involves claiming that revival rather than the Rapture is imminent and denying that apostasy must come. Again, these days are upon us, and we need not quote the many Christian leaders who ridicule belief in the Rapture, calling it an escape theory. Their books and tapes are readily available.[9]

Here is one reason why Jesus has not already returned. Peter said, "But, beloved, do not forget this one thing, that with the Lord one day is as a thousand years, and a thousand years as one day. The Lord is not slack concerning His promise, as some count slackness, but is longsuffering toward us, not willing that any should perish but that all should come to repentance" (2 Peter 3:8–9 NKJV).

Both the Old and the New Testaments repeat the promise of the Second Coming over and over again. At one time, all the major denominations accepted it, believed it, and preached it. But many will not even talk about it today. What does this tell us about the signs of the times?

Apostate teachers have taken over many of our religious institutions. They are denying not only the virgin birth, the inerrancy of the Scriptures, and other long-held beliefs, but also the once esteemed doctrine of the Second Coming. If they do not die first, many of these apostates will be the beginning of the false church that will be so prevalent during the first half of the Tribulation Period.

Dozens of prophetic signs indicate that the Tribulation Period is drawing near, but man's attempt to ignore or discredit Bible prophecy is one of the most prominent. Many pulpits are occupied by people who choose to deny the absolutes of the Bible. Some of the fruit of their ministry is shown in the following chart.

Fast Fact on the Day of God's Wrath

The Tribulation Period	Scripture
False prophets and teachers will lead many astray and they will be punished.	2 Peter 2:1–10

Like ravening wolves, the enemies of God will infiltrate the people of God to lead people astray, but distorting the Scriptures will not prevent the future judgment. Following God through Jesus is the only safe path, as the following chart shows.

Fast Facts on the Judgment of Unbelievers

The Great White Throne	Scripture
God knows how to hold the unrighteous for judgment.	2 Peter 2:9
Severe punishment is reserved for the wicked.	2 Peter 2:17

Three Worlds

The World That Was	This Present World	The World to Come
Changed at the Flood	Changed at the Second Coming	Renewed

1 JOHN

Like Him

> 1 JOHN 3:2 *Beloved, now we are children of God; and it has not yet been revealed what we shall be, but we know that when He is revealed, we shall be like Him, for we shall see Him as He is.* (NKJV)

We have three great truths here. The first is that believers already are the children of God. We do not hope to be saved or hope to go to heaven. We can **dogmatically** declare that we are saved and we are going to heaven. We have what some call a "know so" salvation. This is true because God said it.

The second great truth is that "it has not yet been revealed what we shall be" (1 John 3:2 NKJV). People ask, Will I look like a teenager in heaven, an older person, or what? The answer is, this is something God has not yet revealed so we do not know. We probably wouldn't understand it even if he did.

come down
1 Thessalonians
4:13–18

body
Philippians 3:21

locked
John 20:19–28

ate
Luke 24:36–43

heaven
Acts 1:4–11

The third great truth is that we will be like the glorified Christ when he returns. He will <u>come down</u> from heaven, raise the dead believers, and transform every believer's body into a glorious <u>body</u> like his. This is something we cannot explain, but we know it will be wonderful.

Following the resurrection of Jesus, he suddenly appeared inside a <u>locked</u> room and showed the disciples his hands and side. On another occasion, he appeared and <u>ate</u> with them. And on yet another occasion, he gave them some instructions and then ascended into <u>heaven</u>. What it means to "be like Him" (1 John 3:2 NKJV) is a mystery, but it sure sounds exciting.

Believers are the children of God right now, but new bodies are needed before we can be like Christ. We will receive them when the church is raptured.

Christians have a special relationship with Jesus. He is the Head of the church, and it is his body or bride. He sacrificed his blood for the church and has entered into the Holy of Holies in heaven to make intercession for it. Christians have nothing to fear when the church is raptured. Some of John's teachings are in the following chart.

Fast Facts on the Evacuation of the Saints

The Rapture	Scripture
The faithful will not be ashamed when they stand before Christ at his coming.	1 John 2:28
Because believers demonstrate the love of Christ, they will not be afraid at the judgment.	1 John 4:17
Every believer should strive for a full reward.	2 John 1:8

Abyss
Revelation 9:1–11

judge
1 Corinthians 6:3

Evidence of a nearing Tribulation Period can be seen in a growing opposition to Jesus and his teachings. Instead of interpreting Scripture in light of Scripture, the emphasis will be put on inclusiveness and pluralism. The following chart indicates some of this.

Fast Facts on the Day of God's Wrath

The Tribulation Period	Scripture
Believers will know the last days have arrived because of the opposition to Christ.	1 John 2:18
False prophets and teachers will arise and deny that Jesus came from God.	1 John 4:3

JUDE

An Interesting Day in Court

JUDE 6 *And the angels who did not keep their proper domain, but left their own abode, He has reserved in everlasting chains under darkness for the judgment of the great day. (NKJV)*

Many people are concerned about the future of humankind. Satan and his fallen angels are winning spiritual battles all over the planet and some worry that they will win the war. But the Bible teaches that they will be defeated, judged, and stripped of their power forever. It even teaches that some have already been locked in a dark dungeon called the <u>Abyss</u> and that the time will come when believers will <u>judge</u> them.

> what others say
>
> **The Southwest Radio Church**
>
> The angels who left their estate in Heaven knew the God who created them. They knowingly and willingly made a choice to follow Satan; therefore, there is no redemption for fallen angels.[12]

go to

angels
2 Peter 2:4

deceiving
1 Timothy 4:1

Fire
Matthew 25:41

subterranean
beneath the earth's
surface

Abyss
a deep pit where
demons are kept

Imagine this: It will be spookier than walking through a haunted house at night. No horror film can do it justice. You will be in a courtroom when one of the grossest, most evil demons of the underworld is brought before you to be judged. You will face him and declare his fate.

There seems to be two classes of fallen <u>angels</u>. The worst have been locked in a **subterranean** dungeon called the **Abyss**. Those not so bad are roaming loose on earth <u>deceiving</u> people and causing great harm. Believers will judge these angels during the Millennium and have them cast into the Lake of <u>Fire</u>.

The end of the matter is this, Jesus will come back when he gets ready, and nothing can stop it. The following chart shows it will happen, and man's failure to understand that he is God will be dealt with.

Fast Facts on the Glorious Appearing of Jesus

The Second Coming	Scripture
Jesus will return with thousands upon thousands of saints.	Jude 14
The ungodly will be judged for wrongdoing and speaking against Jesus.	Jude 15

Spiritually corrupt pastors and leaders create their own doctrines and impose them upon the church. As shown in the following chart, the Scriptures spell out in no uncertain terms what will happen to these unfaithful servants.

Fast Facts on the Judgment of Unbelievers

The Great White Throne	Scripture
The apostates will be thrown into hell.	Jude 13

Chapter Wrap-Up

- The old covenant of Law has been replaced with a new covenant of grace. This new covenant will be instilled in the minds and hearts of God's people. And it will be better because it will be accompanied by forgiveness of sins. (Hebrews 8:7–13)

- Some will hoard wealth for the last days, reap misery for doing so, and in the end find that their wealth is worthless. This will be presented as evidence of greed and selfishness at their judgment. (James 5:1–3)

- Patience is required of those looking for the Rapture. They will receive mercy, hope, and an inheritance, be shielded by God, escape the Tribulation Period, and be protected from the Great White Throne judgment. And most amazingly, we will be like Christ. (James 5:7–9; 1 John 3:2)

- The second coming of Christ is not a fable. Jesus performed a miracle on the Mount of Transfiguration to reveal the Second Coming to the disciples. They were eyewitnesses to something the Old Testament prophets predicted long before. (2 Peter 1:16–19)

- People will mock the doctrine of the Second Coming in the last days and use ridiculous arguments in an effort to prove it won't happen. Following the Second Coming believers will judge the fallen angels. (2 Peter 3:3–4; Jude 6)

Study Questions

1. How is the new covenant different from the old covenant?

2. Is the accumulation of wealth wrong? What is it about hoarding wealth that will make people miserable in the last days?

3. What warning is given to Christians who grumble against each other? What has the mercy of God done for believers? Who will we be like when the Rapture occurs?

4. What supernatural event underlies Peter's teaching about the Second Coming? Explain.

5. What foolish argument will scoffers set forth in the last days? What does the judgment of fallen angels imply?

Prophecies in the Book of Revelation

Let's Get Started

Now we come to one of the most awesome books in the entire Bible: the book of Revelation. The word *revelation* comes from a Greek word meaning "uncovering" or "disclosing." This book contains information about the future, beginning nearly two thousand years ago, that Jesus disclosed to his disciple <u>John</u>. It is attracting widespread interest today because the daily newspapers are filled with articles that seem to indicate the end of the age is drawing near. If these truly are "signs," and it looks like they are, the world is on the brink of terrible **calamities**. People need to know these things and be prepared.

One thing that is rarely noted in commentaries on the book of Revelation is the grace of God, which is prevalent all through the book. Here are some examples:

John
Revelation 1:1

revelation
an uncovering of something hidden

calamities
war, disasters, etc.

1. The Rapture is before the Tribulation Period.

2. The Tribulation Period lasts seven years, but the Millennium is a thousand years.

3. The Four Horsemen of the Apocalypse can't race forward until Jesus permits it.

4. Jesus returns to keep the world from destroying itself.

5. Satan, the Antichrist, and the False Prophet are cast into the Lake of Fire.

6. The gospel goes worldwide, multitudes are saved, and the false religion is destroyed.

7. Jesus wins and the earth will be restored.

Church History Before It Happens

the big picture

Revelation 2–3

Jesus dictated letters to seven different churches in Asia Minor. Looking back on history, we now realize he had good reason for picking these seven particular churches and for writing to them in the order he did. It turns out that the good and bad things about these seven churches and the problems they faced coincide with church history. In other words, these seven letters reveal seven phases or eras in church history.

There are many ways to interpret the seven letters to the seven churches. Some say they represent seven different spiritual conditions that existed in the churches (see Illustration #5) of John's day. Others say they are messages to individuals of all ages, and still others say they are messages to the church as a whole. Actually, it seems that all of the above are true, and since the entire book of Revelation is a book of prophecy, it also appears to be true that they represent prophecies about seven eras or phases in the Church Age.

The book of Revelation is a prophecy (Revelation 1:3), and the seven letters provide a panoramic view of church history from the first Pentecost to the Tribulation Period midpoint.

The belief that the seven letters to the seven churches are prophetic is new to some, but it has been around at least since the third century AD. Also, it does not contradict the teaching that the letters are to individuals, those seven churches, and the church as a whole. It simply adds another element of information.

If it is true, and many prominent authorities believe it is, that seven eras of the Church Age are revealed here, then the Church Age is now in its final hours and the Rapture is imminent.

what others say

Tim LaHaye

It is suggested that they also represent the seven basic divisions of church history. A study of history reveals that the Church has gone through seven basic periods or stages.[1]

Map labels:
BLACK SEA
GALATIA
ASIA
AGEAN SEA
GREECE
ATHENS
PATMOS
• PERGAMOS
• THYATIRA
• SMYRNA
• SARDIS
• PHILADELPHIA
• EPHESUS • LAODICEA
• ANTIOCH
Crete
Cyprus
• DAMASCUS
• JERUSALEM
EGYPT
ARABIA

Fast Facts on the Present Age

Church Age	Scripture	Approx. Historical Date of the Church	Prophetic Condition
Ephesus Period	Revelation 2:1–7	Pentecost to AD 100	Will backslide
Smyrna Period	Revelation 2:8–11	AD 100 to AD 312	Will be persecuted
Pergamos Period	Revelation 2:12–17	AD 312 to AD 590	Will compromise doctrines
Thyatira Period	Revelation 2:18–29	AD 590 to AD 1517	Will tolerate heresy
Sardis Period	Revelation 3:1–6	AD 1517 to AD 1750	Will almost die
Philadelphia Period	Revelation 3:7–13	AD 1750 to AD 1900	Will be evangelistic
Laodicea Period	Revelation 3:14–22	AD 1900 to Rapture	Will be lukewarm

go to

trumpet
1 Thessalonians
4:13–18;
Revelation 4:1

throne
Revelation 4:2

elders
Revelation 4:4

creatures
Revelation 4:6

angels
Revelation 5:11

heaven
Revelation 5:3–5

Lamb
John 1:29;
Revelation 5:6–10

reign
Revelation 5:9–10

purchased
redeemed

Let's Go to Heaven

the big picture

Revelation 4–5

John was called up into heaven where he saw Jesus sitting on a throne next to God. He saw a rainbow over the throne, twenty-four elders seated on other thrones around it, seven blazing lamps and a sea of glass in front of it, and four living creatures by it. God was holding a scroll with seven seals and an angel asked, "Who is worthy to open the scroll and to loose its seals?" (5:2 NKJV). Jesus was the only One qualified to do this. Then the four living creatures, the twenty-four elders, multitudes of angels, and everyone else worshiped him.

The Church Age (Revelation 2–3) will end with the Rapture. A voice sounding very much like a <u>trumpet</u> will summon the church into heaven where the saved will appear before a <u>throne</u> occupied by both God and Jesus. The twenty-four <u>elders</u>, the four living <u>creatures</u>, and multitudes of <u>angels</u> will be there. It will be that time between the Rapture and the Tribulation Period and the issue will be "Who is worthy to break the seals and open the scroll?"

In other words, Who can qualify as the Redeemer of the world and open the seals? We will learn more about the seals later, but here we learn that Jesus will be the only One in <u>heaven</u> or on earth who is qualified to do this. He is the <u>Lamb</u> that was slain for the sins of the world and his shed blood **purchased** a people to <u>reign</u> on earth.

what others say

Gary G. Cohen

Once broken, a seal was impossible to repair without leaving tell-tale traces; thus here we are certain that this book with its woes for the earth has never yet been opened. It was certainly not opened prior to the crucifixion as vs. 9 shows; and its contents (Chapters 6–19) do not mesh with these past 2,000 years of church history. The opening is set for the start of the Tribulation Period! The fact that there are seven seals shows that the entire matter—here Tribulation judgments for the ungodly upon earth—will be completely dispatched by these seven seals.[2]

first seal
Revelation 6:1–2

what others say

John F. Walvoord

Immediately after the Rapture of the church, there will be a time period which may be called a period of preparation. In this period there will emerge a ten-nation group forming a political unit in the Middle East. A leader will emerge who will gain control first of three and then of all ten (cf. Daniel 7:8, 24–25). From this position of power he will be able to enter into a covenant with Israel, bringing to rest the relationship of Israel to her neighbors (9:27), and beginning the final seven-year countdown culminating in the Second Coming.[3]

These chapters reveal the Rapture and what will occur in heaven shortly after that. The "shortly after" events will take place during that period of time the Antichrist is rising to power on earth.

It's Time to Deal with Rebellion on Earth

the big picture

Revelation 6:1–8:1

John watched as Jesus opened the seven seals on the scroll in heaven one at a time (the seventh released seven trumpet judgments). As each seal was opened, a judgment that was being restrained in heaven was released. In between the opening of the sixth and seventh seals a pause occurred while God marked 144,000 Jewish evangelists.

All of the judgments on earth will be triggered from heaven. The first seven seals will be as follows:

Seal #1—Jesus will open the first seal and the first living creature will release a rider on a white horse that most experts agree is the Antichrist. He will rise to power with great deception, saying and doing many good things to give people a false sense of hope. He will wrap himself in piety and respectability and his supporters will not sense the evil in his heart. He will talk peace, but John says he will come forth "conquering and to conquer" (6:2 NKJV).

go to

second seal
Revelation 6:3–4

third seal
Revelation 6:5–6

fourth seal
Revelation 6:7–8

fifth seal
Revelation 6:9–11

sixth seal
Revelation 6:12–17

converts
new Christians

Seal #2—Jesus will open the <u>second seal</u> and the second living creature will release a rider on a fiery red horse. This rider will undo the world's fragile peace treaties and spark a rash of conflicts around the world. God will permit this to show the world that the Antichrist is a false prince of peace.

Seal #3—Jesus will open the <u>third seal</u> and the third living creature will release a rider on a black horse. This rider will surge forth with the terrible consequences of war. These include, among other things, economic disaster and famine. Most currencies will be worthless and food shortages will be common. Misery, poverty, and starvation will prevail. God will permit this to show the world that the Antichrist is a false bread of life.

Seal #4—Jesus will open the <u>fourth seal</u> and the fourth living creature will release a rider on a pale horse. This rider will be named Death, and the color of his horse will be similar to that of spoiled meat. A creature named Hades will follow him and these two ghoulish characters will use war, famine, plagues, and wild animals to harvest the souls of unbelievers as fuel for the fires of hell.

Seal #5—Jesus will open the <u>fifth seal</u> and there will be great persecution and death of those who accept Christ after the Rapture. The media and world leaders will portray these new Christians as enemies of world government, world peace, world religion, and the environment. They will blame these new **converts** for starting religious wars; call for their elimination to preserve the dwindling food supplies and protect the environment; and use food, water, and other things as weapons to force support for a new world government.

Seal #6—Jesus will open the <u>sixth seal</u> and there will be a great earthquake, the sun will turn pitch black, the moon will turn blood red, meteors will fall to the earth, the wind will recede like the rolling up of a scroll, and every mountain and island on earth will move or shake. This appears to be nuclear war throwing debris into the atmosphere and affecting the very universe itself. It will cause worldwide panic, multitudes will try to hide from God in caves and bomb shelters, and many will finally realize that the Tribulation Period has arrived.

The First Interlude—In between the sixth and seventh seals there will be a pause in the coming events. Jesus said the <u>gospel</u> will be preached in the whole world before the end comes, but at this point the church will be in heaven because of the Rapture. So God will call "time out" in the judgments to **seal** 144,000 Jews.

Whatever this seal is, it will protect from harm while they preach to the world and win a great multitude to God.

Seal #7—Jesus will open the <u>seventh seal</u> and this will start a new series of tragedies called the trumpet judgments.

go to

gospel
Matthew 24:14

seventh seal
Revelation 8:1–6

false
Matthew 24:11

wars
Matthew 24:6–7

famine
Matthew 24:7

death
Matthew 24:9

earthquakes
Matthew 24:7

heavenly bodies
Matthew 24:29

seal
mark

what others say

Dave Breese

If we want to know the direction in which the world is going, that direction is ahead of us. We are to anticipate not a utopia or a perfect world, but an era of devastating divine judgment.[4]

J. Vernon McGee

The Great Tribulation is the Devil's holiday. That is the day when he is going to have freedom to do as he pleases. We will see why God is going to grant that: it is a period of the judgment of God upon a Christ-rejecting world.[5]

After the Rapture things will grow progressively worse. The world will go through a <u>false</u> sense of peace (Seal #1); several <u>wars</u> and rumors of wars (Seal #2); economic collapse and <u>famine</u> (Seal #3); the death of millions of unbelievers because of war, famine, and plagues (Seal #4); the persecution and <u>death</u> of believers (Seal #5); <u>earthquakes</u> with disturbances in the <u>heavenly bodies</u> possibly because of nuclear war (Seal #6); and then the trumpet judgments will begin (Seal #7).

After the church is removed from the earth by the Rapture, there will be a brief period of euphoria followed by a seven-year period of war, famine, pestilence, persecution, and death on a level so intense it staggers the imagination.

Judgment Will Come Upon All the World

go to

first trumpet
Revelation 8:7

second trumpet
Revelation 8:8–9

third trumpet
Revelation 8:10–11

wormwood
a bitter, intoxicating,
poisonous herb

Revelation 8:2–11:19

the big picture

John watched as seven angels stood before God and each one sounded a trumpet (the seventh trumpet brought on seven judgments called bowl judgments). One at a time the trumpets sounded and each time a terrible catastrophe took place on earth. In between the sixth and seventh was a pause while John received two other visions.

The judgments found in Revelation appear in sets of seven. For purposes of study, each set of seven can be broken down into four and three. For example, the seal judgments fall into two categories: the Four Horsemen of the Apocalypse and then three additional judgments. In like manner, the seven trumpet judgments will fall into two categories: four "Judgments of One-Third" and three judgments called "Woes." The following is an overview of the trumpet judgments:

Trumpet #1—An angel will sound the <u>first trumpet</u> and hail and fire mixed with blood will fall to the earth and destroy one-third of the plant life. This furious supernatural storm will alter the entire balance of nature, destroy badly needed crops hastily planted to curb food shortages, destroy lumber needed to build houses, destroy grazing land needed for cattle, and kill a tremendous number of people.

Trumpet #2—An angel will sound the <u>second trumpet</u> and something like a huge burning mountain—perhaps a blazing meteor, a comet, or a very large missile with a chemical warhead—will be hurled into the sea causing it to turn into blood, killing one-third of the sea creatures and destroying one-third of the ships. The Bible does not say so, but it seems likely that this will cause a great tidal wave that will pollute, damage, and destroy large areas of coastline.

Trumpet #3—An angel will sound the <u>third trumpet</u> and a large burning star will fall from the sky. People will name it after a bitter herb in the Bible called **wormwood** because it will pollute and poison one-third of the earth's fresh water supply (rivers, springs, etc.) and cause many people to die. Fresh water is one of earth's most precious commodities and losing one-third of it will have terrible consequences. Those who think they can submit to God after the Rapture are making a terrible mistake.

Trumpet #4—An angel will sound the <u>fourth trumpet</u> and the light of the sun, moon, and stars will be diminished by one-third. This will affect the weather and every form of plant and animal life on earth. It may even bring about the nuclear winter predicted by many scientists and environmentalists.

Trumpet #5—An angel will sound the <u>fifth trumpet</u> and another star will fall from heaven. This will not be a literal star because it will be given a key and is called "he." Most conservative commentators believe this "he" will be Satan. His key will unlock his subterranean home called the Abyss. He will use it to release multiplied millions of demon-possessed locusts with stings similar to that of a **scorpion**. God will not permit them to kill anyone, but their poison will be so toxic many people will want to die. Some will even try to commit suicide, but they will not succeed. These scorpions will be allowed to torture people for five months, and everyone except the 144,000 Jewish witnesses will be tortured.

Trumpet #6—An angel will sound the <u>sixth trumpet</u> and four of Satan's fallen angels will be released and given authority to kill one-third of humankind. They will gather a 200-million-person army—most commentators believe this will be China and her allies, but a few say these will be demonic creatures—to carry out their assigned task.

Trumpet #7—Loud voices in heaven will announce that "the kingdoms of this world have become the kingdoms of our Lord and of His Christ, and He shall reign forever and ever!" (Revelation 11:15 NKJV). The twenty-four elders will fall down and worship God. Then there will be a great earthquake, a great hailstorm, and the seven <u>bowls of God's wrath</u> will be poured out. These events will happen very fast, and they will come near the end of the Tribulation Period.

The Second Interlude—A <u>mighty angel</u> will descend to the earth with a small book and stand with one foot on the sea and the other foot on dry land. This will be a symbolic way of claiming the planet for God. The angel will announce that the remaining judgments will not be delayed and all of them will be fulfilled exactly as the prophets said.

go to

fourth trumpet
Revelation 8:12

fifth trumpet
Revelation 9:1–12

sixth trumpet
Revelation 9:13–21

bowls of God's wrath
Revelation 16:1

mighty angel
Revelation 10:1–11

scorpion
a small spider-like animal with a poisonous sting

go to

temple
Revelation 11:1–2

two witnesses
Revelation 11:3–14

waters
Exodus 7:14–25

hail
Exodus 9:18–26

darkness
Exodus 10:21–23

Preterists
a group that teaches
that most, if not all,
Bible prophecy has
been fulfilled

The Third Interlude—The Jewish <u>temple</u> will be in existence, but the outer court will be controlled by the Gentiles for forty-two months. <u>Two witnesses</u> will appear and begin to prophesy. No one will be allowed to harm them for forty-two months. They will be able to hold back the rain, turn water into blood, and strike the earth with various kinds of plagues. After the forty-two months have expired, the Antichrist will be permitted to kill them and their bodies will be left in the street for all the world to see for 3 1/2 days. Then they will be raised from the dead and ascend into heaven.

---

what others say

Grant R. Jeffrey

God cannot simply ignore our sin and allow an unrepentant sinner into heaven despite their rejection of God. God's absolute justice makes it impossible for Him to ignore our sins.[6]

John F. Walvoord

These are catastrophic judgments and should not be explained away. In view of the fact that they are supernatural, we should not limit God in what He is desiring to do.[7]

A group of people called **Preterists** teach that most, if not all, Bible prophecy has been fulfilled. They also teach that the really bad things were fulfilled in AD 70 when the Romans destroyed Jerusalem. But one-fourth of earth's population will die in the fourth seal and one-third will die in the sixth trumpet. Nothing like this has ever happened before, but it will happen during the Tribulation Period.

The first plague on Egypt in the days of Moses turned the <u>waters</u> into blood, the seventh was <u>hail</u> that killed people and animals, and the ninth was <u>darkness</u> that covered the land. Since God did these things in the past, isn't it reasonable to assume that he can do them again?

Jesus intends to establish a kingdom here on earth during the Millennium. He cannot allow unrepentant people into that kingdom or they will corrupt it. They must repent or perish before the kingdom is established. The purpose of these judgments is to give people a future and to protect the future of those who follow God.

The Dragon Loses

go to

Joseph
Genesis 30:22–24;
37:3–4

nations
Psalm 2:1–9

dragon
Revelation 12:9

child
Matthew 2:13–18

kingdoms of the world
Matthew 4:1–11

cross
Matthew 27:42–44

flee
Matthew 24:16

the big picture

Revelation 12:1–17

After the seventh trumpet sounded and before the seven bowls of God's wrath were poured out, John was told to prophesy about some of the peoples, nations, languages, and kings of the Tribulation Period. Then he saw a sun-clothed woman in heaven with the moon under her feet and a crown of twelve stars on her head. She was expecting a male child that would rule the world. A dragon stood before her desiring to destroy the child at birth. The child was born and taken up into heaven. The woman fled into the wilderness, and the dragon went to heaven, but God's angels cast him down to earth. He pursued the woman into the wilderness, but God protected her.

The symbols associated with this woman (the sun, moon, and twelve stars) are all found in a single dream <u>Joseph</u> had in the Old Testament about the nation of Israel. This child who will rule the <u>nations</u> is Jesus and the <u>dragon</u> is identified as Satan. When Jesus first came to this earth as a human <u>child</u>, Satan tried to have him killed. When Jesus began his ministry Satan tried to destroy that by tempting him with the <u>kingdoms of the world</u>. When Jesus was dying on a <u>cross</u> for the sins of the world, Satan tried to stop that by having others encourage him to save his life. Following his death, Jesus was resurrected and he ascended into heaven. In the future, at the Tribulation Period midpoint, Israel will have to <u>flee</u> into the mountains, and Satan will lose his place in heaven and be cast to this earth with many of his fallen angels. They will do as much damage on earth as they can. Satan will also try to destroy all the Jews, but God will not allow that. He will help many of them escape and supernaturally protect them.

what others say

J. Dwight Pentecost

According to Revelation 12, the object of satanic attack during the tribulation period is "the woman" who produced the child. Since this child is born "to rule all nations with a rod of iron" (Revelation 12:5), it can only refer to Christ, the one whose right it is to rule. The Psalmist confirms this interpretation in Psalm 2:9, which is admittedly Messianic. The one from whom Christ came can only be Israel.[8]

go to

Jerusalem
Zechariah 12:1–9

what others say

John Hagee

Satan will target Jews and Christians because attacking them is the only way he can retaliate against God. Unable to prevail against God militarily, Satan will seek revenge against Him by targeting the Jewish people, the apple of God's eye, for extermination.[9]

The Bible warns that Israel and <u>Jerusalem</u> will be severely attacked at the end of the age, but God will be watching for this, and all who try to harm this nation will actually be doing injury to themselves. Every nation that attacks Jerusalem will be destroyed.

The return of Israel as a nation is a clear sign of the approaching Tribulation Period. When the temple is rebuilt the stage will be set for the Antichrist to defile it and that will signal the casting of Satan and his fallen angels to earth. The implications for all who trust in God are terrifying, but those who defy God will be in greater peril in the long run.

the big picture

Revelation 13:1–18

As John continued to prophesy about some of the main characters who will be on earth during the Tribulation Period, he saw a beast coming out of the sea and a beast coming out of the earth. The beast coming out of the sea became the primary political leader of the Tribulation Period. He received political support from ten other rulers or leaders, but the dragon was his main source of power and authority. This beast was wounded but healed; he was a military genius, a blasphemer, and a persecutor of God's people. Then the beast coming out of the earth appeared and he became the primary religious leader of the Tribulation Period. He pretended to follow God, but his doctrines were like those of the dragon. He gave religious support to the first beast, forced people to worship the first beast, performed miracles, set up an idol of the first beast and caused it to come to life, and killed all who refused to worship it. He also forced people to be identified with a mark on their right hand or forehead the number of the beast coming out of the sea.

The beast coming out of the earth is the False Prophet. He will be the world's most powerful religious leader during the Tribulation

292 ——————————————— **Prophecies of the Bible** ————————————————

Period. He will present himself as a lamb, but will be a wolf in sheep's clothing; and his doctrines will be like the doctrines of Satan. At first, his authority will be equal to that of the Antichrist, and he will use it to give full support to that evil man. Multitudes will be deceived and forced to worship an idol he will set up in honor of the Antichrist. He will get a law passed forcing everyone to receive a mark on their right hand or forehead. This mark will be like a license to transact business. Those who have it will be allowed to buy and sell, but those without it will be denied that privilege. This mark will be the number and name of the Antichrist. People cannot figure it out now, but after the Rapture when the Antichrist is revealed people will discover that the numerical value of his name is 666.

horns
Revelation 17:12

heads
Revelation 17:7–11

dragon
Revelation 12:9

blaspheme
show contempt for God

Beasts of Sea and Earth

The beast coming out of the sea is the Antichrist. He will be the world's most powerful politician during the Tribulation Period and is called a beast because he will be filled with evil. This beast will have ten <u>horns</u>, which means he will have ten kings (or ten leaders of factions) on earth who will give him political support. And he will have seven <u>heads</u>, which means he will have ties to the seven world governments of past history. The <u>dragon</u>, who was identified in the previous chapter as Satan, will give him power. He will receive what appears to be a fatal wound during his reign, but to the amazement of the world he will be miraculously healed. People will be overwhelmed by his personality, his rise to power, and his ability to win wars. He will boast of his abilities, **blaspheme** God, try to kill everyone who worships God, and gain the worship of multitudes.

> **what others say**
>
> **Tim LaHaye**
>
> Whenever a political leader tries to exterminate religion or the true worship of God, he must use the services of a false religious leader. The Antichrist will be no different. His leader will look "like a lamb" and speak "like a dragon" (verse 11).[10]

The idea of a Global Ethic sounds good. After all, a lot of wars are religious wars. But the establishment of a Global Ethic is the same thing as the establishment of a world religion. And the establishment of a world religion will bring about the persecution of Christians and Jews because they will not comply. Would you switch religions? Would you accept the values of a man who gets his marching orders from Satan?

Throughout the entire history of humankind, the control of all buying and selling and the tracking of all individuals has been impossible. In fact, for hundreds of years skeptics have said such a day would never come. But now we have entered the information age, and many United Nations bureaucrats are giving this idea serious consideration.

Supernatural Intervention

the big picture

Revelation 14:1–20

John saw Jesus standing on Mount Zion with the 144,000 and he heard a heavenly choir singing. The 144,000 had made it through the Tribulation Period unharmed, undefiled, faithful to the teachings of Jesus, and they said nothing but the truth. Then John saw several angels. They first preached the gospel on earth

earth and urged people to turn to God. The second announced the destruction of Babylon. The third announced that all who took the Mark of the Beast would be cast into the Lake of Fire. The fourth prevailed upon Jesus to remove multitudes of unbelievers from the earth, and the fifth removed wicked nations.

Considering the fact that more than half the earth's population will have been killed by this time in the Tribulation Period, it will be truly amazing that every one of the 144,000 Jewish witnesses will still be living. Not even one will be killed by famine, hail, polluted water, nuclear bombs, the Antichrist, or any other disaster that takes place during this **indignation**. And considering all the wicked things humankind will be doing, it is a wonder that God will still love people enough to send an angel to preach the gospel to all those on earth, but he will. Then one of his angels will announce the destruction of Babylon, another will announce the destruction of those who take the Mark of the Beast, another will announce the removal of unbelievers from the earth, and another will announce the removal of clusters (nations) from the earth. The heavenly angels will be very active on earth during the Tribulation Period.

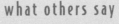

what others say

Billy Graham

It will be a time of nuclear conflagrations, biological holocausts and chemical apocalypses rolling over the earth, bringing man to the edge of the precipice. History will "bottom out" in the battle of Armageddon. We already see its shadow creeping over the earth.[13]

For hundreds of years the ancient city of Babylon did not exist, but here we have a prediction that it will fall during the Tribulation Period. Isn't it interesting that the city has come back into existence in recent years? And isn't it interesting that this is occurring at the exact same time in history that Israel and Europe are being revived? Is this a coincidence?

When the Battle of Armageddon approaches, many nations, cities, and individuals will be removed from the earth by the terrible weapons we now possess. If the people of earth would heed the preaching of the 144,000 and the angel God plans to send, they could avoid this. But they will not listen and they will not escape the awesome judgments of God.

go to

144,000
Revelation 14:1–4

killed
Revelation 6:7–8;
9:15

humankind
Revelation 9:20–21

gospel
Revelation 14:6

Babylon
Revelation 14:8

Mark
Revelation 13:16–18;
14:9–11

earth
Revelation 14:14–16

clusters
Revelation 14:17–19

indignation
another name for the Tribulation Period

angels
Matthew 13:40–42

perish
2 Peter 3:9

first bowl
Revelation 16:2

second bowl
Revelation 16:3

third bowl
Revelation 16:4–7

repentance
turning toward God,
away from wrong

The heavenly angels will be very active on earth during the Tribulation Period.

Fast and Furious

the big picture

Revelation 15:7–16:21

John watched as one of the four living creatures handed the seven bowls filled with God's wrath to seven different angels. As each angel went forth and poured out his bowl upon the earth, a terrible judgment took place. Finally, a voice from the throne of God said, "It is done!" (16:17 NKJV).

During the Millennium, God plans to set up a kingdom here on earth. If the lost were allowed to enter that kingdom, they would corrupt it just like they have everything else. But God will not let that happen again. When Jesus returns at the end of the Tribulation Period, he will send out his <u>angels</u> to gather the lost and cast them into hell. This is not something he will enjoy doing. The apostle Peter said God doesn't want anyone to <u>perish</u>, but he does want everyone to come to **repentance**. So as the end of the age approaches, God will pour out the most severe judgments of all, referred to as "bowls," in one final effort to change the hearts of unbelievers. The first four judgments will affect the earth, the sea, the fresh water, and the sun. The last three will affect the Antichrist and his kingdom.

Bowl #1—The <u>first bowl</u> will be poured out upon the land. Those who still have a chance to repent will not be affected, but all those who have taken the Mark of the Beast or worshiped his image will be covered with ugly, painful sores. The Antichrist will not be able to heal his own followers and the world will know he is a fake.

Bowl #2—The <u>second bowl</u> will be poured out upon the sea, turning it into blood. The pollution will kill every living creature in it.

Bowl #3—The <u>third bowl</u> will be poured out upon all the earth's remaining fresh water, turning that into blood. The angel in charge of it will declare that this judgment is justified because the Antichrist and his followers have been spilling the blood of God's people.

Bowl #4—The <u>fourth bowl</u> will be poured out upon the sun, turning up its heat output and scorching people with fire. They will acknowledge the existence of God, but will curse his name and refuse to repent or give him glory.

Bowl #5—The <u>fifth bowl</u> will be poured out upon the Antichrist and his kingdom, plunging everything into darkness and causing such grave misgivings among his people they will chew their tongues in agony. Their pain will be so intense that they will curse God, but none of them will repent of their sins.

Bowl #6—The <u>sixth bowl</u> will be poured out upon the Euphrates River, causing it to dry up and paving the way for the kings of the East (China and her allies) to move their great army westward toward Israel and the Middle East. The **Satanic Trinity** will respond by sending demonic spirits to gather the other kings of the earth for a great battle. They will assemble at a place called Armageddon.

Bowl #7—The <u>seventh bowl</u> will be poured out and the greatest earthquake the world has ever experienced will take place. Every city on earth except Babylon will be in ruins and that city will be split into three parts. Earth's entire surface will be changed. All the islands will sink beneath the waters, every mountain will be leveled, and people will be crushed by hundred-pound hailstones falling from the sky.

go to

fourth bowl
Revelation 16:8–9

fifth bowl
Revelation 16:10–11

sixth bowl
Revelation 16:12–16

seventh bowl
Revelation 16:17–21

festering
Exodus 9:8–12

blood
Exodus 7:14–24

darkness
Exodus 10:21–22;
Matthew 27:45

hail
Exodus 9:18–25

Satanic Trinity
Satan, the Antichrist,
and the False
Prophet

> **what others say**
>
> ### David Jeremiah with C. C. Carlson
>
> Loathsome skin diseases are significant because they are outward signs of inward corruption. Jesus described those who looked good on the outside, but were rotten to the core, when He spoke to the self-righteous leaders of His day.[14]

God can do anything. If he wants to cover unbelievers with <u>festering</u> sores, turn water into <u>blood</u>, plunge the world into <u>darkness</u>, or crush everything with hundred-pound chunks of <u>hail</u>, he can.

Because of the similarities some writers think the bowl judgments are a restatement of the trumpet judgments. The similarities are there, but there are also many differences including the fact that the bowl judgments will be much more extensive.

seventh angel
Revelation 16:17

Many who go to church no longer believe it, and many who never go to church scoff at it, but this world is headed for judgment. God will not accept a satanic world government, a godless Global Ethic, or a Christ-hating civilization. Whether people believe it or not, the "good old days" are almost over and things are about to change drastically. Those who take the Mark of the Beast or worship the image of the Antichrist will not repent and be saved.

Judgment

Seals	Trumpets	Bowls
Antichrist released	1/3 of plants destroyed	Sores on followers of Antichrist
War breaks out	1/3 of seas polluted	Seas turned to blood
Economic collapse, blood	1/3 of fresh water polluted	Fresh water turned to famine
Death of unbelievers	1/3 of heavenly bodies darkened	Sun scorches unbelievers
Death of believers	Demonic locusts released	Darkness over kingdom of Antichrist
Nuclear war	1/3 of mankind killed	Battle of Armageddon earthquake
Trumpets sound	Bowls dumped	Destroys every city

Some Mysteries Are Truly Mysterious

the big picture

Revelation 17:1–18:24

After the <u>seventh angel</u> poured out the seventh bowl, there was another pause so one of the angels could explain the mystery of Babylon the Great. She had two identities: a woman and a city. As a woman this evil person was a prostitute and she taught her children to be like her. She conspired with political leaders to merge religion and government. At first, she was rich, supported the beast with seven heads and ten horns, and thrived by persecuting God's faithful people. John was told that the beast (the Antichrist) will come out of the Abyss, rule over a world kingdom divided into ten regions, oppose Christ, and be defeated. But before he falls, God will put it in his heart to turn against the woman and destroy her. As a city, Babylon will develop strong ties with world government and become the home of world trade. It will be rich and sinful, will persecute God's people, and will be destroyed in one hour. World leaders will cry when they see her destruction. The city will become the home of demons and will never rise again.

The sun-clothed woman in Revelation 12 is a good woman that represents the nation of Israel. The wife or bride in Revelation 19 is a good woman that represents the church. The woman arrayed in scarlet and purple is a bad woman that represents Satan's effort to replace the raptured church with a one-world harlot religion.

The one-world government will think it needs a one-world religion to prevent religious wars. As a woman, Mystery Babylon is the **Global Ethic** that will exist during the Tribulation Period. Being a prostitute means she will commit **spiritual adultery**, a biblical way of saying she will be unfaithful to God. Teaching her children to be that way too means this world religion will influence all the other religions of the world to adopt her wicked beliefs. World political leaders will love her Global Ethics, her set of one-world religious values, and the two (the prostitute and the world leaders) will be so infatuated with each other at first they will try to merge church and state. The **beast** will support her for a while—she will be rich and will help persecute and kill God's true people. The beast, commonly called the Antichrist, will be someone who comes out of the Abyss, the subterranean abode of demons. He will rule over the next world kingdom, the seventh in history, and drastically change it into an eighth—a Satanic New World Order. At the time he takes over the seventh, it will have been divided into ten regions, each region having a ruler and all ten rulers giving him their unqualified support. He will oppose everything associated with Christianity and be defeated by Christ at his second coming. But before that happens, God will put it in the beast's heart to destroy all those who supported the one-world religion. Before the Tribulation Period is over, all those involved in this corrupt religious system will be killed by the Antichrist and his political allies.

There is wide disagreement among expositors over the identity of this city. Some say it is Rome. Others say it is New York City or the United States. But all the cities mentioned in the book of Revelation are literal cities, and since Saddam Hussein started rebuilding it, a growing number of writers now say this is probably literal Babylon, which they expect to grow rapidly after the Antichrist takes control of the world government.

As a city, Mystery Babylon will court world leaders and support world trade. Some businessmen will become extremely wealthy. It will be one of the most wicked places on earth and the crimes

beast
Revelation 13:1

Global Ethic
government-approved religious values, one-world religion

spiritual adultery
abandoned God

beast
the Antichrist

committed there will not go unnoticed by God. The city will be destroyed in one hour. Her destruction will be worldwide news, political leaders will be terrified, and rich businessmen will grieve over their losses.

No one will be able to buy or sell during the Tribulation Period without taking the Mark of the Beast and worshiping the Antichrist. Therefore, all of these global traders will be corrupt businessmen under the influence of Satan.

Church and state are going to be merged during the Tribulation Period and the result will be a corrupt religious system. The two will cooperate to strengthen each other and to persecute and kill true believers. The world government will destroy the world religion and Jesus will destroy the world government.

The Second Coming

the big picture

Revelation 19:1–21

John witnessed a praise service in heaven, the Second Coming of Christ, and the end of the Antichrist and the False Prophet.

Armageddon
the last and greatest war on earth

Lake of Fire
the final abode of Satan and his followers

At the end of the Tribulation Period, all those in heaven will begin to praise God for his destruction of Babylon and for avenging the death of true believers. The church will be united with Christ, heaven will open, and Jesus will return to earth with his church. He will confront the troops of the Antichrist at **Armageddon** and destroy them. Then he will capture the Antichrist and the False Prophet and throw them into the **Lake of Fire**.

what others say

David Reagan

This terrible carnage is called "the supper of God" (Revelation 19:17). What a contrast we have here between the beautiful marriage feast in heaven and the ghastly supper of God on earth when the army of the Antichrist will become food for the vultures. And the crucial question is which of those feasts are you going to attend? Are you going to be invited to the glorious wedding feast in heaven, or are you going to be feasted upon by the vultures at the supper of God here on earth? At one feast you are the honored guest; at the other, you are the meal! The choice is yours. Your fate depends entirely on whether or not you put your faith in Jesus as Lord and Savior (1 John 5:5).[18]

Wim Malgo

While the Satanic trinity (cf. Revelation 16:13) deceives all the kings of the earth and leads them to Israel (for Armageddon lies in Israel), it is ultimately the Lord Himself who is leading them there, "And he gathered them together into a place called in the Hebrew tongue Armageddon" (Revelation 16:16). Here it becomes absolutely clear what is taking place worldwide. The nations do not want to war with God and the Lamb but with Israel. They do not see that in reality they are fighting against God and the Lamb.[19]

corrupt shepherds
corrupt priests and
prophets

Arnold G. Fruchtenbaum

The thing that should be carefully noted here is that the church is already in heaven before the second coming. Furthermore, the church has been in heaven long enough to undergo the Judgment Seat of Christ. This clearly means that the Rapture and the second coming cannot be the same thing but must be separated by some duration of time.[20]

Because Armageddon will be so destructive people need to pay attention to the reason why God will bring it about. Men will ignore the Scriptures and start a war for their own selfish reasons. Then, God will remember his covenants and put an end to it. Notice the goal of each side in the Battle of Armageddon:

key point

1. Man's purpose will be to destroy the nation of Israel.

2. God's purpose will be to get glory for his name, to rescue Israel and to deal with the nations for (a) taking Jewish land, (b) scattering the Jews, and (c) wickedness on earth.

It is sad that so many so-called brilliant people will go to such a terrible destruction, but it will be the result of their own faulty decisions. What will happen to them will be the result of their own steadfast refusal to abandon their wicked ways and turn to God. They will leave him with no choice.

The Millennium and Beyond

the big picture

Revelation 20:1–15

John saw an angel seize Satan and throw him into the Abyss for a thousand years. He witnessed the resurrection of those who refused to take the mark and watched as they reigned with Christ for a thousand years. None of them suffered the second death. After the thousand years ended, Satan was released for an unspecified period of time and he led other rebellions against God. This brought destruction upon his followers and got him cast into the Lake of Fire. Then the dead unbelievers were raised, judged, and cast into the Lake of Fire too, which is the second death.

Following the Second Coming an angel will be sent from heaven to earth to arrest Satan. He will capture the devil, bind him, and cast him into the Abyss to prevent him from harming the earth for the next thousand years. This thousand-year period is often called the **Millennium**. During this time, the church will sit on thrones and judge the world. The Tribulation Period saints who were beheaded by the Antichrist will be raised from the dead and they will reign also. They will never be cast into the Lake of Fire. After spending a thousand years in the Abyss, Satan will be released. The Bible does not state it, but the purpose of this seems to be to test those born on earth during the Millennium and to prove that sin is a flaw in the human heart, not something that results from a bad environment. Satan will cause many to sin and they will be destroyed by fire from heaven. Satan will be captured again and this time he will be thrown into the Lake of Fire and will never escape. Having done this, God will set up a throne, raise every unbeliever from the dead, open the books, and judge each person by their record. The Book of Life will be opened, but the names of these people will not be there because they will be people who never accepted Jesus as their Savior. They will be cast into the Lake of Fire. The other books are books of works. The unbelievers will be judged out of them because there are degrees of punishment for the lost during eternity in the Lake.

go to

judge
1 Corinthians 6:2–3

Millennium
the thousand-year reign of Christ on earth

what others say

William L. Pettingill

The departure of the Church from the Earth will be but temporary. She will return with her Lord when He comes in the clouds of Heaven with power and great glory to judge the world and reign as King of Kings and Lord of Lords [sic]. Wherever He goes she will go, for she is His bride and the promise is "so shall we ever be with the Lord."[21]

David Jeremiah with C. C. Carlson

The Great White Throne Judgment will not be like any courtroom experience anyone has ever had. There will be a Judge, but no jury; a Prosecutor, but no defender; a sentence, but no appeal. This is the final judgment of the world. God is patient, but at that time there will be no more opportunities to accept Him.[22]

go to

earth
2 Peter 3:13

City
Hebrews 11:13–16

Lake of Fire
Revelation 20:11–15

The day will come when the Book of Life will be checked and anyone whose name is not there will be sent to hell forever. Is your name in the Book of Life?

Some critics do not believe in a Millennium, but a thousand-year period is mentioned six times in Revelation 20. Once is enough, but six times makes it emphatic.

The things mentioned in this chapter are incredible, but many of them are confirmed by other prophecies in the Bible. The return of Christ to set up a kingdom and judge the world is mentioned over and over again. Christians have much to rejoice about and non-Christians have much to fear.

The Holy City

the big picture

Revelation 21:1–27

John saw a new heaven and a new earth. He also saw the Holy City called the New Jerusalem. God and his church were both there. The Holy City had twelve gates, twelve foundations, and a thick wall, but there was no temple, no sun, and no moon. Visitors flocked there with gifts, but nothing impure was allowed in.

In the future, the current heaven and <u>earth</u> will be replaced. One of the features of the new earth will be the absence of large bodies of water. There will also be a Holy <u>City</u>, which will be the future dwelling place of the church. The throne of God will be there and everything will be new. We will not die, cry, or hurt, and we will have free access to the Holy Spirit. This is our Christian inheritance for overcoming sin through faith in Jesus. And there will be no unbelievers there because they will all be in the <u>Lake of Fire</u>. The Holy City will descend to the new earth. It will glow with the glory of

God, have a high wall with twelve gates, have an angel sitting at each gate, and have the name of one of the twelve tribes of Israel written on each gate. The wall will be sitting on twelve foundations and each foundation will bear the name of one of the twelve apostles. The city will be cube shaped, each side being about 1,500 miles long, and will be made out of pure gold. The wall around the city, comprised of **jasper**, will be about 216 feet thick, and its foundations will be decorated with various kinds of precious stones. Each gate will be made of a single pearl and the main street will be pure gold.

The city will not have a temple in it because there will be no sin there and everyone will have direct access to God and Jesus. The Father and the Son radiate light so their presence will eliminate the need for a sun and moon. In fact the light will be so great, it will even light up the new earth. There will never be any darkness or any need to shut the gates. Visitors will be allowed in, but only those who have accepted Christ.

Babylon had the reputation of being one of the most beautiful cities ever built by man. But New Jerusalem will be built by God, and it will be more beautiful than anything man has ever done. It will be a literal city with walls, gates, streets, foundations that will make Babylon look like a dump. It appears that John had ancient Babylon in mind when he described New Jerusalem. A partial comparison is shown in the following chart.

jasper
an opaque, translucent stone such as opal, diamond, or topaz

key point

Babylon vs. New Jerusalem

Babylon	New Jerusalem
Future home of evil spirits and demons	Future home of Father, Son, and church
Had death, mourning, and pain	Won't have death, mourning, and pain
Had Euphrates River	Will have River of Water of Life
Will be plunged into darkness	Will be lit by Jesus
Had famous Ishtar Gate	Will have twelve gates of pearl
Walls 14 miles long and 87 feet thick	Walls 1,500 miles long and 216 feet thick
Will be destroyed	Will never be destroyed
Gates often shut	Will never shut gates
Was kingdom of gold	Will have streets of gold
Had Hanging Gardens	Will have Tree of Life

living water
John 4:13–14

tree of life
Genesis 3:22–24

Wim Malgo

Jerusalem is the opposite of Babylon. The separation of the two is radical and clearly visible, for Jerusalem is situated on the new earth. Today also, the contrast between light and darkness, good and evil, heavenly and earthly, the true bride of the Lamb and the whore, is visible.[24]

Hal Lindsey

This ends the Millennium, and eternity then begins with God destroying the old earth and re-creating a new heaven (universe) and earth. His crowning creation, however, is the New Jerusalem—that beautiful City of God.[25]

Some worry about overpopulation and the earth running out of critical resources. But the One who created it in the first place will create another one that will be better and will never be depleted or destroyed.

Lot's of Good News

Revelation 22:1–21

An angel showed John a river containing the water of life. Then he showed John the tree of life and told him more about God and heaven. Finally, John heard Christ's final invitation, final warning and final promise.

The Holy City will have a river called the "river of water of life" (Revelation 22:1 NKJV). This is a symbol of the living water or the Holy Spirit and it will flow from the throne of God. The truth taught here is that there will be a continual outpouring of the Holy Spirit in the New Jerusalem and this outpouring will satisfy the spiritual thirst of everyone there. Rows of the tree of life will grow on each side of the river and bear fruit for the residents of the city. The believer's task will be to serve God, and each one will see God's face, bear his name, and walk in his light.

The angel pointed out to John that the return of Jesus will happen very fast; many commentators say, "in the twinkling of an eye." Also, those who die without Christ as their Savior will never change and never have a Savior, but those who die with Christ as their Savior will belong to him in eternity and receive rewards for their service in this life. One of the blessings will be permission to pass through the gates of the city. Hell, the abode of unbelievers, will be outside the city somewhere. The final invitation is to come and be saved through faith in Jesus. The final warning is that anyone who adds to or takes away from the words in the book of Revelation will suffer the wrath of God. The final promise is that Jesus will come back and it will happen very fast. The last verse in the Bible is a reminder for his people: "The grace of our Lord Jesus Christ be with you all. Amen" (Revelation 22:21 NKJV).

earth
2 Peter 3:13

City
Hebrews 11:13–16

Lake of Fire
Revelation 20:11–15

what others say

John F. Walvoord

All that spoke of sin and its penalties is wiped away in heaven, and there is nothing left that is a reminder of sin. All are blessed, not cursed. In support of this conclusion, it is revealed that God's throne and that of the Lamb will be in the city.[26]

Larry Richards

We cannot know how wonderful eternity will be for those who have trusted God until we are welcomed into the new heaven and earth God will create. But these last chapters of the Bible tell us that it will be wonderful indeed.[27]

After reading the daily newspaper or watching the daily news on TV, one can easily think the future looks bleak and become discouraged or depressed. But we must remember that many of these troubling events are things Jesus said would happen just before he returns. Today, things may look bleak, but prophetically speaking the future looks bright.

God gave Bible prophecy for many reasons. One purpose is to warn unbelievers of God's future judgment. Knowing these things will cause some to repent of their sins and accept Jesus as their Savior before it is too late. Another purpose is to let God's people know that he is still in control and has many blessings in store for them in the future. The blessings mentioned in this chapter just scratch the surface of what eternity will be like for the saved.

Chapter Wrap-Up

- Many experts believe the seven letters to the seven churches are, among other things, prophecies that foretell seven phases of church history. They are seen as a panoramic view of church history before it happened. According to this interpretation, the church is now in the seventh and last period, the Laodicean period. This places the church in its final hours before the Rapture. (Revelation 2–3)

- The Tribulation Period judgments have been written on a seven-sealed scroll in heaven. Jesus will break the seals and open it after the Rapture. The first will release the coming Antichrist; the second will spark a rash of wars; the third will bring economic collapse and famine; the fourth will take the life of untold millions of unbelievers; the fifth will release persecution and death of believers; the sixth will be something, perhaps nuclear war, that will impact the entire universe; the seventh will release the trumpet judgments. (Revelation 6:1–8:1)

- After Jesus breaks the seventh seal, seven angels will stand before God and blow a trumpet one at a time. When the first trumpet sounds, hail mixed with fire will destroy one-third of the plant life; when the second trumpet sounds, a huge burning mountain will kill one-third of the sea creatures and destroy one-third of the ships; when the third trumpet sounds, a large burning star will fall to earth and pollute one-third of the earth's fresh water supply; when the fourth trumpet sounds, the light of the sun, moon, and stars will be diminished by one-third; when the fifth trumpet sounds, multiplied millions of demon-possessed locusts will be released to sting earth's inhabitants; when the sixth trumpet sounds, four of Satan's fallen angels will cause the death of one-third of humankind; the seventh trumpet will cause a great earthquake, a great hailstorm, and the release of the seven bowl judgments. (Revelation 8:2–11:15)

- After the angel sounds the seventh trumpet, seven angels will pour out a bowl of God's wrath one at a time. The first will cause the followers of the Antichrist to be covered with ugly painful sores; the second will kill the sea creatures; the third will pollute earth's fresh water; the fourth will cause the sun to grow hotter and scorch people; the fifth will put the Antichrist and his kingdom in darkness and cause great fear; the sixth will dry up the Euphrates River and set up the Battle of Armageddon; and the seventh will be the greatest earthquake the world has ever seen. (Revelation 16:2–21)

- During the Millennium Satan will be restrained, the church will serve as judges on earth, and believers who die after the Rapture will be resurrected. After the Millennium Satan will be temporarily released and cause more rebellion on earth; then he will be seized and cast into hell; and then the dead unbelievers will be resurrected, judged, and cast into hell. Following that, God will create a new heaven and new earth. The Holy City will descend to the new earth, and the church will dwell in the Holy City and move back and forth between it and the new earth. (Revelation 20–22)

Study Questions

1. What is an interlude and what is revealed during each one of them?

2. What is wormwood and what harm will it do?

3. What are the two identities of Babylon the Great and what do they mean?

4. Identify two symbols that are used to describe the Antichrist. What do they mean?

5. What will the Holy City be like and what is its name?

Appendix A—The Answers

CHAPTER ONE

1. Prophecy is an important part of the Word of God. It reveals what God plans to do. Up to 40 percent of the Bible is prophecy. Because so much prophecy has already been fulfilled, we can logically expect the rest to be fulfilled. (Introduction)

2. Yes. He allowed Satan to tempt Adam and Eve, the world to be corrupted, and Israel to stray. He will allow a Tribulation Period. (Genesis 3:14–19; 6:11–13; Deuteronomy 4:26–31)

3. His covenants are the driving force behind prophecy. They reveal what God plans to do and they are everlasting. (Genesis 12:1–3; 13:14–17; 15:18; 17:19)

4. God will bless us if we bless Israel. Our Messiah came from the nation of Israel. The covenants tell us who the Promised Land belongs to. (Genesis 12:1–3)

5. He will come from the nation of Israel and from the tribe of Judah. (Genesis 28:13–15; Numbers 24:14–19)

CHAPTER TWO

1. It contains the first use of the word *Messiah* or *Christ* in the Bible and it predicts that the Messiah or Christ will also be a King. (1 Samuel 2:10)

2. The phrase "David's house" refers to the dynasty of David and it will last forever because Jesus, who is a descendant of David, will rule over it. (2 Samuel 7:4–17)

3. It would be one of the consequences of Solomon and/or his descendants abandoning God. If they turned away from God, became unfaithful, lived in sin, and failed to keep his commandments, God would turn away from them and the temple would no longer be special to him. (1 Kings 9:3–7)

4. Never. They are everlasting covenants. (1 Chronicles 16:15–18)

5. It depends. One's relationship with God through Christ is the determining factor. The saved will celebrate, but the lost will weep. (1 Chronicles 16:31–33)

CHAPTER THREE

1. Instead of having verses that rhyme, Hebrew poetry has thoughts that are repeated. The same thoughts are restated in a slightly different way.

2. He would have flesh, see with his eyes, stand on earth, it will be in the latter days, etc. (Job 19:25–27)

3. It makes him laugh at, scoff, rebuke, and terrify his opposition. (Psalm 2:1–12)

4. They will mock him, pierce his hands and feet, scorn him, despise him, cast lots for his clothes, give him vinegar to drink, and accuse him. (Psalm 22)

5. Everyone on earth. Jerusalem. Israel. (Psalms 22; 48; and 132)

CHAPTER FOUR

1. The Jews will no longer defile themselves; they will obey God and keep his laws. Jerusalem will be called the City of Righteousness and the Faithful City. (Ezekiel 37:23–38; Isaiah 1:24–31)

2. The Tribulation Period. It will begin with a seven-year covenant to protect Israel. It will be half over when the Antichrist sets up the abomination that causes desolation. (Jeremiah 30:5–7; Daniel 9:27)

3. I is a covenant that God will make with Israel during the Millennium. He will bless the nation with rain, good crops, freedom, safety, and a knowledge of him. It will be a covenant of peace and it will be everlasting. (Ezekiel 34:22–31; 37:1–28)

4. The bones represented the entire nation of Israel that had scattered into foreign nations; Israel seemed dead, dried up, and without hope. The joined sticks represented the revival of Israel and Judah as one nation. (Ezekiel 37:1–28)

5. Russia and her allies, Babylon (Iraq), and Damascus (Syria). (Ezekiel 38:1–39:16; Isaiah 13:1–22; 17:1–14)

CHAPTER FIVE

1. Yes. Hosea compared the wickedness of Israel to that of an adulterous wife. He predicted that the nation would be punished, renewed and restored. (Hosea 1:10–11; 6:1–3)

2. A lack of food and water, empty storehouses, dried-up pastures, a military attack against Israel, the sun and moon darkened, and the Battle of Armageddon. (Joel 1:15–20; 2:1–11; 3:9–16)

3. The world will be filled with distress and danger. (Amos 5:16–20)

4. All nations. The entire world. (Obadiah 1:15–16; Zephaniah 1:14–18)

5. The Jews will look upon the One they pierced and weep. He is the shepherd, the One who will return to the Mount of Olives, the One who will return with his saints. (Zechariah 12:1–14; 13:7–9; 14:1–21)

CHAPTER SIX

1. Jesus calls blessed those who are poor in spirit, those who are mournful over sin, those who are meek before God, those who hunger and thirst for righteousness, those who are merciful, those who have a pure heart, and those who are peacemakers. (Matthew 5:3–12)

2. The sermon is called the Olivet Discourse because Jesus was on the Mount of Olives when he preached it. That is also where he was when he ascended into heaven and where he will return. (Matthew 24:3–5; Acts 1:9–11)

3. It is better to stop sinning than to go to hell. The worms never die and the fires are never quenched there. (Mark 9:42–48)

4. The one who knows God's will and does not do it will be punished more than the one who does not know it. More is required of those who know better. (Luke 12:45–48)

5. Jesus. When he returns to receive his people in the Rapture. (John 11:25–26; 14:2–3)

CHAPTER SEVEN

1. He will judge each person according to what he has done. They will receive trouble for trouble. (Romans 2:5–6; 2 Thessalonians 1:6–10)

2. The hardening will cease at the rapture of the church when the full number of Gentiles has come in. The Bible says all Israel will be saved, but "all Israel" includes only those people God says are Jews. (Romans 11:25–27)

3. Gold, silver, and costly stones are indestructible materials that represent sound Bible doctrines such as the death, burial, and resurrection of Jesus, holy living, etc. Wood, hay, and straw are destructible materials that represent unsound, feel-good doctrines. Those who build in the church with indestructible materials will receive a reward. (1 Corinthians 3:10–15)

4. Jesus will return in the clouds, he will bring the deceased believers with him, they will be raised from the dead, living believers will be caught up into the clouds with them, and all believers will be with him forever. (1 Thessalonians 4:13–18)

5. No. Believers have been taught so they are not in darkness and will not be caught by surprise. (1 Thessalonians 5:1–9)

CHAPTER EIGHT

1. The old covenant was faulty, required keeping the Law, required priests, was broken by the Jews, and was canceled by God. The new covenant is a covenant of grace, is placed in people's hearts, requires no priests, and provides forgiveness of sins. (Hebrews 8:7–13)

2. No. God blesses many people with wealth so they can use it to do his work and glorify him. But hoarding wealth in the last days will make some people miserable because they will lose everything when it becomes worthless. Wealth will not substitute for faith in God. It will not buy his favor or stop his judgment. Rather, it will be used against the lost as evidence of greed and selfishness. (James 5:1–3)

3. Those who grumble against others are warned that they will be judged. The mercy of God has given us new birth, hope, an inheritance, protection, and more. And when the Rapture occurs we will be like Jesus. (James 5:7–9; 1 Peter 1:3–7; 1 John 3:2)

4. The miracle on the Mount of Transfiguration. Jesus took some of his disciples to this mountain, a change came over him, a voice spoke from heaven, and the Second Coming was revealed. (2 Peter 1:16–19)

5. The scoffers will imply that nothing has

changed since the beginning of creation. The judgment of the fallen angels implies that all who reject God will be judged.
(2 Peter 3:3–4; Jude 6)

CHAPTER NINE

1. An interlude is a pause in the sequence of events. For example, God placed an interlude in between the opening of the sixth and seventh seals to explain the marking of the 144,000. He placed another interlude after the sounding of the seventh trumpet to explain that a mighty angel will claim possession of the earth for Jesus during the Tribulation Period and to explain the two witnesses. Another interlude explains the attacks on Israel, the Antichrist, and the False Prophet.
(Revelation 7:10–13)

2. This is the third trumpet judgment, a great star blazing like a torch that will fall to earth and pollute one-third of the fresh water supply. It will be named after a bitter herb in the Bible and those who drink the tainted water will die.
(Revelation 8:10–11)

3. She is a mother and a city, a false religion and the home of global trade. As a mother she will commit spiritual adultery with world leaders, merge church and state, and produce a Global Ethic that will be opposed to Christ. Her daughters are the prostitute religions (false religions) of the world. As a city, she will be the home of global commerce, the home of corrupt businessmen who have taken the mark and worshiped the Antichrist.
(Revelation 17–18)

4. He will be the first rider to appear on a white horse and the first beast, the one coming out of the sea. As the rider on a white horse, he will be a counterfeit Christ, a fake man of God who will talk peace and produce war. As the first beast, he will be full of evil, blaspheme God, worship Satan, receive authority from Satan, and kill God's people.
(Revelation 6:2; 13:1–10)

5. God will dwell with his people, and there will be no death, loneliness, depression, pain, or suffering there. Jesus, the Holy Spirit, the angels, and the church will be there, but no unbelievers. The city will be square on all sides, have a thick wall, gates of pearl, streets of gold, a river of the water of life, the tree of life, no sun, and no night. It will be called the New Jerusalem. (Revelation 21–22)

Appendix B—The Experts

Wayne Barber, Eddie Rasnake, and Richard Shepherd—Pastors at Woodland Park Baptist Church in Chattanooga, TN, conference speakers, and authors. (AMG Publishers, P.O. Box 22000, Chattanooga, TN 37422)

William Barclay—Internationally recognized scholar, teacher, author, and pastor, and the editor of the Daily Study Bible series of books. (The Westminster Press, Philadelphia, PA)

Kenneth L. Barker and Waylon Bailey—Seminary professors, authors, and pastors. (Broadman & Holman Publishers, Nashville, TN)

Irvin Baxter Jr.—Pentecostal minister, editor of *Endtime Magazine*, and author of several books. (Endtime, P.O. Box 2066, Richmond, IN 47375-2066)

Robert T. Boyd—Pastor, author, archaeologist, and conference speaker. (Kregal Publications, Grand Rapids, MI 49501)

Dave Breese—Former president of World Prophetic Ministry and Bible teacher on *The King Is Coming* television program. (World Prophetic Ministry, P.O. Box 907, Colton, CA 92324)

Charles Capps—Author, teacher, and host of *Concepts of Faith* radio broadcast. (He lives in England, AR)

Joe Chambers—Senior editor of *The End Times and Victorious Living*, pastor, and author of several books. (Paw Creek Ministries, Inc., 5110 Tuckaseegee Road, Charlotte, NC 28208)

J. R. Church—Host of the nationwide television program *Prophecy in the News*. (Prophecy Publications, P.O. Box 7000, Oklahoma City, OK 73153)

Gary G. Cohen—Author and president of Clearwater Christian College. (Cleawater Christian College, Clearwater, FL)

Terry L. Cook—Pastor, author, and lecturer. (Second Coming Ministries, 61535 S. Highway 97, Unit 9, Suite 288, Bend, OR 97702)

Timothy Demy—Navy chaplain and author. (Harvest House Publishers, Eugene, OR 97402)

Jimmy DeYoung—Author, conference speaker, and expert on Israel.

Charles Dyer—Professor of Bible exposition at Dallas Theological Seminary in Dallas, Texas, and author of several books. (He lives in Garland, Texas.)

Theodore H. Epp—Author and host and former director of *Back to the Bible Broadcast*. (Back to the Bible, Lincoln, Nebraska 68501)

Charles L. Feinberg—Dean emeritus of Talbot School of Theology in California, author, lecturer, and recognized authority on Jewish history. (Moody Press, Chicago, IL)

W. Herschel Ford—Former pastor of several large Southern Baptist churches including First Baptist in El Paso, Texas. (Zondervan Publishing House, Grand Rapids, MI)

Arno Froese—Editor of *Midnight Call* and *News From Israel*. (Midnight Call, Inc., 4694 Platt Springs Road, West Columbia, SC 29170; News from Israel, P.O. Box 4389, West Columbia, SC 29171-4389)

Arnold G. Fruchtenbaum—Founder of Bible Institute in Israel and Ariel Ministries in the United States with fellowships ministering to Jews in several major cities. (San Antonio, TX)

Arno C. Gaebelein—Pastor, teacher of the Word, and one of the greatest Bible expositors in the history of this country. (Loizeaux Brothers, Neptune, NJ)

Duane A. Garrett—Professor at Bethel Theological Seminary and author. (Bethel Theological Seminary, St. Paul, MN)

Mike Gendron—Evangelist and conference speaker. (Proclaiming the Gospel, P.O. Box 940871, Plano, TX 75094, www.pro-gospel.org)

Billy Graham—World famous evangelist and author of several books. (Billy Graham Evangelistic

Association, 1300 Harmon Place, P.O. Box 779, Minneapolis, MN 55440–0779)

Oliver B. Greene—Author of several books, radio show host, and former director of The Gospel Hour, Inc.

John Hagee—Founder and pastor of Cornerstone Church and president of Global Evangelism Television. (San Antonio, TX)

Charles Halff—Executive director of The Christian Jew Foundation, host of *Messianic Perspectives Radio Network*, and featured writer for *Message of the Christian Jew*. (Messianic Perspectives, P.O. Box 345, San Antonio, TX)

Henry H. Halley—Author of one of the best-known and most-used Bible study guides in the world, *Halley's Bible Handbook*. (Zondervan Publishing House, 1415 Lake Drive SE, Grand Rapids, MI 49506)

Gary Hedrick—Author, speaker on the *Messianic Perspectives Radio Program*, and writer for *The Christian Jew Foundation Newsletter*. (Messianic Perspectives, P.O. Box 345, San Antonio, TX)

Ed Hindson—Minister of Biblical Studies at Rehoboth Baptist Church in Atlanta, Georgia, vice president of There's Hope, dean of the Institute of Biblical Studies at Liberty University in Virginia, executive board member of the Pre-Trib Research Center in Washington, DC, and speaker on *The King Is Coming* television program.

David Hocking—Pastor, radio host, and director of *Hope for Today Ministries*. (P.O. Box 3927, Tustin, CA 92781–3927)

H. Wayne House—Dean and professor at Michigan Theological Seminary in Plymouth, MI, freelance writer and author. (Kregel Publications, Grand Rapids, MI 49501)

Dave Hunt—Internationally known author of more than twenty books with sales exceeding three million copies.

Noah Hutchings—President of *The Southwest Radio Church*, one of the oldest and best-known prophetic ministries in the world, and author of more than one hundred books. (P.O. Box 1144, Oklahoma City, OK 73101)

Thomas Ice—Pastor, author, college teacher, and executive director of the Pre-Trib Research Center in Washington, DC. (Harvest House Publishers, Eugene, OR 97402)

William T. James—Coauthor and general editor of several books presenting a series of insightful essays by well-known prophecy scholars, writers, and broadcasters. (Benton, AR)

Grant R. Jeffrey—Best-selling author and frequent guest on radio and TV programs. (Frontier Research Publications, Inc., Box 129, Station U, Toronto, Ontario, Canada M8Z 5M4)

Irving L. Jensen—Professor emeritus of Bible at Bryan College in Dayton, TN, and author of dozens of books with more than sixty currently in print. (World Wide Publications, Minneapolis, MN 55403)

David Jeremiah with C. C. Carlson—David Jeremiah is president of Christian Heritage College and senior pastor of Scott Memorial Baptist Church in El Cajon, CA, and host of a popular radio program called *Turning Point*. Carol Carlson has authored/coauthored a total of nineteen books, the most famous being *The Late Great Planet Earth* with Hal Lindsey.

Woodrow Kroll—Pesident and senior Bible teacher on *Back to the Bible* radio and television programs. Author of many books.

Tim LaHaye—Founder and president of Family Life Seminars, author, pastor, counselor, television/radio commentator, and nationally recognized authority on Bible prophecy and family life.

Norbert Lieth—Writer in *News from Israel*. (See Arno Froese)

Hal Lindsey—Many call him the father of the modern-day prophecy movement. He is president of Hal Lindsey Ministries, author of many books, and host of a radio and TV program. (P.O. Box 4000, Palos Verdes, CA 90274)

Herbert Lockyer—Author and pastor of churches in England, Scotland, and the U.S. before his death in 1984.

Marlin Maddoux—Host of *Point of View Radio Talk Show* and author. (International Christian Media, P.O. Box 30, Dallas, TX 75221)

Wim Malgo—Former author, pastor, lecturer, evangelist, and founder of *Midnight Call Magazine* and News From Israel. (See Arno Froese)

J. Vernon McGee—Pastor, author, and former host of the popular *Thru the Bible with J. Vernon McGee* radio program. (Thru the Bible Radio, Box 100, Pasadena, CA 91109)

Chuck Missler—An expert on Russia, Israel, Europe, and the Middle East, founder of Koinonia House Ministries, and editor of *Personal Update* newsletter. (Koinonia House, P.O. Box D, Coeur d'Alene, ID 83816–0347)

Henry M. Morris with Henry M. Morris III—Authors of several books and teachers at the Institute for Creation Research. (Master Books, Inc., P.O. Box 727, Green Forest, AR 72638)

Leon Morris—General editor of the Tyndale New Testament Commentaries, author and former principal of Ridley College in Melbourne, Australia.

J. A. Motyer—Former principal of Trinity College in Bristol, England, editor of *The Bible Speaks Today* commentary series, pastor, and author of several books. (Intervarsity Press, Downers Grove, IL 60515)

J. Dwight Pentecost—Scholar and professor emeritus at Dallas Theological Seminary. (Dallas Theological Seminary, Dallas, TX)

Bill Perkins—Executive Director of Compass International, Inc., and host of *Steeling the Mind of America* conferences (Compass International, Inc., 460 Canfield, Suite 1000, Coeur d'Alene, ID 83815)

William L. Pettingill—Author of more than a dozen books. (Fundamental Truth Publishers, Findlay, OH)

Randall Price—President of World of the Bible Ministries, Inc., and author. (World of the Bible Ministries, Inc., 110 Easy Street, San Marcos, TX 78666-7336)

David Reagan—Founder and senior evangelist of *Lamb & Lion Ministries*, host and teacher of *Christ in Prophecy* radio program, author of several books, and editor of a monthly publication called *The Lamplighter*. (Lamb & Lion Ministries, P.O. Box 919, McKinney, TX 75070)

Larry Richards—Author of more than 175 books and general editor of the *God's Word for the Biblically-Inept* series. (Starburst Publishers, P.O. Box 4123, Lancaster, PA 17604)

Sol Scharfstein—Author of more than one hundred books. (KTAV Publishing House, Inc., 900 Jefferson Street, Hoboken, NJ 07030)

Billy K. Smith and Frank S. Page—Dr. Smith is a former provost and dean at New Orleans Baptist Theological Seminary, and author of numerous articles and books. Dr. Page is a pastor, and the author of numerous articles on Old Testament studies and church administration. (Broadman & Holman Publishers, Nashville, TN)

Charles Stanley—Senior pastor of the 12,000-member First Baptist Church in Atlanta, GA, speaker on radio and television program called *In Touch*, and author of numerous books. (First Baptist Church, Atlanta, GA)

Gary Stearman—Author, conference speaker, and speaker on *Prophecy in the News* television program. (See J. R. Church)

Lee Strobel—Award-winning author, graduate of Harvard Law School, chief legal editor of *The Chicago Tribune*.

Bruce A. Tanner—Writer in *The Bible Expositor and Illuminator*. (See Union Gospel Press)

W. H. Griffith Thomas—Widely recognized before his death as one of the world's outstanding Bible teachers, preacher and lecturer, author of several books. (Wm. B. Eerdmans Publishing Co., 255 Jefferson Ave. S.E., Grand Rapids, MI 49502)

Merrill F. Unger—Author of many books and former professor of Semitics and Old Testament at Dallas Theological Seminary.

Jack Van Impe—Cohost, along with his wife Rexella, of a worldwide television ministry that analyzes the news in light of Bible prophecy. (Jack Van Impe Ministries International, P.O. Box 7004, Troy, MI 48007)

John F. Walvoord—Theologian, pastor, author, past president and past chancellor of Dallas Theological Seminary, and past editor of the seminary's theological journal called *Bibliotheca Sacra*. (Dallas, TX)

Note: To the best of our knowledge, all of the above information is accurate and up to date. In some cases we were unable to obtain biographical information.

Endnotes

PART ONE: PROPHECIES IN THE OLD TESTAMENT

Chapter 1: Prophecies in the Pentateuch

1. *The World Book Encyclopedia*, vol. 15 (Chicago, IL: World Book, Inc., 1990), 274–75.

2. Larry Richards, *The Bible—The Smart Guide to the Bible*™ (Nashville, TN: Thomas Nelson Publishers, 2006).

3. Wayne Barber, Eddie Rasnake, and Richard Shepherd, *Following God* (Chattanooga, TN: AMG Publishers, 1998), 7.

4. Ed Hindson, *Is the Antichrist Alive and Well?* (Eugene, OR: Harvest House Publishers, 1998), 22.

5. Bruce A. Tanner, *Bible Expositor and Illuminator* (Cleveland, OH: The Incorporated Trustees of the Gospel Worker Society, Fall Quarter 1987), 38.

6. Robert T. Boyd, *Boyd's Handbook of Practical Apologetics* (Grand Rapids, MI: Kregel Publications, 1997), 36.

7. Chuck Missler, *Learn the Bible in 24 Hours* (Nashville, TN: Thomas Nelson Publishers, 2002), 30.

8. Barber, Rasnake, and Shepherd, *Following God*, 44.

9. Henry M. Morris with Henry M. Morris III, *Many Infallible Proofs* (Green Forest, AR: Master Books, Inc., 1996), 194.

10. Russell L. Penny, *The Conservative Theological Journal* (Fort Worth, TX: Tyndale Theological Seminary, December 1998), 458–59.

11. Randall Price, *Jerusalem in Prophecy* (Eugene, Or: Harvest House Publishers, World of the Bible Ministries, Inc., 1998), 99.

12. W. H. Griffith Thomas, *Genesis* (Grand Rapids, MI: Wm. B. Eerdman's Publishing Co., 1946), 160.

13. Merrill F. Unger, *Unger's Commentary on the Old Testament* (Chattanooga TN: AMG Publishers, Tyndale Theological Seminary, 2002), 71.

14. Thomas, *Genesis*, 238.

15. Barber, Rasnake, and Shepherd, *Following God*, 44.

Chapter 2: Prophecies in the Books of History

1. Lee Strobel, *The Case for Christ* (Grand Rapids, MI: Zondervan, 1998), 262.

2. Henry H. Halley, *Halley's Bible Handbook* (Grand Rapids, MI: Regency Reference Library, 1927), 184.

3. John F. Walvoord, *Major Bible Prophecies* (Grand Rapids, MI: Zondervan Publishing House, 1991), 101.

4. Thomas Ice and Timothy Demy, *Fast Facts on Bible Prophecy* (Eugene, OR: Harvest House Publishers, Pre-Trib Research Center, 1997), 117.

5. H. Wayne House, *Dictionary of Premillennial Theology*, Mal Couch, general ed. (Grand Rapids, MI: Kregel Publications, 1996), 315–16.

Chapter 3: Prophecies in the Books of Poetry

1. Charles Stanley, *The Glorious Journey* (Nashville, TN: Thomas Nelson Publishers, 1996), 213–14.

2. Arno C. Gaebelein, *The Book of Psalms* (Neptune, NJ: Loizeaux Brothers, Arno C. Gaebelein, Inc., 1978), 9–10.

3. J. R. Church, *Hidden Prophecies in the Psalms* (Oklahoma City, OK: Prophecy Publications, 1986), 43.

4. Thomas Ice and Timothy Demy, *Prophecy Watch* (Eugene, OR: Harvest House Publishers, Pre-Trib Research Center, 1998), 50–51.

5. David W. Breese, *Destiny Bulletin* (Hillsboro, KS: Christian Destiny, Inc., November 1998), 3.

6. Ed Hindson, *Approaching Armageddon* (Eugene OR: Harvest House Publishers, 1997), 231.

7. Charles Halff, *Message of the Christian Jew* (San Antonio, TX: The Christian Jew Foundation), 6.

8. Gaebelein, *The Book of Psalms*, 319–20.

Chapter 4: Prophecies in the Major Prophets

1. Randall Price, *Jerusalem in Prophecy* (Eugene, OR: Harvest House Publishers, World of the Bible Ministries, Inc., 1998), 299.

2. Herbert Lockyer, *All the Messianic Prophecies of the Bible* (Grand Rapids, MI: Zondervan Publishing House, 1973) 61.

3. N. W. Hutchings, *The Persian Gulf Crisis* (Oklahoma City, OK: Hearthstone Publishing, Ltd.,1990) 104–5.

4. Gary Stearman, *Prophecy in the News* (Oklahoma City, OK: Prophecy In The News, December 1998), 12.

5. Tim LaHaye, *Understanding the Last Days* (Eugene, OR: Harvest House Publishers, 1998), 83.

6. John Hagee, *Beginning of the End* (Nashville, TN: Thomas Nelson Publishers, 1996), 93.

7. Thomas Ice and Timothy Demy, *Fast Facts on Bible Prophecy* (Eugene, OR: Harvest House Publishers, Pre-Trib Research Center, 1997), 107.

8. Charles Halff, *The End Times Are Here Now* (Springdale, PA: Whitaker House, 1997), 76.

9. Arnold G. Fruchtenbaum, *The Footsteps of the Messiah* (Tustin, CA: Ariel Ministries Press, 1983), 282.

10. Jimmy DeYoung, *Why I Still Believe These Are the Last Days* (Oklahoma City, OK: Hearthstone Publishing, Ltd., 1993), 31.

11. Henry M. Morris, with Henry M. Morris III, *Many Infallible Proofs* (Green Forest, AR: Master Books, Inc., 1996), 195.

12. Randall Price, in William T. James, ed., *Forewarning* (Eugene, OR: Harvest House Publishers, 1998) 232-33.

13. Gary Hedrick, *Israel: God's Timepiece* (San Antonio, TX: Messianic Perspectives Radio Network, 1998), Taped Message, GT-74, Side 3.

14. Chuck Missler, in William T. James, ed., *Forewarning* (Eugene, OR: Harvest House Publishers, William T. James, 1998), 232–33.

15. Grant R. Jeffrey, *Final Warning* (Toronto, Ontario: Frontier Research Publications, 1995), 125.

16. Randall Price, *Charting the Future* (San Marcos, TX: World of the Bible Ministries, Inc., no date), 53.

17. Marlin Maddoux, "U.N. Says Water May Be Peace Policy for Future," *Point of View* radio talk show (Dallas, TX), Taped Message 990113.

18. J. R. Church, *Prophecy in the News* (Oklahoma City, OK: Prophecy In The News, November 1998), 18.

19. Ed Hindson, *Is the Antichrist Alive and Well* (Eugene, OR: Harvest House Publishers, 1998), 9.

20. Hedrick, *Israel: God's Timepiece*, 39–40.

21. David Jeremiah with C. C. Carlson, *The Handwriting on the Wall* (Dallas, TX: Word Publishing, 1992), 199–200.

22. Charles H. Dyer, *The Rise of Babylon* (Wheaton, IL: Tyndale House Publishers, Inc., 1991), 188.

Chapter 5: Prophecies in the Minor Prophets

1. Irving L. Jensen, *Minor Prophets of Israel* (Chicago, IL: Moody Bible Institute, 1975), 5.

2. Duane A. Garrett, *The New American Commentary,Hosea, Joel*, vol. 19A (Nashville, TN: Broadman & Holman Publishers, 1997), 94.

3. Robert T. Boyd, *Boyd's Handbook of Practical Apologetics* (Grand Rapids, MI: Kregel Publications, 1997), 112.

4. Arnold G. Fruchtenbaum, *The Footsteps of the Messiah* (Tustin, CA: Ariel Ministries Press, 1983), 402.

5. Jensen, *Minor Prophets of Israel*, 30.

6. Garrett, *The New American Commentary, Hosea, Joel*, vol. 19A, 331.

7. Thomas Ice and Timothy Demy, *Fast Facts on Bible Prophecy* (Eugene, OR: Harvest House Publishers, Pre-Trib Research Center, 1997), 24.

8. Randall Price, *Jerusalem in Prophecy* (Eugene, Or: Harvest House Publishers, World of the Bible Ministries, Inc., 1998), 189.

9. Thomas Ice, "What Does The Bible Say About Armageddon?" *Midnight Call* (W. Columbia, SC: Midnight Call, Inc. December 1998), 17.

10. Billy K. Smith and Frank S. Page, *The New American Commentary, Amos, Obadiah, Jonah*, vol. 19B (Nashville, TN: Broadman & Holman Publishers, 1995), 169–70.

11. Charles L. Feinberg, *The Minor Prophets* (Chicago, IL: Moody Press, 1948), 171.

12. Kenneth L. Barker and Waylon Bailey, *The New American Commentary, Micah, Nahum, Habakkuk, Zephaniah*, vol. 20 (Nashville, TN: Broadman & Holman Publishers, 1998), 93.

13. J. A. Motyer, *The Minor Prophets*, vol. 3 (Downers Grove, IL: Intervarsity Press, J. A. Motyer, 1993), 923.

14. David Reagan, "Living for Christ in the End Times," *The Lamplighter* (McKinney, TX: Lamb & Lion Ministries, February/March 1999), 3.

15. Grant R. Jeffrey, *Prince of Darkness* (New York, NY: Bantam Books, 1994), 85.

16. N. W. Hutchings, *Why I Still Believe These Are the Last Days* (Oklahoma City, OK: Hearthstone Publishing Ltd., 1993), 15.

17. Gary Hedrick, *The Christian Jew Foundation Newsletter* (San Antonio, TX: The Christian Jew Foundation, November 1998), 2.

18. Feinberg, *The Minor Prophets*, 335.

19. Ed Hindson, *Is the Antichrist Alive and Well?* (Eugene, OR: Harvest House Publishers, 1998), 41–42.

20. Jimmy DeYoung, *Why I Still Believe These Are the Last Days* (Oklahoma City, OK: Hearthstone Publishing Ltd., 1993), 34.

21. Thomas Ice and Timothy Demy, *Prophecy Watch* (Eugene, OR: Harvest House Publishers, Pre-Trib Research Center, 1998), 184.

22. John Hagee, *Beginning of the End* (Nashville, TN: Thomas Nelson Publishers, 1996), 43.

PART TWO: PROPHECIES IN THE NEW TESTAMENT

1. Irving L. Jensen, *Simply Understanding the Bible* (Minneapolis, MN: World Wide Publications, 1990), 171.

Chapter 6: Prophecies in the Gospels and Acts

1. Henry H. Halley, *Halley's Bible Handbook* (Grand Rapids, MI: Regency Reference Library, 1927), 414.

2. John F. Walvoord, *Every Prophecy of the Bible* (Colorado Springs, CO: Chariot Victor Publishing, John F. Walvoord, 1999), 364.

3. Thomas Ice and Timothy Demy, *Prophecy Watch* (Eugene, OR: Harvest House Publishers, Pre-Trib Research Center, 1998), 44–45.

4. *Life Application Bible Commentary: Matthew* (Wheaton, IL: Tyndale House Publishers, 1996), 268.

5. Mike Gendron, *The Great Apostasy*, Pre-Trib Rapture Study Group, Dec. 14, 1998 (Plano, TX: Proclaiming The Gospel, 1998), 1.

6. David Reagan, "What's the Relevance?" *The Lamplighter* (McKinney, TX: Lamb & Lion Ministries, May 1999), 2.

7. Gendron, *The Great Apostasy*, 1.

8. John F. Walvoord, *Major Bible Prophecies* (Grand Rapids, MI: Zondervan Publishing House, 1991), 213–14.

9. Gendron, *The Great Apostasy*, 2.

10. J. Dwight Pentecost, *Things to Come* (Grand Rapids, MI: Zondervan Publishing House, Dunham Publishing Co., 1958), 148.

11. Arno Froese, "European Union in Prophecy," *Midnight Call* (W. Columbia, SC: Midnight Call, Inc., June 1999), 13.

12. Arnold G. Fruchtenbaum, *The Footsteps of the Messiah* (Tustin, CA: Ariel Ministries, 2003), 676.

13. Billy Graham, *Angels* (Waco, TX: Word Books, 1975), 108.

14. Pentecost, *Things to Come*, 149.

15. William Barclay, *The Gospel of Matthew*, vol. 2 (Philadelphia, PA: Westminster Press, 1956), 287.

16. *The Nelson Study Bible* (Nashville, TN: Thomas Nelson Publishers, 1997), 1620.

17. H. Wayne House and Randall Price, *Charts of Bible Prophecy* (Grand Rapids, MI: Zondervan, 2003), 17.

18. Charles Halff, "False Prophets in the Last Days," *Message of the Christian Jew* newsletter (San Antonio, TX: The Christian Jew Foundation, May-June 1984), 3.

19. "The Beginning of Sorrows," *Prophetic Observer* (Bethany, OK: Southwest Radio Church Ministries, April 1999), 3.

20. Jack Van Impe, *2001: On the Edge of Eternity* (Dallas, TX: Word Publishing, 1996), 99.

21. "The Beginning of Sorrows," 3.

22. Billy Graham, *Storm Warning* (Minneapolis, MN: Grason, 1992), 35.

23. David Hocking, *The Olivet Discourse/Divorce & Remarriage* (La Mirada, CA: Calvary Communications, Inc., 1989), 26.

24. J. Vernon McGee, *Thru the Bible with J. Vernon McGee*, vol. 4 (Pasadena, CA: Thru the Bible Radio, 1983), 126.

25. J. Randall Price, *Forewarning* (Eugene, OR: Harvest House Publishers, 1998), 134.

26. Union Gospel Press Publication, *Bible Expositor and Illuminator* (Cleveland OH: Incorporated Trustees of the Gospel Worker Society, March 1981), 47.

27. Thomas Ice and Timothy Demy, *The Truth About the Signs of the Times* (Eugene, OR:

Harvest House Publishers, Pre-Trib Research Center, 1997), 26.

28. Half, "False Prophets in the Last Days," 8.

29. Mike Gendron, *The Great Apostasy*, Pre-Trib Rapture Study Group, Dec. 14, 1998 (Plano, TX: Proclaiming the Gospel, 1998), 2.

30. Joe Chambers, "How To Discern False Prophets," *The End Times* (Charlotte, NC: Paw Creek Ministries, Inc., November/December 1998), 2.

31. David W. Breese, *Destiny Newsletter* (Hillsboro, KS: Christian Destiny, Inc., June 1999), 2.

32. Grant Jeffrey, *The Signature of God* (Toronto, Canada: Frontier Research Publications, 1996), 196.

33. Sol Scharfstein, *Understanding Israel* (Hoboken, NJ: KTAV Publishing House, 1994), 114.

34. Dave Breese, in William T. James, ed., *Forewarning* (Eugene, OR: Harvest House Publishers, 1998), 313.

35. Charles Capps, *End Time Events* (Tulsa, OK: Harrison House, Inc. Charles Capps, 1997), 146.

36. *Life Application Bible Commentary: Matthew* (Wheaton, IL: Tyndale House Publishers, 1996), 478.

37. Graham, *Storm Warning*, 38.

38. Capps, *End Time Events*, 148.

39. Arnold G. Fruchtenbaum, *The Footsteps of the Messiah* (Tustin, CA: Ariel Ministries, 2003), 443.

40. Walvoord, *Major Bible Prophecies*, 263.

41. Gary Hedrick, *Israel: God's Timepiece* (San Antonio, TX: Messianic Perspectives Radio Network, 1998), Taped Message, GT-74, Side 2.

42. John Hagee, *Beginning of the End* (Nashville, TN: Thomas Nelson Publishers, 1996), 100.

43. Capps, *End Time Events*, 155.

44. Walvoord, *Major Bible Prophecies*, 296.

45. Ibid., 105–6.

46. David Hocking, *The Church Is Born/Who Is Jesus* (La Mirada, CA: Calvary Communications, 1990), 68.

47. William Barclay, *The Gospel of Luke* (Philadelphia, PA: The Westminster Press, 1953), 172.

48. *The Pulpit Commentary, Mark & Luke*, vol. 16 (Grand Rapids, MI: Eerdmans, 1980), 103.

49. Henry M. Morris with Henry M. Morris III, *Many Infallible Proofs* (Green Forest, AR: Master Books, Inc., 1996), 58.

50. Irvin Baxter Jr., "Israel's Future—Through the Eyes of Prophecy," *Endtime Magazine* (Richmond, IN: Endtime, Inc., May/June 1999), 28–30.

51. David Reagan, "The Rise and Fall of the Antichrist," *The Lamplighter* (McKinney, TX: Lamb & Lion Ministries, November 1998), 3.

52. W. Herschel Ford, *Sermons You Can Preach on John* (Grand Rapids, MI: Zondervan, Corporation, 1958), 229.

53. Hal Lindsey, *Apocalypse Code* (Palos Verdes, CA: Western Front, Ltd., 1999), 301.

54. Hagee, *Beginning of the End*, 102.

55. J. R. Church, *Raging into Apocalypse*, William T. James, gen. ed. (Green Forest, AR: New Leaf Press, 1996), 184.

Chapter 7: Prophecies in the Letters Written by the Apostle Paul

1. N. W. Hutchings, *Romance of Romans* (Oklahoma City, OK: Hearthstone Publishing, Ltd., 1990), 79.

2. Dave Breese, *Forewarning* (Eugene, OR: Harvest House Publishers, 1998), 310.

3. Woodrow Kroll, *The Book of Romans* (Chattanooga, TN: AMG Publishers, Tyndale Theological Seminary, 2002), 31.

4. *The Pulpit Commentary, Acts & Romans*, vol. 18 (Grand Rapids, MI: Eerdmans, 1980), 270.

5. Hutchings, *Romance of Romans*, 329.

6. John F. Walvoord, *Every Prophecy of the Bible* (Colorado Springs, CO: Chariot Victor Publishing, 1999), 454.

7. N. W. Hutchings, *Why I Still Believe These Are the Last Days* (Oklahoma City, OK: Hearthstone Publishing, Ltd., 1993), 20.

8. J. Dwight Pentecost, *Things to Come* (Grand Rapids, MI: Zondervan Publishing House, Dunham Publishing Co., 1958), 294.

9. Arnold G. Fruchtenbaum, *The Footsteps of the Messiah* (Tustin, CA: Ariel Ministries, 2003), 108.

10. Breese, *Forewarning*, 334.

11. Billy Graham, *Angels* (Waco, TX: Word Books Publisher, 1975), 39.

12. Theodore H. Epp, *James: The Epistle of Applied Christianity* (Lincoln, NE: Back to the Bible, The Good News Broadcasting Association, Inc., 1980), 67.

13. William Barclay, *The Letters to the Corinthians* (Philadelphia, PA: The Westminster Press, 1954), 169.

14. *The Nelson Study Bible* (Nashville, TN: Thomas Nelson Publishers, 1997), 1950.

15. Theodore H. Epp, *Galatians* (Lincoln, NE: Back to the Bible Correspondence School, The Good News Broadcasting Association, 1974), 83.

16. William Barclay, *The Letters to the Galatians and Ephesians* (Philadelphia, PA: The Westminster Press, 1954),194.

17. *The Pulpit Commentary, Galatians, Ephesians, Philippians, Colossians*, vol. 20 (Grand Rapids, MI: Eerdmans, 1980), 218.

18. Walvoord, *Every Prophecy of the Bible*, 472.

19. Oliver B. Greene, *The Epistle of Paul the Apostle to the Philippians* (Greenville, SC: The Gospel Hour, 1964), 54.

20. Graham, *Angels*, 39.

21. David Hocking, *Israel and Bible Prophecy/Philippians: The Christian's Guidebook to Joy in Christ* (La Mirada, CA: Calvary Communications, Inc., 1991), 65.

22. *Life Application Bible Commentary, Philippians, Colossians, & Philemon* (Wheaton, IL: Tyndale House Publishers, 1995), 225.

23. Charles Capps, *End Time Events* (Tulsa, OK: Harrison House, Inc., 1997), 192.

24. Norbert Lieth, "The Rapture," *News from Israel* (Columbia, SC: Midnight Call Ministries, March 1999), 10.

25. Breese, *Forewarning*, 318–19.

26. William T. James, *Foreshocks of Antichrist* (Eugene, OR: Harvest House Publishers), 8.

27. Hal Lindsey, *The Rapture* (Toronto, Canada: Bantam Books, The Aorist Corporation, 1983), 143.

28. Jack Van Impe, *2001: On the Edge of Eternity* (Dallas, TX: Word Publishing, 1996), 152–53.

29. Billy Graham, *Storm Warning* (Minneapolis, MN: Grason, 1992), 278.

30. Dave Hunt, in William T. James, ed., *Forewarning* (Eugene, OR: Harvest House Publishers, 1998), 28–29.

31. Breese, *Forewarning*, 322.

32. Bill Perkins, in William T. James, ed., *Forewarning* (Eugene, OR: Harvest House Publishers, William T. James, 1998), 55.

33. Graham, *Angels*, 31.

34. N. W. Hutchings, *Studies in Timothy* (Oklahoma City, OK: Hearthstone Publishing, Ltd., 1990), 75.

35. Mike Gendron, *The Great Apostasy*, Pre-Trib Rapture Study Group, Dec. 14, 1998 (Plano, TX: Proclaiming the Gospel, 1998), 7.

Chapter 8: Prophecies in the Letters Written by Other Apostles

1. Larry Richards, *The Bible—The Smart Guide to the Bible™* (Nashville, TN: Thomas Nelson Publishers, 2006).

2. John F. Walvoord, *Major Bible Prophecies* (Grand Rapids, MI: Zondervan Publishing House, 1991), 187.

3. Irving L. Jensen, *Hebrews* (Chicago, IL: Moody Bible Institute, 1970), 68–69.

4. William Barclay, *The Letters of James and Peter* (Philadelphia, PA: Westminster Press, 1958), 136.

5. *Life Application Bible Commentary, James* (Wheaton, IL: Tyndale House Publishers, 1992), 123.

6. Theodore H. Epp, *James: The Epistle of Applied Christianity* (Lincoln, NE: Back to the Bible, The Good News Broadcasting Association, Inc., 1980), 231.

7. *The Pulpit Commentary, Thessalonians, Timothy, Titus, Philemon, Hebrews, James*, vol. 21 (Grand Rapids, MI: Eerdmans, 1980), 76.

8. *Life Application Bible Commentary, I & II Peter and Jude* (Wheaton, IL: Tyndale House Publishers, 1995), 174.

9. Dave Hunt, "Flashes of Falling Away," in William T. James, ed., *Forewarning* (Eugene, OR: Harvest House Publishers, 1998) 36.

10. David Hocking, *Real Truth for True Believers, I John* (La Mirada, CA: Calvary Communications, 1990), 37.

11. J. Vernon McGee, *Thru the Bible with J. Vernon McGee*, vol. 5 (Pasadena, CA: Thru the Bible Radio, 1983), 787.

12. The Southwest Radio Church, *The Whole Realm of Rebellion* (Oklahoma City, OK: The Southwest Radio Church, 1980), 9.

Chapter 9: Prophecies in the Book of Revelation

1. Tim F. LaHaye, *Revelation: Illustrated and Made Plain* (Grand Rapids, MI: Zondervan, 1973), 22.

2. Gary G. Cohen, *Kirban Reference Bible, Revelation Visualized* (Chattanooga, TN: AMG Publishers, 1979), 96.

3. John F. Walvoord, *Every Prophecy of the Bible* (Colorado Springs, CO: Chariot Victor Publishing, 1999), 550.

4. Breese, *Forewarning*, 312.

5. J. Vernon McGee, *Thru the Bible with J. Vernon*

McGee, vol. 5 (Pasadena, CA: Thru the Bible Radio, 1983), 949.

6. Grant Jeffrey, *The Signature of God* (Toronto, Canada: Frontier Research Publications, 1996), 271.

7. Walvoord, *Every Prophecy of the Bible*, 564.

8. J. Dwight Pentecost, *Things to Come* (Grand Rapids, MI: Zondervan Publishing House, Dunham Publishing Co., 1958), 215.

9. John Hagee, *Beginning of the End* (Nashville, TN: Thomas Nelson Publishers, 1996), 172.

10. Tim LaHaye, *Understanding the Last Days* (Eugene, OR: Harvest House Publishers, 1998), 59.

11. Charles Halff, *The End Times Are Here Now* (Springdale, PA: Whitaker House, 1997), 109.

12. Terry L. Cook, in William T. James, ed., *Forewarning* (Eugene, OR: Harvest House Publishers, 1998), 114.

13. Billy Graham, *Approaching Hoofbeats: The Four Horsemen of the Apocalypse* (New York, NY: Avon Books, 1983), 251–252.

14. David Jeremiah with C. C. Carlson, *Escape the Coming Night* (Dallas, TX: Word Publishing, 1990), 188.

15. Hal Lindsey, *There's a New World Coming* (Eugene, OR: Harvest House Publishers, 1973), 225–26.

16. Jeremiah with Carlson, *Escape the Coming Night*, 167.

17. Leon Morris, *Revelation* (Grand Rapids, MI: William B. Eerdmans Publishing Co., 1987), 197.

18. David Reagan, *Wrath and Glory* (Green Forest, AR: New Leaf Press, Lamb & Lion Ministries, 2001), 87–88.

19. Wim Malgo, *A New Heaven and a New Earth* (West Columbia, SC: Midnight Call Ministries, 1985), 73.

20. Arnold G. Fruchtenbaum, *The Footsteps of the Messiah* (Tustin, CA: Ariel Ministries Press, 1983), 112.

21. William L. Pettingill, *The Unveiling of Jesus Christ* (Findlay, OH: Fundamental Truth Publishers, 1939), 93.

22. Jeremiah with Carlson, *Escape the Coming Night*, 217.

23. Thomas Ice and Timothy Demy, *The Truth About Heaven and Eternity* (Eugene, OR: Harvest House Publishers, 1997), 14.

24. Malgo, *A New Heaven and a New Earth*, 146.

25. Hal Lindsey, *There's a New World Coming* (Eugene, OR: Harvest House Publishers, 1973), 268.

26. John F. Walvoord, *Every Prophecy of the Bible* (Colorado Springs, CO: Chariot Victor Publishing, 1999), 641.

27. Larry Richards, *The Bible—The Smart Guide to the Bible*™ (Nashville, TN: Thomas Nelson Publishers, 2007).

Index

J

Jacob
 in Canaan, 27
 definition, 74, 204
 God of, 22, 28, 57, 134
 God's decree to, 41
 twelve sons of, 26
Jaffa (Tel Aviv), 133
James, William T., 249
Jasper
 definition, 305
Jeba, city of, 145
Jeffrey, Grant R.
 on Armageddon and Israel, 140
 on the Battle of Armageddon, 97
 on electronic communication, 186
 on God's justice, 290
Jehoahaz (or Joahaz), King, 42
Jehoash (or Joash), King, 42
Jehoram, King, 42
Jehoshaphat, King, 42
Jehoshaphat, Valley of, 126, 127
Jehu, King, 42
Jensen, Irving L.
 on covenants, old and new, 265
 on Joel's prophecy, 123
 on the Minor Prophets, 115
 on Old and New Testaments, 152
Jeremiah, David, with C. C.
  Carlson
 on the antichrist and temple, 111
 on the final world government,
  300
 on the Great White Throne
  judgment, 303
 on inward corruption, 297
Jerusalem
 attack on, prophesied, 127, 136,
  144, 189, 211
 Babylon versus, 305
 Babylon's capture of, 102
 as City of Righteousness, 65, 66
 destruction of (past), 112, 119
 European Union and, 109, 187
 Faithful City, 65, 66
 rebuilding, 83, 84, 108
 siege of, 136, 178
 temple in, 112, 253
 Titus's capture of, 171
 topography of, 67, 134, 145
Jezreel, 115, 116, 117
Joash, King, 42
Job
 book of, 49

Joel's prophecy, 122
John
 definition, 169
Jones, Jim, 173
Joram (or Jehoram), King, 42
Jordan River, 32, 75
Joseph (father of Jesus), 38
Joseph (son of Jacob), 28
 dream of, 291
Josiah, King, 42, 203
Jotham, King, 42
Judah (person), 28
 Jesus as descended from, 28
 as lion's cub, 28
Judah (place)
 definition, 71
 destruction of (past), 37, 95
Judas
 definition, 181
Jude, book of
 Second Coming prophecy in, 278
Judea
 definition, 210
 as in West Bank, 152, 189
judgment(s), 11
 angels, of, 219
 definition, 11
 God's future, 307
 Tribulation Period, 287
 wrongness of passing, 229
judgment day, 44,
Judgment Seat of Christ, 213,
 224, 229, 243, 244, 272, 302
justice
 definition, 117

K

King(s)
 of Israel, divided kingdom, list
  of, 42
 of Kings, Jesus as, 28
 Jesus as, 32, 58, 88, 142, 197
Kingdom of Christ, 239
knew
 definition, 49
Koresh, David, 173
Kroll, Woodrow, 225

L

LaHaye, Tim
 on the antichrist, 293
 on deliverance of Christians, 77
 on the seven churches of Asia, 282

Lake of Fire, 11, 18, 39, 147,
 168, 169, 184, 203, 207,
 224, 301
 definition, 301
 final form of hell, 304
 Satan and unbelievers cast into,
  303, 304
Lamb, Jesus as, 284
Lamb's Book of Life, 230
Lamech, 13
Laodicean Period, 308
last days, 120
Latin, New Testament translation, 5
latter days
 definition, 33, 119, 134
latter times
 definition, 256
law
 covenant of, 264, 278
 definition, 264
lawlessness, 184, 253
Lazarus, 213, 214
Lebanon, 60, 61, 96
legion, 205
Levi, 28
 tribe of, 28, 98, 99
Levites, 28
Libya, 95, 96, 108
 as Put, 96
Lieth, Norbert, 228
*Life Application Bible
 Commentary*
 on hoarding wealth, 267
 on Jesus, realness of, 273
 on Messiah, return of, 194
 on serving Jesus, 243
 on weeds, parable of the, 159
life, crown of, 234
life, tree of, 306
Light of the world, Jesus as, 273
Lindsey, Hal
 on the City of God, 306
 on the Rapture, 249, 215
 on the seven-headed beast, 300
living water
 definition, 145
Lo-Ammi, 116
Lockyer, Herbert, 27
locusts
 demon-possessed, 289
 plague of, 122, 123
Lord
 definition, 242, 245
Lord's Supper, 99, 266
Lo-Ruhamah, 116

of the sower, 161
of the weeds, 158
Passover, observation of, 100
patience, 269, 279
patriarchs
definition, 26
Paul, the apostle, 155
on the antichrist, 242
peace, 247
antichrist claiming to be man of,
106, 175
covenant of, 87
to prevail, 69
peace movement, 83
peace negotiations, Middle East, 249
pearls, parable of, 167
Pekah, King, 42
Pekahiah, King, 42
Penney, Russell L., 17
Pentateuch, 9
Pentecost, 126
Pentecost, J. Dwight:
on Church Age teaching, 168
on Jews and Jesus, 229
on the parable of kingdom of
heaven, 165
on Revelation 12 (Satan and
Jesus), 291
Pergamum Period, 160
Perkins, Bill, 254
perplexing, 163
Persia, 95
Iran as, 96
Persians, 74
pestilence, 3, 176
Petra, city of, 188
Pettingill, William L., 303
pharaoh
definition, 29
Philadelphus, Ptolemy, 152
Philistia
definition, 60
plague(s)
coming, 125, 144, 145, 176,
286, 287
definition, 29
plant life, destruction of, 288, 308
plowshares, swords into, 123, 134
Poetic Books, 49
poetry, Hebrew, 49
political correctness, 164, 180, 184
politician, antichrist as, 293
polygamist, 13
Pope John Paul II, 186
possessions, attachment to, 209

postmillennial
definition, 163
postmillennialism, 5, 6
definition, 6
power, of God, 94, 225, 270, 271
prayer, 56, 60
premillennial
definition, 163
premillennialism, 5, 6
definition, 5
premillennial view, correct (as),
163, 165
preterists, 190, 290
definition, 290
Pre-Tribulation Rapture, belief in, 83
Price, Randall
on anti-Semitism, 179
on earthquakes, potential, 128
on Israel, covenant of peace
with, 94
on Jerusalem, future of, 99
on the millennium, 67
on the Promised Land, 19
Prince of Peace, antichrist's claim
to be, 175, 286
principles
definition, 133
priorities, 39, 271
Promised Land, 19, 21
illustration of, 19
prophesy
definition, 126
Prophet, the False, 161, 182, 192,
281, 292
Prophetic Observer, 127, 175
prophetic signs, 248, 274
prophet(s)
characteristics of, 191
false, 126, 141, 170, 181, 182,
191
false, as "second beast," 182
major, 65
minor, 115
true, 142, 182
Protestants, millennial theories of, 6
Proverb, 40, 192
psychics, 183
Ptolemy Philadelphus, 152
Pulpit Commentary
on farmers, patience of, 269
on Second Coming, events of, 226
on sin, 239
on the Tribulation Period, 208
punishment, in life to come, 206
purchased

definition, 284
pursuits, 208
put his name on
definition, 40
Put, Libya as, 96

R

rapture
definition, 3
after, 106, 112, 161, 173, 212,
229, 243, 266, 286, 287,
293, 309
antichrist in relation to, 106,
199, 293
Holy Spirit, removal of, 189, 253
millennium in relation to, 201,
235
signs of pre-Rapture, 173
raptured
definition, 189
Reagan, David
on the antichrist and Jews, 212
on Bible prophecy, perversion
of, 162
on end times, 138
on the Supper of God, 301
rebellion
definition, 252
Reconstructionism, beliefs, 7
red horse, 174, 286
redeemed
definition, 165
Redeemer
definition, 49
redemption
definition, 66
regenerate
definition, 89
Rehoboam, King, 42
rejoicing
Christians' reasons for, 271
Crown of, 234
religion
false, 66, 75, 170
world, 105, 179, 286, 294, 299, 300
religions of the world, illustration
of, 299
religious liberalism, 55
remnant
definition, 57, 226, 228
rescued
definition, 271
responsibility, 168, 206
resurrection(s)

two nations
definition, 38
two witnesses, 175
Tyre, 60

U

unbelievers
doom of, 286, 287
judgment of, 203, 207
unfulfilled, 3
Union Gospel Press, 181
United Nations, Antichrist and, 106, 110
world government, as, 103
United States, 211, 299
unregenerate
definition, 67
uprightness
definition, 40
Ur of the Chaldeans, 15, 19

V

valid, 41
validated, 152
Valley of Hinnon, 203
Valley of Jehoshaphat
definition, 127
Van Impe, Jack
on end, nearness of, 249
on warfare and famine, 175
vegetarianism, 256
Vietnam War, 174
vineyard, 123, 129, 169
virgin
definition, 203
virgin birth prophecy, 70
visions, 126

W

wail, 129
wall
definition, 129
Walvoord, John F.
on Bible, cleansing power of, 241
on Davidic covenant, 37, 205
on God's judgments, 290
on God's people, 229
on the Holy City, 307
on the millennial kingdom, 264
on the parable of yeast, 164
on the Rapture, events following, 202, 285
on the Second Coming, 196

on the Sermon on the Mount, 157
war(s), 174
birth pains, as like, 174
casualties, recent, 175
disarmament, 134
nuclear, 286, 287, 298
in Revelation, 57
and rumors of wars, 57, 128, 174, 210, 287
Vietnam, 174
World War I, 89, 174
World War II, 174, 181
water
living, 145, 306
pollution of, 296
wealth, hoarding, 279
weapons
Battle of Armageddon and, 295
biological, 106, 176
chemical, 106
nuclear, 75, 97, 106
weeds, parable of the, 158
weeds, Satan as sowing, 163
weeping, at Tribulation Period, 129
West Bank (Judea and Samaria), 19, 90, 139, 189
Palestine and, 90
western sea, 145
wheat, Christians as, 158
white horse, 172, 285
wickedness, 13
witchcraft, 256
witnesses, two, 175
wolf in sheep's clothing, 293
World Court, end of, predicted, 135
world government, 55, 102, 104, 106
Jesus to destroy, 300
United Nations and, 106
world religion, 105
wormwood
definition, 285
wrath,
God's, 56, 70, 91, 230, 244, 275, 296
wrinkle
definition, 241
Wye River Agreement, 90

Z

Zebedee's sons, mother of, 53
Zechariah (king), 73

Zechariah (prophet), 138
Zerubbabel
definition, 171
Zerubbabel's Temple, 171
Zimri, King, 42
Zion
definition, 55, 124